# HERSELF

# HORTENSE CALISHER

# HERSELF

## ARBOR HOUSE

*New York*

To C. H.

# CONTENTS

PUT your ear to an old faucet, do you hear the lifeblood of art drip-dripping, leaking like tapwater? —it's only the old ivory-tower blues; she hears it every day. A faucet has realms of being for everybody; that is hers.

Meanwhile, ordinary life-under-death waits at the mousehole. She tosses it theater like everybody, learns like them to build honeycomb houses for whoever shall be there with her: the flesh of her body and other guests.

With the years, so much like other peoples', this furnishment, as you know, turns to waxwork, family rooms staring shakily at time. Now and then, in spite of all she can do, one of the bodies she is in fealty with falls into death's gigantic blanket—whooshed out of a mousehole! —they sink down down, lost lost, melded to the planetary hum.

Now is the time she must speak out her life—she never told that story. Of how she has spent her life trying to learn her own name.

Is this an autobiography she writes—when you'll never get to know what she was doing that day in Wardour Street, at half-past three? Never a diary (she wrote other peoples'), partly a journal (travels with love did that), more than a memoir—for who wants to look back only? —she feeds it with fugitive soundings from a past she keeps up with, as with a correspondent more cogent than herself. If life is a minotaur to be found at the end of a confessive thread, then is this a new way of finding it?

Yes of course, it always is; you remember? This is the envelope to the life-bank, paying the interest but not the principal—not that, not yet. It's the apologia played at dawn on the boarding house piano, by the unsuccessful suicide decamping to the West. And it's the fruit carried every day to table with common bowl and knife, under the impression that someday she will fall to the floor in the fit of *grand mal* she always wanted—the great epilepsy-for-once.

"Life-talk, life-letters, that's what it is," she says. "It's what's left over after you've killed yourself laughing."

It's what the graffiti would say, on the tombstones of those who have been cremated. Or the letter one sometimes gets back from the P.O., addressed to oneself in one's own hand.

It's the note modern life leaves behind in the motel, saying "I was waiting for hope."

And it has her name on it.

PART I

# THE BIG APPLE

APPLES. That's what New York-
ers of the 1930s remember. Apples of the Hesperides, neatly stalled
on corner after corner, sold on the last trembling line of decency by
men who were unwilling to beg. Sometimes a man had only two.
We bought them, our Cézannes-to-be, with the nickel carfare home,
and didn't know it was our education we were bringing back. "You
walked again!" said our middle-class mothers. "Forty blocks! My
God, what am I going to do about those shoes?" And, for the first
time, they might mean it.

Depression settled on us younger ones slow as the really big snowflakes. My father came home from a business trip, his face ashen,
though still for *others*. "Decent family men stop you. They say
nothing. When I took out my wallet—one wept." 1929 had brought
his business to the wall, but he still had it. We would always eat.
And did. It never occurred to me that he and my mother were frantic,
within their scale. Then it developed that college was no longer assumed
for me. I mightn't go. . . . I wasn't to. "Go and be a secretary!" said
my mother. "Like Mary. *Work!*" Mary!—my friend from the "wrong"
neighborhood—two blocks away. My father said nothing; maybe he
knew there were almost no secretaries any more.

But I had to go to college. All the books I still hadn't read were
there. And, in the way of the young, my methods were rough—and
clean. Pride of my dancing school, I went and got the chorus job
guaranteed to blow my mother's cool—and me, of course, to sexual ruin.
"I start on Monday," I said. So, to college I went. The $400 for the
first term was found, somewhere. I even had a short, frilled red crepe
I could wear right now, and never wore out, for *boom*—that fall, skirts
fell. And oh, yes, isn't it all tender and charming and somehow gayer
than now—as retrospect always is. But there was still to come the incredible gift the '30s gave some of us. For I still didn't know how
rich we were.

At Barnard, where I took no sociology or economics (which
wouldn't have helped), I thought I was learning—how poor. I'd had
to ask for a scholarship. But when the banks closed, many around
me mourned for what their papas still had there. Another's father
had jumped from his skyscraper office into a large bloody pool of
insurance. Meanwhile, I had one new dress per year, and almost no
pocket money. So I worked. Summers and Saturdays. And a few
more snowflakes fell.

Am I telling you about the decline of the middle class, or the rise
of liberalism among the well fed? Indeed not, I still think sociology
is for the simple-minded. I'm telling you how a "society" girl was
prepared for her debut.

First job—hostess in a Happiness restaurant (later Schrafft's), hours
11:00–3:00, wages $11 per week and lunch. There she learned: (a)
waitresses whose pinched cheeks testify to one meal a day eat different
from a girl to whom it's just by-the-way; (b) professionals, who've
worked up to what they are, hate those who get the job because of
what *they* are; (c) to hate customers. And most important of all, in
later life: never take the first table a hostess offers you. Saturdays, she
worked as salesclerk in a department store, where she learned to
hate employers—particularly, among the buyers, a Miss Siff, whom
she saw snarl to a manufacturer waiting outside the buying office—
hat humbly in hand, a Homburg like *her* own father's—"Get out."

And outside, "society" waited, for him and for me. Not a matter

of the "400," any more. Some of this I saw, of course, though with
a strictly visual eye. . . . Southward of those Hudson River sunsets
behind the college, along the flats below Riverside Drive, a squatter
town had risen, tar-paper shacks that to us flapped carefree, Romany
Rom in the breeze. . . . At the Savoy night club in Harlem, where
a boyfriend was announcer (radio), I stomped almost as good as
*them*, until replaced by a black girl supple as the two-foot bird of paradise on her head. . . . In the newspapers, certain farmers in the West
were raging toward revolution—but when is a farmer ever real to New
York? Or the Okies?—even then trickling toward Steinbeck, and to a
clever, arty still in *Bonnie and Clyde*. . . . Politics was happening to
many, for the first time. At school, the editor of the paper was pulled
off it for writing sympathetically of Russia; we figured she'd met one,
somewhere, at the parties of those parlor pinks ten years too old for
us. . . .

Meanwhile, at home, we moved from ten rooms to four; my mother,
"on the advice of her doctor," now did her own housework; and
the family business, on which so many relatives depended, went bank-
rupt. But we went on managing—my father, aged 70, got a job. How
remarkable this now was for a man of any age, he never said. Soon,
I would know.

And so would my boyfriends—a word deeded to me from the '20s,
along with some of its gaiety, of which we still had our own frolic-
some kit bagful. (For a decade never knows for sure when it *is* one,
or when it is over. We didn't know we were "the '30s" yet.) Among
my male classmates the architects worried the most, having been
taught early that they depended on the promises an economy makes
to itself. "Bodies will still need help," the grinning medics said. "I'll
open a grocery store," said the business types, laughing. "People always need food." And that, of course, was to be—very true. Why,
we were all of us brimming with expectation—of the world, the flesh,
and maybe the devil, too. No one had explained to us that imagination
wasn't the same as "looking ahead." Why should it be? But I'm no
one to talk.

For—see now our society girl, poised on the brink of it, her shoes almost as pointed as they will be again in 1960, under what she doesn't know is a maxi-skirt. She often wears her leotard for a blouse, belts her waist wherever, sometimes wears her grandmother's jabots to fine effect, and under floppy hats, chandeliers her ears—whose lobes are unpierced, however, for that's still only for immigrants. The Smith-Corona she writes her poems on is still partly owed for. Art *is* long. And time does fleet—already June, and the daisy chains breaking. Her greatest shock is that she must pay $20—four Saturdays—for her sheepskin. And when it comes, it isn't sheep. So college has, after all, prepared her as her parents couldn't; she's a cynic now.... And so, full of Shelley in the head, chicken patties in the gut, and chicken feed in the pocket—I came out.

And the snow had fallen all around us. And "the world" had stopped. Or the money had. The world we were being presented to—was closed. Shut-up shop, most of it. No one wanted to let *us* in. But we were all still expected to remain *alive*. That, to me, is the surreal feel of the '30s, and why we understood at once, with our wordless pulses, the inscapes of de Chirico and Magritte, and Tanguy. ...Somewhere back of a landscape jammed to stillness, a machinery has stopped, leaving these dreams and artifacts to stare. We wander, half-dream and half-artifact among them, but *moving*, plasms that must feed, must breathe. We cannot stop our hearts. But no one lifts a finger to help us keep them going....

In the face of nature, one can sometimes scrabble, and seed. But in a city, the metal and the electric, and the money, must move also— and the circulation of money is different from the circulation of the blood. Some eras obscure that; now it was nakedly appearing. I began to understand why the banker had jumped. A circulatory failure. He'd made *his* connection between money and life. We were all being asked to. While outside—or inside the fringe where people like me were —millions were being refused a chance to make any connection at all.

Job, job, job. A larky word now, a grace note, sweet or sour, to life's general song. Then, it was like the tocsin start of the Beethoven *Fifth:* we-want-a-job; who'll-give-us-one? Later, those notes were the victory theme of a war, reminding me. Guns or butter? —the

'30s was a war for beans. Outside the employment offices, hundreds rioted for a single opening. Beggars were not come-to-our-town but from it, dropping in *our* tracks. The poor were with us from dawn to dusk now. And in the end, they got me a job.

In the DPW—Department of Public Welfare—where I went to work, in the former Bank of America on 116th and Madison, we sat on orange crates, posting our disbursements and costs: the dole was the great industry now. Our office was a "precinct," police style, and I was "the investigator." When we went out, it was called "going into the field." There. "How has client managed up to now?" was the query every case record had to answer, in dollars and cents, and in rent and Con Ed bills to show residence—a clear history of starvation in a face was not enough.

Each of us had 175 families per month to visit—all of them, it seemed, on the top fifth floor. I saw hall toilets for the first time—and all polyglot disease. One of my blocks had the highest TB rate in the U. S. A.: another was solidly prostitute. "Family?" a girl said to me. "There ain' no *fam*ilies here." In a dark cell, a 300-pound woman lay, her gangrenous leg glowing like radium: I had found her by a man's answer down below—"Follow the smell." I discovered the slum fear of city hospitals; 30 years later we are authenticating it.

When the city marshal evicted a family, we were required to "cover it"; it was a common sight to see furniture and effects piled at the curb, remaining under snow and rain. Once, I "covered" an eviction on Sutton Place, rent $400, where the maid knew nothing, and the master, appearing over her shoulder, let loose obscenities I've never met since—not even in print. Daily, I was learning the language, and the country—mine. When a man was "away," he was in prison: when a girl got pregnant, she "fell in." The clean, up-tight workers in Yorkville showed me their canceled bankbooks with mute pride; a gangster's family down on Rutgers Street paraded its royalty to me—Dutch Schultz. And we "workers" had our own jokes, some inadvertent, jotted on the emergency tickets we were always trying to give: "Woman in bed with doctor. Pay rent." Or: "Nothing to eat in the house except a loaf of bread and a pot of caviar." Or how, when I asked one kid the result of her Wassermann, she said in skat-rhythm, and with a finger snap, "Positive, hunnah. Poss*it-TIVE!*"

I was married now, to the only engineering grad of his class to get a job within the year; against my $27.50 per week, he earned $25. In the late '30s, if you had that much, you could rent anywhere; after teasing 20 hopeful landlords, we settled in a beaut just off Fifth, north of the Museum: top floor of a former mayor's mansion, fire-place, park view if you stretched, and roof garden—for which we paid $65 per month with concession, which brought it to $55. I bought a white sofa for it—years later, after all the child battering, it was still called that—and I know exactly why I did.

Maybe it was partly those movies you love now, for their fizzy blondes and musical staircases, down which trip the dimplies, singing, *eyes right*, "It payzz to be good—"; *eyes left and a time step*. "Ye-*ah*, but not much!" Maybe I did see them, those chocolate-soda fantasies of the end-of-the-week, already-borrowed-on paycheck. I can't re-member. Hollywood twinkled in our slang, anyway: some men were "Come into my log cabin" letches, and an employer went after you with a "penthouse ploy." But, although the "precinct" was union organizing, and labor was shouting "Joe Hill" to every sky, I never saw until much later those other *documentary* signs of the times, like the I.L.G.W.U'.s revue *Pins and Needles*, or Pare Lorentz' film *The Plough That Broke the Plains*. (Often the '30s never saw its own movies, you see. They didn't know enough to be with-it. Or they didn't have the dough.) The real reason for my sofa was simpler—I knew it was the '30s, now.

I came home of a night, soaked from the urinal a man had thrown at me for not bringing him a relief ticket, or maddened with the sight of two children their insane mother kept starving no matter how much I brought, or wondering what I should do about a former longshoreman who slept with all his daughters as they reached puberty —now that his youngest, weeping it to me in the hallway, had. Or how to counsel the Italian mother of eight who, denied a diaphragm by priest and thrift, had secretly crocheted one. We were supposed to "refer" all "problems" to a "private agency." What was a private problem, as compared to a public one, I could no longer say. But I knew I was in society, now. Only barely in my '20s, I was already so rich with its realities that I almost couldn't stand it. The sofa? That was a dream, from decades past. So every night, after peeling off clothes later to be inspected for the bedbugs the desks that had replaced the orange crates were swarming with, and after a wash in my inside bathroom, I tiptoed guiltily over to my past—and sat down on it.

Then, in a burst of glory-works—Roosevelt, the Dust Bowl, WPA, TVA, NRA, pick your alphabet—the decade ended. Or slipped quietly through the psyche's mousehole. There's a war on now, a real high-class war. Some of the same unity is visible, and gaiety—the bonhomie of a terrible mess that everybody's in. We're in the Army Ordnance now, traveling with a baby, on half the salary, which doesn't always come through on time.

Once, in a new town, we go to the store with $5 to cover the ten days to the end of the month and, after setting aside the baby's milk money, buy beans, flour, lard, a bacon slab, two cans tomatoes, and eggs. Sugar and spices we carry with us; no coffee, a little tea. We could telegraph "home," but we are gourmets now, weighers of experience.At night, for health, we carefully lick the baby's cod-liver spoon, each to a side. I make muffins with a water recipe I know, lard cookies with lemon extract, beans with Bell's seasoning, and bacon with beans. We have a roof, a fireplace, a sink, wood in the yard, toilet in the house, all needed beds and tables, and a musical instrument.

On the last night, I play a flourish on it, and set forth our dinner— a triumph. For each of us, one half of the last of everything—of a muffin crowned with a poached egg, crossed with bacon, sunk in "cream" sauce, and, on top, from some Christmas box, a bubbling rind of cheese. We're not perky or grand; we're temporarily cozy, and fearful. We are ordinary, for our time. The decade I came out to was over. But that night, and often after, I could feel it inside me, reassuring me of what was real.

Every decade sooner or later gets authenticated in every detail, maybe by a later one that falls in love with it. For years, the '20s have been our *belle époque*, congealed by us into a mélange of Riviera tennis matches with Gertrude Stein leading Gatsby, and diamonds-are-girl's-best, dusty answer, to death-by-toreador—in the revolutionary afternoon. That's the easy, highlighting way. Now it's the turn of the '30s, and we can all see that film-fashion image coming, in the berets and the bell-bottoms, and Humphrey Bogart's revisited nonsmile.

Nice, all of it, but it's not the straight story. What is? No decade is ever all economics, either, any more than it is only what it wears, or sings. And a decade is never itself only. For some people, the '30s will always be the time they first heard the Bach *passacaglia* as well as "Those Little White Lies." All the sex in the world is in every decade, and all the subjects of literature. So, the mountain of what I haven't mentioned, from Mae West to dance marathons to the rise of John Dewey to the decline of Jack Dempsey, doesn't oppress me. I've my own dream, or artifact.

I pick—an apple. My nickel Cézanne, it now holds an era, polished by the decent, trembling fingers of the past. In it I see us, then and now. Some men never got over that time; they lost their confidence there, sitting at idle windows, in vague West Virginias of the soul. Others, like me, have merely an odd way with money, call it healthy or ambivalent. At times we can't spend money, at times we can't save it—depending. We're often not good at getting jobs, but are beavers when we do. And many a woman among us, no matter her stock list, and sables, feels safest with an egg in the house. No wonder some of the young, in search of the pure, are nostalgic for our bitter-bright youth. No wonder *we* are. In any decade, men and women have to settle for themselves the connection between money and life. The '30s showed us—the difference.

Still, I had a special feeling for American fashions in decades. Falling in love with a part of the past is a human habit. Surely it must start in those slanted oral histories given the young. Those handed me had had an oddly longer span than is customary. Born of a father and grandfather who had both waited to marry and rear families until near elderly, when I delved into that two-generational perspective which is a child's usual lot, I unwittingly went much farther back. I heard nothing direct from that grandfather who, on record here as an elder of the synagogue in 1832, was probably born in the eighteenth century, and had died some fifty years before my birth, but I could listen to echoes of Civil-War Richmond—and 1850 Dresden and 1888 New York—from his much younger widow, who was still only ninety-seven when I was twelve. I didn't much want to, being understandably more in love with my father's dashing youth, which had taken place years before his marriage to my much younger mother, and in a decade the whole world already called the *belle époque*. Less than half a century gone, in our family it seemed still at hand. A decade? That was nothing. Instead of being timebound by access to such a stretch of it, within the usual terms of the human bondage I seemed to have been set free to wander as a citizen of time's kind of time.

By now, I am old enough to have seen clothing repeat itself, even on me, and to enjoy it. In Hollywood, I have just sported a jacket saved for its marvels since 1947, and once more so much the height of avant-garde fashion that the Fairmont in San Francisco had got into the papers for trying to bar me from the dining room—now that I was wearing pants with it.

But I still know that the history of the imagination never repeats itself that knowingly. In art, you can die for love of an epoch— and die of it. Maybe in life, too. When I was first writing I had a friend so much in love with the '20s that he admitted he would have preferred to have been young *then*, along with the writers he admired. Sad, I thought, for I was somehow sure they would never have given up their time for another—I would never want to give up mine. (And I still recall a remark heard at a play of his: "How can so young a man be so modern in such an old fashioned way!")

The Big Apple, as you may know from heritage or even experience, was a dance. It came after the Charleston, which came after the Bunny Hug (well after), and was followed by all those others it resembles. It was one of those dances—maybe all of them one spastic version of the Lebentanz—which leap up in America like crops. I never danced it. But I was there.

What is the history of a writer, as a writer, outside the books? Is there an internal history, as a writer, which goes on alongside them? Is it worth talking about? I was never sure.

Not yet published, a writer lies in the womb, marvelously private as one looks back on it, but not yet born, waiting for the privilege to breathe. Outside is the great, exhaling company of those who have expressed.

First publication is a pure, carnal leap into that dark which one dreams is light. The spirit stands exposed, in what it at first takes to be the family circle of confreres. Everybody, shaped to one ear, is listening . . . but after that—one must live.

What is a writer's innocence? In my work, I begin early to ask what innocence is for anyone, to examine it.

"I wanted my conviction—no, that is not the word—*themes* perhaps, to rise pure of themselves. In the uncontaminated country that I could sometimes glimpse in the depth of myself, there was another kind of knowledge that sometimes turned its dark fin and disappeared again, that I must fight to keep," the young hero of my first novel, *False Entry* says. "Compromise has no taste, no muscle; one day it is merely there, in the bogged ankle, the webbed tongue."

I myself fear that logic will overtake the dream, and extinguish it. "The young act from a pure, breathless logic still ignorant of the conventional barrier between dream and possibility," he wrote, under my hand. "When a man begins to *act* logically according to others . . . then he has left his youth behind."

In heaven, there must occasionally be recording angels who can't be as objective as required. They won't go along with the theology that everything is known; they know better than that. Yet why has that supra-knowledge, so full of the abyss, been planted on dubious guys like them? It worries them. Even so, whenever one of them is kicked out and over the bars of heaven, it is for shaking his fist at

the hills of grace, and shouting "*I* expect to know everything!"
Adding as he falls, "A prince I know I'm not."

Lucifer takes his hand, or hers, and says "Be a writer."

No stars fell when she was born. Yet she will address them.

All through life she will waver, between that arrogance and
that humility.

Meanwhile, as I begin to practice the word-life, and both to learn
and fear its postures, what gnaws at me most is the gap between
words and action. Given the age I live in, I am bound to see that
gap mainly in political terms; indeed it takes an effort of mind, even
now, to recall that other ages have seen this same gap solely in
terms of religion—the distance between word and action *there*.

By this time, perhaps 1951, I had accumulated a certain amount
of sub-political experience. Most of it in an ancient field to which
my time would give the modern name of "race relations."

Back in the Relief Bureau (as both we and the clients called the
Department of Public Welfare) many of my "co-workers"—a name
slid over to us from sub-Marxist doctrine—had been black, as was
my boss supervisor, Herbert Rountree—like so many of the middle-
to-upper staff a trained social worker recruited from "private" welfare work to public—in his case from the Urban League. (Precinct
heads were usually political appointees.) When I waltzed with him
at an office party, my background silently waltzed with me: —On
the one side, the Southern paternalism of my father, whose voice,
when he spoke of Awnt Nell, the mammy who had "raised" him,
still shook with filial feeling—in the exact timbre, I now realize,
with which he spoke of my grandmother. On the other side, my
mother's murmured "*Die Schwartze!*"—which was the way German
Jewesses of her day warned the family not to talk of something-or-
other in front of the maid. Barring an Ethiopian rabbi my father
claimed once to have met, and Cyril, the West Indian elevator boy
who had once coached me in Latin, educated blacks were unknown
to them. And except for two handpicked brown girls who had been
at Barnard—to me.

I felt that Mr. Rountree's large, gently astute eyes could see this, right down to my backbone, on which his hand was placed with a formality entirely to do not with race but with waltz. Thirty years later perhaps, and I Wasper and blonder, we might have had to sleep together to show our empathy over the world's hangups. As it was, I gave him a provincial New York City girl's peculiar confidence. I wanted to give him something. "Want to know something funny?" It *had* surprised me. "Until I went into the field, I never knew that there were dumb Jews!"

Behind me now are the years between, the early 1940's, spent barnstorming small industrial cities: Wilmington, Elmira, Binghamton, and larger: Rochester, Detroit—in the wake of an engineer husband. Engineers then (and perhaps now) are among the most conservative middle-class elements. As young family men, often with a holy distaste for cities, which takes no thought of what sins their own profession might be committing there, they make straight for the safer suburbs, in which all the prejudices—anti-Jew and black, anti-crowd and even anti-art—are spoken of as entirely natural. These men, one collegiate step above the foundry and the furnace, have little of the rough-and-ready about them, often not even manual dexterity, and none of the individual workman's craft-guild or underdog independence. Instead, they take having a boss for granted, buy cars and houses of a grade deferentially lower, just as in the famous *Fortune* magazine study of pecking-orders in monolith industry, subscribe healthily to the theme that General Motors—or Eastman Kodak or U. S. Rubber—*is* America, and in general are the Eagle Scouts of the corporate image. (Who, by and large, seldom made it to very top executive. This daughter of a lone, cranky but never subservient small-businessman, could have told them why.)

Wives meanwhile, are to conform, up the ladder of the country clubs, which are churchgoing and hard-drinking, in the obsessive way of the American on the rise, who has no other release. As a New Yorker I am out of it in one way, as a Jew in another (almost all engineers at this time were, like my husband, Christians). And as a secret artist (for I continue writing poems in between the housework) in a third way, perhaps the most significant. Except for a "sport" like my husband, whose family was musical, and for certain foreigners in his class at school, like his friends Viscardi and Khrennikoff, all these men, met from city to city, have passed through the college mill with scarcely a trace of "the humanities" to show for it; respect for those is not yet a part of this sector of American life. (As that sector's resurgence, in each war, and in almost every President, clearly shows.)

"Art" is the property of their wives, who paint the furniture à la Peter Hunt, read the gentle *Babar* books even to their boychildren (before dreams, if not before school), press for whatever theater tickets are bought, and fill their houses with a flurry of handcraft. ...If ever I am brought to agree that the "fine" arts and the art-crafts are the same, it will not be the art-gallery weavers and potters who have persuaded me, but the memory of those women—and myself—bent over, flecked with wool and paint and yearning, in the middle of baby's naptime, in middle America. ...

I am not writing yet—except for those poems, flung off in brief single seizures, in trances of regret for the intellectual life I seemed to have lost. I never send the poems out. I am paralysed, not only by the house-and-child life—which is a total-flesh-draining, a catatonia of rest for the beaverish brain, that in a way is craved—but by this immersion in a society where I feel not superior to it, but at first fatally out-of-step Susie, then submerged, and ultimately lunatic-wrong. (And by my immurement in a marriage where I cannot talk of these things to a husband, however kindly, who, brought up in just this sort of life, mildly subscribes to it unless argued to otherwise, which no doubt was *his* immurement.) Again I am learning what "society" is—and again, how different.

Knowledge gotten like that, unconsciously and unphrased, unrecognized even as misery, is the deepest there is. On the surface, I remember the succession of towns by whatever oddities happened to us in them. In Wilmington, the "corporation" lawyer who lives across from us on a country road just recently shaken by the wedding cortege of the two opposing clans united by a President's son and a Dupont heiress, has himself just been married late and for the second time, to Mattie X, an elegant lady, with white hair à la Recamier, whom, however, my mother-in-law, a Wilmingtonian, recognizes as the town milliner—a world of difference in that phrase! (Which Mattie herself—busy faking a lineage for herself via a French grandmother who had eloped here with the gardener and had expired on her deathbed when just about to point out her true patronymic in the *Almanach de Gotha*—is forever trying to repair.)

In her husband's pure white office, the walls bear column after column, goldleafed in Old English—the names of those nationwide companies who have incorporated themselves in Delaware, because of its favorable tax laws, and use his office as attestation. This was the "law" by which our neighbor lived, and the only way he practised it, allowing him to collect old glass, to serve us tomato juice in Napoleon's champagne cups—and his wife of sixty summers to embarrass him by buying a modern "bride's chandelier" out of *American Home*. Through her we are ratified for Lammot Dupont's private dairy-list—the question startlingly put as "Would you like, my dear, to get cream from Lammot Dupont?"—who had by the way been present when she and her husband were churched.

We were learning what a feudal name meant anywhere it sounded, in all the ranges of house and home beneath it, in a state it utterly owned. And how under the pseudo-hometownliness, the tycoons of Winterthur could make this visible. "Up at Henry Bielan's," (the Dupont brothers and cousins being thus called by their forenames), my husband, going with other staff at the Experimental Station, to the home of the Dupont who bosses it, is served drink in Moscow Mule mugs like those at any bar, but of a yellow metal; one gauche experimenter, inquiring of his host what the alloy is, has to be told it is high-carat gold.

I "saw" no blacks that year; in the habit of the country there one did not "see" them, though they were everywhere. Besides, I am busy learning to live in houses with furnaces (of which I ultimately will know every variety from coke to gas to wood to coal) instead of in apartment houses; to can strawberries from our acre of them the night my first child is born, and to live two months alone with her, speaking only to her, just after (all our few friends being summer-absent), while my husband, having lost the chemist's job his training hadn't fitted him for, goes to other towns to find one. Later, in a story of mine, "Mrs. Fay Dines on Zebra," those Negroes would appear briefly in a line or two, turtling on the Brandywine; it would appear that I had seen them after all.

And somewhere along this procession of towns and wildly various houses (huge ones no one else would have, or small ones which "everyone" had) as I see all the social classes in our so-called one-class America, and myself do a servant's work—out of this comes what I am to write in "The Hollow Boy" about servants in America, black or white. As I brood over, and feel in my very knees—in the "housemaid's" place there, and in my shoulders, in the yoke's place there—the peculiar, self-levitating dreams and nonseeing rope tricks which are the diversionary morale of a money democracy.

... Oh, I was seeing. But I still did not write. In Rochester, where the scarce job has been found (through a vice-president of Symington-Gould who is my husband's godfather) I go to Forman's, the best fashion-department store, and asking for a job myself on the basis of two post-graduation prior Relief-Bureau years as a Macy "executive trainee," am told they do not employ married women— "Besides, why would a nice girl like you want to work?" I couldn't tell him the whole truth, because I didn't know it yet, about women, husbands, society or writers, so I said, "We need the money"—godfather didn't pay very much. And am told, after being asked where my husband works and in what capacity, that it would do his status there no good, if I "tried to work."

Businesswomen, in the American provinces of those days, are not college graduates (who go into teaching if they stay single) but of a lower class; since they are perforce single, and have to "keep themselves up," they are often also "racy" and "hard," the kind of company a married man often goes looking for. Proper provincial girls might still not find it necessary to go to college; the bland, local Junior Leagues take care of what they had been reared for. Daughters of the new industrial rich want to be just like them—a young scioness of the Fruehauf Trailer-Truck Company, taking us and her husband to lunch at the Downtown Club (on her father's membership) says, with sincere effort, when she finds out I already *have* worked, "Well now, it's nice to be able to, like if you was a nurse, and your husband got sick. Or if you're left a widow." Then she smiles, with her sharp little muzzle, at her father's employee, her husband.

Half the conversation of these women of the middle industrial society I am meeting comes from venoms and satisfactions of which they are unaware. In their social evenings, sitting across the living-rooms from the men, they speak of their husbands as "He" to their faces, swapping their intimate habits, always barring the sexual ones: "Oh Jim, he always, Dick, he doesn't like to, Bill, he won't ever, for him I have to—" speaking more often of what regrettably isn't than of what is, and never knowing how, in this coy chat, they take their revenge. Or for what reason it is taken. Sometimes, though, when a display of uxorious feeling is required, or even truly felt, they flirt with their husbands in a kind of sorority badinage. One never talks to another's husband except by the way, and of the most womanly preoccupations; indeed the safe topics for either sex, and the great ones, are schools-for-the-children, and redoing the house. Or the cost of dental care. But it is at a presidential election-eve party that I first learn to the full how, as a woman in this society, I am what the employment agencies call "overqualified."

We are in a large group of doctors, dentists, engineers, lawyers and Kodak executives—not "old" Rochester (meaning old industry, a few of whose grandes dames I had met) but the heart of its middle sampling. All are upstate New York Republicans; we are Democrats. My husband is teased for it. The provincial, if he has to be polite to difference, doesn't know what else to do.

"And I suppose you vote along with him?" The nearer truth was that he voted with me; I'd converted him. But when I begin to explain, want to discuss (as all the men around us have been doing, to be sure unilaterally) and which, since I am young, supple, vague, doe-eyed, must sit less shrilly on me than it would later—a quiet coverlet is drawn over my attempt, first with kidding, then with ridicule, and at last stopping me short, with the kind of brute snarl, that we now call "redneck"—meaning workers who haven't had the benefit of the "humanities." Professional men of the time got it in the eye—reddened. Women didn't have views. All they really had, in a case like mine, was hot pants. . . . It is confusing, I suppose, that women of energy, men too, often have both.

As for the blacks, I never see them now. "We" never do. When they riot in the streets of Rochester in the 1960s, I will remember that. . . . Of how, once in a while up there, seated in a bus, I would see one, riding equally with us "up north here" on the aboveground railway, some old figure, dark, starched and Seminole among the white dishclout faces. . . . At the time, the ethnic resemblance of everybody to everybody up there takes my breath away; my heart is homesick for those dirty, spittled caravans where a half dozen flaming nations jostle each other at breakfast time. All riding in that New York indifference which I now see as dignity. Into one of whose buses a lama might enter, pushing like peace against that weirdly resisting middle door (and no one will help him, nor no one comment) to stand between a bitten-off, babyface old Sally of a theater usher in her round white stock, and an eyelashed goldfish of a garment-center chick, in her racing silks. . . .

Up here where I am, in the outland of the real country, not a stone is cosmopolitan, or pied beyond nature. The bus is for the pieced mornings of spinsters, idlers, housewives, cripples, or the evening bird-talk of stenographers. Each person who can, rides his own vein of life, in a car. Sundays, we do it also, driving to Palmyra and Joseph Smith's Mormon dream—only a hillside, to Painted Post—only a cross-road garage, to the Oneida community—a silver Utopia tarnished into a factory for sterling, and to the dying reservations where the squat Indians sit unfeathered, plaiting their fingers in the sullen, wampum-colored air. So we ride on like everyone else, for the standard cheap Sunday with the children in the back, while the old names: Ticonderoga, Canandaigua, lash our faces with history, and the small rain of the present scours the lakes. Transportation is the psychic skein of existence here; it is how the people here hunt whatever lyric winds that blow.

Twenty years later, riding the whole of New York State through the Ontario region to Michigan, I will understand these people *back then*, in their lamaseries of kitchen and field, their strange spas and mountain follies, their stiff springtimes—the men all the time so sexually delicate of finger, in the finite distance between them and the machine. I will see enough at last to write in *The Last Trolley-Ride* about that inland-outland transportational dream, always dying and resurrected, from barge to wagon to rail to car to plane, brought up short only by the easy horizons of the coastal cities, and of mixed peoples.

All this time, back there, there is a war. In the last years of it, we move to Detroit, arriving on the day of the race riots which have erupted at Belle Isle. At the luxe hotel on Lake St. Clair where the U. S. Rubber Company has temporarily quartered us, the management, joining with the permanent guests, decrees that the Negro domestic staff is to be quarantined at the hotel, since if these "good" ones go back the long route to their homes in the slums of Paradise Alley, "it might be dangerous for *them*." Now at last, I too can see those others, the "bad" ones, as in their mythic violence and their real, they hang invisibly from the roof-tree of every white inhabitant.

In Grosse Pointe, we find a huge house for rent, almost the only one anywhere. Not lake-front—only a six-cylinder-fortune house (as we joke to one another)—whose heirs will rent it cheaply until sold. The lease, when it comes, is "for occupancy by three persons only, of Caucasian race." When I ask what will happen when we become four, as is plainly to be, Mr. Sutter, the heir, says that when the baby comes, the lease will be so amended. I haven't the will to ask, "And what if it's black?"—not from fear (though that does exist—where else would we go?)—as from a deeper depression. I am living, possibly for always, among people for whom the words I use as acids and reliefs, the possibility even of verbal solutions to life, mean nothing. "Even in the hat salon at Hudson's—!" Mrs. Sutter, a suburbanly pretty woman, adds "—you can't be sure what you try on hasn't already been on one of their greasy heads."

Detroit itself is in the midst of another twenty-buck silk-shirt war; gas rationing, because of which we had let be carted away our beloved nine-miles-per-gallon classic old Packard, means little here; the lake buzzes with motorboats. Big-wig restaurants and company-clubs serve filet; meat-rationing is for the poor supermarket fools. I now think of the East as more moral; it will take another war, and richer friends, to teach me that bank profiteering is merely more hidden. We are meanwhile meeting the blatant "new" machine-tool-and-electronic rich; by this time I know that there are always these new ones—as opposed to the more elegant, older industrial rich, who have had their "humanities" and sometimes make use of them. Suppliers to the war, these new ones are a thick-psyche'd breed, with the terrifying animal sureness of those who know themselves to be the wave of what is— and do not reflect on it. Fighting a happy, redsnouted, clambake "operation," they have the fat, satined-up wives of men who go to whores, and the expensive, anemic houses which come out of first-generation military contracts. One of them spends thousands to illuminate the local church like a ballroom for the one night of a daughter's wedding—and the church allows it. But all the Grosse Pointes, Park to Farm, ring with anti-reform, anti-Roosevelt "sick" jokes, and the Detroit Symphony goes out over the air under the sponsorship—all it could get—of "Sam's Cutrate Store"—until an older industrialist (chemicals) rouses the new money to civic-mindedness.

I go and do what women are immemorially urged to do in wartime, especially when the bleeding goes on somewhere else. From Balaclava helmets, to Bundles for Britain, to USO, down the ages it's all bandage-rolling—and part of the quieting corruptions to which women have immemorially lent themselves, in the name of good works. Always finding by instinct their proper niches and social class.

. . . Mine has retrograded—or advanced. Early in the war, in Rochester (where on the Sunday afternoon of Pearl Harbor we two and child have been symbolically caught in a bookshop) I have been somehow organized into a group of the daughters and wives of its rich clothiers, women who (as our energetic hostess confides to me) would otherwise not have done *anything*. As we fold and ply, their talk and their diamonds flash equally rainbow; what we could have been sewing for an atomic war, I can now no longer imagine.

In Detroit, I work for election reform with the League of Women Voters, campaign for Roosevelt (under the aegis of the electrical workers' union's notorious Briggs Local), and when I get back to the house hang his picture in the bay (in defiance of the Park, which thinks it low to hang party posters, and knows where it stands, anyway)—and teach the new baby to do his fine razzberry of a "Pffui," whenever I say "Gonna vote for Dewey, Pete?". Sad anodynes of women, when they live cattycorner to world responsibility, sad games of all men, when they live under conditions for which they are indirectly not to blame.

In the Relief Bureau, I had learned that any food tickets I brought— or any emotional welfare I might bring—if as has been suggested, I train to be a psychiatric social worker with one of those private agencies which now took over where public welfare left off—would not be even as much as a thumb thrust in the dike of human economic misery. Now I realize that in a war, unless a woman can kill for it, or will dance for it, she has no honest position in it. To be a woman pacifist is as nothing; since for us (and me) there is no risk. This must be why women, since getting the vote, or one half of Athenian citizenship, now appear to me to have done little since except sit down and let the political facts roll by, until once again it is time to cooperate blindly—wartime. Until women come under full and equal military service (I think to myself)—nothing to do with WACS or WAFS— they cannot hope to have any of the secular powers which men took for granted, including the possible right to refuse to fight. All secular power was related to it. Once they had it, their own pacifism might mean something . . . though I wasn't at all sure that women, given military power, might not show the same divisions of opinion as the men. I could be so bright about all this, and so distant, because I have now faced a fact—I don't want to play any of these roles.

The role I want to play is evermore hidden, not a role at all, but an overwhelming need. Certainly not merely to *be* a writer, for though I have a deep, natural yearning to have an honorable place in the world, co-essential with what I am in the family, and using intelligences that seem to be lying fallow—I never think of the role of the writer as other than on the printed page, have never met a writer, and somehow never expect to.

The urge I have is a personal mysticism, somehow to be worked out between external fate and this self I have been fated with, which has a physico-religious-sexual impetus to complete itself in print. As it remains thwarted, I begin to feel more and more caged off from the realm of those lucky ones who are "allowed" to do as they were meant to do, or who will it; an almost palpable wall of glass seems to be between me and them. I droop (it seems to me now) exactly like those specimen animals, rat or primate, whom the experimenter frustrates into depression or frenzy by keeping them from their natural patterns of life.

I was and am, I think, a species of human *meta* physically; since that time I have met too many in or near my pattern for it not to be so. These are the recording ones, who must forever confirm reality by making a new piece of it—verbally, tactilely, visually, musically, kinaesthetically—and by doing so, bring themselves into the line of being, so confirming themselves. Any worldly ambitions that accrete are after-the-event even for the most greedy of these people; as artists it is only that other hunger which will keep them truly alive. When that dies, then the inborn pattern dies with it, exactly as all other processes in life do—exhausted or diseased, or simply played out in a richness that is now done. Or, more likely, in a combination of all of them. Sometimes, in a long life in-the-pattern, there are little dyings and remissions; oddly, it is when this species is physically cut off from its "work" that it feels most cut off from other people. Immersed in such work, such a one doesn't think about reality; he or she is it. He is being "allowed" to do what he has to. Like those others, or like the luckiest of them.

Curiously, during all those hibernating sub-catatonic years, when at times I cannot read good prose or poetry from sheer despair at what could be done and I not doing it, when I dive into detective books as into a manhole, reading ever faster and more depressively —all along I know very well *who* is not allowing me. And that certainly it is not outward circumstance. (Certainly not because I am a woman, or a woman busy with children and without household help; I was never able to take that excuse route, which applies only to the surface things, and not to that inner life which is non-exclusive for both women and men.)

Psychiatry never occurs to me, and not only because, outwardly, I am performing conventionally. Instinctively I feel that neither the impasse, *nor* the solution, is entirely to be found in my intrapersonal life, present or past. This pattern I am in is, as far as possible in humans, an impersonal phenomenon, (bound to the psyche of course, but somewhere a-psychic), a religious one if you like, with the god-head residing in the work done. To which the personality of the worker, a feeder, a soma, might indeed be "everything," yet have to be so without benefit of a clergy—alone.

. . . My guess is that the best work still is done alone, safe from a stranger's invasion of that matrix which feeds it. Safe even perhaps from any amelioration of that madness which can also feed it, out of those insights which a collaboration, however "freeing" to the person, cannot give. A mind which has been freed to work by a process other than the work, is not the same, can never be the same, as the mind which has found its own precarious balance, murderous insight, and life celebration—within the process of itself. Psychiatry or psychoanalysis can no doubt be an experience within that process, but for writers particularly it perilously apes their own self-process. The examined self—*when the examiner is the unaided self*—is different. Indeed some writers, after the psychological process, though often conventionally kinder, wiser, happier or blander than before, also seem addicted to self in a way that the still-unraveled are not. And of course they have altogether another process to go to. To resort to. Whose standard, however delicately refraining from the older, obvious norms, somewhere generalizes towards these, somewhere pities "madness" and venerates "health." Yet conversely, has no god-head of its own—except *its* process. . . .

Art is its own form of life. Psychoanalysis is. Consider Blake or Genet, Whitman, Colette, Proust, Shakespeare, Shelley, Sappho, Firbank, or Chekhov, Beckett or Poe, the Brontes or Dickinson, Turgeniev, or Joyce or Dickens—doing both. Or the qualitative changes in the work of those, in our lifetime who have.

But, by 1951, I have been writing for four years, publishing for three. What has occasioned it? We are back East. In an air I am more at home in. My parents have been dead since 1942—is it that I can now say what I will of our family life, released from both it and from being a child? Is it that my own children are now of school age? That we have a house from which we no longer move? Among friendly people, of like culture, to whose aims I am almost not ashamed to confess mine?

. . . Hoards of selfhood have had to find their spillway; I have had to burst or break. The line between the two has been very thinned For too long, I have been in that state where one *knows* oneself to be something, someone, other than what appears. (Somebody whom no one else suspects one of being, or recognizes one as being.) This is paranoia then, unless one proves oneself by becoming what one feels one is.

Until I do write, there is a shame in confessing that I want to, so I don't confess it. And in a way, this makes a bind which helps keep me from writing, or from the posture of it—which might have helped. Most of all, to begin, I need my own self-approval—which hasn't come as easy or early or naturally as it does to some. (Yet in the writing schools, whose students are given the posture—of being a writer—on a platter, plus an immediate audience, I question whether they are not often also reduced from the rage of their own instincts, kept from that inner pressure to erupt, which has its own marvels. The attic poet, the attic soul, is often nourished by more than poverty.)

I have had plenty of approval, writing from the time I was thirteen, and through college. Once out, and into the life-shock, what I lack is my own. Even that modicum of self-approval necessary to *begin* writing, to put myself in the stance of it, does not come easy and natural. No doubt, that has its roots in family history. But also, I have been so fed on the wondrous dead of literature; it seems lèse majesté to try to align oneself at their side. Yet I can do nothing less. Harboring all this, I am gauche and private; from childhood I have known that privacy is the bourgeois' enemy.

("He's a very private person," a fashionable prates at me; they know that in "artistic" circles, this is felt to have worth. Yet an artist's privacy is an illusion. Rather, he is a fanatic, on whose scrolled flesh the marks are meant to be read. In some nations this may still be done at a respectful distance from his life. In ours, almost the last to have it so, were the Transcendentalists, in their sweet country commune. Shared barriers help. And a whole later generation revered Eliot for having fled us.)

When the courage to write finally comes, it may be simply because I have lived long enough. Perspective means having lived in a severe state of perception for some time. That I knew I had done; I had things to say; worthy or not, I had to say them. The story I write, almost the first since college, and the first published, is done in my head as I walk the younger child a long hilly mile to nursery school, call for him later—and twice in the routine walk it alone. Often on these solitary parts of the trip, as the story increases in my head, I find myself fighting for breath (though I am strong and have never fainted in my life) barely able to get to the house, where I fling myself down, and recover. Once I leave the child, no longer talking in his process, I am no longer safe. When I am walking with him, he is like an amulet by my side, while that story, which I am making about grandparents unknown to him, can go on.

I do not know that the name of my breathlessness is panic. On my occasional day-in-town, I begin to have it on the long lines waiting for the bus from New York back to Rockland County—going home, is that it? But once on the bus, thinking the story, I am safe. I fight for breath now in crowds, at parties, I who love parties and am a

New York City swimmer in crowds. It begins to happen anywhere. Thought can begin unawares, anywhere; whether it *can* begin, can be permitted to, is what is at stake. The panic comes closer finally— into the house. But the story is some pages now, I can no longer hold it in my head. Writing, breath is forgotten. Finished, these are my people, me. And slowly finding other stories, I write them. I have my breath now. The process that made the panic allays it.

. . . As for "hearing" the sequences of prose at some length before inditing them—(as I have just this moment done with the preceding paragraph)—I have always done that, holding in my head anything from a sentence to a page, just as I would for sections of a poem. More than that amount can often be projected but not as precisely —and only in impressionistic patches to be phrased later: figuratives waiting to be found. (And onomatopoetic effects waiting to be struck out). This makes for a prose that can always be read, often subtly demands that. Sometimes leading dangerously to a rhetoric which, loving its own rhythms, may stray too far from sense, or fall into marvelous accident—but towards a prose that in all its inflections is somehow a voice.

. . . I did not intend any of it, in those terms. From the first, when it begins to be said that I have a style, am a "stylist," I chafe. Doesn't this mean I have nothing to say comparable to the way I say it—or else that anything I say will all sound the same? I do have in mind an image of sentences I would like to read: long lean branches of them, with buddings here and there or at the end—of fruit, or short stoppages, in sudden calm. And a prose, centrally aural-visual, which would make one hear-see. The "disappearing" style once so vaunted by Maugham and so fondled by the hacks—that seems to me merely a "showing," with no room or vision left for "telling"—and done in an understatement which never dares overdescribe. The best style seems to me so much the fused sense of all its elements that it cannot be uncompounded—how-you-say-what-you-say, so forever married that no man can put it asunder. Its elements may be anything; the expression may be as elaborate or violent as the meaning is. (No one ever raises the point, if it is as *mild* as the meaning is.) The word "prose" itself is what should all but disappear in the mind as one reads; just as in poetry, one accepts the marriage of idea and word, but does not too dividingly congratulate. The marriage of meaning and manner is then its own lawful issue, a new object or presence, made accessible. What words make at their best is an open fortress of meaning.

So, in my late thirties, I began at last seriously to write—that is, as steadily as I could in time and vision, on both the hidden and the evident in the life I saw. And almost unwarily, had seen. Like many beginners, in the first work I set about understanding a family—mine, in absentia—theirs, picking my way carefully through injustices collected and just awards on both sides, making my analytic peace with them. The difference from therapy being, that each time I dove into the matrix, I retrieved a shape—a story, true—and in it a shape beyond its shape. Then suddenly, after less than a dozen such close-to-auto-biographical stories, their process is over; I want out, to the wider world.

In other words, I have my health now. That long half-schizophrenia in which I am other than I seem, is over, the pane of glass gone, in a regeneration that seems to me magical; years later, when in the novella *Extreme Magic* I write in its concluding paragraphs, "For extreme cases there is sometimes extreme magic," I will be amazed to have one commentator suggest that I have perhaps venally tried to impose a "happy" ending. What I have done is to stretch a dark story toward that light which I now know can occur in life.

When my first out-of-the-family, "non-autobiographical" story appears—"In Greenwich There Are Many Gravelled Walks," my friend and monitor, Julian Muller, who had become so by having discovered the stories and helped bring them to publication, calls to ask: had I ever known the people in the story?

"No, just bits and pieces of various people. No one person like any of them."

"Congratulations, you've just written your *second* novel!"

There was one remote family reference: my mother, in no way connected to the boy's mother as far as I could see, had, during a postpartum breakdown after my brother's birth, been for some months during my sixth year in a sanitarium in Greenwich, Connecticut. Which name, always said hushed, and of a place where I never was taken, had always sounded doomfully, linked with those recesses we keep, or *in which we are kept*. Once written about, it will no longer have that sound. As, once having set down the family stories, I will find that those incidents the mind had held in escrow until then, those depths that it had shaken me to recall, had now lost their power and even their configuration. But I will write more of mothers and daughters, and quite naturally, as men, in those configurations the world and the family pushes them toward, have written much of fathers and sons.

A second non-family story, *In The Absence of Angels* (later, at the suggestion of my editor, John Woodburn, the title of a first collection), Muller doesn't like at all, viewing it as a trend I ought to stay away from—it is political. It was he who had remarked, on seeing my first unpublished stories, that since they were of "a certain maturity," it was surprising not only that I was comparatively young but also that I had no prior publishing history—he had expected to hear that I had "come up through the little reviews."

In some ways, though I still didn't much read these, I was now belatedly going through the same history as some of those who had, or who had written for them.

.
. .
.

IN 1946-48, the American Labor Party, in and around that small river town, twenty-odd miles north of New York on the left bank of the Hudson, to which we had just moved, was almost certainly all but identical with a group who, it was later to be borne in on me, must have been a Communist cell. They were also my neighbors, all of us in a post-war euphoria, in this gentle idyll of a country still only half commuter, its legend-heavy corners filled with craftsmen who had begun arriving in the '20s, to live perhaps in the loosely collective housing of men like Maxwell Anderson, who financed dwellings for his friends, and Henry Varnum Poor, who built them, or in rentable enclaves, such as the stone cottages of Mary Mowbray Clarke, a sculptor's widow who with him had been involved in that historical Armory Show which had severed old painting from new. New couples arrived every day, from the city, from the war, ready for the dreams which such a countryside engenders—the farm-dream, the art-dream, the ecological one (a word heard early there). "Way of Life" for some meant "Proselyte it," for others "This is our Preserve." Everybody joined in dottily, enthusiastically, in the development of himself and his neighbor; it was a harmlessly effervescent way to live. Under the headlines, somewhere, people are living it now.

In our first year in Rockland, "the county" as it calls itself, with housing still war-tight, we rent an eighteen-room American Gothic whose one wing we sub-tenant amateurishly. First to a nice young man—we chat of *Howards End* at first interview—whose wife however, a former model for Valentina, goes out of the house only once in six months after the birth of the baby, and then in Charles Addams black, and is forever complaining of the old house's woes and our invisible landlord. Calling from the top of the stairs "Robber barons shall not steal my baby's gold!" she refuses, in sub-Englishy accents, our offer to let her husband tend to his furnace, during zero weather, via our inner cellar stairs instead of their outer one. "Naow, naow that would be squatterstown indeed!" Somewhat pitifully, she describes to us how her mother when ill, is carried up and downstairs by her father. Finally, after further complaints we cannot solve, she leaves us, apostrophizing "Robert, call father; father will send the Cadillac for us from Connecticut!"—which he does. In some relief, we take in a nicely nondescript couple brought to us by an American Labor Party acquaintance down the block, the woman plump, homy and *very* outgoing, the man shabby-dour under her umbrella of "just folks." Shortly he will be notorious.

A pair named Carpenter, they give as employment reference a muttered "World News Corp." or some such, which as once-bitten landlords we never check. Shortly after they are in, mail under the name of Zimmerman starts coming to them in our box, since though asked to, they have put up none of their own. (Later, I will understand that in an honest effort to annul the sense of property, they let the practice of sharing it slip vaguely into the art of sharing other people's.) Though I sort and hand over the mail, the matter of the two names is never mentioned—perhaps they know I have voted or will vote for Henry Wallace, and assume the rest (in fact Henry and I at this point are no doubt in the same state of guilt by association). All I assume is that they have translated their name. Settled in, they invite us for coffee; I gravitate at once to the books, finding them to be almost entirely about Russia, evoking no comment from me, though Mrs. C. suddenly volunteers that her husband had worked for a newspaper in the southern town from which they had just come. I ask, which one? "Which town?" she says. "No, which newspaper?" Possibly I was not picking up hints, passwords I should have. Her answer does give me pause. "I forget."

From there it isn't hard to notice that a weekly meeting of some sort does go on behind our common wall, and that Mr. C., whose silences Mrs. C. ascribes to hemorrhoids, commutes to the city by night bus, at what may well be newspaper hours: finally I deduce to my husband, "They're Communists, and I bet he's with *The Daily Worker*." (He was in fact, as the newspapers broke later, their "librarian"—and the David Carpenter who reputedly made the microfilm for Whittaker Chambers's pumpkin.) Although he and his wife never appear at those vaguely open, Saturday-night drink-and-dance parties given by one or the other members of that group we sometimes meet going up our steps.

Though most of the various people who did go to these gatherings may have been close to the inner workings of the Party, they were certainly not its philosophes. Small-business people, one generation away from the peddler East Side, middlewesterners emigrated from pa's hatstore in Oshkosh to Greenwich Village and then "up to the county" (one of these will turn out to be a government spy), couples who had met at the Art Students League, labor organizers and their rich wives, they were breezily different from the other young

"New York college people," professionals or not, who had brought their babies and their liberal opinions to the county also, now found themselves in the then rockbound political home-ground of Hamilton —"Ham"—Fish, and democratically meant to do something about it. One very brawny little man—call him Johnny, a Slav, Hungarian perhaps, or Pole, with one of those felted over, neutered names which are as recognizable as an alias and as forgettable, has had "real" experience in the mines or the steel-works, which others of the group spoke of with respect; though he too rarely appears at parties, he and his younger wife, who has organized a nursery school, often have people in, in what elsewhere is more simply the suburban or Rockland County way of dropping-in, of those years. One's house, if one liked it that way, or was socially eager, or came from the lonely years I had, could be a constantly receiving sieve.

Several times, I am brought to these parties by a stubbornly gentle Canadian-born woman who is to become a lifelong friend; whatever her interest in the Party, its roots are a passionate kindliness toward people and against the ills they are subject to and subjected to (she never much bothers with the distinction), which perhaps prefigures the artist she is to become. One night, when I happen to tag along to Johnny's, we find there a harried couple and their children, excitedly passing through from somewhere; though I am on the outer fringe and we don't speak, their air of being on the run stays with me; years later, I recognize the man's picture, as one of the five, (or was it six or twelve), leaders of the Party who were fugitive from government trial. If one recalls that no one at the time has ever yet spoken a word to me about the Party, that at best I am known to them as involved in the fight to get the local YMCA to open its pool to Negro children, it brings back, as their insistence on capitalizing Negro does, the whole loose folk air of their politics, in which to hum "Joe Hill," or to join in when somebody guitars the "Landlord, Landlo-oord" song (the girl who sings it, I am told, is the actor Will Geer's wife and "Mother Bloor's" niece, but I don't know who the Communist leader Mother Bloor is), sufficiently stirs up the collective Saturday-night sympathies. And to be classified a "good guy" is enough to allow you to be there, even among surely deeper and darker political realities, and conspiracies. . . . It never occurs to me that aside from my vaguely liberal opinions, what makes me interesting to them is that I am a writer. And perhaps capturable.

Intellectually they dismay me; if there is a secret dialectic they follow, it is certainly not one I can join. (I will still have to learn that I am incapable of joining any one group.) They are simple people, often of an endearing friendliness raggedly educated, wistfully ready to believe that group thinking will be high thinking. What attracts me most to them is their plain living, or their pleb experiences of it. In their conversation, even a sophomore's logic, which at least acknowledges that certain traditional truth-questionings have been argued before in the world's history, is unknown to them.

"Facts" they trust far more than I do, to the point of seeing nothing false in a misuse of these. Someone anonymously sends me the weekly *National Guardian*, which indeed has a style—soup-kitchen revolutionary. In the last article I ever read there, the narrator, leaving a certain part of Czechoslovakia by passenger-boat, is given a dockside sendoff by crowds of happy peasants handing him flowers, saying, "Give our love to Henry Wallace." But that part of Bohemia has no seacoast! I confide as much to my friend, but without result; she has a saint's need to see good.

I have a writer's need of it, and some ability to—but a disdain of absolutes. Shortly it must have become clearer that I was not going to settle for this one. At the last party I go to, as I sit on the arm of a chair, probably looking my disaffection, a woman who knows I have published in *The New Yorker* comes up to me. "Looky here, Richard Rovere is coming; just you wait." (He didn't.) Often, others too drop the names of philosophes they "know" (no one yet mentions Party) and so think will be attractive to me, all with the disarming simplicity of worker-ants preparing the way for somebody they judge more fit to meet their royalty than they.

By this time, even if I were to meet the more august Communist thinkers—in New England perhaps, or France—it would make no difference—now that I have met this lower echelon. Whose argument

now worries me far less than two other considerations: that too many
of their members seem to want the coterie as much or even more
than the goal—or else have anti-establishment hostilities, or pro-
cravings, which suspectly have very little to do with utopias, or with
political gains for us all. In the pursuit of any serious discipline:
revolutionary, scientific, artistic, religious, even military, I am asking
myself—how far ought the aim of camaraderie to go? Or the practice
of it? And how purist is one to be in weighing those other archetypal
motives which underlie the reddest flush of human devotion? (A few
years on, at a World Federalist Saturday night, to which the women
always bring fine foods, and where the company is chockablock with
"media" people who are maybe easier on the ear—though let more
years pass and many of the same will be heavy Unitarian—when my
friends Joe and Bob, an editor of *Life* and a writer for *The New
Yorker*, ask me why I don't join—don't I want world union, of course
I do!—I will search these same profundities before I answer, "Your
casseroles are too good.")

. . . Years later, when here and there I will finally meet those by
now documented "former" Party bigwigs of the literary world, it
will seem to me that their former-to-present lives, and their present
appearances, shine out to me the better for having known their proto-
types in that other lower echelon. All have become what every writer
becomes if he and she lives long enough, and publishes widely enough
—establishment. Some—and my prejudice is that these are almost always
those who live closest to the nerve of art—still live lives of passionate
views and statement, whatever their practice is. Others have been
tamed to the power *of* the establishment. Plain living or not, high
thinking or not, they have to me that definable air, meaner than hoped
for, of men and women who once sought the good of others, and
now, softly, have found it for themselves.

There exists a sad, almost schoolgirlish essay—its antecedents a combination of "The Woman Who Sees" (a column in *The Evening Sun*
when I was a child), the "Editor's Easy Chair" columns in our Civil
War *Harper's,* and all the *Atlantic Monthly* essay contests I never

entered, and its stance come down to me from all those minor elegists from Izaak Walton to Cowper, those diarists from Chateaubriand to Amiel to Rousseau, who had together taught me the humble obligation to meditate and observe—which was written in that last, valuable time before I knew for sure I had "views."

. . . Views I will be bound to propagate because, as a writer's, are they not public property?—and to promulgate because people will listen to them. All this to be done of course, in the assumption that these views are "right," and with the attitude that if a writer does this, he or she won't have to do anything else. I am to find this attitude —in which, to be verbally engagé is enough—intolerable as a private person. I will also find that on the barricades, even on such foot-high stiles as I venture, the habit of meditation creates a gap of its own. I would always leap back to the meditation . . . or forward, as I sometimes judged it . . . As a writer always will. . . .

It costs ten cents (I said) to ride the elevator to the top of the Washington Monument; you can walk up the 898 steps and 50 landings for free. The Saturday in early September on which my husband and I, our fourteen-year-old daughter and eight-year-old son, ended there a tour which had included various monuments and divers graves, was a perfect picture-postcard day. As the four of us stood on the hill overlooking the city, with the main points of the compass accurately pinned to earth for us—to the north the White House, to the east the Capitol, to the south the Jefferson Memorial, and nearest us, to the west, separated only by the long dark bar of its reflecting pool, the Lincoln Memorial—the minute, aerial photograph perfection of the scene only added to my depression. I recoil from the prearranged educational experience, on the grounds that anything of real value is usually acquired accidentally, at least by me. At such times, my view of history is dark, my separation from the crowd neurotically deep; as I stroll past the incised marble, the preserved trundle-bed. I keep up a constant, sub rosa colloquy with the dead, in which only they and I know how much less honorable they were, how much less honored they are, than the ladies' associations and the restorers would make them out to be. Only they and I know how rude, philistine, and essentially inconclusive it is to be alive at all.

Some one should have informed the talented retoucher behind the scenes that too much harmony between column and cloud makes the dangerous analogue between the two all the clearer. I looked guiltily at my children, standing next to me in the long line of people encircling the base of the monument, waiting their turn at the elevator. Had it been right for me to indorse for them this cardboard conception of "our nation's capitol?" Ought I not remind my daughter that the real officialdom, out of sight or out of town, petty as its army of civil servants, immutable as its McCarthy, nervous as the hop-head journalese of its dateline, had little in common with the symbolism of the obelisk that rose in our center? Wasn't it my duty to take her and my son (who had once asked, in our own northern town 'Why do Negroes have to live in such untidy houses?') to places not too far from the Lincoln Memorial and say "Here they are—the famous slums of Washington"?

I turned away from the eternally prodding, parental dilemma. To the right of us, a farmer out of Virginia or Maryland, a neat-featured, evenly browned man with pomatum slicked along the one cowlick that shot forward from his cropped head was chivvying his wife on .ie ability to walk up, instead of waiting for the ride. The wife, more than buxom, but still with a look of the Saturday-night belle about her, smiled, droopy-lidded, into the sun and made no move. A boy and girl of about the ages of our children squirmed restlessly around her.

"Mumma," said the girl, "will iyut be dowk in thay?"

A very young sailor, sauntering past with his arm around the waist of a girl, giggled, hearing the remark, and swung the girl closer to him, almost colliding with a gray-haired couple who stood immobile in the path, refusing the contact of the tightly packed line. The woman, in her voile, flowered hat, and sensible white shoes the very prototype of so many sailors' mothers in so many refrigerator ads, moved self-consciously nearer her husband.

"Ha-rry," she said, in that middle-western accent which is almost Scottish, "have you closed the windows of the car-r?"

The husband nodded, swinging his watch chain against his dark suit, and the two of them gazed with satisfaction at the parking grounds just below us, where a Buick, set a little apart from the other cars gleamed like patent leather in the sun.

The guard herded us forward, almost to the door of the monument. As we stood there, four young women, dressed alike in black pinafores over underdresses of purplish blue, with caps like Whistler's mother's tied on their center-parted dark hair, came around the side of the obelisk. The tallest, a strapping, heavy-browed girl with more animation than the other three, was deep in conversation with the uniformed driver of a bus tour. The waiting three all had a similar pigeon-breasted scrawniness which, with their high, domed foreheads, gave them the air of women in American "primitives," a look marred into reality by their dull, pimpled complexions, which contrasted with the purity of the caps.

"Deaconesses?" I murmured.

"Mennonites," said my husband.

"Oh." That explained the complexions. I knew something of the Pennsylvania Dutch diet. "Seven sweets and seven sours."

I watched the women as they walked on with the gesticulating driver. As our section of the line penetrated the monument, and we, the farmer and his family, the couple of the Buick, and thirty or forty others as variegated as a poster, were inserted into the elevator, I reminded myself that crowds always have a specious vigor and significance; I must be careful not to draw from it any homilies on the far-flung strength of a nation. Remember, I thought, the verdigrised crowds in the subway, and Harlem on a Sunday afternoon, with the crowd sweated out of its peeling doorways on to the splotched sward of the streets.

At our backs a loudspeaker suddenly gave tongue in a neutral, unregional voice. We listened as we rose, the perfect captive audience, with, for a minute and a half, no place else to go but up inside a shaft, as the voice told us, whose walls were 15 feet thick at the base and 18 inches at the top.

"In a 30-mile-per-hour wind," said the voice, "the sway of the monument is only .125 of an inch."

The voice rested, in perfect timing with the elevator. We disembarked and took our turns at each of the deep-ledged windows through which Washington was exposed with exquisite arterial mimeography. From the slit at which I stood I could see the narrow bar of the Memorial Bridge, its farther end plunged in the greenery of Arlington, which we had visited the day before. Somewhere in that greenery lay the Custis Lee mansion, in front of which L'Enfant, the planner of Washington, is buried. One end of his small triangular tomb points toward the hideously thick, squat columns which support its porch—columns, as my husband had remarked, more suited in their relative proportion, to Knossus, than to the porch of an eighteenth century house. We had wondered how well that architectural purist rested in the sight of them, and had hoped, with the easy insolence of the sightseer, that his head was pointed the other way.

In the little Hudson River town of Piermont, not far from where we live, there is a house designed by L'Enfant, built in 1839 by John Fredon, then president of the Erie Railroad, purportedly to satisfy the nostalgia of a southern wife. It must always have been too magniloquently grand for its situation, set as it is, out of sight of the river, in a valley whose topography could never have given the high-columned porch a proper approach, the view from its widow's walk blunted by an undistinguished hill. Now, although it is well kept up by its present owner, the blank brick wall of the silk mill further constricts its horizon, the creek which must once have been "idyllic" steams with the exhaust of the paper-box factory up the river, and every so often one of the nearby shacks topples or burns. Although it was built long before the Civil War, it must even then have had a lost confederate air—the look of the revenant. But L'Enfant, perhaps, might have liked to be buried there. It has something of the look of his incomplete Washington—of an audacious plan overwhelmed by the complexities of progress—and its columns, slender and improvidently high, are his own.

As we began to descend, the canned voice of the monument spoke again. This time it spoke of the symbolism of the walls which enclosed us, of the world's admiration for the principles of democracy and liberty, and it ended, in graceful synchronisation as we grounded, with greetings from that Department of the Interior under whose perpetual care those principles might be presumed to be. On the faces pressed close around me, I charted the sway of emotion—not more than .125 of an inch.

As we walked out into the sun again, I fumbled in my purse for the leaflet I had retained from Mount Vernon. Mount Vernon, as restored by the Mount Vernon Ladies Association, its clapboards tidily anachronized with stucco, its servants quarters labeled with the names of the original occupants—*Aunt Judy's* room—as if they too, along with the immobile rockers, the empty bread troughs, hadn't been able to escape the collector. I had liked the tomb however, as simple a one as any of our national heroes is likely to have, designed by its inhabitant. We are lucky in this hero, I had reflected; the plot of his biography is spare and rectilinear, if not easily humanized, not easily debunked either, for the most fallible thing we know of him is that he married a widow and had to wear false teeth.

I opened the brochure. "The estate had long been unproductive; the buildings had unavoidably depreciated; gardens and grounds had suffered. A comprehensive plan of repairs and restoration was immediately inaugurated. . . . Since 1858 the tract has been enlarged to an area of sufficient size to insure the property against undesirable encroachments."

It wasn't hard to imagine which sort of encroachments the Mount Vernon ladies had deemed undesirable. I knew suddenly that it was not the depredations of the present on the past which made me a squirming onlooker in the shadows of obelisks, or at the beautifully cut hair of graves. It was the undesirable encroachment—on an inadequate present—of the historic property itself.

Below us, whitening in the noon light, Washington posed its uncomfortable questions, clarified in marble or obscured in the crypts of the brave. From the Lincoln Memorial, on whose steps Marian Anderson sang, one might draw a straight, though not unimpeded line to Constitution Hall, within whose doors she could not. Such a line would pass, probably, through the Munitions Building and the Atomic Energy Commission—accumulating, therefore, certain other platitudes along the way.

"Where is Lincoln buried?" I murmured to my husband.

"Springfield," he said, with a look of surprise.

"Oh, of course," I muttered. "When lilacs last."

Four young men in black suits suddenly tramped toward us around the bend of the path, their long, Dutch-cut hair swinging rhythmically against their round cheeks, under stiff-brimmed hats identically wide as platters. These were the Mennonite husbands. They plodded past us in a kind of instinctive unison, looking straight ahead of them with a blank, cenobitic stare. In a sense they, and we, were encroachments on one another. Yet if there was a central fact which could equilibrate the presence here of both of us, of all the people in the mural, it was that, tangential as we were to one another, we held certain graves in common, and occasionally paid them mind.

I watched as they walked down to the curb where the women and the bus driver waited.

"Where do you suppose he's taking them?"

"Arlington," my husband said.

"Daddy," my son said, looking at some passing uniforms, "which way is Korea?"

There was a pause. It was of a kind which occurs often these days, more often in the conversations of men, although it happens among women too, when something seen or said tears the palpable modern serenities aside, and we remember, for a minute, that the feudal bleeding still goes on. I call it "the civilian pause."

For its second, my husband hesitated.

"That way," he said, waving a curt hand toward the sun, and

linking arms with one another, we all walked together down the
path to the car.

I called the piece "How Sleep The Brave."


ODE
WRITTEN IN THE BEGINNING OF THE YEAR 1746

How sleep the brave, who sink to rest,
By all their country's wishes bless'd!
When Spring, with dewy fingers cold,
Returns to deck their hallow'd mould,
She there shall dress a sweeter sod
Than Fancy's feet have ever trod.

By fairy hands their knell is wrung
By forms unseen their durge is sung;
There honor comes, a pilgrim gray,
To bless the turf that wraps their clay;
And Freedom shall awhile repair,
To dwell a weeping hermit there!
William Collins


This was to be the one time I would use a title not original with
me. Novels armored with quotes from Donne or Yeats or Kierkegaard
are using another man's effects. But this poem, which in college I
had committed to memory, had a special bitterness for me. Even after
a war, its martial elegy could move me. But I no longer believed a
word of it.

What I wrote under its aegis, was—a prelude. (I am to do this many
times again, this audible thinking before I leap into a short story or
a novel, yet it will take me years to see this connection between my
non-fictional and fictional life.)

Shortly after, in the story *In the Absence of Angels*, my work itself enters politics. This is my answer to the gap between ideas and action —I will write it out. In the way that is natural to me. There I will dare anything.

•
•
•

In 1950 *The New Yorker* prints a story of mine called "Old Stock," about a young girl at a Jewish summer resort in the Catskills, one in the old-farmhouse style, centered among natives of the region—and her first encounter with anti-semitism "outside," inside her own family, and possibly in her Jewish self. Before publication, an editor there warns me that both the magazine and I will get a lot of protest mail on it. "From Anti-Semitic Jews who don't know they are." Innocently, I ask, isn't it brave of the magazine to do this then— publish what they already know will bring them protest mail? He answers that all the magazine asks of any work on a controversial subject is that it be impeccable as art—that is, as nearly as possible invulnerable to criticism on artistic grounds. (I will come to believe that little of art is, or that only *little* art is.) But what he says next will return to me often. "You will learn to expect that when people disagree with what you say, or are offended by how you say it, they often won't admit that; they'll say that the work is bad, that you're a bad writer."

Mail does come, from all sides. When addressed to the magazine, it is answered by them, copies of both being forwarded to me. In accordance with their habit of checking any possible usage with existent authorities, they have countered one correspondent who has protested my use of "race" (as applied to Jews of course), with a citation on that word from B'nai Brith, which has O.K.'d my use of it. Letters addressed to me care of the magazine are sent on for my reply. I answer them all, as I will all correspondence from then on. (Even though you believe, as I do, that the best works of imaginative literature are not primarily or a priori controversial, if you also believe that the pen is a power, you cannot refuse to deal at least once with any response it evokes. Up to a point, and addressed to whatever grain of sense.) Still I am grateful for that editor's warning, otherwise the bundles of hate that keep arriving would really throw me.

A Rabbi Silver of Cleveland—*The* Rabbi Silver, as I am told by friends closer to actively Jewish circles—writes a diatribe in his newspaper. I begin to see that the anger, whether it is illiterate, orthodox, written under a university letterhead or scrawled on an obscene postcard, is all covertly the same. Whether it is felt that I have criticized Jews' life-habits, or have even collaborated with the Gentiles by suggesting that *special* Jewish habit exists—I have in each case touched on the same self-hatred and secret fears; I have dared to imply that Jews are not impeccable. (Like art.) And it is all the worse, all the harder to get at, because I have done it under the guise of art.

I understood their anger well enough, also that it goes deeper than anti-Faganism (Jewish villains in literature, movies, et al). Goes below even the holy feeling of many Jews (more anti-Christian than moderates ever admit) that "now of all times"—after a war in part fought for the six million dead—Jews must stand together, and Jewish artists also, by not letting one "anti" iota enter the already half-poisoned air. By never ever even "contributing to it"—as the phrase often went—with any of the unfortunate humor and self-analysis to which centuries of stress had bred us.

I understood what I had done better than they—or earlier. My sin was double. I had expressed some of these tormenting self-doubts which even the most outwardly impregnable Jew—rich, assimilated, cosmopolitan, living an easy life scarcely subject to slurs, much less oppression—may still be born with: Are "we" anything like "they" say we are? Are we defensively proud of being whatever we are, because we have to be? What are we really, underneath the pride? And: Would we really rather not be what we are? Worst, I had explored what must never be admitted to enemy forces—that there are divisions in our ranks. Not only divisions, but hierarchies. I had turned up the underside of our own snobberies.

I was well equipped to, having been born into some of them. My mother (whose portrait I had given in a story called "The Middle Drawer," as well as in "Old Stock"), had been born in a small, rural town probably not so nearly "on the outskirts of Frankfurt" as she claimed, and of a family at the most respectably petitbourgeois; it pained her to admit that a beloved maternal Grandfather Rosenberg, a refined man, had been a cattle dealer. Her pretenses were enlarged by her ever present consciousness that, in spite of heroically perfect English, she was still in her own mind—must it not always be in other people's?—an emigré. Women like her made the Bovarys, the sighers in all the provinces of Europe; later, as a young woman in New York, just in sight of the city feast, but much too respectable to make anything flamboyant of her beauty, she had waited again to move out of her environment. The maternal aunt and uncle-in-law to whom she had come at sixteen, owners of a thriving bakery company in Yorkville, lived in the brownstone ranks of German Gentiles who seemed to me very like themselves. Most of the women in that family (it was the women who emigrated) did indeed look so "German" that it was hard to believe in their pure Jewish blood, or else not credit the very inheritance of acquired characteristic. In turn, they hated the newer ranks of Galitzianers, Poles, and Russians for their foreignness, and, as I grew to know in my adolescence, for their colorfulness. German Jews of that era hated those others for their presumed peasant vulgarities, which "dragged down" Jews like themselves into the ranks of the "unrefined." Really, it was that those others had been inexcusably late. Even any who had been university-educated in the old country or were already professionals here—(now and then I brought home their sons and daughters)—were regarded by the German Jews with the suspicious contempt of people who had never had the idea of the university in their blood.

What my German family admired was rich merchants, industrialists, which a few became; they had no taste for learning as far as I knew, and may well have thought this a Galitzianer or Russian talent too. Once, as we sit in my aunt's bay-window in Seventy-Ninth Street, there draws up at the door the longest limousine I have ever seen, come to take my aunt and uncle for a drive, and I hear my mother's respectful breath at my elbow "Mr. Littauer." Foundation-wealth, as years later I discover. But at the moment I wonder only why they should think it so exceedingly nice of him to trot up the front steps himself, instead of sending the chauffeur.

In a pre-World-War-Two Germany, my mother's half-brother has risen to a townhouse in Berlin with brocaded-walled dining room, and to a white Mercedes of a length identical with Von Hindenburg's —on occasion standing up in it to bow to a populace which mistakes him for the minister. I learn this from his son, my cousin, who in 1937, fleeing from the Fatherland as the first of a train of refugees to be sponsored by my father, gets off the boat with eighteen pieces of pigskin luggage and a German actress on one arm, and sad memories of a ski-hut in the Dolomites, whose table has soup-bowls hollowed into the wood. I have no reason to disbelieve his legends; none on that side are imaginative, neither the women, with their short straight noses and censorious mouths, nor the men who now keep arriving, thickened and formal, with white-flab hands gruesome to receive in the limp, European handshake. None are in the professions; my father has had to find the once-rich young cousin, who has made a bad investment in sugar en route through Holland, a factory job. And none are artists. . . . It was a good background from which to rebel.

My father, on the other hand, has a towering pride in his Jewishness *and* in his Southernness; how Southern Jews of his era had managed this was a nineteenth-century triumph which has come down to me, diluted. He could read Hebrew, no doubt with a drawl. His sisters, trained in music and needlework at the Academy of St. Joseph, in the Richmond of their day the "only" place to go, see nothing untoward in this nor does he; while Jewish men carried on the heritage of near-learning, they had had to get the education ladies got. They are all comfortable with Gentiles, having had them as close friends and neighbors, but this generation, except for one maverick, would not have married them. Their sons and daughters, including me, will do so entirely.

My father's education, formally stopped at the age of twelve when he jumped out of a school window and ran away after having been rapped over the knuckles with a ruler by a female teacher, never really ceased. A great reader, he had taught himself a little Latin and small Greek, spoke a French patois the New Orleaners did, from some residence there, and could swap fake German with my mother, in an accent that disturbed her as possibly Yiddish. Years later, in a chance quote of his, I recognize it as merely the way a self-taught Virginian might pronounce Goethe. His literary knowledge was a flossy quicksand; often only the names had stayed on top, but he knew what was to be got from books, and wistfully honored it. His own father had had a drygoods store in Richmond, but whatever schooling my grandfather might have picked up in his trek from Liverpool to the U.S.A., he had likely been but an average merchant. (When I stood in the old Richmond graveyard, closed since 1917, I could mourn this with real envy; half the early department-store names of America seemed to have come out of it. Among these Samstags and Hochschilds, and Hutzlers, only the Calishers had not achieved either a brokerage house or an emporium.)

But even as a child, I doubted that only the Civil War had ruined their fortunes—early sensing a Southern illusion carried North. My father wasn't a beaver businessman either, although until the twentieth century caught up with him, his own brand of panache and small-town independence had done him well. But his mother, born in Dresden, must have brought a taint of learning with her; her elder brother, Siegmund Bendan, had been a visiting professor of philosophy at New York University, and some Ben-Dan before them, a rabbi. When, on graduation, I finally confess to my father what I will never reveal to others later, that I want to be a writer—at the moment a poet—he brings out a notebook of his own poems, never before mentioned, flicked now under my eyes only tangentially, and at his death lost, saying "Looky here. I wanted to. But you can't make a living out of poetry, m'dear." Already the family flesh was a little corrupted with art yearnings! It is left to me to make the next transition between bourgeois and bohemian. "I don't *want* to *make a living* out of it!"

Meanwhile, my mother keeps up a onesided battle-of-the-hier-archies. When she is angry at him, usually over his allegiance to his clan of matriarch mother, overbearing sisters and dependent brothers, she will try to bring them down a peg, in the peasant way. For while education is no longer suspect to her—indeed envied for what it can Americanly do, she shrewdly sees that what they do have of it they exaggerate. Besides, it is more than likely the very thing in them that bleeds the money away; somewhere along the line they have become incapable of caring most about money. Though by now her-self an incipient collector, already glimpsing the road between money and art, she still knows, in her own words "what comes first." Her supreme contempt however, is for their secure Jewishness, on which she cannot shame them, even when she voices her opinion that the family name had probably begun as Kaliski—name-endings à la Russe or Pole being the worst she can think of.

It was possible. Somewhere in the England of my great-grandfather, Calishers had turned into Curtises, vide my father's first cousin, Julius Curtis, and even to Campbells (in a notorious case of mistaken identities, in the 1930s, a cousin of ours, Bertie Campbell, spent some years in prison for another man's offense, until pardoned by the Governor of New York State.) Though like many early synagogues in America, the one in Richmond (Beth Shalome) had had the Sephardic ritual, much of the congregation had been "German." We had had a few "Spanish" connections, and also, like any English-Jew emigré I met in those days, claimed relationship with a Chief Rabbi of England, in our case through some cousins named Belais, one of whom, Diana, had become president of the Anti-Vivisection Society here. (Had she got it from watching him ritually slaughter chickens?— I always wondered.) But there is incontrovertibly a town named Kalisch which was always being swapped back and forth across the German-Polish border. And I agree with my mother; we probably came from it.

By now however, my father, in his second-generation southernness, is quite simply a certain kind of smalltown American. In the Richmond of his birth in 1861, everybody either did know everybody else or

had the idea that he could—to which were to be added all the levelings
of a town first under military siege, then suffering the long effects of
it. Jews there were often just people, or if socially mobile, always
from their own centers of racial pride. I suppose this is why Southern
Jews, up to recent times, have been so remarkably comfortable in
themselves. As Jews and as Americans, they had pride-of-birth covered
from either side. I saw that my father, in any company—of which, by
the time I knew him, he had had a varied lot—could not be patronised.
Either Southern comfort, or else what his wife called his "Jewish
cheek," would always take care of it.

What would compromise me with some Jews later, was that I
had no recent *shtetl* tradition. The flaccid "reform" Sunday School
I attended up through confirmation had no flavor of it, nor did the
synagogue itself, where history was making a fast beeline between
Judas Maccabeus and the present, on its way to Long Island—on
which most of the congregation had their eye. Chosen as a nearby
compromise with my mother's neutralized ambitions, my father
shrugged at it and used it only for the high holidays—she never went
at all. But would the Spanish-Portuguese synagogue, where he wanted
us to go, have fed me more of Mittel-Europa? I doubt it. Until I
read of the *shtetl* and met its traces in friends, I had literally never
heard about it. The mass of Americans who had its sub-Talmudic
humors and pogrom legends very close to the ear, would always
find it hard not to believe that I didn't have it too, and was only hiding
it. (Probably I must really know Yiddish and was hiding that too.)
After a while, I did learn to hide our length of time in America,
finding early that the very span itself—which to me was history and
family memory—to them *was* patronage. Finally, it would keep me
from being a "Jewish" writer, in the rising American tradition of
that ethnic. We had been here too long. And I wanted more.

I wanted to be—what I was. After all, I had been taught to be that.
We were merely farther on into the mixed American swirl. It never
crossed my mind that my work would have to deal with this. It
simply never occurred to me not to. The spoor of the crossbred

American, ever in more complex overlay, excited me. I was that mixture myself.

. . . In the lingo of democracy, America has always been a classless nation. Yet writer after writer, from James to Faulkner, from Dreiser to Fitzgerald, has proclaimed the opposite. A work that does so here, or a writer, is always in danger, at least at first. For Americans, to go back in time is to be a recidivist, a snob, unless, like a Lowell, you are already in the national mind very clearly defined. (Then it is patriotism.) Class difference, when finally admitted in the United States, was thrown to the sociologists. Who have treated it as such a stinkbomb of a subject should be—without humor and without human coloration. So that none of us skunks would smell of the results.

In the zoo of the social sciences is where the musk-glands of humanity are removed—for study. A novel doesn't study—it invents. Inevitably, it represents. In the end, the novels a nation chooses to keep, to admit to its heritage, are always those which in some way cohere its own images of itself. Often, in America, these have been class-images, of some class structure the nation doesn't yet know— or refuses to know—it has. Yet among the great European novels I had been bred on, those I most grappled to me were the least naturalistic or realistically representative; I would always choose a Dostoievski over a Tolstoi. My American heritage was showing.

An Englishman of the widest reading once said to me of a novel of Joyce Cary's which I couldn't "see" as I thought I "saw" the others, "You can never understand why we so took it to our hearts. It so represents us as we know we are." As they already know they are, from centuries of being it. Americans resist any classification, or confirmation of what they are—as if from the founding fathers' imperative to do so because *change* will be their greatness. Conversely, we—or its middle class—love the masochistic trendbooks like Vance Packard's, or any of those sociological simplifications which lightly flay us with those forms into which we may already have congealed.

What we ask of literature, prose or poem, is that it give us back our national experience, in myth.

We asked it early. And got it, long before Jung, sometimes in a book like *Moby Dick*—which had to wait. As seekers of our myth rather than our realism, in the novel we were closer to German and Russian literature than to that of the language in which we spoke and wrote. And the genius of "our" novel, in so far as one could still separate it from the ever widening nonnational stream of them, often seemed to lie in those regions where, asked for myth, it could still give it, almost to the farthest poetic reaches of prose.

But all a writer thinks of when he or she first starts is "Well, now *I* am here." And what do I do now? Next? Dare I? Can I?

After that first story collection in 1952, though writing steadily, if very slowly, I did not publish the expected novel, or any book, for another nine years. Partly because I still had stories to write, and because the vision of the novel I dimly saw (beginning in 1953) took its time. I saw it as something literally real enough for a reader to "walk around in," yet non-real enough for those flights from the subscribed-to-ordinary, in which for me the heights of literature lay.

I was beginning to have a host of fragmentary subjects, or mythic preoccupations, but as yet had no "world" to put them in. Certainly no national one. When it came, a novel-of-the-self grafted on a novel-of-event, it took a man, not a Jew, from that England which "we"—nation and family—had in part come from, to a South where that same "we" had in part arrived. And on to New York. Written through the late fifties, published in 1961, the only Jews in it were an English family, half mythic certainly, in the man's beginnings, and their American counterpart, sought out by him close to the book's end. The event-climax of the book (too soon for its length, some said, and until I completed the sequel and saw the whole, I half-thought so myself) was black-white. In these Ku Klux Klan sections, I had hit on a mythic-real we ourselves maintained as a nation. But I wanted more.

That book, *False Entry*, ended with a climax-of-self, in the man's realization of his first "mythic" family through his second and American one, whose members appeared only in a kind of prelude of themselves, enough being left unanswered to set people asking me about them for years. I kept it to myself that when I had finished the book in the usual beautific daze, instead of going to the cupboard for the usual lone, Palladian drink, I had surprised myself by setting down and locking away a page of quick successive notes for a book on them, not to be taken up again until after two novels and other shorter works in the intervening four years. In the "sequel," *The New Yorkers*, which takes place before the action of *False Entry* (I learn to think of them as one chronicle, approachable from either end, fitting together like the halves of an almond and publishable as *A Single Story*) I will take up that second Jewish family, with its Czech servitors and Viennese hangers-on, but in tandem with a Protestant family of like realm, following both through the ramifying world of New York—and time. . . .

By then, novels of consecutive time, written in ours, begin to bore me; I don't think time is that, nor is this the order I would most wish to impose on it. Time should radiate complexly, as it does in life, or does for me. Nothing in art should be in too straight a line. . . . When I take up the sequel, its people impose their own labyrinth, of events and style. I also find in myself an ironic dryness less concerned with self-emotion than it is with society. And either book, will be less than the sum of the two, and better understood, better completed, as part of the whole. Even the West African in the second book (in the present climate, would some think of him as a token black?) complements those Negroes in the first one—a conscious man, Anglicized toward the "real," as opposed to their mythic group-dark.

I see that now; I had no thought of it then, and maybe write here what ordinarily I would only muse—in order to show that later on, one can. Was I trying to express the whole American stream of consciousness in my time, what was in our event-stream, and the blood-directed stream of our collective minds? I can't tell you. Not even now. A writer should never let himself know what he "wants to express" or wanted to, other than in the doomed-to-be words of the actual work. But one thing I did know as I wrote them; this second book *was* about class—here.

Meanwhile, back in the first years, I continue prowling the world of Jews I do know. I would soon write another story, *One of the Chosen*—about a well-assimilated Jew who, like me, had never suffered too many slurs, and thought he was safe—already my guilts were rising, as with non-sufferers all over the world. And all over unscathed America. After living in England again, I would write "Two Colonials," which had to do with the way some tiresome Christians romanced Jews in a way we did not do ourselves. Together with the early piece I quote from, they were all I would do in that vein. I would not write of Jews again until *The New Yorkers*, where, returning as if to the earliest genre pictures of my own childhood, I took up again, in an effort to set down its mythic-real, the relatively unsung world of the Jews I knew best.

"Hun' Forty-Fifth" (originally titled "Hun' Forty-Fifth They Gotta Get Out") is a period piece about the way some Jews felt about blacks. Twenty years ago. And now? During the New York City teachers' strike, one of them, coming up to me at an art show "because I already know how *you'll* feel" all but shouts nigger-lover at me; though as a Jew I should be "one of us," I will not join in the "This is how *we* feel" of her special establishment. I am a traitor because I will not "stand together" with her and them.

It is then, and in the weeks that follow, when black resentment against "Jew teachers," "Jew merchants," also finally gets out into the open, even into the papers, that I think of what happened to "Hun' Forty-Fifth," so long tucked in a drawer. It's only an anecdote, on a subrosa subject to whose complications "nobody" except Leroi Jones and some other blacks "wants to contribute"—not the Mayor, not the Jews—and not me? I already know how it can be when, warily looking around me to assure myself that only Jews are present I mention, only as a contribution to history, those streetcorner "slavemarkets" where Bronx housewives not too many years ago used to bid for black dayworkers. "It's not good to bring these things up," they tell me. I am not sure. I am sure—and have been for years now—that there is a hierarchy among minorities too, which has extended even to literature.

By the time I write "Hun'" I have begun to be aware of what underlies Southern comfort. I know now who it was my father patronized. (When, some years later, I write a story called "Mayry," which begins "My father, born in Richmond about the time Grant took it, was a Southerner therefore but a very kind man," the copyeditor who is checking it for publication, very much a Southerner, will call me up to ask if I don't mean the "but" in that sentence to be an "and"). So by now did many Southerners, and writers. I have been raised in the North; it can never be my total subject as it can for them. I am only half-Southern anyway. And Jew as well. How many sides am I fated to see?

(The side I shall see most and longest will be a matter for literature, not of racial controversy or any other. I will have to learn over and over, that the *blended* subject is the most difficult, anywhere. The normal literary treatment for "minority" feeling is to segregate it by ethnic strain. Certain subjects are sacredly reserved for one kind of treatment, which is comfortably apprehendable, and like a sermon or a good recording ratifies what we already know. Mixtures, of people or theme, only make trouble. They make *new* subjects, new ways of seeing.)

One penny postal from the mail on "Old Stock" had amused me. "Miss Calisher doesn't know anything about Jews. Furthermore she doesn't know anything about the *Catskills*." Its girlish complaint reminds me of the girls I had known so well in the garment district; its undertone of "Us!"—that proud-anxious sigh from the sinuses, is one I have heard all my life. Lightheartedly, I set down their conversation. Perhaps I had literally heard it—and I have a parrot-ear. Their lingo, as they straphang on the Broadway train, is unconsciously self-certain.

Claire Brody, the chatterer, the leader, and on the job-hunt, describes how that day, an employment agency has sent her for a job off Seventh Avenue; they have mistaken her name for Brady. Without once saying "Christian"—but all Jews who read will know—she describes the firm, the interviewer's innuendoes and the turn-down—and her righteous wrath.

" 'Mr. Buck,' I say, 'My brother, an electrical engineer, he couldn't get a job before the war—don't bother to ask why. Right now there's a shortage, he's working, they don't ask about his religion.' They ask, he says, he's going to tell them he's a member the Ethical Culture Society—culture for what he learned in the night school, ethics for what he learned in the daytime."

But all this time in the crowded car, she has been urging her confidante to stand in a certain place. "Hurry up, dope, like I told you Over there." They attach themselves to a new set of straps above two seats "occupied by a very black young man in an eclectic maroon hat and a very light-skinned Negro woman in a severe blouse and horn rims, who was reading from notebooks in a leather portfolio." As the train enters the 145th Street station, the young man gets up to leave; Claire makes Selma take his seat at once. As the woman too gets up to go, the two girls see that her fur coat and Claire's are almost identical.

Claire: (as she sits down) "What'ya know! Maybe I should a gotten beaver after all!" (She looks carefully around the car, almost all of whose occupants are seated now, before she speaks in a low voice: "Honestly, the real black ones I don't mind. But those pale intellectual-looking ones—don't they give you the creeps?"

Selma (nodding) "They say you can always tell by the nails though."

As the story ends, Claire is thanking God for the Eighth Avenue subway. "On the Seventh, you never get a seat." New Yorkers of those days will remember that the Eighth Avenue train ended in environs wholly white.

Claire: "Incidentally—what's the matter your reaction time? I practically had to push you across the car. I told you—all you go

to do is stand in front of a couple of them. Hun' twenty-fifth, practically always. But the next one for sure. Hun' forty-fifth, they
*gotta* get out."

In "Hun' Forty-Fifth" I have dug up an even hotter potato. *The New
Yorker* tells me that the piece will evoke more controversy. And
this time, is not strong enough to sustain it. Downheartedly, I agree.
Jewish conversation is stuffed to the gills with what I had described,
but *reality is no excuse*. I hadn't intended anything on a grander
scale. I should have. In that moment I learned this. Oughtn't a writer
know better the importance of what he was saying? And know it
first? "Old Stock" was a *story*. Out of pure experience. "Hun'
Forty-Fifth" was only a rebuttal. Of a professional experience. In
light reportage. On a killer subject.

Still, what the piece says has a right to be said. No matter how?
Or if "the wrong people" get ahold of it—which is why Jews are
always saying we should close ranks?

I have a sudden itch to know what will happen if the right people
get ahold of it. I'll send it to one Jewish periodical, then put it
away.

They reply swiftly that the subject is not within their scope. Maybe
not.

Or not yet within mine.

By now I know that whether you write well or ill, you will never
write truthfully about any ethnic group and please it; in humanizing it, how can you go on capitalising it? Yet, if I couldn't stand
with my own, what was I? A creature who, when the world cried
"Chicken!" or "Traitor!" cried art? Until I could resolve that work-
ably enough (which meant enough so that I could go on working)
I often thought so.

The work was the answer.

. . . *People* stand together. Art stands with them, in their humanity.
But art itself is not a standing together. I will have to learn that over
and over.

As for "Hun' Forty-Fifth," by now it's a period piece. Nowadays on the subway, they may only have to get out somewhere around Riverdale.

•
•

IN THE MID-1950S Philip Horton of *The Reporter*, overhearing me talk of a year spent working at Macy's as anything from comparison-shopper-for-stocking-stretchers to head-of-stock-in-the-hat-department, asks me to "do a piece for us" on it. The magazine phrase already holds much that I fear. I haven't the sociological stance for either the somber, "in-depth" approach of the serious journals, or the newer, light jazziness that is now growing on our commentators, perhaps from their sense that the "superficiality of our time" ought to be treated in its own rhythms. I had no "approach" and didn't want one.... It is the hazard of all who commentate. And a stylish death for many writers.... Yet I am tempted. In spite of a hated year at that store, spent sunk in the misery of the college-graduate who is turned out, *en grande tenue* metaphysically, into a rough, cheap business, I had had only a smart worm's view of the place. But more, ever since my fellowship year in England, I envy the serene mobility of writer-friends there, where writers as yet did not much teach for a living (or come here to, as they do now) but while working for the BBC perhaps, saw themselves as honorably able to rove anywhere in printed space. "Oh, I was only a Macy underdog," I joke. "You'd have to get me to their President." Next thing I know, I have an appointment with a vice-president; Horton has been told that my lack of reputation as a journalist proscribes anybody higher.

Over a three-hour lunch with him—what fun to come in from the country and the children's lunch to dawdle in the East Fifties like a real reporter!—we discuss this highly intelligent man's—intelligence. He is an art-hungerer, for one thing. As one of the earliest to use good painters like Shahn in advertising, he is shortly to leave Macy's for television, but between he and me and his analysis, we know that he isn't going to be happier, trapped as he still will be in all the Byronic despairs of moneymaking.

... This was my first encounter, in the business world, with what I shall call the phenomenon: Art Hunger As Expressed To Artists. I will learn to meet it anywhere, in all versions: in the college-president who ignores a celebrated banker and possible trustee whom I have helpfully seated on his right, in order to quote poetry to a celebrated poet on his left. In the former novelist, now a movie-writer, who tells me he lives and works abroad, not because he both loves his comforts and can't bear the company of writers who write, but so as "to protect his real and future work from the hurly-burly of American literary life." In all cocktailers who come up to you with the shy disclaimer "I'm only a successful *family* person"—generally female, and all from "A trade rather like yours"—generally male. The message is always the same. They had and have the same talent as yours, and the same art-hungers, but unfortunately "can't spend the time for it"; they have plumped for *reality.* . . .

So I tremulously bring out the phrase "will-to-fail"—not a bad effort in these encounters. Maybe money-making is his will-to-fail at art? And get my answer. "But I'm even a failure at *failure*."

For a second meeting, he invites me to dinner with Dr. Louis Finkelstein, head of the Jewish Theological Seminary—for me another heady glimpse at where journalism can get without 'arf trying—but I don't get anywhere on Macy's.

Next Horton suggests a piece on Yaddo where I am going for the first time. I say no, but while there, in the first days of getting used to it and back to the novel, I write what I think is an animadversion against current theories of "Education," but is actually a celebration of mine, and my lucky similarity of background to that of most good writers—attendance at a "good" but horrible intermediary school.

Since then, I have been asked to speak at its graduation. If I do, one more dream of grandeur will have lost its savor—all the audience I would require are gone. But I have long since written the speech.

I called the piece "Reeling, Writhing—and Grouping." Here is part of what it said.

An all-girl public high school in New York City, Hunter was enterable only by competitive examination, and was therefore known to the rest of the city (as Townsend Harris was for the boys) as a "school for grinds," an epithet not undeserved when one considers the hours of attendance—nine to five—and the curriculum, all required, which consisted of four years each of Latin, math, history, English, oral English, three years of another language (a heady choice here, and the only one—French *or* German), and a year each of biology and physics, these latter a fairly new departure and considered somewhat dilettante, but still required. In addition we had two hours a week of physical education, this consisting of the "Simon Says DO THIS!" type of calisthenic performed, in winter, in a gym whose cellar gloom prepared us admirably for the speakeasies of our salad days, and accomplished in spring in the paved school yard under the eyes of the jeering populace, by which latter experience we almost immediately achieved that "group identification" which is such a premeditated part of today's schooling.

We did not covet this, but we had it all right. It was furthered by our costume—middy, tie, sneaks, heavy serge bloomers whose elastic must not be pushed above the knee, and black cotton stockings—all of which, except for the middies which we wore from home, were to be kept in our lockers like tiaras and under no circumstances to be taken home for washing during the term, lest we forget them and thus have too natural an excuse from our fifty minutes of eupepsia. It is not surprising, therefore, that the only other course that I can recall as being in any way connected with *our* personalities, with *us*—a stray weekly hour of hygiene—consisted almost entirely of in-instructions to wash. For the rest, I don't remember the school's ever being interested in our psyches or our future lives, or worrying about us as people in any self-consciously pedagogical way. And in the light of that, although I can still see my old school in all the Dickensian murk that should properly surround it, I can also see it as a really remarkable example, when you come to think of it, of what might be called "nondirective group alignment" or possibly "formation of student nuclei by closed-door method of group orientation."

Miss Webster, the principal, was one of those deceptively fragile steel-in-lace little old ladies for whom one would cast Helen Hayes if one could do so without the char-rm; she actually did wear, in 1928, high whalebone-cum-lace collars, occasionally embellished with an amethyst "drop" and lace halfmitts to match. She was often to be seen on the crosstown bus in the morning, in poke bonnet or toque, and rustling skirts that just cleared the floor, carrying a wicker basket which must have contained lunch but which I thought of as more likely to contain *lettres de cachet* in a gracefully sinister eighteenth-century way. Despite the crowding in the bus, a deferential space always surrounded her, and she never greeted us, nor did we want her to. Her very presence, a vinegar that might just be poison, had the effect of welding us together in a group as powerfully protective (and mayhap as valuable and healthy to persons of our age then) as any I know. Under her glance we knew that we were canaille, but we knew also without question that we belonged to a very special canaille, one marked by terrible hazard but angry promise—the young.

A rabble we might be, but were all back there *together*. We would as soon have called her Louisa to her face as have tickled the Pope in the ribs, but behind her back we called her Lulu. She herself never learned our names, but addressed us by category only, in that "old New York" accent which must be extinct now, whose diphthongs resembled garage Brooklynese being spoken by a highly cultivated rabbit. When we were caught singly at some malpractice—and almost everything was one—we were "Girl!"—the sound of the "ir" being most akin to the French sound in *"deuil"*—making it "Geuil-l!" When we were caught together, it was "Geuills!" She also had a system of cards to be attached to our records for punishment or reward, these done up in the school colors, lavender and white, lavender for grace, white for disgrace. "Moral turpitude" was a phrase that appeared often on the white cards for infringements so tiny that I would weep now for their innocence if I could only remember them—but since almost all of us were Whites, we had an identity here too. Clubs were not forbidden but not greatly encouraged—they came out shyly in out-of-the-way corners in the spring like the arbutus that was the badge of the poetry club—and died of homework (three hours was about minimum) in the fall. The senior class ahead of us once dared to ask for a dance, and was advised that half the class might dress as boys and take the other half. Boys were otherwise never mentioned; Miss Webster would of course have been happiest in a world where the entire human race, one large group of solid lavender, might stand to attention at the sound of "Geuil-Is!" Nowadays the schools, for all their announced intention of turning out "citizens of the community," foolishly arrange things so pleasantly that only a really degenerate nongrouper wants to leave school to be one. Miss Webster did it otherwise—with the back of her hand. Whatever the world might be, it was not Hunter, and we wanted to get there as quickly as possible. As for the teachers, they were excellent—at least at the now disreputable craft of forcing a large amount of substantive knowiedge into our heads. Neither their psyches nor ours ever entered the situation. Even if either of us had known we had them, the schedule would not have allowed it. There were no discussions, debates, conferences; in class we declaimed, recited, or wrote, but never expressed opinions of our own, having none.

When I went to college and made friends among the girls from "progressive" schools, I admired them exceedingly for two reasons. Whereas we had feared our teachers as our masters, they had only tolerated theirs as their servants; and they had marvelously numerous opinions, round and hard as bullets, which they discharged with the frequency and accuracy of Gatlings. I distinctly remember my sensations when I first realized I had made a judgment of my own; I felt as if I had grown an antler between my ears, and I fondled it for days before I unveiled it.

"Reeling and Writhing," then, is my first piece of published journalism, and the beginning of a pleasant, intermittent relationship with *The Reporter*, during which Horton lighthandedly lets me do as I wish, which more often means that I write something and then submit it. Often, when I ask if he would be interested in a subject, I already have the article in the house.

. . . Looking back on the half-dozen or so of them, I see how quickly the habit of the column, like that of the lectern, can also instil the habit of knowing. What the columnist must always be exceptionally wary of, is his own hates—those black beasts which may in the end collar-train him. The special malice of the sometime essayist, those light jabbings from the bleachers of another pre-occupation—how thin they can grow, in comparison with the tumid rise of the real satirist, whose heart, gut, and growl are down there in the pit! A writer must be measured by how much he risks—but to this must be added the different kinds of risks there are. The power of the daily print, or the weekly or the monthly, may be lethal, but is less rarely interested in the universal. A writer who tells himself this when the reviews come out, may as a contributor forget it. Or become rather too fond of the jousting game. Or dry up altogether into the sweet ephemeral. Yet there hasn't been a time in my writing life when I haven't wanted some taste of all of it. . . .

*The Reporter* gave me scope. Formulating my thoughts, I found them. I was never asked to write down to anyone. My first book-piece was on a male writer; I was never confined to the "women's department" of literature. Therefore I could write of Colette, or review Sybil Bedford, without feeling that I was bowing to such a policy. (In 1963 when the *Times* asked me to do a piece on Janet Frame—a writer who interested me—I told them I could not review a book by a woman for them, until more men reviewed books by women in their pages, and more women reviewed books by men. In these matters *The Reporter* did resemble *The New Statesman* and other British weeklies to which it was often compared.)

In the end, though, I stopped writing for it before it stopped, doing a last piece early in 1966. Partly I did so because of its politics on the Vietnam war; I couldn't see appearing even in the Views-and-Reviews back section of a magazine saying what it was saying on the editorial front ones—which now had that rank flavor of the libertarian gone authoritarian. But I was also beginning to feel what I had almost begun to know at *The New Yorker*. When you write under the likelihood that a magazine will take your work, you will not be able to prevent taking your tone from it. No publication can avoid this, but it makes for stronger magazines than it does writers. Either you will write too much like them, or too much like yourself. In time, I would get sick of the gently roving stance of the reporter scanning the horizon for topics to be topical about. It was training my eye.

•
•
•

Now THAT writing has become my life-habit, the guilt always attached to the role of observer has finally been annulled or numbed by the realization that this is what I am here for. Yet I know that I am now also doomed to observe that role the more. "The heart doomed to watch itself feel is not less worthy," the hero of *False Entry* and I say, finally accepting our brand of the consciousness thrust upon us all— "this lambent perpetual in the skull, this responsible, ticktock, weeping flame."

During the years I am writing such things, I have also begun to teach. Partly from vanity—my own college, where as an undergraduate I had so often been in hot water, never really approved of, and where as an unknown, I have been turned down for an assistanceship some years before—now invites me to. But partly also because from the first, writing has begun earning me good money, and I am already turning a thoughtful gaze on that relationship.

Writing to me is still a privilege, and always will be. What I had since childhood been spiritually forced to do, I have finally—after some thirty years, found myself capable of doing. My relief and gratitude has been enormous enough. And now I am getting paid, as well. What I basically love to do, and must—sometimes a scourge but always my salvation—is also capable of paying for my physical life or supporting it also along many unrelated paths of appetite. How to keep the two paths separate?

I am now in danger of becoming a "professional," if I want to. Which means in part, learning to write not necessarily *what* other people want you to, but *when*. I had long since learned that I couldn't write to any order except, now and then moved along in an inexplicable rhythm, to a sudden command of my own, from below. Even when I contracted to do an article, essay, or review on a subject absolutely of my own choosing, as soon as said, a fell weight descended. Somehow, what I had done was to cede to someone else that authority which should have remained mine. Whatever I would write under such circumstances could no longer be said to have come from the marrowbone of myself.

As for my stories themselves, though they might never marry money, by now I know that if I will be just a bit more . . . suggestible, they might well go where more money is.

Nobody much asks me to. Or to become a fan dancer, which I have sometimes thought of as a properly symbiotic arrangement for the support of verbal art. Or to set me up either as an out-of-towner's mistress, or the front for a Mafia bar. (Mornings free.)

Teaching, however, keeps being offered. I always find it hard to turn down any new experience. And teaching—which is as direct an application to vanity as the possibility of parenthood—is also one of the lesser public roles offered a writer.

So, in order to remain an amateur, I become a professor. And soon begin to examine the role—for a writer—of that.

During a year when I commute once a week to Boston to teach, I have time to reflect on the difference between "being" a writer, and "doing" it. Here are five Monday nights from a journal:

*Monday, the 1st*

Never trust the private journal of a writer; give his confidence your sympathy and before you know it you may be standing in the middle of what is merely another work of art. No, these Monday nights here, after talking the stars into the skies with students, I want the fraternity of some dear colleague whose customary vehicle is not words—and as usual, I find myself with a painter, a habit since the age of thirteen, when, not daring to steal from the public library, I copied out great passages from the notebooks of Robert Henri. What a period piece we are back there, he and I—and perhaps now! For, remind myself as I will, I never buy that book, not fearing to find it less good, but mourning the decline of both situation and passion— in which a book is for stealing. Tonight, howsomever got, I have the journal of Delacroix, along with coffeepot, pound of coffee and immersion heater—all of which gear the university has so far over- looked my keeping on week-to-week in the room in the faculty lodge where they quarter me on these visits. Usually they give me the same room; at least the picture on the wall is the same—an original Eilshemius—and that's certainly my gear in the bottom of the closet, tucked back of the beautiful sliding door that doesn't slide. Elegant as the lodge is, it is motel-style, a long wing of rooms budded on one another—open the door of any, and pop, one is sucked into the beatific light of that roving public cell, the ultimate cellule of *alone*. Someday the room won't be the same—I'll know by the picture—but what if my gear *is* still there? For that terrible philosophic abyss, I hope to be ready. These solipsistic nights, another personality takes over, dropped on my head like a sack, the minute I enter. Suspended here, between the day's process of *being* a writer to all those young faces, and the faraway humbler apparatus of *doing* it at home in New York, I examine these alternatives in the muttering underhand of con- science. And I don't leave Delacroix here; I keep him in my bag.

*Monday, the 2nd*

Comments on the pitfalls and sublimes of art are not what I read him for these days, although his can shake one in those depths of gratitude always waiting for the kindred "ahoy" across the waters. "Style can result only from great research, and the fine brushing has got to stop when the touch is going well. I must try to see the big gouaches by Correggio at the Museum. I believe they were done with very small touches." It's the note of authority, underlaid with doubt, that one loves and shivers to. And these days I hunt it most where he scolds and scares himself for being in or out of his society. "I believe that seeing . . . people from time to time is not such a danger to work and the progress of the mind as it is claimed to be by many pretended artists; to consort with *them* is certainly more dangerous. . . . I must return to solitude. . . . How is one to retain one's enthusiasm about anything when one is at all times at the mercy of other people, and when one has constant need of their society?"

"Society" may have enlarged since his day, but the ins and outs of it for the artist are always much the same, no matter how stated. For Mann—the artist yearned to be loved by the bourgeois for those very differences that must be flaunted but made it impossible; to this he added that guilt, now almost traditional, of those who neglect "life" in order to record it. Whereas it seems to me that an artist may be bourgeois or revolutionary—the in-ness or outness merely shifts ground—and recording may be his treasure, not his burden. And each man, from ditchdigger to clerk, stands aside for some part of his day, from what each has agreed to call "life."

What I am rightly afraid of is those seductions—social, financial, even intellectual—which persuade me to speak like a writer, act like a writer, teach like a writer, even write like a writer, at the very moment when I am not being one. Once the public personality begins, however humbly—I think of it as a paper costume inside which one squirms like a child, mindful that rain melts, paper tears, but still rather proud of the accordion pleats on one's forehead—the problem is how to go about one's real business, assuming one knows what that is. Lately, I've concluded that there's less gap than one would think, between those who clench up on some island, and those who antick the public halls—each is a posture, and the expense of spirit, to say nothing of ego, is the shame. Here in America many still envy the European artist, whose role in society appears more fixed, and it is certainly true that under our curious freedom, where class roles are not admitted, one no sooner strikes a match than an attitude flames. Perhaps it's merely easier in one's own country to see how people play the fool. But surely, of all our artists, our writers seem least able to move without a sociological creaking. After all, America does have so much paper.

*Monday, the 3rd*

"Neither the ardent promises of your best friends, nor the offers of service by the powerful ought to make you believe that there is anything in what they say, as to results."

If ever I hanker after a coterie I've only to imagine how it would have been to have been born into one—a Southerner say, or a true-blue baby daughter of the *Little Aorta Review*. That way one might manage it, the way one bears up to one's nose. Now and then one misses the support, of course, as of any uniform. But my thoughts no sooner go into committee than they want out again, like improperly trained dogs. Is it an oddity that those who don't scorn the influence cabals often look down on those who teach? Much needless worry has been expended over the possible destruction of writers by teaching. If a man is sucked into scholasticism, or silenced, it seems more likely that his stamina for that aloneness which should be part of his gifts has never been strong. Teaching is hard. But every man spends part of his life-energy away from his most personal work. Fashionably considered, the university is not a part of going "life" at all, as against the pursuit of homosexuality in Algiers, or strong drink in Connecti-cut. But I find it impossible to exclude from at least tentative reality any place where so many people are.

Nothing's been said on what the university can do for the writer, apart from boarding him. It should never be his atelier—that sort of thing practiced anywhere, at parties or on podiums, gets into the work well beyond its due. What he represents is a unique approach to literature—the artist's—and this is all he should teach. He can teach that there are no permanent rules, else literature would die, that the best work abides by the "form" only enough to leave it, that one observes the inner discipline of a book, watches how its ideas dance within the framework of its times. He is careful to lean lightly, if at all, on the personal life of the author, and in the presence of good or great work he never forgets to elaborate on the wonder of it—the best place to be lavish with detail.

At first, it's tough to teach without the convenience of the small arbitraries; later, the very arbitrariness of the attitude itself stiffens the spine. The risks to the republic are obvious, which may be why even the braver universities prefer to keep only one of him at a time; the danger to him is that he may act like a poet instead of being one, which can happen anywhere.

Meanwhile, even in a sloppy age some of the young are severe enough to be made happy in the sight of a discipline going on somewhere, even if the pursuit of it is so strait that the instructor himself is often confused. In their society, and sometimes with colleagues, I nearly find out what I think, and that, aside from the human attraction of food, wine and sympathy, is what I ask of society. A university is a place where the currents of the intangible flow continuously, and are paid consistent honor. I must have such a contact in my life somewhere. I'll do the rest, on paper.

*Monday, the 4th* (for Delacroix a Monday, too, Sept. 13, 1852)

"Look here! Fool that you are, you get a sore throat from discussing with idiots, you go arguing with silliness in petticoats for a whole evening, and you do that about *God*, about the *justice of this world*, about *good* and *evil*, and on *progress*."

As a petticoat myself, I note that too much of the podium turns a writer of our sex into either a *diseuse* or a scold—what it makes of the men is another story. As for parties, everybody knows about them, yet we can none of us get rid of a naïve hope that Parnassus is in session somewhere, perhaps *there*. And so it is, often with the non-performing wives to serve at the stewpots. Ergo Mrs. Coo and Mrs. Graze, whom I met there last evening.

I found Mrs. Graze attending the statuspot. As the wife of a critic, she resembles those doctors' wives who are all but able to practice medicine themselves. Give her a push, and she is off. In one sentence she found Fitzgerald lightweight, mildly approved of Mr. Angus Wilson as a man who had entertained *her*, demolished Henry James as a family enemy, and was able to settle any contemporary by bringing in Tolstoi. Authors met in the flesh infuriate her. Secretly, she feels that an author loses caste by being met so—surely if he were anybody he would not be at the same party with Mr. and Mrs. Graze. But as soon as met, it is her custom to dig like a trufflehound to find out whom he knows. Woe betide him if he admits to acquaintance with any of her more eminent name-drops. Soon as he leaves the conversation, she hisses after him: "Snob!"

Mrs. Coo, usually younger, attends the malice-pot, with a zombie unawareness of why she wants me in the broth, although I know; at her age I was a nonperformer myself, luckily without entrée to such parties. She and her editor-mate have just made their home head-quarters for a new magazine; the wastepaper problem is already such that now and then a tiny Coo is temporarily lost. "*You* have a book coming out too, haven't you?" she says. I nod, the hair mean-while rising on my pelt. Her chin lifts like a gourmet's: I see just what roils behind her skinny, post-Radcliffe eye. "Is it goo-ood?" she says.

But one should never be surprised by their arrogance; one forgets that they have always before them what looks to them like the spectacle of ours. I suppose *les artistes* picnic best backstage in house slippers, where, in the company of only the company, there's some chance it may be divine. And even there—how many Coleridges are best left in Xanadu! Mrs. Graze is right, really. Authors should not be met.

*Monday, the 5th*

The worst has happened here. My room has been changed, and the gear in the closet is *not* missing. If it were only that, I could postulate the maid. But I should have known there'd be some variation I hadn't imagined. Room, Eilshemius, gear hidden in the corner, all exactly the same as was—only the number on the door has been changed. Life is a movable feast then, a tour in a post chaise, but who's to be considered as moving, it or you? The answer is—quick over the abyss, and be damned to being. Start *doing*. Postulate a book.

Or a story. Think for instance of yesterday morning at the hair-dresser's, when the voice came murmuring from behind some bead curtain of femininity, "*Sure* you know Pearl, sure you know her. Dirty-mouth Pearl?" A girl with fine potentialities, Pearl. Or re-member going to the dairy farm all that Iowa winter, how the rainbows squeaked in the snow as the car stopped at the milk house, opposite the barn loft where the redbone coonhound sat watching. You thought his rightful name a farmer's joke, and were told his breed never made house dogs, yet all that winter you yearned to have one of him, to take back to New York—and still yearn. Reflect now. Could it be that you want not so much to have him as to *be* him, that red king of the hayloft, looking down? Start the real story.

". . . an invitation to dine with the Duc de Montpensier. Fatigued. In the evening fatigue and frightful humor; I stayed home. As a matter of fact, I am not sufficiently grateful for what Heaven does for me. In these moments of fatigue I think that everything is lost. . . . Got a good night's rest. Went back to my studio; it put me into a good humor."

That's it—the only way to cure the pains of the private journal, and the proper place to end it. Trust us there, where we begin to trust ourselves.

PART II

ON THE
MIDWAY

$M$IDWAY in a novel, I sometimes stop, lodged in space above it, looking across its expanse, up and down its territory, as if it is a natural phenomenon of which I am oddly in command. From its own riverbank, I am seeing the other side of it—the part I have not written down, or am leaving out. I see the flow of light on the side opposite to my dark, my willed dark. Or the black stream of the world's sores, going past my impudently bobbing, saucy light. At times the book then takes a turn —or sees there is no turn it can take. Here is where a book can grow more complex, plashing out almost beyond the maker. Or where it simples down, like the tail-end of a foetus, into its own fixed curve. Here a book leaps over its own boundaries, or holds fast to its own joy in them.

Once, writing a novel whose first-person narrator was intensely searching his own history, the word "I"—that mote forever burrowing under the skin, that tic hiccuping down the page—became impossible to both of us. Next chapter, the book glided into third-person—I can swear I did not do it consciously—and stayed there until the "I," that honing self, felt decent again. To me, in the finished book that point-of-change seemed too nakedly clear. But, as often with nude bathers, nobody noticed it.

Now, here I stop. What am I doing in this "auto" of a book? Under the flag of a prefix that from "auto-erotic" to "automation" always seems to signify the worst side of the self. In the column of "autos" in the *Shorter Oxford* at my side, I don't find much to salve that suspicion, rather some sinister confirmations of it that are new to me. "Autofacture," or self-making. "Autolatry," or self-worship. "Auto-noetic," there's a nice one: self-perceiving! But followed by "auto-phagous"—self devouring. Sweetened again by "Autophoby"—a fear of referring to oneself. "Autophony" gives me pause—"observation of the resonance of the practitioner's own voice in auscultation." Also "Autopserin"—"a patient's own virus administered homeopathically in cases of itch." Is that what I'm after?

Buried among the listings, I find a familiar, a risky comfort. I am making an Autonym—"a book published under the author's own name." This time written against the author's usual habit of thinking: that a writer best ignores the process of writing, that a reader best ignores the private life of these, both of them trembling only in the presence of the work, to which belongs the honor and the scrutiny.

Does a writer ever see his own *oeuvre?* I hope not; that will be the *Ave atque vale* of a shade. We don't laboriously and cannily construct such a totality, or even envision it; we accumulate it. In America, the European concept of *oeuvre*, which compounds a time with a single history, expecting a teleological goal from the writer, and serious language-worship from everybody—is still not admitted. An *oeuvre* is a body of work which, like a true body, interacts with itself and with its own growth. We here in America are not allowed the sweet sense of growing them while in life; even after death, the obituary quickly picks over the works for "what will last."

Yet if a writer's work has a shape to it—and most have a repetition like a heartbeat—the *oeuvre* will begin to construct him.

In 1952, the Guggenheim Foundation gave me some money to get up and go. That's the way I wanted it. Applying, I describe myself as still a half-time writer wanting to be full-time, eager to get out of my country for a year, in order to see it from outside. I want to sit and think, and I want to sit and think in Europe. I warn them that though I won't be able to write during such a time, it would all come out later. Candor has kept me young and foolish beyond my years; this time it may have helped. But when the money comes, I realize that I can only get away for the eight months the children can be in boarding school. I go to New York, to the Guggenheim offices, for advice.

"What do the other women you have given writing fellowships do," I ask "when they have children?" I don't expect a blueprint of how to proceed under the onus of the award (for that it half is). I'm groping for the assurance that other women had done what I am going to do—have left their families for a working period, or a period important to the work, just like any man. . . . Already, being a writer had given me certain freedoms, which though I worked at home may have been only those of any working mother, but I was confused on this, and so were my friends. . . . Guilty or not, I am going of course, but it will help if I am told that in the fellowship of artists, female or not, this is ordinary. "Come to think of it," Jim Mathias says, "I don't know as we've had any women Fellows in Creative Writing who have children." We tally the ones who come to mind. That is so.

I know too well what I think of this to discourse on it now; we all do. But in those beginning years I was often to be the only family woman among serious writers and other artists, and this had its effects. At almost my first editorial lunch, I hear a famous woman fiction-editor of the day whisper to my agent "But she's so *normal!*" and want to snarl back *Naht so normal as all that!*, maybe meanwhile hacking off an ear to drop in her shrimp. Or at least giving her a Lesbian goose under the table. It seems to me that I am mad enough for artistic purposes; conversely, as I get to know artists in all fields, they often seem—particularly the best ones—proportionately in better control of their madness than the general population.

But it could take its toll of one—not to be able to lead the artistic life, not being a bohemian—at least to the eye. One had to react to it.

As a woman artist with a family and a conventional family set-up, I
was being scrutinized with male values for artists—often by other
women artists—and by myself. A curious position, akin to others I
had found myself in, maybe as the only heterosexual in a totally
homosexual drawingroom, or the only city individual in a provincial
one: out of step, and honey, *are you so sure you're right?* (Does one
have to be? In step anywhere?) I am learning that bohemians, aliens,
unconventionals, artist-in-groups or artists who believe in a way-of-
life as part of art, will press their conventions on you as cheerfully
and insistently—as the conventional. With the same failure to distinguish the outer and the inner ways of life.

Socially it didn't worry me, and in our quiet house on the river
I was very possibly kept from more mobile ambitions which might
have been ruinous for work. What did get to me was whether a
demi-bourgeois like me, and a demi-sane one, could really be an
artist of the same intensity as the divinely mad, or dedicated alien?
By the time I belatedly read *Tonio Kruger*—what a relief to find that
dichotomy played upon so precisely!—I have already decided for myself. And not with Mann. Meanwhile that question so touchingly
posed down all the ages of art—"What must an artist be?"—would
help keep me happily unaware of another—"Could an artist be female?"

I had honestly never thought otherwise. I could understand all
the feminine rages at unequal circumstances, over-protected lives and
under-subscribed opportunities, and had had some of them—smiling
through my teeth at the male writers who say to me "What *every*
writer needs is a good wife!", worrying over what the children would
make of me in a world geared as it was, and what I would make of
them. But that all the philosophical rages of the universe, its hieratic
dances of either body or intellect, its whole wild, sad glee of celebration and human fact, wasn't to be equally mine—had never occurred
to me. And hasn't yet.

To Mathias, back there at the Guggenheim, I say "Well, guess I
can't take the money then. Since I contracted to go for a year, and
I can only stay eight months. So I better give it back."

His answer, one I trust all endowers of the arts continue to give,

is substantially that I had been given the award under the assumption
that I knew best what would foster my work—if I felt that buying a
car and going to California with the money would do it, that was
up to me. Naturally, as he must have known, the greatest freedom
lay in that I was not bound to deliver any concrete work, not within
a specific time, or ever. The future of my own work, in any form
and pace, was mine.

So I went. It's easy now to pick out later stories which from their
backgrounds, came to me from being abroad. But that was the least
of it.

"Tha-at's right, get your local color!" an old boyo of a bohemian
(who had been a stockbroker) says to me when I'm leaving. And
who doesn't know how that mezzotint comes crowding in? But I now
have walked into another civilisation, of beings who might as well
be on the moon for their foreignness, yet share my parts and my
language. Sometimes it is sparks and crash-bang, a young man yelling
at me "Why don't all you Americans go home!"—and coming round
to apologize the next morning; sometimes I slide *con amore* into the
warm bath of English living and new company, into the misty days
and hot conversations which have helped make a literature.

An American chatterer, now for months on end I become a listener,
at tables where talk is a living organism, to be tended for the good of
all. In mobile-home America, friendship is increasingly easy, sleazy
and forgettable; here friends could be treated as my parents' had been
—grappled to one with hoops of steel and kept for life. They can be
trusted to brush some of the poetry off me, and I to recover it later.
Walking my rounds, Regent Street to Piccadilly, or down the Strand
to Reuters, head high in the air to catch the street signs, and unaware that to pass three times through the Burlington Arcade is as
good as a work permit, I am regularly accosted by men who ask
"Do you have the time?" My male friends, whose women are still
wearing their post-war "utilities," say "It's that black silk coatee of
yours, and the poke hat" (at home the Lord and Taylor uniform
of the year). "They think you're a Belgian tart."

I am so happy here, going from street to street, friend to friend, experience to experience—is it possible that, intellectually, I am an American one? I tell myself that every American is either a potential Anglophile or Francophile, and I happened to hit England first. Where I have the social mobility of the foreigner who may ask to go anywhere, whom friends pass from hand to hand for whatever unusualness of hat, face, situation, profession or tongue might attract them: as an American I am a nobody who might be anybody. As for me, I am having a temporary flight from that provincial construct, by now both suburban and city-literary, to which I am confined at home. But principally, I am learning—like some new resident of a magnetic field in which all my particles are drawn toward a certain pattern—what it is to be American, to them and to me. What it is to be an intellectual woman, *outside* my country. And what it is to be a writer, elsewhere.

To friends in the Foreign Office who know America well, I can see that we are changing from a dearly-held alliance to a disturbing quantity; we are already the civilisation which is going to have to be stood off. (In 1956, in England during the Suez incident, I was able to get some of mine back, but we both knew that their colonial monster was behind them.) Defending my nativity like a college debater, I learn how to handle chaff and return it: poco a poco, soft-sharp; be slow to draw blood, quick to stanch it; if you're a smiler by nature, don't stop now; if you're not, don't start; always keep a twinkle out somewhere to show you're aware you're taking part in a drypoint of language; watch how the most oystery-eyed do it somehow with posture.

As for the literary world, one may meet it almost in toto on a weekend more or less, but rarely will have to; whenever you find it alone with itself—instead of branching out into politics, or *la danse du ventre*, or whatever its larger tastes are—it tends to apologize. As for reviewers, at this time, their provincial worst is in a different style from ours; their middle-average tends to be better educated than ours, but more narrowminded or without our gusty enthusiasms; often their portmanteau reviews, like those in the *Times Literary Supplement*, link books together with infuriating expertise, while never

seeming to alight square on any one of them. With their best, like
V. S. Pritchett, Angus Wilson, and a host of other writers who review steadily and seem not to have lost juice or dignity by it, we
have little to compare.

As for women, the double-job-standard is bluntly advertised in
the weeklies, with higher male pay for the same post as teacher or
librarian. The power jobs in the print media are as entirely male as
they are at home. But once you get to the arts, and the literary ones
especially, among writers and critics both there is a salving lack of
that male patronizing I am beginning to discover at home. They have
their "kitchenmaid" writers, women who write for household women,
but no one, even the hastiest reviewer, even by implication ever lumps
me with them, or my work with theirs. Or sends me books for review merely because they are by women. In their "man's country,"
I am never reviewed as a "woman writer."

In this the English were continental as they are in so much else; the
language has obscured that to us. I found that they took the same pride
in their bluestockings, present and past, as in any tradition, and gave
them the equivalent amount of chaff; as a woman, nobody ever made
me feel too intelligent or too intellectual for my own good or theirs,
but in the arenas of literature and discussion they made it bracingly
clear that I would have to take my licks like anybody else.

That same year, just before my leaving New York, word had
been passed around to writers who often met at Vance and Tina
Bourjaily's (both before and when he was editor of *Discovery*) that
"Norman" wanted us to meet of a Sunday and get some needed cafe
discussion started, the bar chosen being The White Horse on Hudson
Street—which is how it came to be known as a place where writers
went, by the time Dylan Thomas was taken there. The day we first
go, in a group of about ten, of which I recall for sure only Mailer,
the Bourjailys and Frederic Morton, the bar and its usual patrons,
mostly the remainders of indigenous Greenwich Village Irish, are no
more unhandy with us—don't we *know* whether we want a glass or a

stein?—than we are with ourselves. The White Horse doesn't yet know it is going to be a literary pub. And we have the sad sense, or I do, that stuff like this is hard going in America. At one point Mailer takes out a dollar bill, and pleads for somebody to start an argument going with him, "on anything." Nobody much takes him up on it. (I couldn't, though I sympathized with what he was after in getting us together. He knew only one way to advance or conclude an argument with any woman—and a dollar was a small price for it.) Nothing memorable having been said by anybody, we leave, unsure that we have consecrated the place. When I return from Europe the following summer and drop in there one Sunday with Louis Auchincloss, we find nobody we know.

Before returning home though, I live for a few months in Rome. There I recall an evening when Bill Styron proposes to a group of us which includes John Phillips and Peter Matthiessen, that we discuss a book, the stipulation being that it must be one we haven't read. It is lightly said and lightly taken—a game, entered into half protectively perhaps by writers sick of litry discussion, wanting to harbor their own ideas close to the vest? Perhaps. But I have just come from a place where men who crave exchange as much as I think this company does, go about it less embarrassedly. Deeply as these men care for what they are into, they feel more at ease when acting toward it in the attitudes of Sport. We didn't get far; the drunken record player ruled us out. We weren't meant to. Nobody there or at The White Horse, no good male writer in America goddammit, was a dirty intellectual. A lot of them were Hemingway cripples though, in part. By virtue of sex I had escaped that, but the burden is on me inversely; literature in America is a manly Sport, in which I am not expected to compete.

Leaving Europe that first and fatally instructive time, I still prefer the vivid, brawling possibilities of our crude blue air. Though an enchanted visitor, by every impulse I am not an expatriate. But I can see the damage and the limits on both sides. This is what happens to the traveler, and against it there is no amulet. In the white light of the American century, continental energies, which once bloomed so hardily into classicism, will often now seem to me either sere or cosy. But in testing the tone of our country, often our most energetic writers, sometimes our leading ones, will seem anti-intellectual, all too busy standing together with those who are. This will affect all of us. Sometimes our lives, sometimes our works, will go soft with the corruption of it. . . .

When in 1956 I want to go to England again, *The Reporter* agrees to take three of a proposed list of subjects. The first, which is to be on the New Towns built after the war (which with their green belts, Festival-of-Britain plazas and geriatric housing are of interest to planners here) I never write. As the social scientist Bernard Crick and others gamely take me about, and I gather fistfuls of mock-ups and statistical notes, the article seems doomed to come out good-and-proper sociological without my being orthodoxly equipped; in it I'll be a writer lamely walking a researcher's stilts.

One night before I know this, when I am about to leave for Stevenage, the largest of the towns, I am sitting talking, listening to music with two friends. Guy Wint, an editor of *The Manchester Guardian*, is suggesting I write for *Twentieth Century*, a magazine he is associated with. Patrick O'Regan, in whose flat we are, says "Don't do it; it's only recently changed its name from *Nineteenth Century*." Chaff.

I'm emboldened to tell Guy, who begins every sentence with "Why—" or "Do you feel—" or "Would you say that—" —that I live for the day he comes out with a declarative sentence. (Except for this one characteristic not to be confused with Blount, the journalist in *False Entry* and *The New Yorkers*.)

Sitting on the floor, he blinks upward—I see I am learning—and begins another. "Why don't you write about the Pakistani influx into Paddington? In fifteen years we're going to have race problems there."

I marvel—then and now—at how aware they are of themselves. Later, when we are talking of my "classless" nation, he explains that though the class levels may remain fairly rigid in England, there is always a mobility upward—and down, of course—which insures new blood at the top.

Pat, who is Anglo-Irish (and sufficiently on top) says "Don't believe a word of it." He and I have cut short a Sunday walk—ten miles, which is why I am stretched on the floor—so that he may soon get at his homework for milord his boss; he is private secretary to Lord Reading.

Viewing the mass of pamphlets, documents, I say Americanly, "I suppose you have to digest them for him"—bosses at home being conventionally lacking in intelligence, and milords also.

"Good God no, I have all I can do to keep up with him."

Still later, when we are talking of the position of women in the two countries, he wonders why American ones are so uncertain of themselves, and why we take things so personally—including the American girl who, when that was put to her, said "*I* don't."

I tell them these characteristics are American generally, not feminine. "Especially when we're around people like you. . . . Tell me—all those upperclass girls who don't go up to the university even when they have the minds for it, and whose brothers always go, whether there's money or not, or mind or not, doesn't this bother them? And how come they're still so confident? And when they marry brother's chum from there"—which nine out of ten I know them to do—"how do they feel about the difference in education, *don't* they feel it? How does it work out?"

Pat says "We-ell, after they marry, he raises her to his level—" He sees me rising like a meringue, and twinkling, finishes, very much through the nose "—and hmmm—after a hmmm—while, she raises him to hers."

Yet when, playing the Mozart Requiem which we both find ineffable, he says "Yes, I suppose hearing it is the nearest we ever get to heaven" I make a silent reservation. I suppose, I take it personally.

For sexually, they abash me. Either they seem to take it very much for-the-health-and-here-today—with anything from three whips to love-in-the-round and a lambchop supper afterwards—following which they are gone tomorrow to the steeplechase they really prefer (with horses). Or else they seem to have buried it like a dear dead bird, under a clump of marguerites at the bottom of the kitchen garden, on the other side of a stile which one is never quite sure they leap.

This article on their "nudie" Windmill Theatre (which bombing did not close but peace did) is one *The Reporter* has contracted for. When I get to England, they wire second thoughts. Since the magazine is shortly to come out in Britain, they don't want to "offend"—and besides, Alastair Buchan has told them the Windmill has been journalistically done to death; there's nothing more to be said on it. I wire back, on the first count that one sure way to lose British respect is to kowtow to it, on the second count—that I am not a journalist.

They take it, publishing it while I am abroad, with a zealous editor's cuts and under a catchy title, a "mishap" which we both agree to ignore. I had called it "A Taste for Sweeties."

It was a piece of chaff, of course. Which means—an exchange entered into for love of argument and perhaps love of subject, which often ends in love of opponent.

NOTTINGHAM, ENGLAND, *July 1. (Reuters)—Two girls, posing in the nude in a lion's cage at a theater here, didn't move when the beast attacked its trainer. It's against the law for nudes to move in a show.*

When I saw that dispatch in a New York tabloid, a day before flying back to the London I had lived in for a year and hadn't seen for three, it seemed to me that I had already been transported, without benefit of Pan American, to that corner off Shaftesbury Avenue where the Windmill stands—the theater where the art of the nude still, the still nude, or what the British, reaching guardedly and instinctively for French, call the "*tableau vivant*," has been refined to a kind of high-tea perfection.

I grew up in the 1920s, when it first became chic to draw deadly inferences about a nation from its livelier arts, but I should be understandably wary, for instance, of any foreign attempts to analyze life in the United States on a pure basis of Disneyland and the Tootsie

Roll. Nevertheless, as I held that clipping, I began to laugh as I remembered the first time I saw the Windmill's selected pekoe blend
of galvanized pony ballet, sweating comics, and stone-cold nudes.

On a pedestal in the far center of the stage, a comely nude girl
reared her classic cockney form divine. Under a great silver wig whose
chignon streamed to windward in the general direction of Greece, her
whole profile, powdered and Medusa-struck, stared sternly into the
wings. Although she must have been there for quite a while, indeed
since the beginning of the scene, I hadn't noticed her immediately,
first because downstage left a young man in dinner clothes was singing an innocuous song whose topical references were straining my
newly arrived ear, second because four pretty young girls dressed in
dance-team gear were doing an arduous tap routine in front of her.
They bounced energetically but asymmetrically back and forth, wearing jolly soccer-team smiles varied now and then by an occasional
*moue*. For the life of me I couldn't decide whether their bobbing
energy was there to call attention to her who could not move or to
cover her up.

Their costumes had a similar combination of allusion and artlessness.
Made of the usual stage stuffs—electric satins, flimsy tulles, and spark-
lers—they were cut to point adroitly to a thigh, a navel, or other
interesting places. But effects that might have been daring were blotted
out by confusion; each getup was composed of so many colors, textures, and foci that the final impression was that of a costume going
off purposefully in all directions—exactly like a dowager's Fortnum
hat. Each girl wore something in her hair too, such as a string of artificial roses or a little coronet—one wore a butterfly-shaped parure
with waggling antennae, the like of which I had not seen since my
short stint, at the age of eight, in the De Braganza Academy of La
Danse on the top floor of the Audubon Ballroom in New York.

Meanwhile the scene had shifted. We were at a hunt breakfast now—
at least the soubrette, tenor, and chorus, all vigorously singing and
prancing, were done up in smashing pinks, stocks, crops, and boots,
and the tenor was spurred. But this was a hunt held, apparently, in
the gardens of Versailles, or possibly in one of the Roman temples

that had once underlain these streets. For, gradually, one became aware again of those pedestals in the rear, four of them this time, and it was interesting to note that while one immobile naked girl might be news, four sank to the level of scenery.

As it happens, nudity doesn't startle me, but on this occasion I felt distinctly uncomfortable, because it did seem as if no one was noticing those girls except me. In the brown light, I glanced stealthily at the audience. This particular show had started at one in the afternoon, and in the queue outside (the queue starts around ten in the morning at the Windmill) there had been a fair number of bowler hats, striped pants, and tightly rolled umbrellas—City gents, I assumed, hesitating to believe they could be from Whitehall. We had arrived at change-of-show time (the Windmill has six shows a day), and as we came down the side aisle to the stalls we had been caught up in what still lingers in my mind as the ultimate example of the triumph of English disciplinary manners over human impulse. Silently, bumbershoots hooked on wrists, hats in hand, faces rigid with noninterest, the brigade oozed forward. Not an elbow dug, no bunion was trod upon, no whiting pleaded haste to the snail, but in the end the advance guard landed, as if its muscles had unwittingly carried it there, in the choice seats in the front rows.

Since then I've been to the Windmill many times: as a paying customer out front, as a hanger-on at rehearsals and canteen causerie, as an onlooker at auditions, and as a guest bidden to what surely must be the most *gemütlich* dress (or undress) rehearsal in show business— an every-seventh-Sunday-afternoon affair attended by a packed audience of the company's parents and families, including small brothers and sisters, and friends.

This afternoon, however, we are late on account of the weather, without mention of which no study of the British would be complete, and this one not true. My train, bearing me away from more intellectual weekend society in East Anglia, has been delayed an hour by an August flurry that has, among other things, dumped two feet of hailstones on Kent. We find the street door locked, and must be led, via backstage, up and up through the flights of offices, wardrobe departments, canteen and rehearsal floors that make the Windmill a peculiarly self-contained theatrical organism and give it the air of a raffish home away from home.

We come out in the back rows of the dress circle to a view of the chorus that must have its own devotees—the kind of plunge-line perspective that a giant basketball center might have if he were ringed by an opposing team of lady pygmies in décolletage. It is interesting, but the audience, fanned out beneath and around us to the full capacity of three hundred seats, interests me more.

The front rows of the dress circle are lined with about thirty-five photographers. This is the Camera Club, which pays a sum to charity for the privilege and regards it "as a wonderful opportunity to try out various lens systems and high-speed grain-free film stock." Elsewhere the audience is solid with middle-aged couples who may be parents or aunts and uncles; and just in front of me is a white-haired pair of a type more often seen near the band pavilion at a watering place or on a golden-wedding tour at Torquay.

There on the stage is Chastely Unclad, as usual, but everyone is watching the fan dance going on in front of her. As you must know, this consists of a bare girl manipulating two ostrich fans with a wing-spread of at least five feet each, in such a manner that, although she and the fans are in constant motion, one never sees more than a small slice of girl. To this the Windmill has added two other girls with fans that, in flowing rhythm, cover the center girl just as her own fans rise.

From behind me, I hear a small voice say, "Coo, isn't the red one lovely," and an even smaller one answer, "I choose the pink." Turning, I see, sitting behind me under the duennaship of their mother— their starched skirts spread, their lapped hands prim—two little girls, ages about eight and twelve.

For the children who, as I now see, dot the audience, the time may be written off as educational: Art is present, all right, and a flicker of current events, as when the News Girls blame the scantiness of their leopard-skin panties on the credit squeeze. As for the book, there's scarcely a leer in it, unless you count the tenor's impassive, castanet-charged singing, in the Spanish fiesta scene, of "The secret things we *did* (click click click) In *Madrid* (click click click)." There's nothing else your daughter shouldn't hear, really—unless you prefer yours not to pattern her metabolism on Albion's damp version of a torch song: "I've taken a *slow-ow* burn, for a *fah*-ast man," sung, with the faintest of struts, by an asbestos blonde.

When the ballerina, executing a comic version of Giselle, enthusiastically loses her costume to the waist and carries on bravely without it, I do steal a glance at the mother behind me. Better bred than I, she stares me down. *Her* girls, she seems to say, are not the sort to exclaim—if they notice—that some of the empresses down there have no clothes on at all, and I remind myself that they come of a nation where once almost a whole town did not look at Godiva.

As the afternoon wanes toward the cancan, I almost fall asleep to the innocent rustle of the girls' candy papers and their gentle litany of "I choose the red one," "I choose the pink."

In the aisle seat of the last row there is a handsome old man, nodding and smiling at the stage, whom I notice because his morning suit is exquisite and because he is the only one in his row who isn't munching. Now that I think of it, although most London theaters have a peculiarly recognizable odor of must and dust, the air of the Windmill this afternoon smells much more nimble, if artificial. Everyone is eating candy; the house sibillates with it.

It occurs to me that if Sir Osbert Sitwell can claim that the genius of English life is characterized in the names of its butterflies and its fruits—Beautiful Pug, Light-Feathered Rustic, Brixton Beauty, and Cambridge Veneer—there is no particular reason why I shouldn't try a similar interpretation via British sweets, whose light-feathered names I adore. On the stage down there, four girls are doing their tap routine around that statue. Take Number One, the jolly team captain, whose teeth are not her most remarkable projection; one knows her at once—a Nuttie Crisp. Next the shy one with the coronet—a Sherbet Bonbon, I fancy, a pensioner's dream. Rum Truffle for Number Three, a girl with a knowledgeable smirk and moiréed hair. Four does a handspring as I ponder and comes up *moue*-ing; there, if ever

I saw one, goes a Fizzer Fruit. I leave the statue unnamed; she is nobody, she is noumenon. But before I go I cast a glance of respect at the old boy on the aisle. Whoever he is, he's the only one I've ever caught looking at her.

Outside, the weather is fine, all hail melted, and I walk home along the Embankment. The sky is suddenly weirdly beautiful with platinum cloud castles tumbled straight out of a Virginia Woolf sentence, and the sodium flares on Waterloo Bridge make the lurid river below the Thames that Turner saw. At such times in this country, in the all too sudden presence of the awe and mystery of life, one wants only to be comfy, not exacerbated as in America. And I am prepared; I take out of my purse a piece of something called Raspberry Fuzzle.

So, fuzzling, I enter the Middle Temple, that bastion of law, where I happen to be staying, and climb the stairs. And as I pass names still worthy of Dickens's law courts—Ponsonbys, Widgerys, Hurle-Hobbses—I remember those girls in the cage at Nottingham. They too are the law's embodiment in this most orderly of nations: English Daphnes standing firm, perpendicular, and above all fast, in the lion's den. But that lion must have come from somewhere else. Must have been some aggressive foreign beast not yet weaned to treacle toffee—still ravening after good red trainer. Might have been some vulgar old reprobate from the States, left over from Ringling's. Wherever it came from, that certainly was no *British* lion.

Yes, my eye is being trained to the genial reportial near-insolence which sees everything—countries, people—from the slim vantage of its own idiosyncrasy. Here I have taken cover under the comic, but daily I can see it neatly done in the highest seriousness, for "our tragic times." A novelist must have his "authority"—cricketese for what wins his readers' trust, and keeps their hand and eye in his. A reporter has his assurance, which he must be able to give the reader. For the few moments they are spared to jog together (and it is useful if the reader can be made to feel that their time together is snatched from even more important matters on both sides) the reporter must give his reader the same conqueror's sensation to be got from finishing a crossword puzzle—that for the moment the reader is on top of the subject and that if only all subjects could be as conclusively run through, he would be on top of life.

My pen has been ruined for this, or saved from it, by being unable to make points quickly *and then run*. Nothing to do with length, but with the thickening of life that a novelist hopes for. The quick take is fun anywhere. Literature all the way to Shakespeare is full of them. But running also beside them is a horse of another color and rougher coat, bearing a less easy rider. Who carries the extra weight of his own fallibility in the presence of mystery, and will never concede that any subject in human life is *done*.

*The Reporter*, trimming the article down, had inflated the title, to "Bowlers and Bumbershoots at a Piccadilly Peep-Show." I hadn't learned that economy yet. But I might.

With some relief, I get on to the second piece and back to books and writers, who, steeped in commerce though we might all be, were continually scrambling to be spiritually on top of it. C. P. Snow's recent novel *The Masters* had interested me, partly for reasons close to home. I was trying to find a world to write a novel in. Or to see that world, where, somewhere about me, it lay. He had one, though not as so many of the British seemed to, with a dulling sense of having been given it outright. Snow had made his own world as a writer does, in the act of seeing what is offered him roundabout. Had the stratifications of society over there helped?

A neighbor, his editor, offers an introduction to him which I take, though fully intending, for the sake of all writers, to keep clear in my article the battered distinction between man and book. *The Reporter* has agreed to the piece only if it can be "tied to" a forthcoming book; luckily there is one. This is not my first encounter with what helps keep magazines transient; I had already been asked to change the weather in a story so that it might be printed at once, in another season. But I miss entirely the blunt warning that the business of writers, *for* business, is to be forthcoming (ten years

later, with second book, an editor, bleakly looking past Parnassus
to Brentano's will say "You must remember, you're an utter unknown
at the bookstore.") As a courtesy to *The New Yorker*, with whom
I have a first-reading agreement, I check my plans with an editor
there. The New Towns and The Windmill are passed on without
comment. "Snow—do you really think he's so important?" she says.
"I don't think he's so important." Now, Tippy O'Neill, an auctioneer
I knew, could always raise a laugh by standing over some wildly
awful antiquity—a camelbacked sofa, say—and prosing "Now this is
an important piece." When the word is used of a writer, I tend to
see a sofa. "Well, I don't know," I say, "but sooner or later you're
going to have to deal with him. Maybe even in one of your long
articles at the back." (Snow later tells me that what I wrote had
been the first piece over here to treat his work with more than
review perspective if not length, and as a whole. *The New Yorker*
has a much longer piece about him within a year.)

It is odd, going down to Clare to lunch with another writer as
the interviewer instead of the interviewed; I know I will not like
to do it more than once, after which I would no longer be an
amateur. But I am finally seeing the world by way of my own pen,
as generations of pens have done, and I am almost relieved to be
released of my provincial dignities ... the sense of freedom, mobility within the language-world, of real dignity as a writer, that
England gives me is the same as what my father has bequeathed me
as a Jew; the virtue of being what I am.

In the train, sitting next to a sweet, chatty Suffolk woman on her
worried way to a hospitalized sister whose travail comes to me in
bits through the dialect, gazing past her through the window, I vow
not to ask Snow any of the queries which, even in my short career
I knew are conventionally asked of a writer; to ask professional questions of an artist, even of another artist, was to be automatically asinine.
I felt it with painters and composers, close friends or not. I suppose
dentists and doctors feel it with each other. Some arcane processes
are merely too simple to be intelligibly spoken of; do it smart-ass or

dumb-ass, a Bottom was what you became. . . . "Eeeah," says the
woman, "they cut 'er from ear to ear." Startled, I turned from the
window. She is drawing a cutlass line across her diaphragm. "Eeeah.
From 'ere to 'ere."

It was much easier than that. Snow, with his wife Pamela Hansford
Johnson, novelist too, biographer of Proust and at the moment member of a critic's program on the BBC, clearly cover the scene between
them, and at once flip me the proper professional tone; they ask
questions of me. Mostly he does, and she, not at all the panjandrum
that some female critics at home made of themselves, leaves us until
lunch. Three again, we exchange tastes. If pushed to a choice, he
asks, would I choose Dickens over Proust, as he would, or side with
his wife? Such a juxtaposition has never occurred to me.

I say that the division for me is more as between Dostoevski—in
whose low-life depths of spirit I feel most human, and even the
best of Tolstoi—in whom there always lurks for me the *Kreutzer
Sonata* moralist and the apostrophiser of the norm. As for Dickens,
I tell them that by chance only *Barnaby Rudge* and *Little Dorrit*
were what I had read in childhood, in whatever the bound Harper's
editions of the 1860s on our shelves had pirated from his works. So
I had escaped the Sairy Gamps, Pickwicks and all that other host
who seem to be embedded like waxworks, or like Jungian archetypes,
in the British childhood. Reading the rest of Dickens very late, what
I prefer over his people are the great environmental passages everywhere in his books, like those on London in *Great Expectations*. But,
if pushed—"Well then Proust. He's no juvenile."

He shakes his head at both his wife and me. I scarcely know as
yet that I am making a point conventionally made, often by the
British themselves, on British character. Alone with Snow again,
I ask after Christina Stead, whose work Randall Jarrell, and I and
others, are hoping to have reprinted in the States; no, he is not
familiar with it. I describe the early British praise of her, the parade
of novels, her virtual disappearance from the "known" scene, adding
that tracking her down some years before, I had briefly met her in

London with her husband William Blake (originally Blech). Snow says ah well then, perhaps she has stopped writing; often women do once they are sexually satisfied. Neither of us blinks. Chaff?

On the train back, my next seatmate, a burlapped woman with the foam-flecked voice and subhysterical stare of the born acquirer, reveals herself as a collector of Lord-of-the-Manor rights—which in England one may buy up as one does real estate—just returning from a successful purchase of several, which will allow her, among other things, such perks as the right to graze her sheep on a particular Village green. No, she has no sheep; she's a Londoner.... I still think of her, after some purchase of my own. And apparently, once a reporter, these incidents flock as to some scent, for I never again find such quiddities on London trains....

Later that month, Snow takes me to dinner at the Jardin aux Gourmets, as it happens in the middle of my writing the article on him, not mentioned between us. That night, feeling the delicious oddity of me in forever England, I finish it. Next night, taking Angus Wilson and a friend to dinner at the Jardin, on their chancing to order the same entree as Snow and I had, I assume a host's privilege of ordering the wine. Both my friends keep their eyes lowered as I deal with the sommelier. Deliberating, I order the same Volnay—no doubt exactly suitable, in vintage not too showy—which Snow had. Both look me in the eye; nobody says anything. But on the following night, when I turn the trick again with my friends the Gatehouses—I am leaving England and doing what women of my mother's time called "reciprocating"—I burst out laughing and tell them. All this reportial insouciance, with its pretty predicates and conclusions linked by the quickest-to-hand copula, all this ready objectifying which I guess must be Grub street anywhere, no matter how close it seems to Parnassus—how enjoyable it is! I know I can't maintain it in America. And I know I do best in my other work when humility overtakes me. "But there's something hypnotic for me, in your air. I can make people choose their entree."

Doing the piece on Snow, I have made other discoveries.

.
•
.

THE NOVELIST who makes his lifetime work the continuous chronicling of some closed world—one that is limited to a certain set of characters usually further confined by geographical or class milieu—has at once immense advantages of scale, unity and familiarity, if he can live up to them. If social historians are to be trusted, the actual world behind the shadow play of Barsetshire was almost as immutably fixed in its rules and as limited by congenially narrow horizons as were Trollope's characters.

My own opinion, which is no more likely to be confirmed than other estimates of the dead by the living, is that past eras were never quite so categorically neat as hindsight would make them. Nevertheless, in those days even so socially aware a novelist as Dickens both raised and solved his issues in terms of the sentimental situation, still sharing with his readers and characters more premises than many are likely to share securely in our time. The novelist, thus freed or healthily restricted, could preoccupy himself with human weakness in an environment already assessed, could still accept a great portion of his world as having been deeded him by a fiat for which he did not hold himself responsible.

Since then, the world, and the novel with it, has been busy investigating its premises. Meanwhile, the pure national currents of literature have long since flowed together, until it is no longer possible to say whether the expression of our underground spiritual agonies derives from Dostoevski, Thomas Mann, or Céline, our erotic trends from Joyce, Lawrence, or Gide, or whether—as so often seems the case—present-day American writers inherit everything at once by nervously reading one another.

It has become a truism, particularly with us, to note that a world of uncertainty may be good for the democratic process but hard on the novelist, who saw his way so much more clearly in the blessed time of slow trains and few termini. Nowadays he has the double job of finding some homogeneous pattern before he can sit down to describe it.

Certainly the American novelist, who draws some of his vitality from taking things harder than anybody else, takes his uncertainty harder than anybody else. Some commentators believe that, as a younger country, we have a national flux added to the general—yet it is a long time since Oscar Wilde observed that America's oldest tradition was her youth. Could it be, contrariwise, that for the first time we see ourselves solidifying into a national character, and that this affrights us? Our unique contributions—Mark Twain, Melville, Faulkner, for instance—have all had a bardically strong regional base, and we now see those regional differences disappearing. Where the canyons have so far escaped the leveling process, the inhabitants have not. Geographical isolation will not be of any more use to us in literature than it will be politically.

Whether or not we like what we see solidifying is another question. Historically it has often been useful for a writer to dislike what he sees, but still more valuable for him to know what he likes, and ours is a nation where everyone is heartily pressed to be "individual" but eccentricity is not encouraged. (Not even oppressed—for Americans, despite fugues in that direction, are very tender on the subject of oppression.) Meanwhile the artist, who knows that his eccentricity—in the sense of being outside the circle the better to see it—is important to him, knows also that it cannot be cultivated on short notice, like a Barrow Street beard. The best thing that can happen to him is to be born into a tradition that respects eccentricity, sometimes before understanding it, and will give him time to develop it.

It is no wonder that the American writer, who for so long has been carried on the energy of his great national eccentricity—that barbarian-fresh point of view on which he has leaned as on a tradition—feels lost now that he sees this heritage fading. He is losing his folklore of newness, as an endlessly rich source book or as a substitute for a personal point of view, and he knows it.

Given time, he will go beyond newness to something as yet undreamed. He *is* given time, but not too much of it, and not without grumbling. If he pauses to write of his childhood, he is "retreating"; if he writes of the mad, who sometimes illuminate the sane, he is deserting art for psychiatry (everybody conceivably having forgotten that the one considerably antedates the other); if he begins to feel, with Juvenal, *"difficile est non satiram scribere,"* then he lacks compassion. So it happens that if he does desert "larger issues" in the hope of finding some limited world he knows well, he is sneered at for being aphilanthropic. Cornered in self-consciousness, he often finds himself half agreeing with those who predict the death of the novel, and fearing that he has lost his own faith in it as a "form."

When, then, in the midst of such broodings, one encounters a continuous *oeuvre* like C. P. Snow's "Lewis Eliot" sequence, which he has been publishing piecemeal since 1940, one thinks suddenly of how much less often such sequences appear in American literature than in British. As against those British ones which come first to mind—*The Forsyte Saga*, the Tietjens novels of Ford Madox Ford, Lawrence's Brangwens, the works of Henry Handel Richardson and Henry Williamson, the "Eustace" trilogy of L. P. Hartley, the novels of Anthony Dymoke Powell, the work of Joyce Cary and of Snow himself, we have what?—perhaps Thomas Wolfe, Farrell's Lonigan, and Sinclair's Lanny Budd. If we exclude Faulkner as *sui generis,* we cannot do so without noting that the coextensive nature of his Yoknapatawpha County, his creation of a matrix world into which he can plunge at any point, is the one path on which his imitators have not chosen to follow him. The same might be said of those who were influenced by Wolfe.

Our novelists tend to write enormous books but discontinuous ones. Whatever may be made of this, it is certain that the American writer's sense of acceptance is far more discontinuous than the Continental's; his reputation rises and falls with each book to a far greater degree, and even when established he cannot hope to have each successive book taken as part of a total work until very late in the day, often when his creative activity is almost over. Although he may know in his heart that he has only one theme, he must conceal this from himself, as well as from others, in some mask of new-ness each time, and he does not dare any such progression as Gide's, who unconcernedly wrote the same book again and again.

The French, of course, have long since solved the question of what art may or may not deal with by refusing to see that the question exists. But the fact that the American novelist no longer worries over the content of art in any moral sense may have obscured the truth that he does worry over what subject matter is "proper" to it in a metaphysical sense. He is still propagandizing by selection, out of a feeling that a novel will be a better work of art if it not only "settles" something artistically but does it now. He wants the life he saves to be his own.

What this urgency does for him is by no means all bad. It may have produced that peculiar split in our fiction whereby we have hugely competent "realists" whose view of life is organized, enter-taining, yet too opportunely glib, and an opposing breed of "literary" novelists working in beautifully polished bas-relief, in some savagely intense corner of adolescence, homosexuality, or racial sensibility. Yet it may also contribute to that primitive intensity of concern which does not fight shy of poetry, that basic ability to confront feeling which so often seems missing in our drier British brethren. We may learn a good deal about ourselves by studying our opposites, particu-larly in the work of a writer like Snow who, by very national habit, seems at times so much more at home in the novel than we are, and at others too much at home in a way that we might not care to be.

(In this kind of writing-about-others, where the great, attemptable projections of art-emotion are missing, where only now and then I can risk a lurid language-bubble from the floral ponds below, I am really examining myself. In terms of that only, could I dare to pass judgment on others. I must try only to pass printed judgment on a writer when it more than a little concerns me. Then, on entering that drier, theoretical air, I can better keep in mind *caritas*, the human warmth, the human rarity. For the sake of us both.)

•
•
•

I CAME BACK aware. Doubled. And praying to love *my* country best. Why should this have filled me with confidence?

If I stood still, ideas dripped from my fingers, oozed like wax from my ears, tumbled toward my lips. I sneezed, melted, opened to the world's presence. It was all true, and utterable. The world was not my oyster, but everybody's. For life.

"Back in town," but twenty-five miles up river, I ignored the muffled telephone calls which kept coming from New York like a heartbeat from the year before. I lay on the hillside behind the house, head toward the mountain, feet toward the Hudson which ran below, and all summer re-read books I have never before finished to the very end—Proust, *The Brothers Karamazov, War and Peace.* Now and then I went dazedly to parties down the road, when I answered the bright, loving, intense American questioning with the secret smile of the traveler returned. I touched the children with care and some fear, they of an age now to be surely quaking with dreams beyond me, who could only labor and bake for them. My marriage was slowing down; five years later it would come to a stop. Meanwhile, the four of us were, each in our own ways too busy, terrified, or enchanted with growing, to consider this. I was growing not a baby but a book. More total than a child, at least in the making, and a birth that I only could manage, or transmit.

I had been carrying it about for sometime now, not really knowing; I had even signed a contract for another. Turning down *Tale for the Mirror*, a novella, *The New Yorker* had said it sounded more like, or too much like, the beginning of a longer work. At times I too had thought it might be, and had outlined its further projection to an editor, in a page I still have. One should never do that, or I should not. For me, that book now stopped. Or had I stopped it? Yes, I knew further projections for the people in it, but this was often my case both before and after a story—until it was forgotten in the welter of new work embarked on. Probably *Tale* ended where I wanted it to, having said what it was meant to say perhaps a little too soon for its length, but I had obeyed its dictates.

Meanwhile, for several years now, I have been carrying everywhere with me a small bit of paper, on it a few sentences which have for me a sacramental import beyond their meaning. Once I show it to Marion Ives, my first agent, who wisely nods and says nothing. It reads "For the past is a doll's house. It stands there, finished and clear, centered in the attic of the mind. We stand outside it helpless, swollen with the giant present. Inside, where everything is known, charm, joy, and terror chime with the limited pangs of clocks. Outside it I stand, I the enormous Alice, and there is no little bottle from which to drink, or bit of cake that will shrink us in. At its windows the dustless curtains billow perfectly, and below, the pavements sparkle mica-sharp, in the uneclipsable light of a small but steadfast sun." The odd thing is, that I know it is the *end* of something itself not yet conceived. Then, suddenly having written thirty or forty pages, I send word to the editor, Nicholas Wreden, that I want to honor the contract but switch books on him; could this be done? He replies, no doubt tongue-in-cheek, that it has been known to happen; would I send him the pages? Shortly he writes to say that I must go on with it. When it is delivered, seven years later, that passage appears in its last pages, verbatim with one exception: "I, the enormous Alice" has been changed to "we, the enormous children." Why? The book is written from within the mind of a man.

Now I would not be that consistent, or see the need for it. But during the long writing, I had begun to wonder how it would be received, this interior confession—"search for identity" as the jargon of the time tended to call any self-searching book—written entirely in the male person, by me. I even dally with publishing it under an alias. "I'll be one of the Georges," I half-joke to my publisher—but he shakes his head. My own name is what they are buying. I give up the idea with regret; in a way I would always rather be anonymous.

(Waiting, of course, to be found out.) Why have I thought of it at all? Am I afraid of being thought a Lesbian?

I think seriously about this, as my generation has been taught to do. Is it possible I am a submerged one? Tall, and capable of summoning a baritone voice, I was always given the male parts in the all girl high-school dramatic club, and a couple of girls fell in love with the way I looked in a tuxedo. I have a powerful body, curved though it is, and have a certain dominance, though it doesn't always last. I have close homosexual friends but they are all male, many of them married to one other man, all of them leading full lives. I have never known a lesbian well, though I have known couples; in love they often seem to me to tend toward the perfervid, the subhysterical and the sentimental, all the worser qualities of women. I have close women friends whom I love, but like me they are interested in men, or one man. I have never been bodily shy; years as a dancer did that for me. I used to be shy of kissy women, but not for sexual reasons. Since having children I'm much looser at touching people I like. But I can't excite myself over the thought of sex with women. For one thing, there aren't enough parts. I loved my father, though not blindly, partially hated my mother, though I admired her and wanted to be like her too; that editor who so insulted me with the norm may have been reasonably right. No form of sex seems to me innately repellent; any form of it is probably natural to somebody. Saddest for me, as an imagined lesbian, would be not having children. Even if I managed to to adopt some, as homosexuals now and then do, I cannot believe that I wouldn't be sad at having to miss that experience in the ordinary way. From here, where I stand. But I could be having another experience that I do not have—here. We tend to exalt the framework in which we are. Perhaps I am doing that?

There must be something wrong with a personality which seems to have everything so neatly covered. My "mind"—as far as I can disinter it from the rest of me—seems to have no particular sex. I hold no special brief for "the family." I am greedy for experience, but more greedy for some than for others. What pulls me deepest, moves me darkly and lightly, is what I can only think of as ordinary experience. *Sunt lacrimae rerum.* That's me. *Et mentem mortalia tangunt.* I find that line untranslatable, yet am willing to spend my life at it: Here are tears for the affairs of men. They touch mortal minds; they touch mine.

Far as I could tell, I was not a lesbian. If I were, I doubted I would be afraid, silent, or submerged. Then what do I apprehend?

By then, it has been borne in upon me—in a professional way—that to some I will always be a "woman writer." Some, critics and readers both, will not bother to read me. Others, when they do, will express to me their surprise at having done so and admired it, often much as Andre Gide had to Colette. Though I am printed generally, women's magazines are especially accessible; I have to be careful not to confine myself to them, even though at the moment some of them are printing internationally known writers of both sexes. I will begin to notice that when a biographical dictionary (or an academy or a university) excerpts from my dossier, these are the publications likely to be left out. Now and then *I* leave them out. I learn that the best way is not to notice any of it, and push on. When a woman is sent a book of mine for review, I have to hope it is out of respect for what she is literarily; as more men are sent them, I welcome the tribute and learn the risk. I can never be sure of being reviewed as a writer and not as a woman. I learn to know the watchwords when that is happening to me, even when well concealed from whoever pens it. I remember the old warning, from the days of "Old Stock": when people dislike what you say, they will say that you are a bad writer. When they dislike what you are, or cannot admit that you may be an equal, they will do the same. In other words, of course. Maybe slanging the style, or the subject matter. But often in my case, to imply that I am "a woman writer" will be enough.

Yet all this is, as I well know, merely the professional hazard, like the money, and the personality pouncing and the party cauldrons— like the whole worldly loss of innocence. To heed it unduly is to be one of those shriveled devotees who live by the calendar of saints but have forgotten the godhead. None of this must enter the work.

Is there a fear that has?

Not a fear, but a knowledge. Which has entered the writer. Who is a woman.

All around me, women of the richest sensibility were writing. Sometimes they lyricized the world, sometimes they classicised it. Sometimes they grotesqued it. And sometimes, without a tone altered or an honesty shifted, it was possible to feel—in the way one senses a closed window—that they had daintified it. Often they wrote from the interiors of women and children, or of the old. Men they wrote of as lovers, fathers or brothers. Seldom did they write from the interior of a man, or in the male persona altogether, as women had long since been written of by men.

I had done several stories that way, even before the novel. Now and then I idly wondered about this. How far could the adaptive imagination go? I wanted to think it could go anywhere. One enormous shadow then loomed over the American male writer, and through him, over me. War. With all its attendant virilities of sport and sex. Only one—Faulkner, after writing of it in its natural frame, and its current one (*Soldier's Pay*) had gone on to a wider human comedy, hunting the past in the present. Fitzgerald, who had done the same in more immediate terms, was dead, and then largely unappreciated. The rest, senior and young, hunted the war novel, that great bear. And women were civilians, their only connection with war being the bed or the bedpan, the Red Cross doughnut or the office type-writer, or the entertainment circuit, which included those few female correspondents who flirted equally with generals and with death. For the mass of women, the war-connection was as wives, lovers and mothers, all Gold Star. All women were joined to this "larger" world by the same single thread—men. So deep was the human race sunk in war and all the effects of war, that this seemed to us entirely natural. As women, we could be Lysistratas, or Florence Nightingales. As writers, we could ape the men by seeing the world as militarily as possible, or we could popularize ourselves in the image always ready for us—as sweet sprinklers of sachet in the sickroom of experience. Or we could stand back or aside, the better to see the whole range, and the whole other range, of human experience. Including our own.

Although my male confreres who in one way or other imitated Hemingway could still make me feel small punkins in front of a bar or behind a gun, secretly I thought them and him provincial in some way, though I couldn't yet have told why. Their cult seemed to me both narrow and exaggerated. Hunting the blood dramas of war and ambulance as if out for game, tied to the physicality of events, they were becoming the male journalists of literature. Hindsight, not too much later, would tell my why. Men, and women too, who make a sentiment out of physical prowess, need a neo-primitive culture to sustain them; in ours, bloody as it is, physicality pursued to the end keeps one an eternal juvenile. When the prowess dies, the importance of such event dies, and the sentiment, even of combat, dies with them —as Hemingway's suicide gun perhaps signaled. The price paid by some male American writers of the period would be that of an intellectuality refused. But this would be nothing to the price paid by all Americans, whether they know it or not, for fighting wars at the peculiar modern distance. While they sent their sons, the middle-aged stayed at home, to rot in silk, under safe skies. To tranquilize themselves for lesser tragedies. To psychoanalyse themselves for fears of cancer and death. To beat their breasts over the disappointments of educational and social meliorism—and social change. To yearn secretly for the cleansing violence that a nation has, when it defends itself and its ideals *at home*. All the falsities of that America could be laid to it. *We were not bombed at home.* We were the first nation really to live by the electric button, in our souls. Or in our balls? Men writers of the times were telling us that, sorrily not by their prophetic tongues but by their barometric actions. These samurai were having to cross the water, the air, to find gests emotionally worthy of them. Europe, in the bloodiest way, was still attracting Americans. Over there. Too late. In the bloodbath, women are more and more equal. War, no longer a gest, is civilian now. No one, not even a child, need be envious.

Back then, my own progress toward such ideas is slow. When the novel appears, its subject will after all obscure the fact that a woman wrote it. One writer friend will question me thoughtfully. Was is necessary for it to be written through a man? "Oh yes—" I flash back, from depths that surprise me "you see—he had to be able to go anywhere." He sees the point.

By the time I write a second novel (1963) I will have come full circle. It is to be, as I tell him, "about the power of the little events that creep up on you while you are waiting for the big ones. And it'll be as female as I can make it." (It wasn't. I would have regretted that. But it was more so than many serious novels by women. It was, I think, as female as things sometimes are.) A year or so after, a friend who has always admired my other work very vocally, calls me out of the blue. "You know I never read that one (*Textures of Life*). I was afraid to. To spoil what I think of you." I worm out of him that friends have told him not to bother—it is a woman's book. "But now I've read it, I want you to know that they're wrong. It's going right up on my shelf with your others. *Now*." Victorians segregated the books on their shelves by sexes. But I refrain from mentioning it. Let it be.

Now, in the 1970s, I may be in danger of being segregated with women by women, by those ultra-feminists for whom, if I am not totally "with," I will be "against." I will wonder whether they have ever read Virginia Woolf's *Three Guineas*, which so long ago said so much of their litany rather better, in turn getting much of it from another writer, Dorothy Richardson, whom all feminists might explore. No, art is not a standing together. It is a statement by an outsider, from within.

When, in 1957, I wrote on Maurice Goudeket's biography of his wife, Colette, I had this to say:

When Sidonie Gabrielle Claudine Colette Gauthier-Villars de Jouvenel, known to all the world as Colette, died in 1954 at the age of eighty-one at the end of a life extraordinarily inseparable from her work, she had long since received from her own country that national esteem with which France rewards its writers. True, although she was the first woman member of the Académie Goncourt, she had never been a member of the Académie Française. So much the worse for them, rather than for her, to whom even the chary Gide had forced himself to write: "I myself am completely astonished that I should be writing to you, astonished at the great pleasure I have had in reading you," and to whom the more generous Proust had already written, in 1919, "Your style and your color are so full of perpetual finds that if one noted everything one could write you a letter as long as your book."

In her long progression she was to have a life as multiple as one of the cat race she loved—Burgundian schoolgirl, provincial child-wife in Paris, hack writer, music-hall performer and dancer in the nude, actress as one of her own characters, theater critic, seller of beauty products, housewife as perfectionist in domestic lore as she was over a sentence, and writer—perhaps the first great French woman writer to come from the middle class.

Of the *Oeuvres Complètes*, published by Flammarion in 1950, only a small portion of the fifteen volumes, comprising more than fifty titles, are available here in English, although more are promised. And here, too, she has never been given the critical attention awarded either her contemporaries or the younger generation of French writers. Her world, no more feminine than Virginia Woolf's, was less bluestocking, her style too sure to be classed as experimental. And her supposed sensationalism, garbed as it was in the décor of the demi-monde, seemed to many too frivolous for dignified consideration. One might say of her that her art was almost too accessible for criticism, at least for some American critics.

Actually she was her own best commentator, continuously reassessing her life and work, stalking its persistent themes from another angle. After reading Goudeket's account, one understands better Colette's extraordinary gift for the particularities of sensuous detail—a gift that was based in nature perhaps, but was to be equally sharp when turned on the tailor-made world.

"But above all she used the exact names of objects in daily use. . . . She knew a recipe for everything . . . furniture polish, vinegar, orange-wine, quince-water, for cooking truffles or preserving linen . . . this country wisdom impregnates all her work. . . . Looked at in one light it would not have displeased her if one talked of recipes for writing."

This household imagery is to appear everywhere in her work, bringing a curious solidity to her demimondaine worlds, and used in contexts light or powerful, from the casual, conversational aside when she could call Bach "a sublime sewing machine" down to the details of Léa's ménage in *Chéri*, where, in the language of cuisine and nursery comfort, the relationship is described without a psychological word, and no symbol of anguish is more apt than Léa's turning out her cupboards after Chéri is gone.

Which brings us, brooding on the particular, to the question that often rears its silly suffragette head in critiques on women writers, and not infrequently in the hearts of the women themselves: Are female writers more limited in their world than male? Should they ignore all the special data they have as women or use it, try to be men or stand upon what they are—and in so doing any one of these things do they consign themselves to narrower than male limits and to less chance of greatness?

The answer, I think, comes better from Colette than from any other woman writer I know, and is to me a token of her stature. She is no more essentially feminine as a writer than any man is essentially masculine as a writer—certain notable attempts at the latter notwithstanding. She uses the psychological and concrete dossiers in her possession as a woman, not only without embarrassment but with the most natural sense of its value, and without any confusion as to whether the sexual balance of her sensitivity need affect the virility of her expression when she wants virility there.

Reading her, one is reminded that art—whether managed as a small report on a wide canvas, or vice versa—is a narrow thing in more senses than one, and that the woman writer, like any other, does best to accept her part in the human condition, and go on from there. . . .

But let us return to Goudeket, who, while modestly disclaiming critical authority, scatters understanding everywhere in this quiet, graceful book. "It is not enough to say that she loved animals. Before every manifestation of life, animal or vegetable, she felt a respect which resembled religious fervor. At the same time she was always aware of the unity of creation in the infinite diversity of its forms. One evening she gave me a striking example of this. We were at the cinema, watching one of those shorts which show germinations accomplished in a moment, unfolding of petals which look like a struggle, a dramatic dehiscence. Colette was beside herself. Gripping my arm, her voice hoarse and her lips trembling, she kept on saying with the intensity of a pythoness: 'There is only one creature! D'you hear, Maurice, there is only *one* creature.'

It is no wonder that she was able to treat every variation, singular or regular, of the sexual or half-sexual relationship, with never the slightest false touch of lubricity, for, seeing every creature as an aspect of one, she could never really regard the sexes as antithetical.

And this in turn was only part of a larger attitude that never made too much of the distinction between the animate and the inanimate, that was at any moment, witty or profound, likely to describe one in terms of the other. . . .

It is an attitude that accounts for much; it is for instance one reason why she translates well, for whatever nuance or idiosyncrasy may be lost, there is almost always some basic image, native to us creatures, that does not escape. It accounts in part, also, for that earlier mentioned "accessibility" which perhaps so depresses the interest of the modern critics, particularly those more interested in displaying themselves. There is nothing much to emend in Colette. She treats of the basic mysteries, but with the utmost care not to add any mystification of her own, like a midwife too busy getting the baby born to stop for the philosophical "Why?"

As for her "daring," it is there, but is not of a sort to compel, for instance, those who love to brood on the eunuchoid element in James or to extrapolate a national homosexual dream from Huck Finn. It is the daring of an eye that looks on the world with the directness of total health—an eye somewhat chilling at times, possibly because, like those of the genus Bufo or Rano on whom she often drew for imagery, it occupies so very much of the head. One finds here perhaps the reason for the accusation that she did not create individual character, that she saw people to be as inchoate as those other fauna or flora through whom life blooms, droops, and is cut down, and that she never moved from her microcosm either to the metaphysical or to the "world at large." Certainly it would be just to say that she never seemed to have much time to consider things as they might be, so busy was she with the morality of things as they were.

By the time I wrote on Colette, I had come to terms with being a writer. And for all my surface rages in the past and to come, with being a woman among us. I feel I can go to any war I want to. To all the wars of life, and of mind.

In the depths of the world, of the sky, there's a rhythm that must be listened to. Anybody can. One day—who knows under what cloud or circumstance?—that beat may seep from your wrist to your pen. Like blood—which has no ultimate sex. *One must give back the stare of the universe.* Anybody can.

•
•
•

THE STORY of a man aided in his pursuit of art or war by his love for a good woman, or a bad one, is an old literary occurrence. The spectacle of a woman encouraged in life, companioned in art and in certain of her own wars through love of a man—is not. Because of that, I break a self-imposed rule which was to have been—"Except for where it appertains to the work; keep your private life out of it.

I know that in that other work, *the* work, no matter how seemingly objective, I somewhere lay my own life on the line. Yet I have no desire to make my own life a public work of art. Should I—as some have? No, I am not that kind of artist. I have a need to push myself through the human extravaganza the *other* way. Yet this book, like those others in their way, has to be true to the happenings.

Since 1958, I have had among my papers a certain "Journal From The Far East," kept by me and sent in lieu of letters, in exchange for one kept and sent similarly, from Iran. I decide to include it here, abridged for length and lesser trivia. And to reveal the necessary background. I do this for a reason as personal as you want. A life looks hard, vain, empty, without its love. In my case, it would be a lie. For extreme cases, sometimes—an extreme magic. Once again.

When you look at Iowa City, seat of the state university, from one approach at sunset, it still looks (then) like the last movie-set of a frontier town. That low, paper-cut facade still clings to the prairie at its base and to the turn of the century at its square, dribbled roof-line, promising in its center the feedstore and the horse-trough. You know otherwise, even if the streaking cars aren't advising you. Behind there is the usual university-town prospect with its seedy porches, null college buildings, and perhaps one Palladian hall. Yet it is still a western approach.

It was the farthest west I had yet been.

I had never heard of the Writers' Workshop, and when I arrive there still have little idea of what such a workshop is. Each time I had turned down the offer of a year's teaching, the price had risen. At home, my earnings had begun to be counted upon. And I had a divorce to settle, dragged out by a partner who would not assist—or leave. So, accepting the offer for only a half-year, again I left the children behind me, to schools and father. Once I had the divorce and some modest situation, I intended to devote my time to work, *the* work, and to them. I had found I was unfitted for casual sex, which depressed me. Or for short passions, which in my case were really the obsessional outbursts of a personality still on-the-search. For that not-impossible, born-at-the-other-side-of-the-world (I always knew that) Platonic half whom one at birth had become separated from. In whose existence I at the moment did not believe.

At the depot, I am met on the one hand by the couple who are my landlords-to-be—he with a long, Grant Wood neck, she with what must be a hundred spit-curls, set in rows like Papuan teeth. On the other hand are my friends the Bourjailys with their Anna, Tina calling out in her amused voice, "I recognized the coat!" (Worn since London, a long, hooded, pocketed jewel of a reversible, in which it is possible to live like a tent, it will serve me as a *chadur* in Persia, though I can't know that yet.)

And in the middle, a tall man, with a face. I see it yet, with its strange look of recognition, that it doesn't want to make. It is seeing the same look on mine. He has come out of courtesy to meet a traveler, not a woman. I have not come to meet a lover—the lover. Because the face is handsome, I even wisecrack to myself like a smart chorine— "Uh-*uh*, Hortense. No." The last time I say it.

We become an accepted couple, the beaming faculty displaying a restraint softer than New York's would be, and effortfully more cosmopolitan. As for the rest of the place, the Workshop especially, it is a blend of a rural Athens with a Greenwich Village when it too was doe-eyed with its own dreams, set down in a campus autumn ringed round with football and "homecoming" queens, where we play handball with an all-poet team. It is the perfect place for an idyll we don't know is going to last.

The Workshop is a shock. They really mean to *make* artists. Much of the student work is mediocre, sometimes rising to good, though with that fell tone to it which tells one it is doomed to remain what it is; an alarming proportion of manuscripts is bad—and a few students, maybe one or two, are first class. They are already *made*, by God or the Devil, California or Brooklyn, and are there for time out and money—in order to make. I tell the head, Paul Engle, "When they're no good, I want to say to them 'What are you *doing* here?' When they're good, I want to say to them 'What are *you* doing *here?*'" He says brightly "That's what we pay you for. Your personality."

So I am for this lovely moment absolved. To be for the first time in my life with a man whose intelligence leaps with mine and is capable of outrunning it, whose sexuality does the same. From differing lives, we find constant points of similarity. We listen alike—to the rest of the world. And we know too much to think this merely the entente of love.

A Lutheran boy with six siblings, from a working farm where country skills were taken for granted, and a Jewish girl with the streets in her blood, an only child until she was seven—we both felt

that we had become writers, or humanists, from having sat young in
the outer shoals of large, anecdotal families. We both wrote mornings,
after which we craved physical activity and then perhaps, company,
although we had a capacity for silent, inner living—which unnerved
other people. His wife had felt shut out when he closed his study
door; my husband, though compliant, had been at a fatal distance
from what I did there.

I have since known many artists who live with non-artists; there
is always a separateness. The non-artist is forced to admire, or to
stand off, or to serve. And there is always a rub between the two
routines. I cannot now imagine living with someone who doesn't
share that other unspoken rhythm. Days when one or the other was
not working and was feeling it, were likely to be our worst; then we
were like anybody else. To people who find one artist's life queer
enough, two together are a riot; the prospect of two writers getting on
seems to pique most of all. Or perhaps it is the old concept that every
artist is doomed by his demon never to get on in that way, to be
alone, emotionally. We were to be, in a way, but knew that. We
were never to "share" the work, until it was done. But we belonged
to the same cell.

Meanwhile, we had no thought of marriage, on this rebound, ab-
sorbing though it was. Too much was unsettled, in any case, and not
only divorces. His so recent wife, though now with the man of her
choice, wrote often of returning after the child she was bearing was
born. I had my children, and my resolve. During the next year we
separated several times, I to Stamford, in the spring of 1958, to teach,
where he visited me, he to Iowa for the summer, where I visited him.
(Once, when I was flying to Mexico for divorce papers, we arranged to meet in Chicago on my way back. On the flight down, the
president of a Texas Methodist university gave me his card, no doubt
tabbing me as one of those divorcées—he laughed when I said *I* was a
professor—and tried to persuade me to stay overnight in El Paso—
presumably with him. I refused, and from the plane watched him
being met by a woman no doubt his wife. Saved his card though; it

was such a classy one. We left it stuck prominently on the mirror of the Chicago motel.)

By now absences were a travail. We solved the problem with visits ever wilder. In the fall, he was to go abroad as a Fulbright lecturer, and had opted for Tabriz, in Azerbaijan. That past winter, the International Educational Exchange Service, which during those years specialized in exporting our culture (and to whom I had once applied, on the suggestion, both of us full of drink, from Richard Blackmur, who was going to Japan for them) had asked me to join a summer symposium in Japan. I had turned it down—the novel was going too well—and I cannot take seriously either summer programs or symposiums. (Once, I heard a woman say proudly that her son had gone "to a supposium"—which seems to be apt.) As a writer, my application to the I.E.S. had languished, except for a reply, ominous during this McCarthy-probe era "Yes, Miss Calisher, we know who you are and what you are doing."

But now I am a professor, no matter what Texas Wesleyan thought —and on their preferred list. So I write asking to join whatever program they may have in Iran. Just then Iraq bursts into flame, curtailing their Middle-East projects, but after some bargaining it is suggested that if I will do a three-month tour of Southeast Asia for them, they will drop me in Iran as I have asked to be—I hadn't said why.

I have brought love and the U.S. government together, but the joke is private. So far. We plan to live together in Tabriz, perhaps even to the end of my children's school year. Because of the place being both Islam and a tiny foreign community, we weigh whether it will be easier for us to live as married. Decenter too, for them. Though we dislike the pretense. As for actual marriage, we haven't spoken of it. His marital status is still in question; his wife and the other man had once flown to Mexico for "papers," but she had reneged and come home without—later sending on mail-order ones.

Perhaps we ourselves are trying out marriage, in our own way. "Marry him!" my friend Alma—on whom I have relied for the conventional approach—says when I bring up the differences in our ages,

I the elder. "He's older now than your first—(five years my elder)—will ever be." Her acerb look adds, "And in some ways, my dear, older than you." Right. My friend Mickey says lightly "Oh do marry him—it's so much easier in hotels."

And on the Southeast Asia diplomatic circuit as well. For very soon, some weirdo—one of the gods perhaps, fresh from a summer conference course in fiction—takes over our script. We have never been certain whether or not his wife—now hopefully "former"—knows of our connection, though we hope that perhaps the academic grapevine has done its work. Shortly we do hear that she and her new husband and baby have been posted to Bangkok. Where, in discharge of their duties and mine—we will most surely meet. (In the Journal they are J. and R.) Proprietary letters from her to my friend still keep coming, indicating she feels that the option to return to him is still hers. When my friend, leaving the U.S. ahead of me, gets to Tabriz, her greeting awaits him. "Welcome to this side of the world!"

We too are struck by how small it is. Since I, in my modest way, am to be a public personage over there, we decide, consulting by letter, to spare ourselves and the U.S. any domestic drama. The prospective lie bugs me—like somebody else's mucilage I have got stuck in. Not my style. Nor his. But we shall try to be as seemlily married as the occasion appears to demand.

Meanwhile, we have decided that during the separated part of our travels we will keep journals, and exchange. The following, somewhat abridged, is mine.

PART III

# SEIZURES OF
# LOVE AND WORK

*September 11th or 12th, nearing the Aleutians*—(Somewhere we cross the International dateline.)

Washington was bland and brilliant when I arrived at about one in the afternoon. Although the airfield is in Virginia (where, as some said, it always feels warmer than D.C.), the atmosphere already had for me, as it always does, the reflected memory of central Washington, the white, null buildings of a nation's public grandeur. I did not see these this time. Instead, after tucking myself away in the Presidential, a small hotel, old-fashioned but pleasant even to price ($5 per diem as against the Statler's expense account $13) I walked around the corner to the offices of the International Educational Exchange Service. Housed in a separate building away from central bureaucratic Washington, it is, as one of the staff informed me, somewhat a stepchild of the State Dept. It felt strange, after so many months of corresponding with titled names under the august blue S.D. imprint, to meet Mrs. G., inhabitant of a small office, and suffering humanly from a bad cold. Colwell was out ill also; mortality runneth high perhaps, among these step-children. Man next to her handles Latin-American cultural requests; said Vance had written to him giving my name. (They need people who speak

Spanish.) Gave V. a strong recommendation—imagine he will be asked to go next summer.

The main impression of my visit—that I was told nothing. It was assumed that I knew why I was going and what to do—I cd not decide whether or not this was intelligent on their part, or the resignation of routine. Appointments had been set up however—first with Miss Wilkins, the financial head, who explained, in hallowed tones, about 'per diem'—pronounced 'per dye-em.' In any case, it hangs heavy over every S.D. person—all women of this type—the figure-handlers, bursars, comptrollers, have an air of the religious about them; they affect me like certain librarians of my childhood—with the best will in the world, listening to them, as I do, with the prim air of the very good child, I know I shall be in Dutch with them ere long.

Then the briefing. Two hours approx. for 4 countries. A Mr. Gregory, eager to get back to his car pool, escorted me thru various divisions of the Bur. of Far Eastern affairs. On Thailand—Mr. Buschner; Manila—Mr. Brand; Japan—Mr. Derr. It was my strong impression that they did not know why I was there—I was ill-equipped to tell them, and cd scarcely ask them whether they had heard of the IEES. Mr. B. was outraged at the limited time given. Intelligent man, but he cd but tell me bits and stuff—such as—it is an insult to cross legs and point the toe or sole of foot at the Thais. Suggested I hear some of their music. Gathered he loved the T's; his face brightened when I spoke highly of those I had met at Pat's in London. Suggested I contact the man sent by New Asia Foundation to teach journalism at Thomasat U. Gave me a pamphlet—of which I already had 2 copies, and, I suppose, his blessing.

Mr. Brand (Mr. Gregory told me *sotto voce*) might be a bit of a wind-bag. Certainly B. loved to talk, but he did it well, and was by far the most informative. I gathered that he had earned the reputation the enthusiast often does among staff with more routine incentive —or else Mr. G.'s ride home was in extreme peril. B. showed me a copy of the *Phil. Free Press*—comes out bi-monthly, article on the short story by N. V. M. Gonzalez, their most eminent novelist, a member of Santos's group. I gather that these are the more conservative nationalists—the younger and more arbitrary, leftist or whatever group —this was not clear—cluster around the *Manila Chronicle*. Their idol, however confusingly, is Claro Recto, Japanese puppet gov't member during their regime. Other names—Nettie and Fred Ramos—leaders in the group of young writers at the Univ. of P. Also a litry lady— Mrs. Nakpil, very energetic, has ulcers. Random comments—the Islands have a long super-cigarette the size of a cigar, that I must try.

*Morning—Saturday, Sept. 13, Imperial Hotel Tokyo.*

I see that I have just escaped Friday the 13,—perhaps that was the day that went over the line. What a satisfactory thing a journal is— or perhaps it is just the sensation of resolve fulfilling—I always wanted to keep one and never have. Then too, it is a companion when one is touring alone. And one forgets so quickly. I meant to put down, back there over the Aleutians yesterday (how I love such an off-hand phrase, flinging my still new-found cosmopolitanism over my shoulder like a scarf) that *back there* in Washington, Mr. Derr, the man to brief me on Japan, and I throw up our hands over the impossibility of same. Again I had the impression that he had no idea of why I was going, or whom sent by. I imagine (from the way I have heard Foreign Office gents refer to the Br. Council) that information services are usually viewed dimly by the official services. But, feeling that this was no reason for *me* to be embarrassed, I told Mr. D. that I supposed the IEES simply picked someone who cd be trusted to fare forth on his own, etc. Mr. D. quickly and relievedly seized on this, returned my own remark twisted neatly around a compliment, rather like a napkin folded over a hot roll that he had buttered for me, and said "Yes," he imagined that most of the briefing had been done in Personnel, when they had chosen me.

Dick Kearney, in the Legal Dept. of the Bureau of European Affairs, friend whom, with his wife Peg I had met in England in '52, picked me up and drove me down to their place in Bethesda for dinner. Nice evening with him and Peg, who appeared the next morning to see me off. NWA is the best airline I have flown—I remind my self that it is the first time I had flown first class. En route to Detroit, over the champagne, seat-companion Joe Maher (pronounced Marr) of the legal dept attached to the Senate. Very pleasant, interested in my "mission," discussed, among other things Norman Mailer—he is an admirer of *The Naked and the Dead*. "Approved" my ideas on various subjects which he extracted neatly—(few people have trouble on this with me, I say, rather pointedly to myself) with the constant statement "Ve-ery good. Very good"—that somehow seemed to be already infinitely American. In a nice way.

As soon as I start a journey to another country I already find myself looking at my compatriots from a certain severe, measuring distance. Champagne floated me to Seattle, steadied by a ceaseless flow of food. Plane out of Seattle was to have had only a 2½ hr. stopover, however was delayed 4 hrs., so I slept in the terminal lounge intermittently, writing letters in my head to the designers of air-terminals (Seattle's is a new and handsome one) asking why they persist in installing doors that must be PULLed instead of pushed by passengers and porters with hands already encumbered (why not the photo-electric doors that every supermarket has?), and why they do not have a room with couches and SHOWERS.

On plane to Tokyo sat with a Miss Vivian Denkhahn, whom I had seen in terminal and already tabbed as an old hand, probably a social worker. (Blue serge suit, sandals, frizzed gray hair, neat and durable all round.) Not far off, I—she turned out to be a regional director for Southeast Asia, of the World Health Organization of the U.N. (headquarters in Geneva) recently working out of New Delhi. Bits of info mostly on shipping—although I tried to get her to talk of her own work—by asking about yaws in S. A., where she may go, etc. In Bangkok said she, I must buy jewelry at Johnny Siam's, silks at Jim Thompson's, an American who came originally to install Amer. methods in their silk industry and stayed to open a store. We floated over the ocean, and sozzled by the omnipresent champagne—I began to feel, and at this writing still do, that if slit neatly down the middle I should appear like one of those Russian doll-puzzle-toys I had as a child—a wooden oval doll inside which is another slightly smaller, inside which is—and so on down to the infinitesimal. Or like one of those *cordon-bleu* recipes out of *Gourmet,* which starts with a large bird, say a duck, inside which is a Cornish hen stuffed with rice at whose heart there is an artichoke which contains a crabapple which contains an olive stuffed with, I was going to say a toucan, my still air-addled head having intended pecan. But perhaps "toucan" is what I meant after all—it feels rather like.

Shemya airport, our only stop, formerly an airbase, is one of the last in the chain of the Aleutians, a 2 mile island that served us tea and more snaks (Aleutian spelling—Alaskan influence?) in the middle-middle of the gray Pacific. It is so small that we seemed to hover dangerously over the waves, scarcely more than a few hundred feet it seemed before we glimpsed its mud and gravel. An hour and a half there, during which most of us wrote letters or cards on forms ac-comodatingly supplied by the airline, which will mail them on free. I sent cards, knowing that I wd never do so from now on, and be-cause not to send mail from an island so situated, when one can, is to slap the face of wonder.

At Tokyo airport, the official tour began. Met by Nancy Downing, very pleasant assistant to the cultural officer—one of those poised, cool American girls with a prettily indented profile, charmingly assured clothes and a perfect, lissom, if slightly unripe figure—all of it with a businesslike femininity about it that seems only slightly related to a sexual quality, and is almost too trim and virginal for it. I had for-gotten how this comes out in our women so much more clearly when they are abroad. (Miss D. is by Decatur, Illinois, out of Wellesley, six years in Japan, her first job with the service.) I suppose it is this quality—the boss-virgin in them, which draws them plenty of beaux—(one thinks of these as beaus, not lovers, although this may often not be the case) but about which European men ultimately complain. I imagine too, that if one took a census of American women working abroad, a larger number of them wd prove to be middlewesterners, in the same way that the majority of our good correspondents come from there. More intrepidity, plus more desire for coastlines and seas. Anyway, the combination of good—quite good, or "solid" midwestern family and an eastern education is unbeatable in this sort of job.

Miss D., with the help of the NWA rep—a Mr. Watsunabe or Matsumoto—some Jap. equiv. of Smith-Brown, got me thru customs with a smooth and very acceptable V.I.P. treatment—the customs officer questioning only the traveling-iron, still packed in its anonymous wrapping from Abercrombie's. I wondered how I should explain the packet which Donald Keene had given me to carry to Mishima, Keene's wedding present to him. Since M. had asked for "a Western antique," and D. had left it for me at the Beekman already packed, while I was out, I cd not have told them what it was if asked, but was not.

Japan, which I had hoped to be already cool, and Donald said might, greeted me with a gray-green humidity, something thick and sweet about it. Used as I am to New York, this was different—and my knitted sheath was no help. As we drove on, the rains came; it is the typhoon season, but I am told should already be cooler than it is. This is my usual luck, especially about heat—I had the familiar sensation of trying not to sweat in my unsuitable clothes. Miss D. gave me my itinerary. Only my plane's being late saved me from appointments that same afternoon with embassy officers (these therefore delayed until Monday); they waste no time.

I therefore had Sat. and Sunday free—Miss D. asked if I wd like to go to Hakone, the national park area around Fuji, or Nikko. Although I might—I thought it wd be too melancholy and wearing to do alone and at first and said so. (What a bad tourist I am—one year's residence in England and a second visit, and I still have never seen the Tower. It wd be entirely in line if I got out of Japan without seeing Fujiyama, which of course was shrouded when we came in on the plane—the steward said he had seen it so only once in 8 yrs.) Miss D. accepted this, questioned me very little in general—to her I was an entity in the business way, quite like the sports personality sent by my program last month—who "spent all his per diem on shopping and was difficult over being denied PX privileges." I humbly indicated that I wd not be. Since I had no Jap. money and she had to be at an embassy reception at 5:30, she recommended that I wait to cash a check in the Imperial. They put "all their visitors" there, she informed me—again I had the sense that I belonged to a category which they were prepared to find unmanageable in some inconvenient way— Faulkner had undoubtedly got drunk, the sportsman had his Achilles heel—what wd be mine? I chatted with a heady air of competence and worldliness—when Miss D. got back to her own she wd be able to say "This one seems O.K."

We drove first up to the Old Building—of the Imperial—regrettably I am quartered in the New Annex, not the old one, (Frank L. Wright design). Rivers of water came out to meet us—at least on this score I have been provident. Boots of light rubber and heavy in my bag, umbrella, raincoat. The Imperial is undoubtedly one of the great hotels of the world. Arranged for foreigners—almost all personnel speak some English—and now of course definitely oriented (in two senses of the word) toward Americans, as it might once have been toward Germans and then English. (Kippers still on the breakfast menu—I had them the next morning.) At the last minute Miss D. invited me to the reception—probably to her horror, and mine, I accepted. It was partly the inability to stop that comes from exhaustion, and partly habit begun on my first trip abroad in London—never, however weary, spend the first night in a foreign country alone in a hotel. Claustrophobia, even xenophobia, might set in. She lent me 200 yen, enough to get me to the Sanno hotel from mine, cautioned me, in answer to my question about dress, to wear nothing too barely cock-tailish, no thin straps—the Japanese don't and Mrs. MacArthur had so decreed.

The room was quite lovely in the J. manner to which our own recent craze for their interiors—the motel in Suffern, the house exhibited at the Museum of Mod. Art, and countless lampshades in the houses of my friends and myself—had already accustomed me all too thoroughly. Once on the bed, released from the air-motion but with it still inside me, I placed my forehead on the sheet and all but conked out—"smiling, the boy fell dead." Exactly so—a poem was never more convenient. Southey? Not what one wd have thought one wd think in Japan. But of course I was not really here as yet—or there. My atoms, streaming behind me, had still to be collected—from Washington, Seattle, from the house in Nyack, Josh's place in New York, Mary's with Curt, the Earle with Curt. Lulled by the motion of the DC7, hedge-hopping up and down through the last clouds of the voyage, and probably seduced by the penultimate glass of champagne, I dreamed of him, of making love. In my dream we did so, then still atom-confused, we met at the airstrip in Tabriz, I fell on his breast and said "I have come a long way to be with you," and scanned his face for traces of Italy where, even in my dream, I knew he was at the moment.

I woke up on the bed, trifled with thoughts of calling Miss D., now dressing at her home whose number I had, and begging off. No. She had suggested a stole if what I had was too bare. Not sure it was—the black Lanz silk jumper without blouse—the white wool stole, though smart, was too impossible for the weather, the long black lace scarf, my grandmother's, properly aristocratic but bad against black. I was too tired to be chic; went off draped in the lace, feeling rather—and looking, what with my black hair and gold earrings, as if I were about to tell fortunes. But I was glad I went—even though I began to feel ill from the standing. I had never before had the symptoms of real lack of sleep (very little in four days)—and I have the writer's greediness to know all such sensations—rather like Colette's insistence that she not be drugged even when dying of arthritis—although my version of it is pale beyond comparison—I shall never be that brave, when the time comes.

Went down a reception line, mouthing appropriately, in a sort of daze. Miss D. no where to be seen at first, but met people rapidly, Nickel of the embassy, an odd bird Joe "Skelly"—(certainly Irish-sounding, but he appears to have a somewhat-garment-district was it? —not quite—accent) turned out to be named Szekely—Hungarian, of the U.S. Information Service at the embassy. Many Japanese. An Army-Navy Club reception. I remembered one such at the A.N. club in London, with Mickey, where to her delight, when I got stuck

SEIZURES OF LOVE AND WORK

with a Haw-haw who had to tell me, or let me know, that his daughter had married a lord, who had insisted on giving her a Bentley ("Dear me, the improvidence of the younger generation"—especially those who marry lords), I had let myself be chatted to for just so long—(it wasn't the upmanship of the gent that bothered me but talk about cars, any cars—from a lifetime of it with H. I cannot bear it—and had then moved off with the airy statement—"Ah, well, you know, I am American, I have only a Cadillac." A 1941, so I cd speak with truth, even if with my own upmanship. I thought of it now because embassy receptions must be the same world-over, though I have been to few. Here the Japanese ladies were bow-crouching, in the curve I knew from woodblocks and prints—graceful as they are, it does not go with the western dress most of them wore. With so many other Americans in the room I did not feel my height, as I had expected to, and may, when, if I am lucky, the company is all Japanese.

I say lucky, because part of traveling-luck is to meet as many of a country's people as possible, as intimately as possible (and this will be hard in the Orient). Also, I know that even embassy Americans, who are trained to "meet the native" in a job way, and are often intelligent and adroit about it there, really continue socially to congregate with their own, (except for the really bright or freakish ones who do not and are rarer) and tend to regard with benevolent indulgence those, like me, who show signs of insisting on the other. "Jobwise" they are proud of knowing "the Japanese," "the British," etc., and "all about them"; they fancy the cosmopolitan touch as well as any, but it is only the rare and really top-in-the-field ones, like Donald, who do not to have to "let-down their hair" in the bosom of their own kind, etc. And already I had met several with the familiar practiced American bonhomie—too experienced of course to back-slap literally, but still the conversation, the manner, has a backslap about it.

Severity is with me again—unsympathetic as I think I basically am toward the craze for things Japanese which is rampant at home—I am already looking at this big, blond jovial gent, that young lady secretary, through almond-eyes. Miss D. chaperones me—two labels will suffice to identify me—I am "an American writer who is going to lecture at the universities," and I have just got off the plane, isn't it wonderful of me to come?

Well, it is rather, I think as I bow, mutter, enunciate clearly, bend double to this fragile male Watsunabe, that trio of gentlemen from the Tokyo press. I, who have never felt faint in my life, feel as if I were going to—and know I am not. Two Japanese I remember particularly—they are standing together; in different ways they have the imprimatur of aristocracy; my libertarian-trained blood no longer disapproves but is grateful—it means manners; it means that they will make the effort to seem as if we are "talking" together; we will each act as if we are at ease even if we are not. They are Professor Kotani, emeritus from Tokyo U., in Amer. History, and Mr. Koizume, former Pres. of Keio, tutor to the Crown Prince, so introduced. I like Kotani particularly—he has a delicate and beautiful face, a faraway voice that speaks a somewhat ghostly, precise English, which I bend to hear more of, not because of his height but because of the cocktail hum. We talk a little of what I have been reading—the books Donald recommended—Tanizaki's *Some Prefer Nettles,* Kawabata's *Snow Country.* He is no more interested in them than an American professor of Japanese history wd be—why should he?—but he nods and (I was going to say that his face lit up)—it did not, but there was a kind of postural wince of pleasure—at the mention of Keene, whom he knows. I should like to know more of the professor, but doubtless shan't.

The tutor is a big man, tall as I almost, heavy. His face is a mass of scars from burns, the runny type of scar with probable plastic surgery. He is more the pompous aristocrat, or perhaps he merely wants me to *know* he is one; with empressement he repeats his identity, his tutorship, wants me to know that he has been several times in America. Asks me if I know Mrs. Vining's book, (Tutor to the Crown Prince, it was, or some such; I saw an installment or so in the LHJ). I meet a prof. from Keio U. (best private U.) where I am to talk next week. I tell him that I do not lecture, only seminar informal discussion (I know that this will be difficult with J. students particularly, since tradition, respect, inhibits them, probably more than other foreign students, many of whom still do it with difficulty). He looks dubious—the seminar, I remember, is a distinctly American habit. I am dubious too, but am determined not to lecture. Determination easy, since I have nothing cooked up.

I meet several Japanese embassy wives, all of whom speak English, a particularly august one, wife of a "big" there, in kimono, has daughter at Wellesley. Miss D. had promised to take me home, but she cannot leave until the personages do—I must go, or drop. I borrow another 200 yen and cab to the Imperial, unfortunately the driver leaves me at the entrance to the Old. By bridge, underpass, corridor, stairs, I reach the New, half in one of those unending subway-train dreams I used to have as a child, wrong stations melting into others equally wrong. I take the wrong elevator, but at last I make it. I am to call Miss D. next day.

Arise on Sat. at what I fondly take to be 5, have my kippers and a huge breakfast when rm service opens at what I think is 7, write in the journal, and at last call Miss D. at what I think is 9. It is 12, noon —my watch, still going, which I set by hers last evening, I know—has had its atoms scattered too. We are to meet for lunch right now, and a Mrs. Betty Larsen, a wd-be writer, works for a paper too, will be with us. I am too tired to evade the beginnings of the embassy-wives deal. We go to lunch to a pleasant restaurant with magnificent gardens which I merely regard and thank for their cool—named *Chinzan So*, Emperor visited in former days, says the little pamphlet, "unfortunately, however, on May 26, 1945, all the buildings were reduced to ashes and the whole garden devastated by fire." There is no need to say by whom, why. But, resumes the pamphlet "restored thru the great efforts of Mr. Eiichi Ogawa, Pres. of the Fujita Kogyo, that extended over 6 yrs after wars end."

The girls gossip intramurally after Mrs. L. interviews me "—ooh weren't you excited when you were first in *The New Yorker*"—and we make some conversation about me—I hate to be a duty to them, know I am, and resent them a little because I am stiff with them and conscious of possessing charms that wd not charm them, that Mrs. L. particularly wd not have the wit to draw from me. Miss D. is brighter, or perhaps only more experienced—she is Embassy, Mrs. L. merely the wife of Amer. Express man here. Both of them wear splendid double ropes of cultured pearls—I resolve to buy, and immediately not to—I know how that will end. They discuss a dress, "Stateside" purchased by Mrs. L. which she will sell to Miss D. (since Mrs. L's husband doesn't like) for $59.95, and the mink jacket which Miss D's sister in Chi., who has a "mink-entree" as Mrs. L. puts it, will buy and send here. "Oooh, Nancy," says Mrs. L., "the man who marries you will get you with everything, mink, pearls."

I ask where to buy pearls, and intimate that what the gals at home are wearing is broadtail. They ignore me—what shd a "professor," which they think me, know of this, and I am wearing a blouse and skirt. And no pearls. Momentarily I regret the jewelry left in the safe-deposit, like a good girl, at home. Especially when Mrs. L. adds "Now, all you need is diamonds." I'm a bad girl, and know it. But what do embassy people get paid here, anyway?

Miss D. shows us a ring, worn for the first time. Given her by a Jap. friend, male. She had refused of course but he had replied "from my chi-chi" (the intimate word a J. uses for father, although a stranger may not do this) and had run off "before she cd do anything about it." We giggle, *en femme-ille*, and admire the lovely mauve lustre of its two pearls. "But I can't get over the lustre," says Miss D. over and over. I call her Nancy, asking permission, God help me.

We go then to Mitzukoshi, dept. store, ostensibly to show me the exhibit of Brides' Kimonos—Oct. is the season, but Mrs. L. manages to hunt for a bathrack, buy a lampshade, and Miss D. prices transistor radios and binoculars. We drive back. Tokyo center is rather dullish at first, as I had expected. I do not know whether I will have the incentive to tour here. My instinct, in art objects, etc., has always been to prefer the Chinese—although, as I well know, the modern Jap. ceramics, pottery—we saw some Hamada which was very good—are beautiful, they are so in somewhat the same way as the Swedish—and we at home have already seen as much of them. Woodblocks, yes I suppose if I were smart I should pick up some —I do not particularly wish to. Miss D. is having a kimono and obi designed by a mod. J. artist. Etc. Etc. I don't know. Already, in the States, I have been somewhat sickened by the ease at which the conquering have invited the conquered to conquer them. But will explore this anon.

Purchased an apple, some J. biscuits, and a lime, in M.'s grocery dept., came home, fell in bed and slept without supper until ten, ordered tea and pastry (a pale green—which was even less sympathetic than a fish, complete with lizardlike head and white eye, that was on the hors d'oeuvres at lunch, soused in cream.) Ate my apple and wrote all this. It is nearly 3 A.M., I am time-boggled. Tomorrow is empty Sunday—had tried to get Mishima on phone but he apparently, like the hard-working writer he is, has none. Will write him. And so to bed, feeling that time, which I have so beat about in my book, has at last beat me.

*Sunday in Japan—9/14/58*

It is already nearly three of the following morning. Sunday began by being one of those vacant Sundays which bring the prospect of terror to those, like me, who connect melancholy with such days even from childhood—listless afternoons even then, worse in adolescence, and in my case worst in those early years of my maturity when I seemed to be accomplishing nothing. As it turned out, it became one of those reverie-days that I may remember better, later on, than others stuffed with activity.

Found that Mishima had a number after all and had the temerity to phone his home at 9:30, probably very rude, but I leave Jap. Tues. and his present is on my mind. Was of course told that he was "sleeping"—"until three." He called me then—I am to phone him tonight at a restaurant where there is some sort of party, 6 to 9—the Hyo-Tei. Although he speaks excellent English, it was somewhat difficult to understand over the phone, and cd not be sure that he was not inviting me—but I thought not, so said I wd call him there and perhaps see him after dinner. Asked about Kawabata (am read-

ing his *Snow Country*). I know he lives in Kamakura. M. said he
was "suffering from stomach trouble," and had gone away to "avoid"
either it—or perhaps callers like me. I am of course too new here
to know when I am being too pressing, or when an excuse is real.
I told M. I was a writer, at which he seemed relieved. Think it will
clear up when we meet—they must often be plagued with visiting
Americans—publishers, editors, or worse.

The lobby here is well supplied with our unique brand of "worse,"
the gray-haired Amer. matron, usually in twos or, if with a husband,
those of the bony, hard-skulled type strong enough not yet to have
left these wives widows. Almost universally these ladies have middle-
western voices—the voice of the Chicago grackle is heard everywhere outside their land. But I could not quarrel with the lobby, where
I sat alternately reading Mishima's *No* Plays and fascinated by the
motley—a Japanese family, man in business suit, woman in kimono,
younger generation (college) two young men and a girl, very deferential of course to the elders, the girl bowing deeply even in her
"sack" dress out of the latest Amer. movie. A group of Jewish
businessmen who, from their conversation live in the Orient, yet
spoke with a Brooklyn accent as powerful as Steve Greene's. A
worried man, Malay-Eurasian, who waited for a half hour looking
desperate; then was met by an Amer. couple. A girl from, I think,
Manila, met by two swains similar, flirting all get-out. The hotel
itself is staffed with hordes of pretty Japanese girls. How pretty
they are, here and on the streets, but even though one of course
begins to distinguish physical types, and they do not "all look
alike" as in the ancient joke, they do, I think resemble one another,
fall into types, even more than other Orientals, such as the Chinese,
for instance. I suspect that if the J. are an "imitative" race, then it is
even true that their imitation begins here, in the physical. The
beautiful J. woman looks like an archetype of such. I might think
that this is merely my Western eye, did I not already know that
Chinese do not seem so to me.

Later I went out for several walks; dallied with idea of going to the *Kabuki* Theater which is around the corner from the hotel—the Takarazuka, but decided to wait until the embassy interpreter cd go with me, as planned. Another troupe, possibly better, is playing elsewhere. The *No* plays do not run as regularly.

The streets were crowded with a Sunday-morning-on-B'way-crowd, rather like parts of London too, on that day. Japanese schoolgirls seeing the latest foreign movie—in this case a German one—*The Best Day of My Life*. Walked thru the hotel shopping arcade—Uyeda, the pearl dealer, apparently august enough to close on Sundays, but other shops open, all of them with that same world-wide specious air of the souvenir shop. From Atlantic City to Bucks County antique dealer, lacquerware to bad jade Kwan-Yins, the tone is the same.

In Mitsimoto's one of our ladies was buying pearls, or rather telling the bland dealer the history of what she owned. "No nothing like that," I heard her say, rejecting a pearl ring—they are usually of fairly unobtrusive design. "I want a pre*ten*tious one, a conver*sa*tion piece!" Bad as she, I wandered outside to one of the open-stall drug stores, and in an access of nostalgia—and providence—bought a pot of Ponds.

Mostly I yearned for C., with whom such a perambulatory day would have so much meaning—some of our happiest times have been when we have been doing nothing but such, idly walking, observing, in Iowa, Chicago, New York, anywhere. That kind of exchange, basic sympathy, has become a need now; as I warned myself early when we first met, I have somewhat lost the power to be romantically alone in a strange place. Reminded myself that it should not be for long—we will be together in a foreign place—and that, after an early breakfast, I was probably in need of food. Lunched in the hotel on smoked salmon, buttered bread, and the coffee that is better here than in almost any hotel in N.Y. and went out again, this time intending to walk past Hibaya Park to the Meiji shrine. But I always forget that maps are upside down or I am—must have walked opposite, ended up at the Nippon theater. It did not matter, walking is the only way to see a foreign city. One sees the people and buildings not at their apex—the monument—but in their off-moments.

Ended up quite happily in the Sukiyabashi shopping arcade—very like ours at home, modern, air-conditioned, shops open-fronted the only difference. Had a coffee-float in a tea-shop. Saw, with mine own eyes, in a Rexall drug store (Jap. Rexall) there, among the piles of Vicks Vapo-rub (very popular here apparently), Jap. drugs, and their brand of nail polish (Kiss Me)—the square red box of the "Once More" Famous Condom (quote marks not mine), which, in addition, bears a second legend beneath, quotes also not mine—"Where Particular People Congregate." I guess this made the day, spirits lifted.

Outside, in the un-air-conditioned street, tried to pin down the unique Jap. street-smell. It is not as bad as Henry Adams recorded it—he was here at the height of summer—but it is strange to Western nostrils, used to bad stinks but their own. It is a sweetish sour blend of soy, fish and fry, a vegetable steam not quite decay, not only perfume. It reminds me that I shall get tired of Oriental cuisine; sweet-sour-and-hot gets to be a bore to teeth uncompromisingly taught to chew. The cheap restaurants display simulacrums of their wares in glass cases outside—the way Woolworths sometimes still does at home—here sundae-frappes piled huge with cotton batting, gamboge cutlets, salads with fretted radishes, and a dozen other convincing minces. There is something dreadful about imitations of food, much more so when it is done so well, as it is here, and is an assumed part of life.

And so home, where I fell heavily into bed at five—partly time-trouble, and partly a case of traveler's trots. Woke at one—to what time am I really waking—to N.Y.C., or to Italy-Tehran where Curt must have arrived? This journal will eviscerate letters, I cannot do it twice—shall be reduced to telling him how I miss him, recording itineraries etc. And must not write this at such length. What, still no Monuments! I shall blame it on the Japanese—if I put down so much trivia it is partly because of being in a country which has

made such a delicate art of arranging trivia to look *significant*—
and perhaps of the reverse.

## Tuesday, 16 Sept. '58

Well, the week began with a vengeance yesterday—no more
vacuum—I expect I shall pine for latter shortly. Embassy car picked
me up at 9:15, spent an hour or so with Mr. Boylan, head of the
Exchange Service in Japan who showed me their publications, explained their aims, delicately tried to help me understand that things
might be difficult since the J.'s did not know who I was and prefer
the "top" in everything—no symphony orchestra will do here, except
the Boston; they have accepted the advent of the Cardinals (instead
of the Yankees) as a second-rate team—Martha G.'s dance team no
reception, etc., etc. This I know. Then saw Frank Tenney, the regional field supervisor of the USIS. Said I wanted to meet some one
who cd tell me what was taught in colleges, wanted to meet with
P.E.N. Club, in other words I *wanted*. Things started rolling.
(Lunched in snack-bar, met a man who has a record agency here
and have folder, plan to get some samisen and Kabuki records when
get to Iran. N.B.) Then at last met X, an interesting man, good
friend of Mishima, and of all things of Ben Santos. I spose specially
interesting because he knows my work—is himself a critic. Extremely
helpful—Later sent a note he wished to introduce me to Hiroo Mukai,
who had studied with Stegner. Noted critic. Works with International
House. (Has written few articles for *Pacific Spectator*, translated J.
short stories. Knows Angus.) (N.B., Later found out Miss D. loathes
X. Homosexual, with wife and child, says she.)

Rushed home to meet with Prof. Ichiro Nichizaki of Waseda and
Ochanomisu U.'s. Typical prof—armed with catalogues, literature
lists, etc., but exactly what I wanted. Presented me with a Jap. book,
one of the 20 vol. set on Amer Lit which Leo Picon of the Embassy
is editing (spent time with latter in morning—doing fine job)—in
which N. had a trans. Asked him to sign it of course—now how can
I throw away! Also presented me with a vol. of letters of Faulkner

he had exhumed from the *Times-Picayune* and edited. Later took me to the bookshop street, woodblock, print store—loved this—as he said, the Charing Cross of Tokyo. How nice to be doing this so soon! Nichizaki taught last year at U.C.L.A. *Send book.*

Then home, feeling ill again—the trots—fell dead on bed, but had to call Mishima, who thru X I had found was at the Hyo Tei restaurant to judge a litry contest of the *Chuō Koron,* the *Partisan Review* of Japan. He asked to bring a friend—arrived earlier than planned, took them to the Skoal bar downstairs. Friend was Tsutomu Shimamura, ed. of the *Chuō Koron* (looks all of twenty-five at most.) They charmed me, and, I think, I them. We laughed and had a great time. Shimamura has trans. Capote—their veiled laughter about Truman was funny—Mishima has met Mailer, was on extended tour of U.S., Europe and Mexico last year. Brilliant I'm told, highest scholar ever at the Peers school—his *No* plays may be produced on B'way. I liked them both extremely. They both wanted to help me in every way, say Kawabata does not speak Eng., but Ooka does, and some of the others French—I am to get in touch with them when return on the 22nd. They are pleased of course, at how much I am impressed with the new J. writers—well I can say that with honesty.

And so to bed, after packing, vǎshing etc. Tomorrow, lunch and meeting with Lit. (Amer.) Society of Waseda U. (private U.), then off to Kyoto in the evening—overnight by JNR (Japanese Nat'l Railroad).

Travel plans would prevent our meeting again in Japan, though I would briefly meet Mishima once more in the States at the time the *Nō* plays were produced. Later, after his death, I would write in a review for *The New York Times:*

In Tokyo I spent an unofficial evening with Yukio Mishima, who came to my hotel with Tsutomu Shimamura of *Chuō Koron,* a leading intellectual review. We got on; the memory must affect what I write here. But that alone does not entitle me to brood on his life and works. His death however was a public act and the work a public offering; the world is invited, commanded to brood. The way we live now, our deaths are seldom even personal acts, much less publicly declarative ones, nor are they much expected to have a direct consonance with our lives. To be otherwise, death must be constantly present in a life—a familiar. As for acts, writers of any power crave them, always under the anxiety that writing may not be one—or one which can have temporal and above all immediate influence. Some take to religion as an act of faith or community, some to politics; some canonize their lives through excess, of illness perhaps, or of sex, alcohol, drugs. And some, letting their lives simmer or sputter, put all the balance on the work.

Mishima's ritual death, as the culmination of years of training for such an act, side by side with a body of work increasingly invested with the idea of death as the everpresent blood-beneath-the-skin and the possible grail of action, asks us to put his life on the level of his art, and *past* it. What does it mean when a writer wants to transcend words? And knows to the end that we must and will re-examine his? Mishima's death *and* words put these matters once again in their vital juxtaposition. Even if one ascribes his suicide to a certain madness, either by occidental terms or modern Japanese ones—as I do not— there are few writers at the moment of whom one can say the same. Re-reading all the novels and plays available in English, plus the "confidential criticism" as he called it, of *Sun and Steel,* an extraordinary essay of the most compelling clarity published early in 1970, the year of his death, and *Spring Snow,* the first volume to be translated of the tetralogy *The Sea of Fertility,* whose final words were written on the day of it—one conclusion, of which he was aware as any of us, rises preeminent. Visualize that extravagantly formal, mutedly blood-slippery act, as one will, as most of the world has, even aided by a few pre-lim shots on television. Scrutinize that last day of his, plotted for a hero. Place his suicide in the Western context or the Japanese one— or in both, where I think it most significantly belongs. Trace his progression toward it, hear in every book its pure, fell sound. True, only his last act has given us this after-event wisdom. But has he succeeded in that final coincidence of flesh and mind he hoped for, of dual chariots whose crash was to be the final bloom of existence? For himself, perhaps an assumption into the tragic life, for us an echo. Perhaps he attained the non-reflection he wanted. He leaves us with his lifetime of reflection. The words—to the end his avowed snare, yet as much his weapon as the duelling staves he used in *kendo*—are what remain most clear.

The world usually puts an artist's work ahead of however pertinent a life. Equating them, one enters the realm of saint and hero, and finally—myth. This too must have been part of his intent—can a spectacle-death ever be without it? The Japanese are now republishing everything Mishima ever wrote, including even photo-captions, a well as a separate edition of those novels he wrote as potboilers. Internationally, his facts at the moment overshadow him. Assessment of his full work must wait for translation; English has merely a small part of 228 works, which include the 20 long novels he considered "literary," 13 articles, 143 short stories, 21 full-length dramas and 31 one-act plays.

The work we do have—for the most part grave, somberly exciting, formidable with self-analysis, able to canvas the crowd and the ages, but more often with fixed, internal stare of the diarist—is in some ways peculiarly fit for Western eyes. The violence we so mouth over, but would relegate to the atom-ashheaps of the military, and are facing with such difficulty, hypocrisy or extravagance in our daily life and art, he gives us simply, domestically, in all its subcutaneous horror and myth. Like the Greeks, he pours the blood that is there. And taking into account the samurai gestures surrounding his end, and so at variance with the exquisite sanity of his self-explanation, I have come to believe that, as often with us, his was a cross-cultural death.

I came to Japan knowing only the cliches, mistrusting these only for being that, and having read a few modern novels that Donald Keene, my mentor for years to come in all this, had hastily listed as available: Tanizaki, Kawabata, Ooka. The gap between a writer's place in his own country and abroad is often between fame on the one side, near oblivion on the other, and foreign publication is often non-consecutive; at the time, Mishima had published here only *The*

*Sound of Waves*, his early prize novel, and his *Five Modern Nō Plays*. The first, a tale of island lovers, told in the "legendary" manner that an educated and probably urban young man might adopt, had an authoritative finish—Mishima had struck the absolute tone of such people and such telling, hewn but not rude, a bas-relief that moved lyrically in nature without introspection. What was most impressive was the natural description, detailed, exact, even studied, the emotional motive behind it somehow more than beauty as the West would have it, and less than pantheism, as if the Japanese psyche had some formal relationship to the natural scene, whose conventions the writer could play upon and enlarge. The Nō Plays, returning to a classical mode as we perhaps might go back to all those early seventeenth century marvels that were *not* Shakespeare—to Dekker, Webster, Fletcher, and Massinger, those mordant players of funeral lays and darker madrigals—did seem to show just such a dark modernity cloaking itself in past models. This was all our literary world knew of his work.

Actually at that time, in 1958, Mishima, a prodigy at nineteen and then thirty-three, had behind him twelve novels as well as many other works. Of these *The Temple of the Golden Pavilion* (surely one of his best and among those we have, along with *Confessions of a Mask*, closest related to the progress of his own philosophy as set forth in *Sun and Steel*) would be published here, to praise, the next year. *Forbidden Colors*, written in his twenties and remarkable on any score, wouldn't get here for another ten years, in what is plainly an inept translation, and touted as "an invitation to the world of homosexuality." I would find its subjects and worlds complex, dealt with by an appetite and expertise consciously on its way to the Olympian, and spanning from the bisexual hero's friendship with a famous writer (very possibly a partial portrait of Kawabata) to an account of the young man's presence while his wife gives birth, in a childbed scene comparable to none I know. Yuichi may be in part or at first that beautiful youth beloved of homosexual male writers, who in Mishima's own division is the "seer" rather than the "seeing," but the novel's sexual worlds are several. Old and young, married or

inverted, innocent or "decadent," the people revolve in their other
social statuses as well, with an easy, Trollopian illumination from
behind; Mishima, even this early, is never limited enough to treat
of sex alone. This novel would have a poor reception here.

We had met once before Tokyo—in New York at a Gotham Book
Mart party for James Baldwin, where Mishima had looked as anyone
does under such circumstances: tentative, interestedly afloat on a
sea of foreign contexts whose base-game is second nature to him. This
second time, I had brought Keene's wedding-present to him, and
introduction. To this I could add only my awareness that a writer's
presence is always less subtle than the actuality. We did not really
talk of literature. He was a handsome man I thought, with a coherence
of face and form; though I felt very tall in Japan and he was shorter,
he did not appear small. Though Japanese faces had already lost
their "masks" for me and begun dissolving into types, I couldn't
tell whether his face was as guarded a one to other Japanese as it
seemed to me; some triangular proportion in it, broadbased at the
brows, made one look at eyes and mouth separately. Hindsight sees
how such a face might empathize alternately, as his work would, with
both the ugly and the beautiful. We laughed a lot that evening, and
most of it was laughter over intramural jokes, not embarrassment or
an occidental misinterpretation—reading the glinting humor of *After
the Banquet* five years later, I remember this. When he and his friend
kept saying how Oriental I looked, I told them how my daughter's
boarding school had surreptitiously asked her was I Eurasian; we sat
bright-eyed, sympathetically comfortable, language-hampered. The
one remark I never forgot he made with utter seriousness. He told
me was building "a Dutch Colonial house." It had its pertinence.

Very shortly, as my journal shows, I was to be sick with what the
world glibly calls cultural shock. Though this was the first time I
had been enclosed within a language not cognate to mine, that was
minor. As the weeks passed, always in meeting many people very
fast, as the state-sponsored visitor does, I kept thinking that it was
really our souls, American and Japanese, which were not cognate. An
ancient sailor-joke I had picked up somewhere—that in Oriental women

the slit ran the other way—kept returning to me. If there were a canal—I visualized it—throat-to-groin of any human, carrying not that being's alimentation, respiration, or circulation but the psychic equivalent by which that same being persevered, then here was a country of beings in whom such a path ran some other way. A Japanese professor to whom I put the question of why I felt this difference—in my travels from Tokyo to Fukuoka I was always putting it—answered: "It's because we lack your *Christian* sense of sin." But though this helped, in revealing what he knew about us, both of us, smiling at each other in our excellently cognate English knew that there was more—the whole, massive anthropological past, more imperial even than empires, which yet could localize itself in two people at a table, whose closest rapport lay in that both were aware of it. I have spoken much in my journal of the smells; perhaps because my family's business had been perfume, that sense was developed in me, and its imagery very accessible. I kept analysing a smell of the country, to me as clear as the unique odor of a person, into what its components might be: food, hair-oil and the specific soap, open drains? All the time I knew what it was, but hadn't the wit to say. I was smelling the sweat of the dragon-fight, that odor of burnt ideologies, smoked-out shrines, commingled loins and potsherds, which down the ages must hang invisibly over those silent, inner battlegrounds wherever two civilizations are trying to engorge one another. I was seeing how a nation under occupation was dealing with its "conqueror," and how we dealt with them.

What are artists for, if not to embody this? There had always been those of whom it would afterwards be said that they were born for it. Or are spewed up by these life transferences? To have more than national ideas swaying their heads, yet these doomedly vying there.

Mishima, born in 1925, educated at the Peers School where the Spartan fires of militarism still burned, graduating as its highest honor student mid-war, spent half his youth under the clangor of historical glory, and all his manhood with the American conqueror standing sentinel at every streetcorner of Japan's culture. Grounded deeply in his own literature, he was widely read in Western, classical and modern, and evidently far beyond that French influence, so marked in writers like Kawabata and Dazai, which was now waning, though it would linger in him in his debt to their diarists, from Amiel to Gide and the early Sartre. Eventually he would range and adapt at will, from the Greeks to De Sade, while all the while his novels and stories swell with the most intimately proud mapping of his own country's topography, the people in it, on farm or shore, in town or temple, forever referentially hemmed in by whatever hills face where, and what weathers come from them. Behind all, always localized like another hill, is their ancestry.

We tend even now to forget, under the stereotypes we have managed to maintain ever since Commodore Perry's expedition (and even under a war, seventy-five years on, that has all but completed his task) how Westernization of Japanese spirit and object has been going on since the roughly coincidental Meiji restoration of 1867. In the continuous dialogue between the two young male classmates of *Spring Snow*, Honda, whose father is a Supreme Court justice trained to respect German logic, and who is a law student (like Mishima himself, who graduated from the School of Jurisprudence) says at various times, of history and of Kiyoaki: "To live in the midst of an era is to be oblivious of its style ... The testimony of your contemporaries has no value whatsoever ... You detest that bunch on the *kendo* team, don't you?" ... In the midst of turmoil, each man builds his own little shelter of self-awareness. ... You have one characteristic that sets you quite apart; you have no trace whatsoever of willpower. And so I am always fascinated to think of you in relation to History."

Mishima's first account in *Sun and Steel* is of a child, himself, who, as it were the opposite of one of Bettelheim's autistics, refused to perceive the body, and was let into reality through words. In time "words" however useful and powerful a fetish, become the corrosive evil, and "ideas" foreign to that romantic ideality of the body which he craves. In his attempt to straddle and manipulate the two he becomes the novelist, but only increasing further his "thirst for reality and the flesh." In this small book, most certainly a classic of self-revelation, his pursuit of that "second language" is examined with such dispassion and self-insight that paraphrase must only distort; we are in the range now of a metaphysics where every sentence counts, and delivers its poignant message with a kinesthetic shock. "As a personal history it will, I suspect, be unlike anything seen before," he says, and he is right. In his journey from the black Styx of the inner life to the blue sky of the outer as reflected in ordinary men's eyes, he sees at every point the parable of his own life. He is taking us down that psychic canal, in very nearly complete consciousness.

Having experienced all the glorification that the verbal arts can give, he seeks "the essential pathos of the doer" and "the trimph of the non-specific," learning that for him "the tragic pathos is born when a perfectly average sensibility momentarily takes unto itself a privileged nobility . . ."? and "endowed with a given physical strength, encounters that . . . privileged moment especially designed for it." Imagination is now arrogance; he is intent on pursuing the words through the body, whose muscles will elucidate the mystery. "To combine action and art is to combine the flower that wilts and the flower that lasts forever . . . the dual approach cuts one off from all salvation by dreams." He is led to explore the lapsed concept of consciousness as passive. He will seek to replace imagination by duty; since that word has so faded in Western form, I take it in the more Japanese sense of "obligation." Concluding that what dignifies the body is its own mortality, he seeks the *sought* death that will give the most solemn proof of life. And finds that "the profoundest depths of the imagination lay in death. . . . I could not help feeling that if there were some incident in which violent death pangs and well-developed muscles were skillfully combined, it could only occur in response to the aesthetic demands of destiny. Not that destiny often lends an ear to aesthetic considerations." That is everywhere the tone —of an ego stretching beyond itself, to an appreciation of what the ego is. And giving us, in that so human extra, the one thing that Mishima himself may not see.

It happens, I think, at some juncture in his own painfully exact report of the romantic attraction a beautiful, doomed death comes to have for him. At some false jointure of the samurai gesture with a misconceived ideal of Christian martyrdom—"I yearned for the twilight of Novalis"—the analysis begins to serve the yearning. Up to then, he has pursued his own awareness, as he says, as one pursues erotic knowledge—both in *Sun and Steel* and elsewhere. Set a group of graduate students to count the blood-images which beset every book, to clock where the blood begins—is its psychological source in that dream in *Confessions of a Mask* where the narrator eats the entrails of the boy who is a belly suicide? Does the blood-bath culminate in "Patriotism," in the mad formality of the marital double seppuku? "There in my murder theater" they will find Mishima before them. No doubt a legion of psychiatrists with whips (for each other) can attribute it all: the black-mass sadism of *Madame de Sade* (madame!), the sexual-sensual transliteration which make a mortally ill man die "groaning like a bride," the lack which makes woman a *bas relief* or a ritual—to the arrestment of a homosexual personality. Such simplification won't do. In *Confessions of a Mask* Mishima has already said: "The thought that I might reach adulthood filled me with foreboding" —and much more. Just as in *Sun and Steel,* he is mortally aware of what "the destruction of classical perfection" must in practice mean to him.

Often, even if we refuse the psychiatric labels, we will attach the sociological or literary ones; we tend to think of writers outside the western framework, if not as "simples" or "originals" then as the primitive genii of other anthropologies or thought-systems which attract us for their qualitative difference—as Buddhism does the solid Madison Avenue matron or the floating intellectual—rather than for their intelligence. In dealing with *Sun and Steel,* as with all Mishima's work, one is encountering a mind of the utmost subtlety, broadly educated, in whose novels for instance, the range may even appear terrifying or cynical, to those who demand of a writer steadily apparent, or even monolithically built views. These are there, indeed touchable at every point in his work, but the variation of surface, and seeming reversals of heart or statement, sometimes obscure this.

And the Western split may have done it, in his work as in his life. So that, as he foresaw, his death better explains both. Leaving us to review the explanation.

Mishima's Western scholarship is very touching, all the more for the possibility that as he rejected words for body, dead literature for live action, or tried to bring the two down to the "average" co-herence, he was also denying the Western impurities that had early ensnared him. For everywhere, his references to *our* literature, *our* martyrs, are hallowed, reverent to what he borrows or admires, and sometimes as oldfashioned as our own youth. (When since, have I heard mention of Amiel or seen a modern writer lean on him?) He takes our classics as seriously as we did once, as a matter for life and death. And death he does illuminate and widen for us, but—in a paradox he might well have anticipated—only when he takes his own unique path of experience and learning, not ours. For though he makes analogues with the martyrs of a Christianized West, in the end, the once-proud grail of Western existence, addled and dusty as this has come to be, eludes him. What does not occur to him is that the sought death may be as artificial as imagination, against the sought *life*.

Still, he is telling us that death is one of life's satisfactions. We may not be able to believe it, or may wish that death had not so enhanced itself for him. But he tells us how he came to this pass, with a sanity that ought to be exquisite enough for our own. And crosses cul-tures to do it, to tell us how a man bent on *seppuku* might come to it by way of St. Sebastian.

Can Westerners understand such a death as easily as they under-stand dying like a pricked gray flab in a hospital? Or accept the artist who tosses his life in the balance, as easily as they do those who jerk to the very end of the galvanizing money-string, or distil their life-knowledge only in teaspoonsful of ipecac for the applause of a liverish coterie? Mishima is explaining his life and death in admirable style, in words that hold their breath, so that the meaning may breathe. In a low voice just short of the humble. On the highest terms of that arrogance which decrees him the right to. Our souls may not be cognate, but he makes us feel again what it is to have one. And understand the persuasion of his. If he had been otherwise in his youth—a porter, a woman, a dancer—the tower of his symbols might have built another way. But to ask him to break out of the mystic cage of his logic is like asking it of Thomas a Kempis or Augustine, or to be a Catholic praying for the conversion of the Jews. What he is telling us is that he is *a priori* this kind of man, and that insofar as we cannot break out of the cage of our bones, so are we. Here is not a man with an opinion; he is telling us how he was made. To paraphrase him in words not his, or with muscles not his, is to try to build a china pagoda with a peck of nails. *Sun and Steel*'s power is that it is a book one must experience step by step, led as if by a monk, or by a great film-master, from inner tissue to outer and back again, along his way. It is not necessary to accept that way. But only the frivolous will not empathize with what is going on here; this is a being for whom life—and death too—must be exigent. And were.

### Thursday Morning—in the Kaneiwaro Dekkan, Kyoto

A J. hotel which I can recommend to anybody as charming, clean, exactly as in the best movies with Marlon Brando—and that I wish I were out of. The JNR—little did I know—but I am ahead of my story, though scarcely strong enough to pen it.

Waseda, on Tuesday, was a success. Beautiful private U., rather like Stanford in status I should say, founded by Baron Okuma some 60 yrs ago. Rolling, usual garden which we looked at through fine rain. Professor Tatsunoguchi, fat version of yesterday's professor (as to ego—much fatter) translator of Twain, etc., etc. Also had interpreter. They were very dubious about the question-and-answer or seminar method—I finally suggested we ask the students to write their q's thus evading the horrid necessity of their standing up. This we did—the interpreter rapidly translating both my prefatory remarks, and later, the interchange. As a matter of fact I was a howling success.

I began by referring complimentarily to the J. writers I had been reading—this, the compliment, one must do here, even more than the usual politeness, and even if one believes it! Told them I did not lecture, that I was interested in the past—as all writers are, but not as a scholar—this is the line that divides the writer and the scholar. Paid a passing compliment to scholars, of course. But the writer's time was now—he cd not wait for the respectability of being dead. And since the students' time was also "now," I hoped we cd talk together. We wd do this as it was done in America—explained process etc. They did ask all sorts of questions—"Why can I get no knowledge of Am. local customs and dress from reading Faulkner" — explained that it was an imaginative world—that they wd not find their favorite Faulkner and Erskine Caldwell a trustworthy guide to a tour of the average street, even in the South. They asked what we thought of new Rus. lit.—I explained that we didn't know much of it, told Pat's synopsis of their state-approved novels, "Boy meets Girl, B. meets tractor, B. gets tractor." Interpreter asked, puzzled what was a tractor—when I spread my arms and said—"a great big farm machine"—they rocked. A good many serious questions which I answered so. Found myself declaiming, in answer to q.: "What do you feel is the function of place, if there is a place, for literature in today's scientific world?" Answer—"To reinterpret humanity to science." This, I was told later, went over big—one forgets that Hiroshima is always in their minds. And so on—anyway I was glad to have "vindicated" the Amer. method to some extent.

Then that evening, off for Kyoto by rail—pure hell, though funny. Found out later, had 2nd-class tickets—1st class almost imposs. to get. Had a lower in a 4 berth watchamacallit. Airless, the sheets perfumed. Three Jap. gents in other berths. Kimono and slippers come with each berth—I lay rigid, telling myself *not* to be Western. Compromised by stripping to underwear, which meant I had to close curtains. My downfall therefore on my own head. Fan going above, but even with curtains ajar in the dark—awful. No chance of going to john as a persistent stream of gents all night, and one who was apparently perishing of tuberculosis or senile bronchitis, spent the night there. In morning, the gentlemen stand about reflectively in underwear, in aisles and berths, anywhere, leisurely tying their ties,

donning their trous. I saw no women—all at home apparently, where
I should have been.

Met by John Reinhardt of the Cultural Center, extremely nice as
is his wife—just out of Manila post. Says Mrs. Nakpil is brilliant,
shd meet. Doesn't think much of B. Santos's writing. Says all those
boys have a knack for getting Rockefeller grants, grants of all kinds.
Mrs. N. and Nick Joaquin prob. the best writers, not N. V. M.
Gonzalez. Had a Western shower and breakfast, then off to this
hotel, where they understood my statement that I wished to nap,
not eat, for a "Bath"—so I had it. Terrible solecism, soaped in it, not
yet knowing. No one saw—but they will know. Discovered that the
dreadful sickly-sweet smell, which I had shed at once in Reinhardt's,
by taking off everything but my convenient sack dress, had returned
*after* the shower. Of course, it *is* the soap, all the cleaning stuff—
and inescapable. I wish I had not such a sharp nose. (N.B.—Can an
action, like soaping, be a solecism—no, but I am too humidity bloated
to find words. Hands, eyes, etc., are puffed. Oh me—and Manila and
Bangkok are to be worse??)

Had tempura lunch, attended by giggling wife of hotel-owner.
Wiggled chopsticks, drank the sauce the tempura should have been
dawdled in, giggled and pantomimed too, and managed by placing
my hand horizontally at the top of my gullet to say I had had enough
just at the crucial moment when the course next in line was revealed
to be apparently a section of flying fish with the wing still bravely
aloft. Pity of it is that if were not feeling effects of heat cd have
done well—have feeling cd perfectly well eat that fish if it were a
cold crisp day, the air nothing but Air.

Then off to sightsee with Hamada, R's assistant—told me he had
been "nowhere except Siberia as a R. prisoner." (When, in compli-
menting him on his Eng., I asked if he had been to States.) Saw a
few shrines—like pictures of them, that is all I can say. Nijo Castle
is however beautiful. Has the "Nightingale floor"—built to give off
squeaks, so the shogun might hear anyone coming to murder him—
many enormous empty rooms matted as usual, but with sliding panels
of lions and tigers (imaginary since Japan has none), beautiful float-

ing panels of trees, painted by court painters. "Paintings on gold-foil screens are attributed to Kano Tanyu and his school. Brass plates in oblong and other fancy shapes on cross-bars and upper parts of pillars etc. have hammered work on intricate tracery, decorative but also serve as cover for nails and jointures beneath." Was particularly interested in side panels in corridors, some where ceiling joined side wall, others on south wall. Beautiful abstracts—waves, nebula-flocked squares, large and small, in gold and white, waves indicated by white. Might be in the Modern museum, and wd outshine much of the current Whitney. Then to dinner with the R.'s, wonderful Kobe beef. (Cows are massaged daily, and fed beer.) This morning go to "Detached Palace," and Osaka for lecture. I wonder if I can take it??

*Friday—Sept. 19, 1958—Kaneiwaro Dekkan, Kyoto*

Well, I lasted and handsomely, thanks to the weather, which took an enormous turn to the cool—result of a typhoon which flooded parts of Tokyo, but not here. Today is hot again, but at least I can now remember there is another world outside the billowy cotton one in which I float in humid weather. Realize too, how ill I had been feeling. Went off bright and early with a Miss Suzuki assigned me, and wandered thru the Katsura Palace, formerly the seat of the shogun, or of the Takagawas (sp)—they all are one or the other, or the same. As is J. architecture—if one makes a virtue of space, rice-paper panels and some painting, how can it be otherwise? Very lovely frame for the outdoors—which it is meant to be—I liked specially the principal room for moon-viewing, where the frame between the panels encloses the outdoor picture meant to be seen. The gardens, all shrubs of course and no flowers, wander with intent from one summer-house to the other, different names, different seasons for each house. At one point there was an artificial seaside-shore of smooth black stones—the feudal court could "go to the sea-shore" or picnic in the country, or have tea at a spot of another character, all as if it were traveling, actually within the bounds of the palace gardens. *Is* this not the fantasy of a nation crowded on a small island and making the best of it? This suggested by Miss S.'s remark that she wd like to go to America, J. being so crowded. (So many want to—girl in Imperial who handles theater ticket desk, asked wistfully if I was a professor, and spoke of *her* wish, etc.) In our wanderings we followed a J. group of sightseers, as always very respectful, attentive to what is being seen. Apparently one cd *not* go unaccompanied—nor did they expect it, or wander an inch from the prescribed path, although I should have liked to, in fact to have spent a day by one of the lily ponds or squatting on my haunches in the moon-room—but alone.

Thence to Osaka, the Milan of Japan, by fast suburban train, Mr. Hamada, escorting me to station. Many formal good-bye's—some talk on the status of J. women. His wife is a designer—school of dressmaking. He says they are "modern" and she exercises judgment in the house. He has bought a Western-style home vacated by Army, but has added one J. room.

Osaka ACC was a surprise in comp. to Kyoto, which is small, with ragged, somewhat untidy look of the Civic Center, whatever was it called, that I visited in one of the British New Towns—Harlow. Osaka's in a modern office building, and the offices themselves very extensive, a film room, etc., might be any place on Madison Ave. Met by Mr. Osada, graduate of U. of Washington as is his colleague Mr. Kitamura—a former newspaperman, as he quickly informed me. They are so quick to give themselves status. He did have rather a more informal manner than any Japanese I had yet met. Was unable to get more than a faint smile from Osada at any time, although I imagined here and there that he "appreciated" a sally or so. He said the English-Speaking Society to which I was to talk, was too well grounded in English for me to need an interpreter—seemed to be a matter of pride, so I let it be. (At the moment I am typing this the maid has come in to serve luncheon—now there are 4 of them—apparently they have never seen a typewriter close up—I am typing this in the center of a nosegay of kimonos.)

*Saturday, Sept. 20th, '58—Grand Hotel, Kobe*

My yesterday's talk to the Osaka Society had seemed to have gone quite well—they did know English better, many of them. Asked questions. Always one is asked about Poe. One lady asked about the change in Hemingway from early bks to *Old Man of Sea* (change in philosophy) when I told her I thought his ethic had always been the same—man's virility against nature, etc., etc., she seemed puzzled—not by what I said, but that I should not universally admire and be in accord with reputation. If a writer, or anybody, has attained prestige, one accepts that and does not judge. Then a young man asked a long socio-political question in two parts—the 1st purporting that writers cd not write what they thought politically in America—was it not so?—2nd—wasn't that the reason Henry Miller was persecuted in America? Said "I am happy to tell you that is not so." A laugh when I said Miller's trouble was due "to pornography." Yng man said "I mean Henry Miller who has married Marilyn Monroe." But all seemed well at time, ending amicably. Reporter from Mainichi came up, asked me apologetically what he called either an impohtent, an impehtinent, or an impuhdent question—which I hope I answered clearly.

Later Osada and a Dr. Suzuki (medical doctor who—status again—was quick to tell me that she had just attended some big International Christian Med. Conference) took me to dinner at a tempura restaurant. This very diff from temp. I had had in hotel. Beautifully styled little place, every detail in order, in a posed and lyric order. We sat first at a table and had the excellent J. beer, with hors d'oeuvres, all good. I found I could use chopsticks—once one learns the rhythm it isn't hard. Then we went to counter and sat while the counterman fried us delicacies, a single one at a time, in a great conical vat of oil just beneath the counter. Each tidbit was then placed with tongs, on a napkin in front of us—a peeled fried chestnut sprinkled with sesame seed—beautiful and good—a small oblong

of fried bread, a shrimp with its tail, ditto, a quail's egg. I was greedy
—had two, on the principle that quail's eggs are scarce in my life.
Wd not have known it was an egg, had I not been told. Then shrimp
and rice, which I ate ignoring sticks. They do not seem to end meal
with tea here—what tea I've had is pale yellow, not much aroma—
no connection with good China tea.

Thence, by prior arrangement (they "consult one's wishes") we
went to the puppet theater. This, the antecedent of *Kabuki,* can be
seen only in Osaka, or the general region, I was told. Since it requires
3 men to a puppet it is very expensive, thus a dying art, Osada said.
We went behind stage first, saw the puppeteers—one of them made a
doll work for me, shake hands, weep, etc. It made me feel like a
child being taken on an extraordinary treat. As it was, we saw only
the last act. Samisen player a noted one—a commentary kind of
music it is. The second actor, a declaimer, narrator, singer—all in
one. I had heard D. do something similar from a *No*—it is very en-
trancing to listen to, and the puppets gliding along with two men
in black, conical hats and all, and master-puppeteer, in full view,
garbed grandly in white with spread collar—had a ballet fascination
that probably grows with watching. We had too little time. Took
the train back to K., found the hotel without trouble, and so to bed.
And then at breakfast the next morning, pick up the Mainichi and
read the attached clip, "Calisher Repudiates Present US Writers."
Wrote letter of protest, which Mr. Baskin in Kobe is going to show
the Mainichi. Baskin said he knows the reporter, who has a chip on
his shoulder—remarks were deliberately twisted. Ah well.

Meanwhile in Kobe, that afternoon (9/19) met the small group—
all professors, who came in one by one to meet me and talk haltingly.
A Mr. Pehda, former Fulbright who has stayed on, returning to
States and here again (when Americans fall for J. they get it bad) was
very very helpful. Great interest as always in our homosexual writers
—Capote, etc. Asked me if they were a group—I explained. The
brightest prof., whom I liked, said that the chief difficulty that J.
had in understanding our literature was caused by the fact that the
Japanese are without a sense of original sin. I told Prof. Sanno that

this was the most interesting thing I had heard in J.—which I think it so far is—perhaps this is responsible for the continuous western complaint that J'nese have no "reaction" or no "emotion"—which we confuse with all the variations of guilt etc.

Thence to dinner at a private home in Kobe, Mr. Will Rogers—home approached through walled hillside path rather like that outside some villas in Italy, etc. Large group of Jap.-American cultural soc. I was infinitely weary, still suffering from diarrhea—had had a Jap. lunch—no more of that. (I know why the whole land smells of fish—after all, it is an island—but I shall have no more.)

Discussion of the position of women—marriage in Japan—etc. (Sat next to Mr. Baker, consul, an amiable Southerner who made amusing comments—which nettled the serious younger Americans, on our own civ.) I too, am now less eager to project our Amer. attitudes, particularly re women—than I wd have been yrs ago. Spoke with Joan Greenwood, doing her Ph.D. with Stegner and now teaching in Kobe Co., for women—she very hot over the injustices of J. women, but less eager to admit our women were not all rosy-happy. Very bright girl. Baker, on my right, explaining meanwhile that the J.'s here constituted perhaps 1% of all J.—this group mostly being men and women who had had some college training in U. S. Such girls, returning, found it difficult to marry here, even to their opposites, the men who have also been to U. S. Americans in group asked abt arranged marriages etc., etc.

I made Baker ask a q. for me—were all the J. women anxious to exchange their "feudal yoke" for Amer. female attitudes? A beautiful and intelligent J. girl spoke up—said she thought things were happier in the home if the man had a certain "dominance." (B. said she was one of the ones who was finding it difficult to marry.)

Sad, what we are doing to them—I think often of Mark Twain's essay on missionaries, which applies as much to the eager-beaver mod. American emissary as it did to his 19th century missionary counterpart. The USIS people all extremely good types however—Baskin and others I heard speak—also their wives—Mrs. B. very charming and intelligent—this unusual as embassy wives go—but they are different from straight For. Service wives I fancy. Thence I was to go to the train—when lo—it was found that all trains wd be delayed owing to a great accident—after much back-and-forth, it was arranged that I stay here in Kobe instead of having to bear the train again, and take the plane in morning. Unless the plane falls down, the gods are with me, for my weariness had begun to be serious, and my mental state poor. Heat, as I know, always makes me hypochondriacal—the heat has lessened, but I still have all the symptoms—maybe it's the stomach etc.—*mal de peche*, etc. Anyway, looking in the mirror—drawn face, skin broken out, and insides melancholy, I told myself that the East was indeed hard on a white woman—what wd C. think if I deplaned looking and feeling like this? At dinner, when someone asked me the ages of my children, and on hearing, made the accustomed remarks on the unbelievability of same, I thought they must be out of their heads, since I looked to myself like that woman in Lost Horizon at the moment just before she crumbled with the weight of centuries of age, into dust.

*Sunday, Sept. 21, Hakata Imperial Hotel, Fukuoka*

I am somewhat recovered, thanks to an evening of rest in the Kobe Hotel, where I wrote the above, just before embarking for here on the JAL plane. And thanks to a pleasant day spent here, which I shall "presently recount." To date I have written this journal without even glancing up to correct the typos, much less read back. It is a curious experience for a writer accustomed, as I am, to mandarin concentration on every word. Perhaps I could not have done this straight from the short story, but the necessary telescoping of that impulse, which has gradually crept on me during the writing of the novel, has helped.

Yesterday, George Iseki of the Kobe A.C.C. came early to drive me to Itami airfield, some 40 minutes drive, and we had a pleasant drive through the rice paddies (Agricultural note for C.—they alternate rice and wheat; G. said he thought they had always done, though not sure.) He had had a year in the U. S., at Northwestern and U.

of Texas, has less accent than most of the other men, many of whom have also been—but he is considerably younger—looks like a young football player, stocky, with carefully crewed hair. I had impression I was talking to someone far more westernized inside than most. Itami air terminal, small and handsomer than any of ours I have seen, even Seattle-Tacoma, which still runs to dull green and henna chairs and sofas of the "public room" variety. The seats in Itami are the brilliant J. yellow, backed with royal blue—imperial colors? —the wood smooth and handsome.

Very bright weather. Followed the map provided, on from the rt side of the plane, seeing the inland sea. Mountains on left. A J. next me, who spoke some Eng. pointed out first Shodo Is., then Inno and Eda—one or the other a shipbuilding base and a naval academy—no doubt I have got them wrong—but sufficient to remind one—if the omnipresent and fresh fish had not—how maritime a nation they are. Near Kure, I had half-hoped, half-dreaded, to look down on Hiroshima, fancying that from the air I might still see that historic and dreadful crater, but H. is inland.

The stewardess announced it, as she did all pts of interest, meanwhile serving us with cake and eclairs. Someone here has told me (an Amer. of course—perhaps Baker) that the J. at Hiroshima are proud of their distinction in being "the first to be atom bombed." Part of the insistent J. reliance on prestige, perhaps? —Thence we landed at Itazuke airfield, about 40 minutes out of Fukuoka, the inevitable A.C.C. truck meeting me, Mr. Kuriya in command. Left me at the Hakata, to repair myself until 2 P.M. when the talk is scheduled —mostly professors, he told me.

The A.C.C., housed in the same building as the consulate, was a surprise. Downstairs, I stopped to note several books enclosed in a case on the wall near the elevator, J. and Eng. among them. And there, staring at me, was Curt's name and mine—on a copy of the O. Henry collection. K explained that 2 other J's were to talk at this meeting—we evolved a scheme whereby I say a few words first, then the other two wd deliver their papers, then I and my questions and answers.

First paper was delivered, in English (at some pains to compliment me I'm afraid)—on James's *Portrait of a Lady*. Beforehand we were each given a mimeographed paper containing, first, the *Oxford D. of E. Lit*'s synopsis of the book, a historical acct of the pub. from Leavis, etc. The speech was in effect, merely a going over of the printed matter (though it is probable it wd have been more expanded in Japanese). But emphasis was placed on Henry James having had a "success" with his bk. The prof. (name not caught) did speak of the ending, left up in the air—why was Isabel Archer left to return to Europe? —this not explained by James, etc. I have always felt this abt the ending also, and later said so.

It was opportune to have something to say, since the lecture was primitive, and this not entirely owing to language—although it was sometimes difficult not to laugh when I finally translated such a sentence as fell on my ear thus: "Isahbel Ochah's seedpod, o, razzer, hah rubber"—as "Isabel Archer's sweetheart, or, rather, her lover." I am beginning to be slightly more deft with J. names and syllables and used to their accent: "In leeding the lurks of," for "in reading the works of," now strikes me as quite natural, and nothing to be reported really. An advance.

The next speech concerned mass-culture in the U. S., a very young and eager-beaver prof. who had lifted some stuff I saw in the U. S. —lists of the popular best-sellers since the 1880s with some interpretations of popular tastes, etc., nothing more than statistics really.

Sakae Murioka, pres. of the society, invited me to a party for the consul Mr. and Mrs. Herndon, there at the lecture and just returned from leave, and for a Mr. Gardiner who has been teaching here and goes to Ochanimasu (U. for girls in Tokyo). The Herndons drove me back to the hotel—he a former language-school grad in Fr., she from the South, plump and talky, rather bright or merely pleasant. She sweet-talks the J. men—this goes down very well with them.

Party was a dinner really, in an impressive walled villa—later the Herndons said they did not know to whom it belonged and may well have been a restaurant. (Now I remember what G. Iseki and I discussed—the reluctance of the J.'s to entertain in their homes, he said, is not due to any large sense of personal privacy, as with the French, but because they feel that their homes may not be elaborate enough, problems of service etc. also being easier in many ways. How like us they are in this, as in their sense of the future, and mechanical talents, though they have infinitely more talent for painstaking handicrafts than we—this because we are at farther distance from our handcraft era?)

The Dinner. Long table, oblong, at which about 18 of us sat, Mr. Gardiner, a rather typical Anglo-Irishman of a certain sort, at my left. He loved being *intime* with the J.'s, not particularly interest in talking to me, altho his teaching will be Lit (Eng.). May not like women. Not interested in talking abt London—I careful not to pursue. But the young Amer. and Eng. who stay out here (Burton Martin at Waseda is a prime example) interest one, since one always suspects —at least Americans do—the expatriate. And it is true that many of these (like the rather-dreadful and pathetic S. K. who spoke to me after the lecture at Kyoto—who has left U. S. because "poetry should not be in the marketplace," who published works of bad poets and probably writes poetry himself—gave me a thin folio by Theodore Enslin) have the flavor of the intellectual remittance man. Undoubtedly, I suspect, many of them stay or return because homosexuality is easy, etc. —Though not all. The foreign service people here, for instance, return for many tours, and obviously love it. —I speak of the single men, teaching at a university, and with a certain air of entente with the Japanese, which seems more than superficial—to them.

But the dinner. First taste of saké, clear, warm—was told it might make me sleepy but not drunk—it did relax, poured from a tiny-mouthed small urn. And getting used to the tidbits one dips in soy (latter first mixed with a mustard—nothing like ours—this is a chopped green smoothness, rather like mashed avocado), then in the main dish that comes swimming in clear sauce. Main dish, kept in a chafing-dish at either end, was chicken giblets etc., particular dish of this region. At intervals, serving maids brought other things to be dropped in the simmering sauce along with the chicken—crinkled Chinese cabbage, which was delicious, not stewed à la the West— and a kind of white, jellied consistency, in squares, which might be fish, might be part of an animal, *quién sabe*—very good. Not bean curd. Had had a delicately salted fish of some sort before, cold, not salmon not crab, but in between, pink—to be dipped in soy. Several chestnuts.

The idea of the J. meal is of course "several"—not too much of anything, a taste here and there, except for the rice, which melds all. Rather a little like Fr. cuisine in that—they of course are sympathetic, very, to Fr. culture, and some of this may come from a natural, native resemblance in the spirit of the two syles of life. Certainly it was a relaxing and civilized way to spend an evening.

The men assume the lotus position, legs crossed in front, but often vary this with one knee raised, or other casual positions, feet stretched under table. I contented myself with kneeling on haunches, luckily, since I am such a floor-sitter, and still fairly supple, this not hard for me, though tiresome. Murioka came over and teased me: why did I continue to sit in the *proper* position for ladies. Glad I had instinctively assumed same—although it is apparently O.K. to sit sideways, as I then thankfully did, though never, for a woman, to cross legs. My sheath dress, which happens to look so Oriental had saved me from this anyway. The dinner had started somewhat before 6, ended a little before nine, with a J. fruit, nameless to me still, a cross between apple and pear. We all exchanged our flowery compliments—I am getting fairly good at this, in fact enjoy it, having an initial taste for formalities and flowerinesses hardly satisfied by life in America. Murioka in particular went into a long speech, describing how, before meeting me, he had wondered was I young or old, now he was infinitely happy to discover that I was young, might he call the hotel tomorrow? —I thought he perhaps might have been a little saké-ed—also the men had had whisky from complimentary bottles of VERY RARE OLD LIQUEUR Sun-Tory brand—anyway I repeated my promise to leave my copy of Keenes' Intro to J. Lit for him, and to send him a copy of my book.

Talked quite a bit with Gunther Rosinus, the dir. of the A.C.C.— Harvard Edct, German background I think, mother a child psychologsit—he brought me home and we had a brandy in the bar. All the liquor, western and J., that one wants—I had not happened to want any to date, but may be sorry for this, as about the fish, when I reach Tabriz.

A wonderful night's sleep at last, stayed in bed until after 9, had breakfast; it is now 1 P.M. Like many hotels in J., Rosinus said, this one is built into a dep't store—I may investigate—they are open Sun. and closed Mon.—tried to get a yakata (cotton bath-kimono) in Kyoto, but they are out of season. Driver commented they w'dn't be able to fit me anyway. Hardly worth having made up, but I w'd rather have these than anything elaborate. Fun to get one for C. too, if I cd. Rosinus said that the tanzen, winter kimono with lining, has a wonderfully pleasing texture to wear, warm and comfortable.

I am still a little dizzy and suffering from that other woe, but not as hysterically tired as I know I must have been. Fukuoka from above —my room on the 8th floor has fine view of rooftops and distant mountains, has a distinctly seaside air—the bay can be seen from the restaurant where I had lunch yesterday. Two J. boys were playing catch with a ball and mitts, on the rooftop of a building just below eye-level, when I lunched. City seems cosmopolitan on a small scale geared to visitors—the way Atlantic City might though it is not a cosmopolis, and Fukuoka of course is at the top end of Kyushu. (How proud I am of my geography!)

I have time to think of C. now—or rather again, for when I felt ill this was part of it—as well as homesickness. I have put his picture out —though Dita in enlarging has hexed it and it does not look as I remember him best—it is nice to see. Perhaps there will be mail when I return to Tokyo tomorrow. I concentrate hopefully on the day we shall meet, in Tabriz, or Teheran. We have had so many partings— the way I see him best is the way he always comes forward as we meet, his face eager and somehow questioning, as if he is asking himself:

(The telephone has just rung. Mail for me at desk!)

Alas, I went down in hopes of mail forwarded from embassy— nothing but a note from Kuriya, saying Mon., is their holiday, so no one may escort me to plane—suggests I ask JAL office downstairs. So I did—although I feel competent enough to get on airport bus

which after all starts in front of hotel, there is always the language
difficulty—and besides one gets rather used to being shepherded about,
things made easy, as a state visitor. *Sic transit amor democratiae.*

This diary is getting far too extensive, but it serves as a companion
too, and C. won't mind my maunderings. I wonder what his will be
like—far more pulled together—plus no climatic or other troubles I
hope. And perhaps not so subjective. When I was interrupted, I was
about to say, almost to *see* his face coming toward me. He always
looks as if he is asking himself: Are we still together? Do we still
love? Is she as she was, for me? Am I still, for her? But always the
same interest in what *will* be—in that we are very alike. At the core of
each of us, something anxious to know, not unfeeling but always accompanying feeling—it is this in us that must sometimes make others
think us hard at the core, that he and I, understanding, know is not,
but recognize. . . .

I did go down to the JAL office, queried the girl about yakatas—
she insisted on accompanying me to the Haikata Daimaru store next
door, where, after pricing "Reblon" lipsticks—they hadn't the color
I wanted anyway, I bought a J. one. Not as many colors as ours, but
quite good I'm sure. Smells of that insistent perfume, which may turn
nostalgic when not so pervasive, and which C. may taste. As I sus-
pected no yakatas made up. Contented myself with the lipstick and
some razor blades for C., then walked down the main street. Foggy
and dusty today, small resemblance to yesterday's seaside Dufy air,
when I cd see a distant white lighthouse on a prong of land in the
blue bay. Nipped into various shops—a record place crammed with our
cheap jazz—it plays all the time in the restaurant here—a food shop and
wine shop where they have many familiar brands—Hennessy cognac
tempted me but they had no small bottles. Bought cheese crackers—
bad reproductions.

All this sounds transitory indeed, but I am rather certain that by
walking in streets and shops, making little random purchases, etc., I
already know a bit more about J. life, (though very little) than I
might if I had done the routine bit to Nikko. And now, I shall read—
alas I thought I had brought *Under the Volcano,* but have left it

with baggage checked at Imperial—nothing except K.'s book which I finished this morning in order to give Murioka—and my own! Well, I shall muse. Empty Sunday, rather nice Sunday. Still Saturday in New York, just beginning to be so in Tabriz?? Not sure.

*Wednesday—returned to the Imperial on Monday—this is 9/24/58.*

After last entry went and blew myself to an enormous dinner—ordered vodka, glass was enormous even after I had extracted all the ice, a huge steak, and Marron *à la crème*—which I thought wd be a tiny taste of, as it is in France. The most enormous pile came—a cone-shaped child's dream of an ice-cream pagoda—cake, piles of ground chestnut, and such festoonings of whipped cream as must have occupied the happy cook with a pastry tube for quite a while. Then sogged off to bed. Since I have read C.'s journal, it is quite apparent we are both drugging ourselves with food.

Flight back cloudy—glad I had seen something the trip down. Met by the Embassy driver, thank goodness, letter from Miss Downing saying that I was to meet a group of J. writers invited to tea for me at the International House, if I had a photograph please to give, otherwise come to embassy to be snapped. Zippo, the routine started again. Also in the packet was a briefing on the various authors (which I shall keep but carry separately and not append here), and at last, C.'s journal.

I saw little of the long ride in from the airfield. Curiously, at first I felt farther away from C. than before. He was writing in London—but at the moment I was reading had already passed thru that experience, also Italy, and was at that moment in Teheran as far as I knew. My own transient state, coupled with his, almost too much to bear—no fixed point—and I am a person who craves same—though not necessarily a geographic one. Being at my desk wd be a help—the journal is at least a little—and I have not written here for the last two nights.

Mr. Boylan (not Black, as I have it earlier) came with me and Downing to International House—built with joint Rockefeller and Japanese funds, werry handsome, as are all their new buildings. One sardonic advantage of being bombed is that they have all these new ones. The writers—ah well. Mr. Hino (author of *Faeces and Urine*) was as one might expect, a bohemian type in long hair, dark blue shirt—they affect the past Parisian style, some of them, still. Perhaps only his vintage—most of these I met were born 1901 or thereabouts. Again the prestige deal: before our exchange was over he had shown me the prize watch won for something or other 28 yrs ago. (Sad reflection however, that he still wears his 28-yr.-old accomplishments as if they counted—in America, last year's book, prize, is no help for this year.) He also had a secretary, very handsome, pallid, and utterly silent young man—asked me one question—how many times I had had the O. Henry. So help me, I said five—what the hell—I had no prize watch!

Others were the ladies—Enji—delicate as the author of her lyrical titles should be, ditto Koyama, tho' less so. Kirayabashi, the gal who's been in prison, was plump, vigorous, smiling—a good proletarian dame. She and Enji had been to the States together recently—the standard tour from Wash. to San F. Hino is to go next week. Thru an interpreter (Boylan said he thinks H. understands Eng. and can speak too), he made it clear he is interested only in the "back streets" of U. S. A. Doesn't want to be corrupted, a vigorous bohemian pose. I said he should look up Algren in Chi. He met Steinbeck at P.E.N. conference here, expects to meet Mailer. Obviously puts me in the mandarin class but I warmed him a trifle and he is sending me his book. Komatsu, translator of Malraux and very *au courant* France, also there—embassy had given me the wrong info—there is another K. who is a music critic, so having learned my lesson v. well in the car on the way, promptly got off on the wrong musical foot with him at once.

*Tuesday—the Autumnal Equinox Holiday*

Went to *Nō* theater with Mrs. Kobayashi, Bryn Mawr grad, husband a botany prof. Very sweet. *Nō* plays extraordinary—one is supposed to be bored, since they are classical, followed by most people there with text—but I wasn't bored, possibly because of interest in dancing. Mrs

K. told me "story" of each, and it wd have been tantalizing not to know
—a baffled American came up in interim and craved info. Very slow,
symbolic mixture of *joruri* declamation, (or some kind of) significant
movement, exceptionally stylized. Old, old. Like the dust of the
hills moving slowly, doing a turn and stopping again. Head actor
wears mask sometimes. Also saw some dances, and a farce. I cd have
watched for hrs.

Tantalizing, but had to leave for Ambassador's cocktail party, and
was sorry afterward I had. MacArthur very nice, also his wife—one
would call her a "zippy" type—but why I was there was apparently
known to no man. Maybe they mistook me for a visiting economist—
everybody there seemed to be in that division. One nice woman just
down from Seoul, who knows Kim Yong Ick, says he is teaching at
U. of Pusan. Rest of time I was nougated down among the Faulty, I
mean Faculty, I mean embassy wives. (First slip a typo?) Should
have got to talk to Ambassador, but didn't.

It is hard having a faculty or an official job as a woman—one always
gets put with them. Was asked whether sack dress was still in, was
crooned over—"ooh isn't that a lovely trip you're having!" etc. Many
of them nice and not stupid—but they have learned the accepted
social responses involved with their responsibility, and live conversationally within them. This kind of thing—the separation of the sexes
even at an intimate party which this was, sadly American—not as
likely to happen at a Fr. or Br. embassy. House handsome, called
Hoover's Folly originally, built in that era. Then I went home and-
so-to, for tomorrow was to be a heavy day indeed.

Forget to say that in the morning I received expense check. Think
how many lunches I have skipped this week. And after all, one must
build up an "estate." Etcetera. Upshot, went down to Uyeda's (recommended by Downing) and bought pearls. Cd have had better lustre
with small ones but look silly on me, so bought bigger of adequate
lustre but baroque. Came upstairs consumed with guilt. Still me.
Maybe feel better when see pearls (being strung). Will have to wear
all the time in Persia. Very sexy bead, pearls, so don't mind, and C.
shouldn't. But these thoughts n.g. for now. Even communication is

difficult. Asked at embassy whether a "ms" cd go in pouch, but only dip. stuff can. Secretary advised me not to mail any mss. of which I had no copy to Persia, since "they pilfer." Even registered and insured stuff. So shall mail this to A.P.O. number. Goodby little ms, perhaps forever. What will Azerbajani make of youz? (Persian sp?)

And so to bed last night. Heaviest day yet today. Morning talked at Tsuda, an hour out of Tokyo—went with driver and Mrs. Kobayashi, who is an alumna. The same blue-stocking girls college atmosphere I wd recognize at ends of earth—very like Barnard when I went there. Miss Kusiya, President (Bryn Mawr also) not unlike the deans of that generation, but softened by Japanese manners, much easier to take than a Gildersleeve. Two others of a similar type, the spinster of good Anglo-Saxon ancestry and educ., teaching in a far land—Miss Chappell, a Canadian, Miss Sechole(?) American. Both of certain age. Had lunch with them in their residence, rather like Eliz. Ames's house at Yaddo. Mrs. Takano, Henry James expert, also there, but spoke little in deference to older ones. Food fine, American taste but J. elegance. Tomatoes always peeled here for salad—barbarians we. Cashmere Bouquet soap in john—far from home little squeak of nostalgia. Questions went well—I am beginning to repeat jokes and ideas like a seasoned academic—feel rather like an actress doing a two-a-day. But this was the last but one.

In the afternoon went to Keio U. in Tokyo. Prof. Kiooka had sent me his trans. of the autobiography of his grandfather, the famous Fukuzawa (Yukichi) who founded the place—one of the first J.'s to visit U. S. in the sixties. Nepotism rampant in the Univ.'s, as everywhere in J. life. On the other hand, they make go-between marriages with selected stock and thus probably usually continue the talents (Sly reference at Tsuda, by Miss Kusiya, that Mishima's marriage with the daughter of Sugiyama[?] famous painter, had been a go-between one—young wife is still at school. Makes me think M. is probably a homosexual—he is so westernized in other ways—he is building a Colonial[!] house, he told me—that he wd have made a Western marriage, I fancy, had it been more than "duty." Apparently comes from rich family—peers school open to all, but takes money, acc. to Mrs. Kobayashi.)

Faculty room at Keio, built by Noguchi is extraordinarily handsome, and the furniture—a long wooden table shaped like an ellipse, beautiful curved divan subtly curved to match, ve-ery long, rattan and reed, exquisitely shaped. I have seen nothing like, and wd rather have this furniture than anything I have ever seen. Lecture O.K.—they warmed up at end. Kiooka no help—Downing told me his subject is *Eng*. Lit, and she suspects he has never read any Amer.—there is no course in it at Keio. Have a noted medical school, engineering and business schools—many of students there in economics, one doing grad thesis in Faulkner, an intelligent girl—immediately told that she was daughter of the J. translator of Baudelaire. Etc.

Made grand exit by falling down one of their unexpected flights of steps and skinning knee. Picked myself up, veddy British. Home to hotel, and there just as I entered was call from Radio USIS station, for "interview" which I had forgotten all about. So recorded on tape for half an hour—nice note: the girl assistant so enthralled by my eloquence that she stared at me, forgot to insert the tape, and we had to do part of a roll over. Then Mr. Hiroo Mukai called—critic, knows Stegner—I shall try to see him tomorrow, between last-minute errand and maybe a Kabuki—Oh God—I want to, and yet. Day after tomorrow, off to Manila. Downing doubts they will send me out of M. during my time there. I hope not. Am already wincing at the thought of the heat to come. Understand they have a workshop set up for me for first day. George Saito of embassy called to say N. V. M. Gonzalez is returning to M. from Tokyo tomorrow and hopes to meet me there.

Good-by dear C. I hope this gets to you. Next installment I hope, from Manila.

Love,

H.

*Saturday*—I did not write after all. Fell asleep.

*Hotel Filipinas—Pearl of Orient Hotels—Dewey Blvd., Manila—Sunday
—Sept. 28, '58.*

Now it is 7:30 of a bright morning. Outside it will already be hot
and moist, but inside here in the room, the air conditioner is roaring
on, I have just had a shower, and the combination of physical coolness
—I slept with a blanket—and bright sun outside, makes me think
speciously of fall, of fall in America, the first fine feel of wool, intensely blue mid-afternoon sky and the crisp, windy tinge that comes
with evening. Best days in the world, fall, I think, and my heart lifts
at the hope of spending some clear cold days with Curt—although perhaps it will be quite cold already when I arrive.

I have just had an international breakfast on my own here. Powdered
coffee, made with tap water, which, never more than lukewarm, is a
shock after the burning excellence of J. baths—then some of the tiny
sour-sweet Phil. limes, then a roll I had previously saved from the
NWA largesse on the plane, day before yesterday. The matches with
which I have just lit my cigarette are from Schrafft's, probably the
one near Josh Cahn's. En avant.

After the suave elegance of the Imperial—how elegant I only now
realize—this room, though not uncomfortable and much larger, makes
me laugh when I look at it. The hotel was built after the war, but
just recently; outside is very tropical-postcard-swimming pool, some
attempt at smartness. But the temperament here does not do this sort
of thing well, in fact the decor is *exactly* Hotel Earle. Terrible dirty
browns, bleeded-out tans, the overstuffed furniture a very sick,
slightly iridescent green, the backs of the chairs showing the pomade
of past heads. The coffee table, long, glassy, and bound in dreadful
wood, the rug a faded straw mat that might just have well been a
handsome beige but is a dirtied rose, that clings to the legs of things,
so that nothing can be shifted for ease. Two daybeds that have to be
made up daily. Grisly 1930—"modern" lamps hooping out at iniquitous
angles. In the bath (no tub) the shower head has merely been pushed
thru the wall, the hole in the plaster left jagged around it. In toto one

feels that these objects were all chosen by someone who did not understand why Westerners liked this kind of thing but manfully have supplied it because we must have it.

My coffee cup is actually the little teacup for travel—blue and white, in a little wicker and cotton bag for safe carrying, that was the parting gift of the innkeeper of the Kaneiwaro Dekkan in Kyoto. Cost a few yen. A remembrance of that almost sinister elegance of everything in J.—one remembers that the trains always ran in Nazi Germany, or was it Mussolini's Italy? —why is it that new democracies cloth themselves like this room, and the authoritarian country has the Ph.D. in plumbing? But already, after yesterday and last night, I begin to get some sense of what the SD people call "Southeast Asia."

My last day in Tokyo I went to see *Kabuki,* moved more by duty than inclination. (Shopped first for yakatas at Takashimaya's but did not buy—decided was silly—now regret. The usual pattern.) *Kabuki-za* theater—large one was somewhat of a disappointment—had heard the staging was better than anything we have in West—this not true—although I did not see the famous production *Kinjancho.* Went to the 4:30 performance, and only stuck it out for an hr. and half. Acting superb, audience brought out picnic boxes—girl next to me eating, with chopsticks, things that—for all the world looked like Peter Paul coconut rolls with a thin outer coating of chocolate—actually rice rolls in a skin of fish. (Fish and perfume again.)

I much prefer the slow, hieratic music dance of the *No* plays—in this, I was told, I have the classic, intellectual taste—most intellectual J. feel that this is what they should feel, and at the *No* plays there is something of the same conscious, superior duty that one might sense at an audience in the Village seeing a fine production of Massinger. Once again I discover with wonder, as I have at intervals thru my life—that I have been speaking prose without knowing it. I seem to have the proper intellectual tastes—only some—but not always for the right "intellectual" reasons.

I felt that there was something less esoteric, broader, about Kabuki —almost "West End" or "B'way" abt this production—if within the scope of the mind that can still be applied to a play in which a man commits *hara-kiri* belly-forward to the audience, in about the same length of time it takes Tristan to expire, and at about the same pace. Meanwhile wife makes exquisite moan, in a ritualized, infinitely varied weeping, no gestures any larger than the radius in which one might swing a spoon. The key to all this, my hopeful profundity told me, is in savagery done with delicacy. And in the audience, which, whether in its gray kid shoes, half of them, or in its traditional ki-mono, still was rapt and approving at the sight of the honorable act of the hero, the stylized anguish of the father who, emoting grandly, sits by while his son kills himself because he has offended HIM. Are these people, the audience, the same who deliver lectures on H. James, who entertain me in offices as smart as anything on Madison Ave.—indeed smarter—whose plumbing slides on slippered ease, whose imitated Dupont glue works as well or better than the original? Yes.

That evening spent with Hiroo Mukai, works at International House. Born in England, left and returned there, perfect English, many times in America; knows Angus W. etc. We talked "Flankly" —as much as one can. He said it was regrettable J. thought one had to be all black or white on subject of Americans—I gather his coun-trymen think he is too pro-us. Downing said later, "He does not like us." I was probably too "flank"—but the hell with it—we discussed the lacks in Amer. culture, the lack of individual judgment that I had noted in J. students, etc., etc.,—it was probably healthier than the usual clichés. I felt M. to be a weary man in some ways—it must be infinitely tiring to live in his position. Yet a tireless man also—his ideal and hope, he told me is to be a J. journalist in Hong-Kong, writing back for newspapers here. We exchanged agreement that one cannot write for one's country without returning to it often—he had done it once, and found he no longer knew what the J.'s wanted. Etc. So to bed and up at dawn for the plane, which left late.

While in terminal with Downing, met a John Morgan, here in Orient for some months past, for Nat'l City Bank of N.Y., lives in Westfield, N.J.—had spent much time at Amer. Club in Tokyo etc. Routine businessman of the hearty-pleasant type one thought at first, except for the earphone he wears on one side for deafness. Carried my typewriter to plane, sat with me as far as Taipeh, and was very helpful. Scolded myself for typing people; this one does of course have all the marks of the businessman in Orient—but a younger, smarter breed, with manners. Majored in philosophy—we talked of Russell and Josiah Royce—both of us, I suspect, leaning on college backgrounds long since dim. He told me of a cormorant-fishing trip he'd been taken on, in Nagano or Hakone or somewhere. An excursion in the J. manner, on river barges, fishing boats, etc. The boats have the cormorants, which in turn catch the fish. Much business with lighted lanterns, etc. Ultimate end to catch the tourist, he said, but still a sight he would not have missed—(especially the geisha girls) and I was sorry I had.

Flying into Okinawa was one of the most beautiful sights I have ever had from the air. Trip to then had been excessively bumpy, white clouds and up-drafts—we were apparently flying out of the typhoon that was on its way to Tokyo—little Ida of the vicious small "eye." (It had bn explained to me that typhoons are the more dangerous the smaller the "eye" and the slower the pace—this one was crawling at 12 mi. per hr. and was expected to attain the strength of the historic one of 1934.) But finally we opened up to beautiful brilliant weather, and Okinawa which had always been a grim, long gray word in the war dispatches, first in the aura of death on the beaches, later, in the news dispatches post-war, a picture of quonset huts—peace-time soldier boredom—turned out to be a long craggy jewel set in a jade-patched purple sea very much like the sea that the Carmel painters attempted but never attained—a thin creaming line of white, where the reefs are, bordering the whole. Morgan had been there, said swimming was wonderful, barring moray-eels, groupers (bloody-mouthed fish, with retractable mouths, that I had seen in Bermuda) and poisonous jellyfish. The whole island, he told me, was crammed with their peculiar kind of cenotaph or gravestone—they having no separate yards but burying anywhere, and we had hoped to see some from the plane, but cdn't.

The place is of course restricted—our passports were taken from us and not returned until we were again aloft—we cd see little from the barbed-wire enclosure around the terminal. Queer things these terminals set in various seas. Little limbos, equipped with postcards and a tired array of goods to take into the "other" world—and not the world of the living perhaps. Tins of Van Houtens Cocoa, American cigarettes in fly-blown cellophane, jewelry that might be hung on a tree but rarely by any mortal woman on herself. Odd to see automobiles, mostly service, with the license marked "Ryukyu." Usual feeling that it cannot be me who is here.

Morgan obviously loves this travel, tho he has a wife and 4 children at home—told me that the two things he knew best were "soldiering" and—I forget the other, since the first, so obviously the wistful adventurousness of a N.J. banker, impressed me so much more. Then on to Taipeh. Could it be I was going there too! Conscious of being for first time in area near a war area, conscious at same time of how silly it seemed to make something of it, especially when a pleasant typical Amer. elderly matron, wife of some commercial tycoon traveling with us—hair marcelled, and with the token orchid given by some "company" at emplaning—said, awed, as we deplaned—"Well, this is historic, isn't it!"

We all love to insert ourselves into history. But I am ahead of myself. Formosa, from the air, was as brilliant as Okinawa but in another way—it looks as rich agriculturally as anything I had ever seen—rice paddies the most brilliant green I suppose, but every inch within the circle of hills that encloses and intervenes, cultivated in some way. A flat green jewel this—no wonder China wants it. The surrounding hills are beautiful—the island from the air seems to have fine highways, considerable commercial areas, etc. A Chinese dignitary traveling with us was met by an enthusiastic horde of admirers— Chiang Mun Lee I was told—a doctor—and the usual Oriental popping of flash bulbs on any occasion. They want to be history too. He a nice old man, quite tall, refined face under floppy Panama. I prefer the Ch. physiognomy to the J.

Morgan left at Taipeh. Flight uneventful, dark. Tried not to have too much Scotch and champagne, but cd do better if had yogurt and raw carrots to substitute. Solemn thoughts, buoyed by liquor, of how long it will be, probably, before I see a raw carrot again. Wonder idly if C. realizes the awful responsibility of having separated me from all such amenities. No doubt. And possibly by now realizing some of that from which he has separated himself.

Is he by now hunting Tabriz for a home for us, having a hard time, wondering if Hortense will approve, can take this . . . or that. I must write to reassure him. To tell him that his company is well worth. Anyway must not play game of "wonder what he is doing now." Have done a minimum of that. Too sterile. Yet moments jump, when it's sharply sad not to be sharing. Then I do play it. Hope he is well, and no longer plagued by stomach, or possible woes of settling. Drive off concern, by cynically imagining possibility that while I so melt, he is at very moment with nice Curt—nose pressed hotly on some tumescent Persian navel. Very unfair that Oriental women shd be so much more attractive to Western eyes than most Oriental men. Or that those of the latter who appeal to me are the Indians and the Chinese—neither of whom I am likely to meet in numbers—altho many Chinese here. Stop the game.

Where was I? Ah, I arrive Manila. And this time they know me—or think they do. A real V.I.P. arrival, flash bulbs popping for me, reporters. Nice, very nice Embassy Cultural Officer Bill Dunne. Fresh from Laos—in the cab, free of all reporters and representatives except Alfredo (Fred) Morales, Pres. of the P.E.N. and head of Fulbright business here, discover that Dunne knows my old and first boyfriend, Herbert Stone, who was in Laos with him. Says H. is now in Wash. with Voice of America or S.D.—still somewhat a recluse—brought a fantastic library to Laos, also records, tapes, etc., also a fantastic bundle of experiences. Still single, tho hard to believe still for love of me.

In hotel, the three of us talk—I still wound up, unload far too much of my bag of tricks to Morales who is concerned about what I shall say Sat. morning to first group I meet—Eng. faculty of U. of P.

Trot out most of ideas on literature that I find myself to have
gathered from psyche during tour—and that shd be saved for morning.
Getting thrifty on ideas as well as meals.

Anyway, ego gratefully expands at welcome—reporters trotting at
elbow, everybody saying "we have been waiting for you—your
heestory has been in all newspapers," etc. Hotel staff very admiring,
next morning sends in a dozen roses to rm—Bill says to his knowledge
they have never done this to visitors he's squired before. Hotel has
swimming pool in back. In morning wd like to swim, but no suit—
anyway Dunne and Morales come at 9:00.

Drive to U. of P. in embassy car—M. very explicatory on what we
see. Many new buildings to replace bombings—Manila and Warsaw the
worst sufferers of W.W. Two. Suspect however that they have always
had a kind of tattered mishmash here—Spanish patio elegance whose
concrete paint quickly peels, much Western-style building by those
who do not understand it, side by side with incredible, really incredible slum. A cold country's slums can be more concealed; these,
open to the weather, tell all.

At University, meet head of Eng. Faculty, whose name I never
catch. Difficulty is that, whereas in J., since I do not know their
language, I can ask name to be repeated, here, since their language is
English, and they have an excellent command of it, it is insulting to
ask. But their voices are soft, accents sometimes severe—as with Ben
Santos—tho not always. Anyway was given a long introduction—lots
of Iowa students on faculty, will have a group meeting with them
later in week. Among them one, DeMetillo—poet, critic, etc., who was
at Iowa. When I ask who was there when he was, he says (knowingly?
—via Santos?) "I was there when Curt was."

I did well. I am becoming remarkably glib. Still, I remind myself,
I merely have a few basic convictions, some basic prejudices—and
happen to be able to manipulate them fairly gracefully, but no shame
to it, since it is au fond simple, and WHAT I BELIEVE. However this
constant glibness is wearing; the familiar academic fatigue, in which
one's own ideas, daily presented begin to seem tawdry, specious, superficial, unendingly obvious. And, as always, a false position to go on

talking abt writing when one is not writing. Tomorrow talk to the P.E.N. group. Suspect I shall be meeting the same group of people everywhere.

In afternoon went wandering and got lost. Streets look built on square—ain't. Discover am back of Dewey Boulevard, facing Manila Bay. Forgot to say that Morales, after lecture, took me and Dunne to tropical soda parlor. No other word for it. Same air of cheap sweetish color and shabbiness abt everything. Exaggerated or "real" counterpart of what any walker thru Sp. districts in N.Y. knows well. Had a dreadful concoction which is known in Tagalog as "mara puno hala," coconut "with everything." Stylistically correct, that phrase. Begins with shaved ice, on top of this a ball of ice cream—Morales substituted for my safe "vanilla" flavor a more adventurous one made from a coconut indigenous here, in which, unlike those we're used to, the milk fills the fruit, is not confined to just inside the hard shell. Shaved ice filled with the milk. Whole thing topped with slices of custard—yes, slices—with a faint aroma of mace. Under ice various things discovered, retrieved, swallowed. Something shaped like long oval grapes, jelly consistency, rather like a chewy honey cough lozenge I used to have as a child—these palm nuts, I thought I understood. Also something looked like raisin, wasn't. Chips of coconut. All vaguely sweet—too vaguely.

Upshot—in the afternoon walk—wandered into a Phil. version of supermarket, bought coffee and limes, and paid one DOLLAR for a box of Ry-Krisp. RESOLVE. Lost my way, in quite a sweat when returned. Climate wd be unbearable for constant consumption if thought of cooled room were not safely in mind. Anyway only me and mad dogs, Englishmen go out in noonday sun. Not the hot season here, I'm told. Really not too bad for short intervals—merely the constant problem of clothing getting really wet. One needs a fulltime laundry and endless cycle of cottons. Western men here wear the embroidered shirt (barong) outside the trousers—Philos conversely often affect the hotter Am. shirt, just as some, I am told, will carry Amer. cigs for show, at a party.

Came in for siesta and did. Smiling the girl fell dead.

Bill called for me at 5—took me around corner to his very hand-some flat, where he was throwing a party for me. Guests USIS and P. intellectuals—no, mostly newspaper people. Met Mrs. Nakpil and husband. Tops, both. She, not the shriveled Ph. type woman who is so unattractive, but the more beautiful heavy-featured, dark—coffee-au-lait—something Malay in the features? Wore adroit pleated white chiffon gown I coveted—also envied long Manchu fingernails coated silver-white. Husband handsome, though didn't covet—architect shortly going to states—I chatted Mies Van der Rohe, Eero Saarinen, talk very glib still. Told him about Des Moines museum. Also there: N. V. M. Gonzalez, who had been at lecture—teaches at U.P.—and is, as I already knew the "man of letters" preeminent—although Rein-hardt says he's not as good as Solianco and Joaquin. Neither of the latter there. Solianco very hard to meet especially.

Guests at party included Morli Dharem—critic for *Times*. Rather mincing, slightly self-important. Used to write short stories. Almost no Male in the Phillippines, except for Americans, has *not* used to write short stories. Mrs. Nakpil, on my other side, compliments him across me—"Morli, you are so versatile, you do everything—plays. . . . etc. etc. If she is vitriolic, she conceals well. Morli replies with a mincy-wince—"Ah no, I fear I spread myself too thin."

Also talk to Frankie Jose, editor Sunday *Times Mag.* and Rosalinda Orosa, who very shyly asks me how to begin to write—should she join a class like Ed Fuller's, as I once did. Have already discovered that everybody knows everything ever printed about my life and hard times in U. S. papers—including old interview with Breit in *Times*, *Sat. Review*, when collection came out—biographical notes from old O. Henry's. Apparently papers ran this all several days ago, thereby producing some confusion. Clips being old, I am represented as having children some 8 yrs younger than they are, etc. Orosa said one article said I write and devote a certain time to career, "squander the rest of time on children." We discussed "squander."

Virginia Moreno—lecturer at U.P., this one tiny-type, excessively matchstick of bone, very shy and nice despite being a "litry per-sonality." Easy to be one here, I think. Mrs. N. said Miss M. had written a "brilliant play." From converse find, from Miss M., that this was in 1951—"Since then I have written a second, but opinion is divided into 2 camps as to which is better." Curious combo of surface shyness—no putting oneself forth à la Calisher, conversationally—and a sense of importance, underwritten by belonging to "the group"—in fact she's a mover and doer in all of them—that I would hesitate to own. Everybody calls her Virgie. A virgin perhaps too—wore engagement diamond. Had been at Bread Loaf. We talked of Frost. All these people have been to States on one grant after another— Amer. Leader Grants, etc., Rockefeller, Asia Foundation. The Morales there of course—she looks nice. N. V. M. Gonzalez the omnipresent. Someone, can't remember who, says he's heavy for symbolism—then he wdn't have fancied what I said that morning, about "new criticism."

Americans included Lewis Mattisons—they new here also. She attractive, grew up in Haiti. He very man of distinction handsome, but very quiet, and I think, lack of confidence underneath. The USIS gets a lot of former newspapermen, former radio and TV, former . . . former. So, they are not quite usual S.D. types, and sometimes one wonders, as here, as to why the "former." But being less routine they are often—well, less routine. Mrs. M. did not know Ann Kennedy or Sheelagh, though had heard of—especially S.'s rep and marriage to a Haitian, no doubt. Wasn't stiff at all abt it—as S. had said so many American old-hands in Haiti were—but said these marriages were an old story—and usually didn't work. (Had read reviews of S.'s novel, tho not the book, and said it seemed to be the "old story.") Very nice gal; liked her. Something wistful, and Fitzgeraldish about her somewhere. They invited me to go on with them to the "Barrio" fiesta to be given that night at the Manila Press Club. The "barrio" is the name of the P. village which (today's Sun. *Times*. [Fil.] in an article on the lack of literacy, says) constitutes 80% of the pop.

The U.P. club was decorated as much as possible in that style —straw booths, and stage-bamboo lattices on the ceiling, both hung with fruits and an occasional iron or stoneware pot. Beautiful vegetables—a squash like a long gourd that someone ought to paint or eat immediately, etc. Crowd mixed, Fil., Amer., Chinese mostly (Chinese

pop is of course large, tho not as large as in other non-Chinese countries of S.E. Asia). There was to be a voting for a popularity-beauty
queen; we were campaigned loudly, mostly by Amer., the minute we
walked in the door. One candidate from each race, campaign manager always another race than candidate. Bar was full, there was to
be dinner, native dances. On paper it sounds like the dullest possible
comb. of the Iowa-Beauty-Queen or whatever-dance C. and I attended, plus the usual Saturday-night do of that country club in a
dozen different colonies where "natives" are now admitted.

Nothing cd have been more wrong. The main impetus was supplied by the Filipinos themselves, their gaiety and liveliness. The
dress of the women is quite lovely, after the eye gets used to the
idea—variety of color, rather than blending or contrasting. The
"mestiza" dress typically has a sleeve shaped like a flat, large pancake, with the thin edge up-ended over the wearer's shoulder, sleeve
often transparent tulle, with a border, sometimes sequined—whatever
the wearer's fancy has indicated. Beyond that it is fitted, sheath, tho
it may have harem skirt, or other modernities or conventions. One
woman was wearing a long one all in black with gold embroidered
figures at set intervals—this was called something else—"terman"—
something like. The queen who won was Chinese—very beautiful. But
other things count in the voting—(last yr's was C. also)—father an
influential C. newspaperman, commonly called "Jimmy Go."

The dances were charming, ranging from sedate, Spanish-style min-
uet—our women, except for one or two were terrible—Filapenas and
Chinese far more graceful. Two professionals, man and woman, then
did a fandango, a wonderful dance where the lady carries first one,
then two, and finally three lighted candles in glasses (these like the
Jewish jahrzeit memorial lights) while dancing—one on her head.
Very lovely—lights in room turned out of course. One group dances
with castanets. Last dance, the tini-kling, is done by two people in
an intricate stepping in-and-out between two long bamboo poles
clapped and parted in set rhythm, on blocks on floor, by two players.
Broken ankles if you miss.

During the performance, we sat on the floor on newspaper, many of us, because the seats at sides, constructed of long light logs on blocks, collapsed twice, dumping twenty or so elegant beauties on the floor. And once a large squash fell. Nobody hurt, everybody gay. Somewhat like a square-dance atmosphere—or the one suburban Americans try for—if one could substitute for our fake farm-dirndls very polished dress on women, tiny, very elegant shoes, the heaviest of perfumes— with my usual luck I sat next to something that made Tabu an innocent floral essence—and a gaiety we cannot counterpart. Ladies passed us handfuls of a wonderful greenish-yellow flower, long, curled leaves rather than petals, and a heady smell I liked—the ilang-ilang. I held on to it for a long time. Handfuls of pennies were passed for us to throw, as a token of appreciation to dancers—not the equiv. of a catcall.

Before this we had dined on a somewhat French (head of kitchen is a Mme. Dupont) version of local foods; suckling pig, a fish mousse rather Swedish, Spanish rice tomato-style paella, with tiny whole clams with shell, embedded in it. Chinese rice balls—dead-white dough —ignored by all old hands but I had to taste, and then ignored also. Huge platter of cold fish beautifully boiled, trimmed with the usual fancies. Large shrimp, or perhaps they were a kind of crayfish, also in shells. Very nice. I was squired by Mr. Mattison and a heavy genial gent named Tull—Press attaché I think—as American as a dentist on a spree—whooping and cat-calling, and a brush moustache. Not unpleasant, and not stupid. Still. . . . Very tiny wife, rather typical embassy, living better than she ever wd at home, servants, etc., and getting rather "colonial." Sample, when talking of her new boy-cook "I don't care what he gives me for lunch, my tastes are simple— I just don't like to walk in at 12:30 and be *asked* what I *want* for lunch!" At home she wd fix herself a sandwich, and no such airs. But generally it was very pleasant, sorry not to get to know Mrs. Mattison better. So home—hotel is all of a block from U.P., but everybody travels even a block in cars.

Today, Sunday, I have loafed, written this, and am just back from the Chinese restaurant. Nothing until 7, when I meet the P.E.N. club at the U.P. club. Up since 6:30 however—cannot seem to sleep late, and it is now 5. Shall siesta. Later perhaps write about the awful slum just in back of the hotel. A bombed building or just the foundation of, in which people are living, hanging clothes—roof made of odd bits of rusted iron, tin, whatever, insides and outside curb strewn with filth—it is hard to know where the "building" begins and the refuse piles end. Yet people do seem to live here, opposite an elegant, white-washed very modern Riviera-style apartment house—opposite several, as a matter of fact. One end of the bombed-out place has walls made of the wooden boxes whiskey comes in, some distillers name still on them, all neatly stacked to fill in the interstices between whatever girders, etc., are left. I have also been reading *Six Filipino Poets*—a small book. Full of their own sensibility, very romantic. Shall I ask them, tonight, about this back alley where the clothes are washed and laid on the curb to sun, on filth? Wondered, as I passed it, how they manage for toilet facilities, etc. *Will* ask. Lighter note for the day—large, very clear sign in the window door of the beauty shop in the hotel "WE ACCEPT BODY MASSAGE." I suppose they mean provide? Or maybe not.

And here it is Wednesday, the first of October. So many things one cannot put down, and hopefully may remember—the corner sign large as life (only two Sundays ago was ?) not far from the hotel in Fukuoka, saying NUDE PHOTOGRAPHS . . . the one on a bookshop not far from *here,* elegantly gilt, saying BROWSE IN. Phillippines have had us and our language for 50 years, and it is required in schools; however, they develop their own version—in another 50 or less they may have a version of English as subtly different as Amer. is from British.

The Sunday night affair was at the Manila Press club. Small dinner in private dining room, a handsome big building. Passed the squatters on my way to breakfast—whiskey-box wall is Peter Dawson boxes—a whole wall of P. D. Dirty urchins everywhere, a music box (how cd it be a radio?) blaring within. Dunne says they have a squatter's assoc., refuse to vacate to allow building on the sites—buildings of course that wd have nothing to do with housing them. Abt 45,000 families in M. live this way—since families are large, this may mean 250,000 people.

Dinner consisted mostly of journalists, though everybody "writes" here. They are quick to award the names here—even at the U.P., where I met some who cd be only undergrads, one and another wd be introduced as a "poet," a "dramatist." Remember, at such times, how I craved such identity at that age, and wd have relished it. Might have helped too. If people *say* you are a writer, then you begin to feel yrself to be one.

But, to the dinner. I have talked so much that the questions and answers are blurring from group to group—here I remember I was asked about what a writer's "integrity" should consist of, much more talk about professional questions, etc. Rony Diaz, one of their better short story writers, was there but did not talk much. Woman writer—Alfon, just hauled into court by Holy Name Society and convicted of pornography—she is appealing it, but the Caths are all-powerful. She was fined. Has 4 children—beautifully dressed and probably rich. When found out ages of my children (this interchange all in the ladies' room) she said, "Oh writing is not difficult because of the children. It is the husbands who are difficult. I want to travel like you" . . . and she sighed.

Two gate-crashers had arrived at dinner—Nina Estroda Puyat, a beautiful woman (Chinese-Malay) whom Morales, on my right, whispered was a rich dilettante writer, and her escort, a Baron von Hagen, whom she introduced enthusiastically as having an interest in Lit., "and of course never had anything to do with Nazis." He, at opp end of table from me, was my focus as I talked, cd not avoid sight of him—face screwed up toward a vanished monocle, twirling what looked to be a silver pencil on a chain, endlessly, somewhat after the manner of *The Caine Mutiny*'s Queeg. Asked a question or two in the English accent educated Germans used to have. He sells machinery. I wonder. Good-looking man, in the straight-backed, somewhat repellent way his type is.

I am getting extremely adept at repartee—always a game I have loved but try to restrain in normal society—fear this constant seeking of my "opinion," the deference etc., is giving it far too free rein. Cd not help knowing that I was doing well. But for some good reasons too. Much talk—of the burning question here—shall they write in Eng. or Tagalog? Later in bed it occurred to me that the only answer I cd give was that the meaning must come first. It will depend on what audience they wish to address, also since every writer decides most such things for himself, it ought to be on an individual basis. But, they have romantic, Latin-revolutionary selves, like to travel in groups (also self-preservatory here, since they are not well known in the world) and think they can decide such things by ukase. Not likely to be so decided—or any literary matter. Alfon writes both ways, as she chooses. Said problem did not trouble her and I felt the others disapproved of her for this. Women are obviously the real individualists, the real revolutionaries, when once doing something apart from family circle.

On Monday I met late in afternoon, their "merienda" time, with a group in the "Listening-room" at the U.P. Recently set up, with mikes, phonograph, lounges, etc., for all-purpose meetings. "Fair Lady" Album was playing as I entered. Very lively discussion; the Pres. of the Club was a nice young man, eager to pin me down abt "ideologies"—didn't literature have an obligation to portray man in a "social situation"?—etc. I won them over pretty quickly—me and my jokes—said that surely a social situation was a part of lit., being a part of life and inextricable from, but that writers of past had been writing in terms of "ideologies" without consciously carrying such imprint, all thru history. Delivered usual imprecations against writing from labels. Was asked, by one soft-voiced girl about "pornography." Delivered usual imprec.—(without mentioning church)—about restrictions, censorship, serious art containing whole of life not being pornographic, etc.

These students, grads, yng faculty, etc., most of them, belong to U.P. Writer's Club, which has published a review *The Literary Apprentice* for some 30 yrs. Showed me some back numbers. Very respectable job—better than some of ours, and remarkable, when one considers fact are writing in Eng. Poetry, however, (like Leonard Casper's *Six Fil. Poets* collection) a court poetry of sensibility, love-moans, etc., mostly free verse—frequently can't be sure whether an image which is odd comes from the intended violence to the language that a real poetic image achieves, or from a certain insecurity abt language. Was asked if, from whatever I knew of Fil. lit., I cd say what I thought wd develop from it. Said I knew little, but from sight of city—mentioned squatters, lightly—I wd think they wd have a lit. that treated of these problems and concerns—cd not see how they cd avoid.

Afterward went to a restaurant with a group, Dunne, Miss Moreno, and about 8 students, of whom the most noticeable were Rony Diaz and Christobal. They have read everything—more than I probably. Intense, vital young men. Diaz, who had applied for a Fulbright and failed. Quieter Christobal (who has been at most of my talks and asked insistently abt function of critic, plus slightly pointed and Anti-Amer. questions) is flashier, but very brilliant. We even got into such byways as Herbert Read—they know all of Bellow, Gold, and contemp Amer. (Later, in talking to Dunne and Morales, found that C. had been one of kids who picketed embassy during the Roe case—sailor of ours who killed a F. and was whisked away for home-trial instead of being tried here). One remembered remark (most of this group is anti-Cath): Adrian C. said, of my projected talk at the Ateneo de Manila—Jesuit College—"They will kill you with dogmatic kindness."

*Tuesday*, which was yesterday, went to embassy in morning to do the elaborate fiscal business necessary to being paid, and had the radio interview. Not nearly as good as in Japan. Interviewer read my dossier aloud—which had to be corrected as it was an ancient one—insisted on briefing me "I will ask you this, and then this . . . etc." I tried to stop him twice—saying it wd be better if we did this cold, but he obviously cd not get away from his blueprint. Behind me the gals of the recording room engineers and staff, incl. McGill (former radio and crime-story writer, for Cavalcade of America) were watching. McGill runs the thing on routine lines, I fancy. Interview probably successful from Amer. viewpoint—he proceeded to ask me set questions and I to try to get away from "set," but he went doggedly on. A dud, as far as I was concerned. Capistrano, Bill's assistant, looked on sardonically—I think he understands.

Later to lunch as McG.'s guest, with Bill, at Overseas Press. Wonderful prawns again. Mrs. M. joined us, recognize her as rather drink-faced dame I had met at Barrio Fiesta. Their 15-yr-old son came in too, from American school—hamburgers, coke, and talk of school paper. (Me homesick for Pete.) They are all enjoying themselves here: as McG., who is nice, bluff type, said he found he was too old to try the TV rat-race; this is undoubtedly a fine haven.

Then to hotel for siesta before meeting with "Chip" Bohlen, our Ambassador. Naturally wanted to be in gd form for this—and naturally, of all times, fell asleep and awoke 2½ minutes before embassy driver was reported downstairs. Dressed in 5 minutes, but made it, feeling the oddness that daytime sleep always brings—from Mars I come. Had some ten minutes or so talk with "unidentified escort," probably Barnsley, head of USIS here, before I was invited in by Bohlen to handsome office with full view of harbor, Bataan and Corregidor in the distance.

Bohlen is a stopper. Pat of course knew him in Moscow, and had told me that to their minds, and many others, he was the top career man in our For. Service, the peer and better of most top men in other services. And of course, there was a loud outcry in the papers when Ike sent him here, a relatively minor post. He's a linguist, knows Fr. perfectly, studied Rus. before it was necessary to, etc. Pat of course, had not mentioned his looks—sooperb. He has an air of authority without having an air of an air of—easy manner. Talked smoothly—not yet knowing of course that I wd have no trouble there. Discoursed on the Phil—obviously a trained and subtle observer. Broke ice by showing me a clip from one of their papers (when we were talking of their language troubles), said—hoped he wdn't shock me—no, guess if I wrote for *The New Yorker* I was old enough to take.

Was an indescribably funny news clip abt a F. man attacked by another who had cut off his testicles. Yng man "disgustedly" retrieved same from garbage can where thrown, ambulance called, and testicles were sewn back on, but last statement of victim, "What's the use?"

In talking of Nakpil (Carmen) I said heard she was convent-bred—this seemed to breed female satirists, as with M. McCarthy. A glint of amusement in his eye, and again, of amusement when I said I had talked so much this tour, was thinking of taking a vow of silence, and getting rather doubtful of myself as I heard me being inexcusably glib. He quickly interpolated—"a very necessary and useful thing." Apologized for not knowing my work—Barnsley who was with us and had not said one word, asked about novel—I said its locale was "in the mind"—and added, or muttered, "a safe place."

Also we talked abt students of previous night—I indicated I thought too many middle-aged grant-getters were taking their share. Bohlen obviously interested in my reports on the Question and Answer business I had made to work on Japs, also in that I was going to meet Senator Claro Recto on my own own request. Upshot—asked me to dine informally with him and wife—only day we both had free was tonight, if dinner is not planned after the Iowa writer's meeting. Hope not—hope can dine with them—as certainly wd like to see more of the A., and have learned from somewhere that wife is in his class too.

Sent back to Hotel, almost exactly opposite embassy, by car, because "Dewey Blvd is hard to cross" said Barnsley, and it is—and because no one walks, including me. At 5:46 Fred Morales called to have me dine "informally with him and wife." I safely in black—not sure of informality. They have very handsome suburban walled house —rather a F. version of Stegners'—as he teased later, wife, is top dentist in F.—which allows him to be a professor. He delighted that I liked Diaz, who is his pet, also Christobal. I asked if I cd help get them to States—he said of course if I dropped a word to Bohlen. Dunne, who is new, and whom I'd asked, said it was all done by committees and he didn't know how to see that I cd help—though obviously he wanted to help me do it. (Nice guy, former Fulbright in France, literature. Short, about 28, Southern but not egregiously so, nice features with long curly eyelashes—my height makes these unavoidably evident. Have told him abt C.—decided to because I wanted to—nice to talk about him with some one—explaining that the "husband" in all the newspaper articles about me was not the one I was going to join in Tabriz.)

*Friday, Oct. 3rd.*

Morning and rainy. Wrote the above just now. Pace has increased here, more people want to meet, so a lot of spaces in itinerary, originally blank, have been filled. Cd not dine with Ambassador and probably will not see again, since our programs will not allow.

Back to the Morales house. . . . Fed sherry and "atis"—custard apple. Looks like a hand grenade. Delicate flavor, many seeds about size of watermelon seeds—meat bland, more like mango than papaya, very good. (Fruits are in incredible profusion here and they make ices and ice creams of all of them—many new to us.) Two other guests, one a very shy man whose name I did not catch—writer of the '30s, old friend of Fred M.'s. (Later Fred told me that his shyness—came to restaurant with us but not theater—was caused by second guest, Dr. Alzona, since she is upper class, he not.)

Dr. Alzona was at first incredibly charming—a tiny bluestocking (Ph.D. Radcliffe, studied at Harvard and other grad. schools—history) —with her dainty, wizened brown face, I took her to be in sixties, but she might be younger—told me she was in mourning for her recently deceased mother—encased in the beautiful high-draped folds of a black tulle mestiza. This style is infinitely flattering to all—even old crones look elegant—their matchstick shoulders swirled with clouds of net. How much nicer than the styles which at home often decree that the boniness of age, or just thinness, must nevertheless be revealed. She has traveled widely, though before the war. Father an attorney—she is of the older Spanish-oriented generation, I imagine, like Recto. Very civic conscious—very involved on innumerable committees, and probably a pillar of high life here—as we drove to restaurant I heard her gossiping with Belen Morales, in the back seat, like any club lady. Belen is plump, downright, nice as can be—a devoted gourmet cook—gave me recipe for chicken adobo, and was delighted to hear how to roast a turkey in a bag. (Aluminum foil is expensive here—though the M.'s appear to have plenty of money.)

We dined in Chinatown, my first taste of Peking-style, since U. S. A. is all Cantonese. Very good—innumerable dishes, shrimp in sherry and in shells, hot spiced beef in shreds, the steamed bread—like dough half-baked and no crust. Etc. Later Fred took us to the "Manila Grand Opera Theatre"—half apologizing, half eager for me to see low-life theater—and right he was.

No opera, it is actually a kind of "Palladium" music hall, vaudeville or what you will. One long feature-movie, American, just ending as we came in. A very large theater—crammed to roof. We saw a 3-act play, hr. or so in length, in Tagalog. Tale of infidelity in their equiv. of a penthouse—three comic servants—a fairy, a Chinese, and a dwarf about the size of a six-yr-old child. The Filos dislike and fear the growth of the Chinese community—merchant class which controls most of the retail trade in the islands, keeps to itself, used to inter-marry but now does not, maintains its own schools and does not take out citizenship. This hotel, the newest, is owned by one, tho not, alas for me, managed by them apparently. Manager is named Covarrubias. Chinatown is one of the oldest quarters—still use vehicles out of another age—looked like a high barouche or fiacre to me—seats about two—horse drawn, very high wheels. Relic certainly of the sixties or not much later—one cd imagine ladies of their Spanish period, leaning out of them. Only vehicle usable in Islands during last war, Fred said—called "calesas."

The whole quarter lacks the neatness of San Fr. Chinatown; this is tropic slum-style. Vendors, seated at braziers, selling hot-anonymities every where, the eternal profferers of lottery tickets, Amer. cigs, pearls —usually two big and *very* anonymous ones half concealed in a piece of tissue paper in the vendor's palm—much more insistent and serious than around the big hotels on Dewey Blvd.

The Tagalog play was a riot to them, and sometimes to me—farce-style one minute, melodrama the next—husband finally knifes wife while tangoing with her, then shoots himself. Rest of program in-cluded a very smartly done modern dance jazz ballet—Fred told me that the girls had adopted mod. musical comedy undress, etc., only recently, since the tour, some months ago, of Katharine Dunham! (So, Dunham, who started out with us as an "ethnic" dancer on a Rosenwald fellowship, is now having the reverse of ethnic effect here!) Last number was a soprano who has done a version of Carmen in Tagalog, but also appears on pop. stage. Opening chorus however was "Stout-hearted Men"—the "Mounties" number usually done at home by chorus boys virilely effeminate in Canadian M. uniforms. Here, done by Filo version of, in uniforms half military police, half I dunno. Also on program—an Amer. Negro—F. said he would be returned G.I. Crooner—sang in both languages, very appreciated by crowd. As to the fairy servant in the play—F. said they are quite Elizabethan abt that sort of humor here.

And so home, after a pineapple sherbet at a coffee shop—how they like sweets! And to bed, unable to scrape from my mind the picture of the two little boys who stood to watch us as, emerging from F.'s little Br. car, not an elaborate one, we crossed the road, no more than a half-paved muddy ditch, to the theater. They were possibly wanting to watch the car, or just to watch us—but unlike the kids in our slum districts ("Watch your car mister, watch your car!") there was no impudence. Our "poor" are nothing like these. There was a solemnity, a deep inborn awareness of difference and of resignation to it. I could not pass, and I could not give them money, which I wd have done if alone (even knowing the hopelessness of that—a sop to my conscience) because Fred had ignored them or rather passed them with a tiny shake of the head—embarrassed perhaps that he had to, in the company of the American.

Now, I must to lunch with Carmen Nakpil—and still yesterday to recount. Will send this on.

(Dear C:

Your journal, so welcome, came from Italy. I am well. Only three weeks now.

Meanwhile, this Sunday I fly down to Cebu and Dumaguete, southerly from here I think. No railroad, and no time for car.

Everything so quick. I look down at a blue bruise on my knee and think, wherever did that come from, then recall that it matches a hole made in my stocking when I fell down the step at Keio U.— way back there, another country, another civilization—and only a week ago. And you must be feeling the same.

Social pace continues fast here. More soon from H'kong or B'kok. I miss you.

Love from me.

H.)

*Saturday, October 4th*

Mailed journal to C. yesterday, and have forgotten where I left off. When one adheres to a schedule one has not cooked up for oneself, the days tend to blur. Where was I?

Well, Wednesday noon, went to visit Claro Recto (Senator), Possessor of the largest legal practice in the P.I., he is also one of the fast-fading Spanish-oriented generation. Handsome offices. He is also reverenced by the intellectual element among the younger Nationalists—there are rumors that he was a J. "puppet," but Bohlen said he had heard nothing to substantiate this. Meeting him—he is cagy, vain, intelligent, a wary old lion in his own concept, perhaps his legal mind wd inhibit any real breadth of thought, though he has the breadth of manner that comes from long dealings with many meetings with the "important" etc.

Of course he had no real idea why I was there, nor I—I cd not make him "give" though I pranced about conversationally from several tacks, even giving my best imitation of a silly woman in order to draw him out. Rather fazed me by saying that he always ended up by "interviewing the interviewer"—since of course I do the same. Had a quote from Toynbee under a glass on one of his desks in the anteroom where we waited for him—something to the effect that it is useless for a patriot to die for his country if the country dies with him in a last grand and glorious—etc. From Toynbee, —he wd not commit himself— I got him on to Russell, or rather he got me, and seemed to agree that R., whom I said I admired more, was the clearer writer. I mentioned that T. was a Jungian—no response. Showed me a sort of style dictionary—Updike—from there I tried him on Fowler, little response. Asked me if I had read *Zorba the Greek*—Kazantkakis—hadn't alas. Neither of us got much out of our "interviews."

Took Bill and Morales to the Overseas Press Club, where B. had kindly got me a press card. Then rested briefly before driving out to U.P. again to record story on tape—I did "In the Absence." They played it back and I tried not to listen, rather horrified at my voice, which comes over "urban-sophisticated" and rather "superior" in tone. Clipped. Not right for that story. Then to the Ateneo, Loyola Heights—the Jesuit college. Father Bernad, the head, writes for their journal, *Phil. Studies*, leading Catholic scholar in town apparently, as well as of course one of leading Catholics. Was determined to give it to them within terms of courtesy, and did. Wish I had tape of *that*! Can't remember all, but did emphasize that artist's voice must be "single"—no labels of *any* kind—said this in one way or other several times. Said Artist was comb. of arrogance and humility—for duration of creating his "world" he must believe in his own judgment—but only for moment— Humility is that of the search. All great and good artists interested in moral values—but must be unhampered in search for them.

One student asked typical Jesuit query, "Which is better, good ideas written badly, or bad ideas written well." Answered—what did he mean by "good" and "bad"?

At this point Father B., who remained on platform next to me at all times, started explaining *me*. This, in the pleasantest way (I think), I wd not tolerate.

He said he "thought I wd agree" that a book abt a murderer, approving same, wd not be a valuable book.

I replied, "Ah that's too black-and-white a way of putting it; a book by one of the greatest novelists in the world, Dostoievski, is about a murderer, who, though not "approved" is so presented that we "understand," and no one who reads it can ever fail to understand the little spark of murder that we may carry about in our hearts.

It went on like this, and thanks to the practice of recent days I was able to do right well.

Was asked by student whether the "sordid" should be portrayed? Went to town on that—said although I wasn't sure what he meant by "sordid," certainly what I presumed he meant was a part of life—the human condition was of all kinds and had to be so represented, otherwise we get a glossy, sentimental 19th c. etc., etc. And worse—or rather better. Was asked what Student shd read. I said—"Everything." Forget what Father B.'s comment was—again an attempt to "explain" or qualify me.

I turned to him and said: "Father, I believe one must be allowed to read everything—without censorship of any kind." How else to form taste and judgment? Said that "some people" when they thought of liberty of expression immediately thought of license—I thought rather that liberty implied self-control; latter came only from it.

Was asked whether writers came more from lower classes, didn't I think so? Again took off—said we did not have div. quite in the upper-lower way they had—rather one long, gray middle. Laughter on this. Said we had poor, but fewer so poor as here—our differences in class were economic, but mainly we were a middle-class nation.

One of the Irish Fathers, at the tea and cakes we had after, said, rather worriedly that it was "a good experience for the boys." How regimented they were, standing up politely—all thru the question, clapping when signaled! Only place I was asked for autographs. Bill D. said after he was sorry he wasn't present; Sam Capistrano, his ass't, a Fil. of Baptist descent, had reported all in high glee.

That evening went to dinner at the Francisco Arcellana's, to meet all the ones who had been at Iowa. Very dull evening, enlivened only by fact that one of the boys who teaches at Ateneo came in saying that he had pre-arranged some days ago to drive Father Bernad to join us—but went by, and Father cd not be found.

Thursday, did my little act at Far Eastern University. As I now know all these U.'s (other than the Catholic)—all private ones, are run as profit-making establishments. Thousands of students everywhere, night and day—when they arrive and leave in the evening they create their own traffic problem. Some of these U.'s necessarily low standard—F.E.U. is apparently fairly high, tho probably not as good as U.P. Very nice young woman, Miss Legarda who had heard me the day before at Ateneo, warned me that her classes here, and much of audience, wd have some lang. difficulty and not be as advanced as U.P. or Ateneo. This true, but we managed to have a lively time—again the "sordid" question. Since this is not a Cath. college in effect, but almost all students wd be, I rather think fame had preceded me.

Lunch at Harold Scheidmans of the Embassy, Cultural Div., not sure what his job exactly. Handsome villa —the nice ones here run to very large rooms opening into one another, wooden paneled walls, some use of bamboo etc. Mrs. S. a sculptor, some pieces around. He is earnest as opposed to serious, bet there's an advertising bkgrnd in the woodpile, loves polls of opinion and used wd "media" etc. Teased him consistently about polls, but he has no humor, same with wife. Very competent at his job, which must be some variant of turning paper into ideas, ideas into paper (effect of Jesuits on me!), well meaning and full of the patter, advertising "liberal" with a slight taste for modern art, and with a Mercedes. Which I envied. Much better off, the Merc., in hands of liberal writer. Wish C. and I cd acquire one. Even better off in hands of two liberal writers.

Liked their guest Ben Legarda, brother of Miss L., as I later found out, economist, Harvard trained, influential family, heads Manila Symphony Board—mother has just been appointed Ambassadress to Vietnam—was much amused at my comment on polls. (Must remember not to carry this salon-manner with me when once tour is over—how awful it wd be—but it is well-nigh impossible not to, just now, given me, and being given my head like this. Legarda invited me to Sat night's concert—all Strauss conducted by a grandson of Johann. Other guest of honor is Strickland, conductor, here again after a triumphal tour a few months ago. Much talk abt S. —very handsome, all Filapenas (ladies) adore—also a good conductor. L. said he wd try to arrange to have Strickland accompany me, saying nicely "what an entrance that

will be." Found later, thru sister, that this cd not be arranged, have
to go with the S.'s. Shall I wear black puffed sleeves, dangerously like
the "mestiza" sleeves, and be regal but not so conspicuous, or the white
sheath. Burning question which wd surprise some of my auditors of
late.

That evening went with Bill and Fred Morales to "Traviata" done
in Tagalog. Language is soft and very suited to song, much better than
Eng. which is awful in opera—did not miss Italian, until a few arias
where I realized diff. in words simply because I knew the Ital. Very
well sung by a beautiful F. soprano. Costumes good, real flashy-dainty,
in the F. way. Later Fred took us to a restaurant where had ice-cream
made of carabeo milk and custard-apple. Try that on *Gourmet* mag.
(Saw Barnad at opera—we shook hands. Church will survive.)

Friday, lectured at Santo Tomas, the less intellectual Cath. U.
—Dominicans. More of same. Sam C. said he overheard two of fathers
saying afterward "We shd have screened the questions." Was asked
about F. Sagan, as I had been on several occasions. Also the "sordid."
This time I mentioned sex. Right out loud. Said some people equated it
with sordid; I did not. Was asked some complicated Jes. question
about "truth in being, error-in-being" for the Catholic. Said I cdn't
answer for C.'s, wasn't one—a kind of sigh (horror or "I thought so"
—an "Ah") from audience. Very silly audience, high-schoolish, giggled
at everything and anything. Some nuns and teachers. In interval three
boys came up and did crooning, with a guitarist. First time ever
shared platform with crooners. Sorry to say, rather typical of the
lower echelons of Cath. educ. Head father nice however afterwards, as
well as two women teachers. Third, younger, said very shyly she had
heard that yesterday, at Ateneo, I had advised reading everything,
"even things on the Index." Said I hadn't mentioned Index, but wdn't
mind saying that I wd say this. Cdn't advise Catholics, but came from
a country where freedom of speech was guaranteed for all; I believed
that any constriction of freedom protected the few at expense of
many, and even this doubtful. Etc. Even spoke of Mrs. Lefon's pornography case with Father Panizo, who indeed was kind (I remembered A. Christobal's remark that they wd kill me with dogmatic

kindness.) Father said action had been brought by citizens of Holy Name Society—had *nothing* to do with church. I went along with this, wide-eyed; "then if they were wrong, these citizens, cdn't the church do something abt?" Oh no, said the Father. Presented me with his autographed book—on function of art. *Art and Morals*—it is entitled— glanced thru—familiar.

Whole thing a waste of time, as cd not speak on higher level cd at Ateneo. *All* a waste of time. Went home and washed hair, and thought of Tabriz.

### Monday, Oct. 6th, '58

Am down in "South," in Visayen country, at Siliman U. which is on the sea, and at the moment houseguest of Edith and Edilberto Tiempo, both writers—he head of Eng. dept here—she a teacher in it. Very open-air villa, climbing orchids outside blinds, lizards running up and down walls, ants along the window sills, and not much water in the pipes. A Presbyterian college, rather *sec*, I'm afraid, from tone of luncheon guests—but am ahead of myself.

In last entry, forgot to record that on Thursday Scheidman took me and the Nakpils to lunch. At her insistence we went to the Manila Hotel, Bamboo Room (on the water, and very posh—wish they had quartered me there) so that I might have real F. food. Rice, fish, wonderful salads and vegetables—all somewhat too sweetish for my taste.

Carmen Guerrera-Nakpil is the columnist for the *Chronicle*, deemed by all to be most brilliant of all, very easy in Eng. Had met her before at Bill's party—handsome woman, this day very elegantly attired all in pale blue, down to handmade leather handbag and shoes. (The shoes in this country very elegant—good thing I don't have time to have some made up.) She and I got along very well—talked of many things alone first, since Scheidman coyly said the scheme was to leave us together. At table however, he was his earnest, heavy self. He was surprised that Faulkner was not "like his works" etc. —I said few writers were, and a lucky thing—Carmen and I agreed loudly that we wd hate to look like our works—she has similar problems with children in schools (Catholic)—she tells them one thing—the school another. Part of her ability to say what she thinks comes from belonging to family she does—father Amb. to St. James; all family has some history of being aristocratic malcontents, I gather. Americans say her position as a writer, and as a woman is limited here, by her being outside a circle, no place to go further. She is reserved, felt we liked each other, but naturally cd not get in deep first meeting. Afterwards Nakpil took me to see the cathedral, now being restored. Exciting to see a cathedral in process, tho indeed nothing like Chartres. Stuff is all being imported piecemeal from Italy, beautiful marbles, bronze angels standing around in crates. Ocampo, the architect took us around—occasional interpolations "The Immaculate Conception will be there, and will arrive shortly." Downstairs to vaults, where there will be burial room for eleven or so Archbishops, or perhaps a round dozen—I'm always so weak on statistics. Outside the cathedral—squatters. Carmen told me they had been *in* the bombed cathedral—Archbishop offered them 65 pesos per family to move—obligingly they accepted, and moved—outside the doorstep.

Saturday, Virginia Moreno of the UP writers took me to market (stall) where I bought material for a Maria Clara blouse, of *jusi*, native woven material, if washed in rice-water should last forever, bought me lanzones—a native fruit, utterly unanalogous to any of ours, fed me a merienda of their special tea and a bibinka—pancake made of rice flour, cheese melted in, and hard-boiled-egg—a fritter, really, eaten with masses of shredded fresh coconut—then we—she, Bill and I—went to the party scheduled for me of the "working" writers. A Miss McIntosh, Barnard, on U.C.L.A. language project out here, also turned up, wanted to talk about language problem, spoke of F.'s as "they"—rather bewildered by what "we" writers began to say to each other.

Rushed back to go to all-Strauss (Josef and Johann) concert, conductor a nephew, of same. Wore the black with the big sleeves, because sheath just too warm for this country—and glad I was that formal, since discovered that newspapers had announced Strickland and me as "honored guests for occasion." Afterwards Ben Legarda, sister, S.'s and I went to the "Old" Selecta, taken by his aunt, a handsome aristocratic type—lovely face—though not an *elegante* like a Mrs. Paterno (a sugar baroness), who met us on the way to her limo— they are as dainty as Parisiennes when beautiful, and with something of the same taste—elaborate, but superb. Had mango ice cream. Nice gay party.

Sun. morning Bill took me to plane to Cebu, said the time I'd been here had been a week to remember, etc.—this in answer to my thanks for squiring me around so kindly. Both sad that one meets so many nice people whom one may never see again.

Plane ride to Cebu (in cramped small plane—but am told PAL is more trustworthy than other mechanical things in this country) was very clear. Terrain around Cebu—rings of small regular cone-shaped hills, rather terrifying since we flew so low—near enough to count the branches on the palm trees, a green doll-country rather like the models-to-scale that museums build, with cottony green vegetation, fuzzed, balled, strung and shaped, matchstick and papier-mache—only this was real and we were very near—and these are the mountains over which Magsaysay crashed. In Cebu met by Charles Ransom and wife—she Barnard again. Very nice both. Very intelligent, alert, thinking people—USIS again as distinct from Embassy. Good we have people like this abroad.

Handsome villa on sea, ten miles out of Cebu. Drove along road at sunset, and this was palmy postcard country indeed. One of the nine novena nights before a feast, people carrying lighted candles and singing as it got dark later on, now gathered in stalls along roadside—each barrio has its own festivals, each group of houses, its people carrying home their suppers, in baskets on heads, dead hens in hand, etc.

Showered, then into Cebu to "Eddie's," a very American place where had a very welcome American steak. Had martinis—in preparation for missionary Silliman. Good talk with Ransom. They are blding extra room but haven't it yet, so spent night in Capitol Hotel, a facsimile of a hotel. Shower and complete bathroom (no tubs in Islands) but no water runs in pipes, nor did they call me in time for plane—as instructed. Luckily my inner clock worked.

Plane had extra passenger, one too many, turned out to be me— apparently someone hadn't entered the reservation made in Manila. But I rode—a man took the jump seat. To such close weight-tolerance were we, one bag in which I had traveling iron was left behind— turned up somewhere in Vocational School at U. hours later—a boy scout troop had got it. Shall take all 3 back on plane with me today, and hope plane stays up.

Staying with Edith and Edilberto Tiempo, 4 yrs in Iowa, old friends of Paul Engle.

## October 13th—Bangkok—Monday

In retrospect the evening with the Ransoms seems especially nice— both superior people—he very keen on his job, she natural, intelligent, friendly—comes of an old vaudeville family. Sorry to leave. Silliman is a Pre. Mission school, very enlightened in some ways comp. to Catholics—in comparison, their somewhat eupeptic Protestantism isn't as unpalatable as it might be elsewhere. The Tiempo's met me—I stayed in their house. Embarrassingly deferential, but this became a trifle more natural as they saw I wasn't the sort. Both write—they are rather funny together and sometimes spat with each other in class, to great entertainment of all. She has adopted the "American" woman's attitude toward hubby—what a shame! He has just had a book published by Avon—she does learned reviews, poems, short stories— supposed by some to be the more talented, but rather think she may be the more academic—his mind seemed freer to me. House incredibly hot—thought I wd perish the first night. No water in taps—a pressure problem everywhere in these parts.

At 7 they were ready for breakfast—oh the missionaries—had

workshop in morning—had had one in evening at the Tiempo's home the night before. Told them they had to read writers other than Americans—they are far too oriented toward us. Truth. Wonder if State Dept. would approve of that.

Man whom I'd met before—Dr. Alden of San Jose College, here on language project, came and complimented me on my "stamina." He had heckled me mildly at one gathering—asked whom I preferred in Amer. Lit, past and present. I'd not mentioned Twain—he asked why, what wd I take on a desert island, of Twain's? Said I had to confess a preference which might seem odd in this company—T.'s Epistle to the People Sitting in Darkness (his vitriolic essay agin missionaries.) It wasn't only the old debbil rising in me; I do love that thing, and quoted it in "Two Colonials."

Had lunch with Gordon Mahy and wife—minister and in Eng. Dept. Old China hands. Discussed *Sat Eve Post* writers of my child-hood—T. Beer, the Glencannon stories. Pleasant, but same air of Protestantism in tropics. Grace before meals—amid orchids—some presented to me by Tiempos—and all the exuberant wild graces of the people and foliage. Left that afternoon with an enormous spray of white orchids E. had made for me, dripping halfway to waist.

So back to Manila Tues night. V. came with the beautiful Maria Clara blouse, but was as usual late. Bill came over to hotel, and we had a nice talk waiting. Had a beautiful penthouse room this time, double—B. took off his shoes and reclined on one bed—don't know what little V. thought—but she has been in Kansas. Tried to take them both to dinner, but he insisted on taking us—an Indonesian place—rather good.

Left next morning—Fred Morales and B. at plane. Also V., who gave me a beautiful *jusi* handkerchief—with a card—"for you to get homesick about"—this a laughing reference to her occasional home-sickness for U. S. A. Sad to leave. Who shd come up as I am clutch-ing gate-pass, coat, mss., and typewriter bag which I wd release to no porter—but a vaguely recognizable young man—Morales said, "You remember him?"

I looked. My God, it was the reporter who had tried to get my views of love-and-life when I deplaned on arrival. He ran alongside us, real correspondent fashion and thoroughly conscious of same— I said "oh it's you again!" Everybody gay. Told him how I loved Manila, etc.—he seemed abt to board with me, Fred Morales laughingly tailing us. Said to reporter "Young man you will go far. But not on this plane with me!" Said to F., B., and V., "I kiss you all," and was swept off. Last sight of B. and F. waving. Sad.

HONG KONG that afternoon. View of the utterly superb harbor— something like San F.'s. Was met by an embassy asst (Thompson), taken to tea at—my God the name of hotel escapes me already—oh, Peninsula, on the Kowloon side. Wandered across ferry to H'kong side, too tired to take funicular to top—decided that since I came from city which undoubtedly had the Indian sign on aerial views of a lighted city, cd skip. Thought of how nice it wd be to have C. along now. Wandered H'kong business dist.—everybody returning home 6 P.M., bought an Olivetti typewriter ribbon (3 H dollars, their dollar five-to-one of ours). Should have bought more. Had a hot bath at last—god bless the British—snaked thru some shops and resolved—oh the clothes, the fabrics—to buy nothing except C.'s present, which promptly did. Left at 11 A.M.—sat briefly in airport bus— with priest (F.) on his way to Rome to study Canon Law. First time he had ever traveled alone. Very impressed I knew Father Bernad.

Arrived in Bangkok unmet. Mary Sanford, the cultural attaché's wife and a Miss Z. came to meet, were stopped by official who declined to let them past gate, because they were of insufficient rank. Siamese most rank-conscious people in world. Liked both Sanfords immediately · Had dinner with them. He, as she said—he did not mention—is disappointed writer. Back in Foreign Service after 2 yrs they spent in Va. on savings and her earnings, while he tried to write—just starting when they ran out of money. She's a pip —they have a fine marriage. As always, that is pleasant to be with. She writes too, knows all my work and has followed. (Not reason she is a pip, though!) We got on fine.

*Next day—Friday*

Embassy reception to me, covered in letter to C.

> Erawan Hotel,
> Bangkok, Thailand
> Friday, Oct. 10, '58

Dearest C:

Arrived here yesterday afternoon from Hongkong . . .

Last night had dinner with USIS Cultural Officer Cecil Sanford and wife. Both from Baltimore, both nice—as USIS people uniformly are. He explained they are all mostly Democrats exiled by present Administration—no wonder I find them all so sympathetic . . .

And now, no more stalling—I've been thinking it over—do we or do we not inform your former wife, and if so what? As you say, we have a simple story and the obvious thing to do is to state it. . . . I can't envision going through all the alternative stories, comparing of notes as to what to say, and other nonsensicalities J. put you through when you and she and R. were in transit toward divorces. . . . In other words, I can't participate in her neurosis about "what people will think." . . . One can't enter her world of general deception . . . Casualness is the best: will give no pretext for drama—anything else will . . .

So as we agreed, I'll just have to play it by ear. I shan't go out of my way to say anything unless pressed, but I can't say one thing in one part of the diplomatic world, and something else in another . . .

Yesterday I was handed a large engraved invitation inviting me to meet myself at the Sanford's reception for me at the USIS center; it has also been announced in the paper; I should think it odd if the R's were not there. A reception line of at least ½ hour duration, Cecil says, then we break into smaller groups. Remember that J. cannot be any more anxious to have her "past" recapitulated. I should think if we talk she'll want news of you . . . may wish yr. exact address . . . from then on is where I shall have to take it as it comes . . . if I'm placed so that I have to tell her, I shall hope to do so where it will be the least shock—maybe better done publicly than privately. I think so, rather. Perhaps if revelation cannot be avoided, it will come best in R's presence—wisest of all, perhaps. Occurs to me I may find myself quite naturally making it to him. Oh well, maybe they aren't even there . . . I really go on talking about it only because I'm talking to you, and don't want to stop, whatever the subject. I miss you . . . And my spirits lift at the thought, exclusive of bed, of being in your company, working in your company—all the rest . . .

. . . Well, it's over, and nothing much happened—no revelations as yet, though we met, and I have a rather clearer picture, which I will now give. Stage set, I must say in my favor—a very handsome and well ordered (by Mrs. Sanford) diplomatic reception. I wore the white wool after all, green-gold Italian earrings. My mirror had been reporting horrid things to me lately—fatigue-drawn, diarrhoea face—and it was nice to know I'd exaggerated—a day in bed here yesterday and all was well. Every woman has days when she knows herself to be at her best—nice to have this one of them . . . Last night was Double Ten night for Chinese (10th day of 10th month), and most people going on to other parties. The reception line, Sanford and me and a Serene Highness (male) was well in order, trays of gimlets passing, all the American staff there, when the R's finally walked in, something after 7. I recognized them at once before they reached us . . . Gals here go in for the beautiful Thai silks which are heavy, ornate, and take height and figure to wear, as well as un-American looks. J. had got herself up in gold lamé . . . R. thinner than his pic . . . I felt rather like my own hero Pierre Goodman (who knew so much about other people's lives, without their knowing). Gazing at the gold lamé, I remembered the gold lampshades—hers, and her remark you quoted, "If there's one thing I'm sure of it's my taste." Well, that's enough—it was over in a minute. She was very cordial and plunged in at once: "I know of you through my former husband, Curtis Harnack, who was your colleague at Iowa last year." Since she looked to me exactly like one of the faculty wives she so looks down upon, that put the final touch to the picture. I smiled, and said, "Yes." And that is all I said.

R. quickly intervened: "I am wondering—how does one get to

go on a trip like yours?" I explained—you've heard the story, of how, meeting Dick Blackmur at a party, he told me to write to a Howland E. Haroldson at the IEES, then the IEES' letter to me, just during McCarthy-time, saying ominously, "Yes, we know who you are and what you are doing"—etc. R. said, "Ah, I see. One goes to a party." . . . I think he was trying to get past J's mentioning you; no doubt it bothers him. The line pressed behind them and they moved on, she saying she hoped they would see me again. I felt that normally it wd be unusual for a woman to refer to past husband in order to make time with honored guest. She must want to talk to me of you . . . and is still using you against R.—the old ploy. Doubt if ever in the world I would prefer him to you, but am sincerely grateful to her for being giddy enough to do so . . .

This will probably be my last to you from here . . . tomorrow speak at PEN group—Prince (and Princess) Burachatra Prem. Met them yesterday. I asked the British Council gent, very nice, to "heckle" me, British-style. Will be a difficult talk otherwise, since I'm told they know so little—and I can't and won't condescend—but will manage. No doubt the R's will be there. Don't worry. Think about us. As I shall.

My love.

H

*Saturday, Oct. 11th*

Brooded too much on my responsibility to C., to do as he wants about not telling J. we are to be together. Was there a bitchiness in me that wanted her to know, regardless? Was it not better to clear air as matter-of-factly as possible, and have done? Etc. Wrote too much about it to C. Repeated to myself what his earlier letter said to me. "You see, I need you dear." Yes, for perspective, I need him too. Ultimate decision—I cd not skulk. Think he will agree. We have told the one lie—which doesn't seem too terrible a one—since to all intents he and I are more married in spirit and flesh than those who are legally. But further, I can't seem to go.

*Sunday, Oct. 12th*

Sat aft Mary had taken me to see the temples and the statue of the reclining Buddha. Wonderful gay, ceramic temples, with snakepoints at roofline, orange-clad monks all about. Many Chinese figures, large and small, at temple doors and in gardens, brought over as ballast in ships. Palace is 18th century. Loved it all—a gay architecture, un-Christian, with the pervading Buddhist sense of the "avoidance" of suffering, which so explains the "East." This is in part what is "mysterious" to us. In morning M. had also taken me to Jim Thompson's famous shop. Bought white silk, and went to M.'s dressmaker to have made. Jim invited me for dinner, for Sun. night, and is taking me to see weavers on Wed.

*Sunday aft*—had the P.E.N. club, which was a riot. Their first meeting. Hours of Siamese speeches, then Nilawan Pintong, the guiding spirit, introduced Cecil to intro me—me with orchid on shoulder etc. I talked a bit—Ninon then interpreted me at length—but only about two questions were asked, then suddenly things got wildly off track, Vietnam had been mentioned. Person after person came up, grabbed one of mikes and spoke. Books, literature, P.E.N. and me left far behind. Prince Prem asked one question—was Amer. interested in S.E. Asia books (he has been courted by Russians—we haven't courted him) and another pro-Communist asked abt book clubs with intent to point up commercialization of U. S. A. All Amer. and English hilarious about what happened—"a typical Thai business," said they. Went downstairs—we were in Auditorium of Priests Hosp—for tea—Princess Poon, a tiny gem of abt 70, who had taught in San F., came up and sat next, also the Stiers, Cultural Asst.—another nice type—and wife. Mnwhile I had glimpsed the R.'s in the audience, and they had followed our group downstairs, along with the Enrights (Denis—Donald Keene's friend, who had spoken to me at reception and promised to see me again). J. had on purple dress so cd follow with tail of my eye—obvious she intended to get to me no matter what. Much business of being stalked—she of course cd not know I was watching

maneuverings—I left one group, attached myself to fringe of another
—she determinedly following, all innocent-eyed. They hung around
to very end; at one pt she attached herself to Princess Poon behind
me—I ignored—after all I had met scores of people day before and
cd be excused for not remembering. To no avail. Nobody left but
Sanfords, Stierses, and Nilawan and me—we were invited to Stiers's
for cocktails—but still the purple dress was on my tail.

Mary Sanford paid them no attention, although she is a very polite
Virginian. Said later there was something about J. she didn't like
although she hadn't the slightest idea what it was, and hadn't pursued
the acquaintance. So maybe my reaction isn't as biased as I had feared.
Gathered this might be general fem. reaction to J., and possibly accounts for their social position here, or lack of really "in" one—
women are very important in social life here, handle invites, etc., etc.
In J.—I think it is the "little me" attitude, which contradicts an air
of calculation, or "plotting," which comes out in eyes nevertheless.
Manner is sweet and poised—but something, whatever it is, is false. I
think she is jealous of most women.

Anyway, calculation prevailed. R. came up to me and suggested
I talk to some of his Thomasat students in Journalism—his school is in
session. She right at his elbow—suggested it wd be better at their house,
and invited me for dinner. I pleaded prior booking, referred her to
Cecil—she said insistently that session mght go on for hrs, students
might never leave, we had better plan on dinner. Cecil said O.K.—later
I told Mary I might like to get out of dinner there and she said she
cd manage it. So—the tete-a-tete I had hoped to avoid is all set I suppose. R. is to call for me in car.

Later had cocktails at Stierses—such nice people again—frank, open,
educated—and dinner at J. Thompson's wonderful Eastern house. In-
describable, will describe to C. President of Thaibok there—a British
woman, very attractive, obviously formerly in dip. service thru husband—old China hand—30 yrs in East. Talked of Lewis. Invited me
to look her up when I return to U. S. Wonderful Siamese food, silent
serving-men at elbow, international talk. Longed for C. to see this
hse. Home very late.

Today get interviewed by Eliz. Ortiz of *Bangkok World*, paper owned by Darrell Berrigan who has writter for *Reporter*, etc.—met him at lecture. Miss Ortiz does women's page—I suppose I shall be asked about family, husbands, etc. Irritable impulse to tell all in paper, and have done. Tomorrow to be interviewed—on TV I think—by Prince Prem. Wednesday dinner with the Piersons, Asia F. head. Sunday, dinner with the Prems. Etc. This will be a social time, but still exhausting. More dates coming up. All this will be romantic to remember—wish it were over—fretted by—Left at this point. Embassy car downstairs to take me to get routine work over—finances, ticket to Tehran, etc. Asked to go on 24th—gives them 2 weeks here.

Was going to say—fretted by a lot of things, still slight waves of dysentery—feeling is like that of top of head slightly above rest of it—modest recurrence of period—Mary S. says everybody has trouble with that out here, climate does it—general feeling of impatience with myself for being so ungrateful about this "experience"—with suitcases and doors for having to be locked and unlocked, with J. for being such a nuisance, and again myself for being bothered. Curt will understand all. Bless him.


*Thursday—Oct. 16, '58*
Have been lazy, tropic-affected in various ways, but real reason haven't written is because soon shd be able to talk to C. —and some of what I have seen wd take long verbal effort to describe—this is a country suited more to color-movies than to words. Or, if words, Somerset Maugham country even yet. Mary and I have had much fun about that—she's a dear, and a woman I wd be happy to have for my friend. Yesterday, at the Sports Club, reclining like two Mrs. Pukka Sahibs, she said, "Hortense, those flowers on the other side of the swimming pool—they're frangipani." I said "Oh"—"Oh Mary—honest"—I *was* really awed—being here, seeing what one had read of since childhood—it was all in my tone, she understood perfectly, and we burst into gales of laughter. But I'm ahead of myself.

Monday, as far as I can remember, did nothing but laze in room, have a dinner in dining room. Tuesday Mary took me to Johny Siam's, the famous jeweler—he's a Chinese Catholic. I bought a set of the wonderful brass and horn cutlery-ware; each piece only costs abt 50¢. C. and I shall need anyway. For largesse, bought a betel-nut container for an evening bag, and one for Bennet. Resisted—quite easily, Johny's "Why you no want star sapphire—very cheap." They are, too, as are star rubies, etc., but unless I were going to deal in precious stones, or sell in States, or had lots of dough, the Siamese jewelry doesn't interest me much—even earrings. And I can't see carrying an unset ruby around Persia. (N.B.—the cutlery must not be washed in hot water.)

In afternoon was interviewed on radio—round table headed by Prince Prem, a young Britisher, Peter Bee, who is P.'s asst at Chulalongkorn (amid his multifarious activities—and Prem is always telling you how mult, 54 committees, P. is head of For. Languages and Eng. at Chula) and Irene Something—British woman who is in business here—Carrier Air Conditioning—has a typical TV personality—asks seemingly idiotic questions to warm up. Also a Siamese, name unknown, lecturer in Sanskrit at U., has idiomatic command of Eng— and whenever an idiom came up, interpolated in tape for Audience— Sample, "unsolicited mail"—what he did with that I'll never know— Cecil had briefed me a bit—thinking Prem might get Anti-American on air, but thanks to dizzy Br. dame, and Peter B.'s real interest in writing—etc, we stayed mostly on me and writing per se—although Peter and his lady compatriot said right out loud how little Siamese lit. there was, and how poor—saving me from asking.

This is a unique country—pleasure-loving, fascinating in many ways I shd love to explore—what one must not do is to bring preconceived notions to it—searching for what one will not find, and ignoring what is. Cecil has given me the book of beautiful prints of life of the Buddha, which I shall treasure. (USIS publication—"most important gesture we have made." Unique for U. S.).

Afterwards, Prince P. took Peter and me to tea—in the car I managed at the same time to ask him innocently about his trip to Russia, and to get him to agree that "we writers" (flattery) simply dried up when we were not allowed to speak freely. His trip to Russia may have flattered him (Cecil says they rolled out the carpet—even printed his book in R. and gave it to him—possibly a limited edition of three, but still.) But after all Prem is a product of Br. schools, I think Eton as well as Oxford—and he knew damn well what I meant. Also the British-reared love frankness, and I was. Told him about *Dr. Zhivago*, and Pasternak's troubles in getting it printed, gov't trying to get it back, etc.—and mentioned it was best-seller in U. S. Cecil highly glee-ful when I reported. Had informal cocktails and dinner with them, folded at 9:30 and went home—Jim Thompson to take Mary and me to the weaving compound where his silks are made.

This trip was where movies were needed. Jim was of course written up in *Time*—he has revolutionized or rather created a silk industry here—it is a fabulous story. (The full story of Thompson's career, and strange disappearance in 1967 is told in *The Legendary American*, by William Warren.) The compound is located right behind one of the "modern" streets—as is all of Bangkok really—the modern thorough-fares are undistinguished, characterless. Smack behind it, one comes to the canal, wooden house after house built on teak poles, catwalks between—water beginning to rise over these. Boat-woman in huge coolie hat rowed us across. The houses, shanty-like at first to the West. eye, are actually made of water-resistant teak (as are all the beautiful highly polished floors in the villas), here gray and water-logged, but sturdy, often carved and fretted very prettily. Weavers have actually grown rich—run to lino and awful middle-class furni-ture, etc.—inside their houses the looms, naked babies, women crouch-ing, vendors going up and down with huge communal vats of food —children swimming off the door-step—washlines strung along the cat-walks. An incredible and wonderful mélange. And an absolute melt of heat of course.

We went thru, Jim talking to the weavers thru his S. foreman—silks in all warps and woofs, princely all the way. Then went to see house J. is building right on canal—Prince of the weavers he. An extraordinary life. He is lonely, divorced, and I think. looking for a lady—very nice—a bit of a name-dropper. (Barbara Hutton had come here in high heels—he was glad I hadn't.) Was nice to be coupled with B. Hutton—or was it? Anyway we got on, might even have got on better—what an opportunity I have let slide—Queen of the weavers, life on the Silken Canal! His house will be beautiful. Presented me with a really gorgeous—no other word, silk stole in the reds and oranges I particularly admire. Left after one last house, presided over by betel-chewing old beldame who had just thrown her daughter-in-law out. Most of weavers Moslems—daughter-in-law was Buddhist. A son or a nephew studying in U. S.—at Johns Hopkins! When we meet foreign students in the U. S.—how can we possibly understand the gap that lies between? Mary says she has a Siamese friend, educated Radcliffe, a princess, whose mother is a betel-stained crone. Understand one gets quite a charge out of betel—wd try. But am told it comes in a kind of gum which is handled in the bazaar covered with flies, etc. The mouth of a habitué is a terrible sight.

Back to hotel, where I had to walk thru lobby literally wringing out dress which clung to me like a bathing suit—dunked everything, including hair—one washes it here every two days—or at least I do, since its thickness increases so with heat that I cdn't be dinner-tidy otherwise. Surprised to find that it was only 10:30 A.M.—we had started at 8. In afternoon, M. and I went to Sports Club—it is, as I said, absolute Maugham. Magnificent pool, louvered-shuttered clubhouse, very swish and white with a glittering bar—roofs of Chulalongkorn Univ. in background—very gay with henna tiles, ending in white snakepoints. Rather nice and breezy—M. said they lived here during dry season as much as possible.

Pleasant enough—I shd think one cd make a highly tolerable life for oneself here as long as one was not doing too much brainwork— the climate is pretty de-energizing for that—one needs a lot of sleep, etc. But for pleasure, company, social gaiety, I shd think a woman ought to find it fine—what J. is crabbing about can't see—this is just the sort of place where she and R. cd devote hours to her and to "life together" as she had told C. that R wanted to do for her. Not the place to devote oneself to work in an art—but she didn't want a man like that anyway. Well, n'importe. (But reading over what C. said her letter contained, I am rather sure that she may even harbor ideas of joining him—if asked—in Iran—her fantasy will easily extend there.

SEIZURES OF LOVE AND WORK 217

After all it is on this side of the world—what easier?) And since instinct has called the turn on what she will do so far, I shall try to make things quietly clear tomorrow.

In evening had dinner with the Piersons, the Asia Foundation head —dinner for me. Beautiful house, formerly occupied by Noel Busch and wife, (Jesus—the "boy" just walked in no by-your-leave, to take breakfast tray—and me at a typewriter in bra and nothing else)—whom Sanfords miss much. (Mary Busch unique, knew more Thais in different and opposing parties, political and social, than any other Amer. woman ever has—Prince and Pr. Chumpat, who are very anti-Amer and cranky in one way or tother, gave her a farewell party the like of which Bangkok had never seen.)

I sat next to Mr. Bruce, delightful Br. Council man—a Scot—we twitted each other in the Br. way and had a wonderful time. Then he rose to make a toast to me with the wine—asked me—"What is your other name?"—I quavered "Harnack"—and he thereupon toasted Miss Calisher—Mrs. Harnack—and a toast to the absent Mr. Harnack. He had already heard I was going to Iran. Criminy. What if the R.'s had been there—a Somerset M. situation indeed—but they weren't. Forgot to say that on Monday, after Prem broadcast, when had been interviewed by Eliz. Ortiz, beautiful Britisher married to U. N. rep here, I asked her to leave out names of husbands, children, etc.—she very tactful about same, but did ask to say that I was going to Iran to join husband.

Today, *Thurs* go to lunch at Mary's—some Siamese women to be there. Not air conditioned, I am told—so shall have to wear cool black, but all right since it is here. Siamese do not like one to wear black to their homes—ill omen—so I can only wear it where hosts are Western. Nobody briefed me on this!

*Saturday, Oct. 17, '58*

The luncheon Thursday had that familiar aspect of ladies luncheons all over world. As Mary said later—"We none of us want to give them or attend them—everyone knows it—but there we are." Something

dull and a trifle wrong about ladies sitting down to glittering table,
many courses—we had champagne to toast the "departing"—Rachel
McCarthy, very nice gal who goes on to Taipeh—had lived yrs in
Hongkong, which she adored and hated leaving, now sorry to leave
here. She's a very tall, handsome girl who Mary said loves clothes–
the "Mme Recamier" of Bangkok, said M. introducing her. We got
on very well, also Mrs. Rims, a white-haired beauty of about 30—in
fact there are either a great many pleasant and attractive women here,
or else, what's more likely, Mary's friends are particularly so. Rachel's
husband is departing head of USIS. Later that afternoon we went to
the embassy for a reception for them and the incoming Garnishes.

Embassy not air conditioned; had been warned it was black-tie–
had one gimlet and sprouted sweat like a fountain—had to mop me with
gloves. If here wd have dresses made like bathing suits with skirts—
no straps, etc. Very dull business, such receptions; talked to a great
many people, fended off the compliments that are a part of dip. life.
I know that I am apparently a success with what little the Thai have
seen of me—Cecil has told me and several others—it's funny actually.
They don't care a hoot about my "intellect"—but they approve looks,
manner, and curiously enough my voice, which they keep comment-
ing on—maybe have been subjected to too many dames from Chicago.
But it wd certainly be ruinous to the character—what little I have
left of it, to go on with this tour. *Only the book will cure.*

Yesterday, Friday, continued the waking at dawn, which makes it
very hard to stay awake for all the social dos in evening; went swimming in pool. Latter is one of loveliest I have ever seen—free form,
rather like my blue Italian earrings, paving has grass interstices all
around, little bridge over a stream at one end, whole pool marble–
rimmed and fringed with rosebushes, —lovely to come up from water
to hang on and meet a velvety dark red rose, or a yellow-monk-colored
one, as you open your eyes. Has the typical Thai posts, like flagpoles
with crowns on them—four on the right-hand side from my window—
on the other a kind of pagoda-niche with the gay Thai roofline.

As I swam I found myself liking the life better and better—sybaritic
me. Hope an attack of dengue (break-bone fever) won't arrive to

SEIZURES OF LOVE AND WORK

change my mind. But I am beginning to catch the special flavor of the place, feel friendly toward it—as in Manila. One nice thing—no real poverty here—to be a privileged foreigner is far easier than in a place like Italy for instance. The missionaries don't make much headway here, tho they work hard—one of the maids here is a Christian, she told me—I imagine these are fairly declassée. Have met several young Thai Princesses, Momrajahwong class, who divorced their prince-husbands. This is "not done"—one does not divorce anybody in the Royal family and keep class. These declassée ladies have found a simple solution—marry white men, who are of course slightly declassé to begin with, in Thai eyes. Quite well-placed young men, sometimes. Foreign service etc.

Mary came—went to dressmaker's for fitting on white dress. Handwork lovely—Dress wd be in the $100 or more class at least at home—abt $10 each for material and sewing, here. Since was to go to the R.'s in afternoon, found myself again irritable, wondering why J. was not happy here—this country built for personal pleasure. But I know really. One wd have to really love the man one was with, feel close, in order to trail happily through all the gay detail of living here. Dead-sea fruit without it.

Returned, had much too much lunch—Muslim-style curry—fascinating (for once, not always). R. called, asked whether I had transportation, said interpreter was not necessary, had Sanford got one?, wanted to know what time we were coming, etc. I had asked students to arrive at 4. Didn't know exactly why he called me, instead of Cecil. Over phone his voice is very tentative, pauses, next door to a stutter or stammer, but not quite. General impression of indecision, pleasant enough—but just not a very firm personality.

Cecil came for me—very glad he was to go with. He said he wanted to see what went on—thought it might be rather a futile afternoon; he wd stop things and get me out of there if "things went on too long." (We were to go to a play in the evening; command-performance, King and Queen to be there, so again black tie.)

I had told Mary some of the situation—that J. had been Curt's wife and did not know about C. and me now. Also told her she was at liberty to tell Cecil—I never think it is fair to ask a wife to keep anything from husband—also impossible. Disliked not revealing that C. and I were not yet married,—since they are honorable, and wd certainly understand—but cd not put further burden on them. Cd not tell whether Cecil knew, as we drove off. But he was certainly a rock to have along. A fine man—works like a drover at his job, too.

The R.'s live very near the Sanfords. Very charming, adequate villa with exceedingly pleasant garden, lawn, shrubs, tucked away down typical walled road. R., J., and baby in carriage with baby-amah (native nurse) grouped in doorway as we arrived. Had feeling that she had "arranged a family group," and that she was constantly posing in one way or another, during afternoon. Felt that this was always so—she is busy "creating an impression" and goes about it in a very poised way. But one is conscious of the poise—think I wd have been even if I were total stranger. She was discreetly but firmly "behind" everything—and not too far behind either. We had no sooner got into living room than she "suggested" to R. that it wd be better if we had students move to terrace, we followed, she had a chair planted in a circle and "guided" me into it, saying "Chair of honor for you is ready." She was the "hostess," and R. followed amiably, altho it should have been his show. About 6 students, only two who spoke fair English, one, who work's for StanVac and edits the house organ, had been in U. S. for yrs, spoke very well—this the "interpreter." Conversation mostly with him.

When she has arranged us, J. comes and sits right behind my right shoulder-blade and places baby in carriage beside her.

I began to feel like Gulliver, as the Lilliputians wove their strings. Use of baby interested me—since everyone has an amah here, J. was not in position of Amer. wife who has to have baby with her—felt again that she was "posing" as charming mother-and-child. Baby very blond and blue-eyed with knitted brows—looks like R. even more than like J.—not a trace of Curt that I cd see. If one cd determine paternity for sure by looks, then one cd say almost unequivocally that baby is not C.'s. I put on glasses for sure. No, it was as I had always thought—she must have good reason to know that child is R.'s, and indeed had never averred otherwise. So that at least I can tell him.

Then R. chilled my blood by saying that since students were journalism, he had had idea that they cd interview me—like a real inter view, me, my life, my writing, etc. I had the presence to say "Oh let's keep it to me as a writer."

Young man on my very near left said—beginning valiantly "Is Miss Calisher your pen name?" I said, Oh no, it was my real name—that writers had about given up 19th-century practice of *nom-de-plume*. Cd see questions about home and husbands looming, but managed to turn question on to writing, and there we stayed.

Interpreter-guy had done a thesis in States on Confucius—so luckily questions became very metaphysical. R. said almost nothing. Cecil helped valiantly too. R. is strange, indecisive manner, but observant, one *must* think, underneath. J. had drinks and cakes brought, then moved herself and baby facing me, and scrutinized me. Later the conversation took a turn as to whether writers shd stay in Universities and get Ph.D.s—with a great swoosh I launched into C.-and-my favorite diatribes on this. Said it produced writers who ended up writing about writers who were writing novels in universities—like a succession of mirrors reflecting one another—everybody laughed. And here J. made her only contribution; saying indignantly "But what about support. How are they going to support themselves!" My inner comment—she meant, "How are they going to support ME!"

Answered J. by saying that the problem, of support, had to be solved individually—I had taught for a year for economic reasons—idea was not to go on doing it regularly, or rather not to fool yourself that could be a prof. and a writer too. Question of Penn Warren and A. Tate brought up. Said that they had professorial position *because* of being writers—and that they didn't rate with the real ones anyway—Warren vs. Hemingway and Faulkner for instance. Mentioned Trilling's "Of This Time" as the only real story by a prof.

J. continued to scrutinize me. Am pretty sure now that some news of C. and me had trickled over here. I finally ended converse on this topic by saying that writer's lives had problems, just like anybody's —personally I wd feel it better for a writer to dig ditches to support his family rather than study for Ph.D.—of course there was a hazard here too—a tractor might fall on him. Cd see J's attitude, so often indicated by C—she feels that one ought to be able to "square away" every "problem" by pre-intellectual consideration of the "pamphlet" covering same. I know, as C. knows, that life is too slippery and evasive for this; pursues its own tragicomical path, and can never be "squared away" in this fashion. As my father used to quote—"a little knowledge is a dangerous thing."

Anyway, Cecil finally brought rather fruitless discourse to end— we rose to go. J. got him off in corner, seemed not to want to let him go. (Mary had told me that she had remembered why she avoided J. —evening they first met, M. & C had rose to go, having a pressing engagement at embassy and having clearly said so, but J. continued to talk to C. and kept on stringing things out; they cd not get away, were late and annoyed.) Meanwhile R. talked to me—asked me where next stop was—I said Teheran, and that I was looking forward to cool weather. Was I going home then? Etc.

So at last I took the plunge, and said no, I was going to stay in Iran six months or so—and I suddenly had a feeling he knew about C. and was waiting. So I said I had been meaning to tell his wife, C. and I were married you know, and were going to be there.

R. said "Oh, I thought C. was going to be in Tabriz. Teheran is dry and dusty isn't it? But we have been looking up Tabriz on the map—it seems higher."

Replied that it was in mountains 4,000 feet up—I looked forward to, as like cold weather, etc. Asked if R. had ever been to Iran—he said no, asked if C. had found a house?

I said yes—we were going to write there, as C. reported teaching wd not be too arduous for him—C. had finished his book.

R. asked if he had submitted—I said he had left with agent before departing. R. at no time evinced any surprise when I told him abt C.—since I do not know him cd not tell whether this was his regular, noncommittal manner or not—but hardly think so. To be that controlled, when a woman tells you she is so connected with your former friend, your wife's former husband, and in view of parlous history shared by all—is hardly credible. Felt that Triems or Springers or somebody must have hinted, and that it was indeed a good thing I had calmly stated what I had—whether or not they believe. (Getting ahead of my reportage.) I mentioned that C. and I were exchanging journals—in order not to have too big a backlog, mails being bad on a tour like this.

He said—"Yes, we have not heard for over two months."

I said, "You mean, from Stateside, family etc?"

He said, "No, I mean from Curt," and again said they'd been looking up Tabriz.

I did not have heart to tell him that C. had asked J. not to write, but she had. It is apparent that C.'s letter to J., terminating correspondence, never was seen by R. I remembered how annoyed J. was before, when C. wrote his letter to R. saying he was really through. She wants all to be under her control, to manipulate as necessary. Ordinarily I wd feel that I was being paranoiac about this—how can one suspect that baby-face air of normal American wife, of such undercurrents? But there it is—as it comes out, piece by piece.

So we were off, the group again at the door. J. took baby from amah and followed us to car with it—leaned in and asked me, of all things, was I well provided with mosquito lotion. I said yes, Sanfords had long since indoctrinated me, etc. At last she let Cecil, already in car with me, drive on.

Mystified. Was she still posing, mother with child? So that in case I was with C., I cd report on pretty picture or observe for myself? Was the picture "You may be going round the world and be Miss Calisher, but I am the real woman, with child, home, husband, etc.?" She cd hardly be concerned about my mosquito-troubles at this point —on the terrace wd have been the time. Or is she simply a woman who can never separate the wood from the trees, details mixing inextricably with important things? Dunno. Final conclusion—if had met her under totally casual circumstances—we would never have struck any sympathies. She would have been slightly jealous, as she is of

women, particularly those who are not her inferior in taste, equip
ment, or achievement, but she wd have tried to cling slightly nevertheless because it is important to her to believe that she belongs with a
"preferred" group—whether celebrities, minor and for the moment,
like me, or big-shot-on-campus, as R. may once have seemed to her,
etc. And I? I am afraid I wd have found her attitudes rather dull and
passed on anyway, since her warmth is rather patently one of manner,
not, as with Mary S. for instance—both—of manner, and from the inside. And this, which I have written at such length so that C. may
read and we may both proceed to more fruitful mullings—is the END
OF CONJECTURING.

*Later Sat. Morning*

Indeed. That's what I thought. Almost precisely when I had put
down this last and decided to go for swim, phone rang—R. calling,
had I had breakfast (11 A.M.) and cd I have coffee? Met him in lobby,
went to small bakery tea-shop in hotel arcade. (Immediately greeted
in passing by Mrs. Unger, wife of Deputy Ambassador, whom I am to
dine with on Monday.) R. very nice, said there had been a lot of marry-
ing—wanted me to tell Curt that "his wife" (E.) had just got married
to the lawyer in Philadelphia. Said when one's former spouse married
there was always a "feeling"—went on about this in a tentative way—
point he was making was that J. was doing a TV program tomorrow
—he hadn't told her my information as "didn't want to disturb her."
Also didn't want me to feel strange, being in a foreign country, in this
situation.

Said I didn't feel strange. We had a long talk. I said that I had
seized opportunity to tell him since thought it wd be better to have
him break to J.—he agreed. He wanted to know where we had married
—I lied and said N.Y. Discussed Mex. divorces—said my lawyer had
told me cd be disbarred for absentee ones—I had gone for mine—but
did not indicate when. Did not feel need to be devious with R.—he is
a nice person. But he is not his own person. So I kept to simple story.

R. suggested possibly that when he had told J. we cd all have dinner

together on Sun. I declined—he pressed me to say why. I said I thought
his wife tended to want to involve people in her personal dramas—I
simply didn't wish to be involved. He said there wdn't be any drama
—this of course contra to fact—otherwise why is he afraid to tell her,
afraid she wdnt be able to go on TV if knew etc?

I said—of course, "I don't mean she'll throw a plate at me, or I at
her"—but we wd either Not talk about or Talk about—and I didn't wish
to, either way. He said he was sure she hadn't an inkling about C. &
me, persisted in wanting me to be "frank" about why I thought she
wd still be concerned—so I said I had been rather embarrassed to tell
him, that the reason he had not heard from C. was that C. had written
earlier asking her not to correspond. He smiled and said his wife was
a "great little letter-writer"—I said "yes" but this had been a direct
request by C. And two letters since.

He wanted me to be "frank" about letters further—but I simply said
she had said her parents were worried sick abt C., rest of letter long
one abt herself. But farther I wd not go.

Cd not possibly tell the man that J. had written C. about her dis-
satisfactions, about "moving on." Have distinct feeling that J. in my
spot, wd not have been so protective of me—viz what she did to R.'s
wife—but nevertheless cd not. Poor guy.

I did ask what he thought wd be gained by our sitting down together
all cozy-like. He flushed and said that when one felt guilty about
having injured a person, one wanted to repair. How mixed up he is,
or how mixed she has made him; How cd our being cozy smooth over
things, if C. was still hurt? I think she has made a great thing of how
hurt C. still is—apparently she thinks he has rushed off to Persia to lick
his wounds, and probably keeps this picture well in R.'s mind. *Merde!*

So I repaired this picture at once. Said he need not feel guilty; that
I didn't think C. had any great resentments toward him now—or
brooded abt J. to any great degree. Drew a deep breath and said
that C. had said that the only thing he cdn't forgive her for was playing
one man against another as she had. R. nodded. I said we were in love,
that we were not jealous of each other's work but tried to foster it—
that this was the delight of my life, as with C. That we had been "at-

tracted" first (I didn't want him to think we just held hands) but had found out how well we did together—told how we had worked in cottage. Said that in mismatings everything fretted one—but that when one had basic aims the same, these frettings tended to disappear—that C. and I did not mind when left by each other to write—it was a mutual "desertion"—we met in evening and exchanged—worked well when we were with each other. Etc. He said he was glad to hear that C. was happy—that he should be with "such a glamorous and charming person" as me. I tried not to simper. Told him more about C.'s novel, what Snow had said of his work, what I thought. Said he was a real writer, that oftentimes the sacrifies a writer wd make for his work seemed hard-minded to outsiders—but that C. and I did not have this to come between us. He asked what C. wd do next—I mentioned California, but said we didn't know. R. thinks he will go back to teaching. Likes it and magazine world too hectic.

And that was about all—we had talked a bit about divorces, agreeing that Mexican ones wd "hold up" pretty well—he said that his lawyer had told him that in any case they cd not be requestioned or fought by people involved. In other words, C. cd not protest J.'s and vice versa.

Wonder if he had idea, kept warm by J., that C. might protest? I don't know. This is tne mélange one gets into anywhere in her aura. It is obvious that he has to move on eggshells with her. Not me. So I thanked him firmly for coffee, for talk, but made it quite clear that as sensible people wd be best to drop whole matter, live our own lives.

He did persist a bit, saying he hoped I wd get to see more than embassy people, who tended to circumscribe one. (Probably she has already begun to propagandize on stuffy embassy, as she did on "stuffy" Grinnell faculty—the technique of disabusement) I said yes, but Sanfords were perceptive people—a delight in fact, that I was meeting lot of Thais, dining with Prem, Prince Suphat taking me to Temple and to Palace, etc, going up-river tomorrow. He was nice all the way thru—but I think for some God-damn reason, I can't tell why, thought that things wd be better if I would come to see them, make everything all right, etc. Too nice to press. But I was not going to fall for "let's all be civilized" lesson from Pamphlet 3 of Liberal

American Attitudes. Look at all the time, breath, ribbon, ink I've wasted already!

And more. Forgot to say that R. said he thought C. "would have written" to J. about us. I said since C.'s wish was to drop correspondence, there was no point in his taking up pen to so inform. C. assumed she wd eventually hear, as people do. Tried to make it clear to him that we had our own concerns, not violently concerned with "What will *Jane* think!" As of course, he is.

FINIS—GOING FOR A SWIM, dammit.


*Monday, Oct. 20*

The dates get near, am now preyed on by usual fear that plane will fall down, on final lap of this endless journey. BOAC has a ground strike, so must change original plan to fly Cathay Pacific to Rangoon and BOAC there. Going to embassy this morning to check.

On Friday night went to Command performance of the play the USIS staff was giving—*Teahouse of Aug. Moon* with mixed cast. Not at all a bad performance for amateurs—they were afraid that Sukini, the part of Okinawan interpreter, might blow his lines because of the presence of the King—but he hammed beautifully.

The Sanfords and I sat in the second "diplomatic" tier, slightly to the right of and behind the Royal Box—two armchairs set in a small enclosure and several feet from each other. I was so placed that I cd see the right eyeglass lens of the King from behind—as if I too were looking thru it. Very thick and cloudy. He has one glass eye—a boyhood accident. (This is of course the King whose brother-King was found shot dead in bed.) He seemed absolutely reactionless thruout—this, I am told, is his usual demeanor. Loves jazz, however. Queen is as lovely as I had been told—movie-star caliber—with one of their incredibly narrow-beautiful torsos. (Mary said almost all of them have this, but invariably bad legs, same as Chinese women. Well, I'll settle for torso—as long as legs are not fat, don't seem so bad to me, though are no Dietrich's to be sure.)

The royal Siamese procedure is that all servants, even other princes, approach on knees—saw his secretary, etc., do this, some of the prince's old men, knee-shuffling forward. Gave me an extraordinary feeling— my blood ran the other way. We listened to national anthem—everybody facing the box. All Westerners bowed as they passed it; ladies curtsy. In front of us sat Chinese Amb. and wife—he an exceedingly handsome man, a scholar—he and wife both delightful, said M., "in spite of being Republic of China." Saw Prince Dhani again in his navy blue pakata (like plus-fours)—he the elder statesman who cannot be bought —Prince Chumpot (sp?) the disappointed, (might have been King) stalking around in black, with a big cigar. A Royal Prince cannot be approached nearer than 3 ft. by those of lesser rank. Kind-hearted M. greeted him from this distance, since nobody else wanted to, and Grant Mead, the ranking person near him (this in intermission) can't bear him and avoided him. Lovely, lovely intrigues of all kinds in this country. A toy kingdom I thought—the S.'s said I was just.

After left R., on Sat., had free day without appointments—wandered in Monogram shop here—saw a tiny reclining Buddha that I will regret not buying. People buy heavy gold bracelets and necklaces here as investment and saving—the servant class as well—no Thai wore costume jewelry until we came.

Sunday at 6:30 we were off to Royal dock to meet Gen. Partridge and his boat. Since we cdn't decide which dock, had wonderful dawn-tour of markets, docks—all inadvertently. The city was still gray— against it the monks—most of them still boys, were beginning their morning pilgrimage for food—in their orange robes against the gray, carrying their bowls. They eat at 8 and 11, not after that. At some of the big houses, servants stood waiting to feed them. My heart ached —since they seem about Pete's age—but apparently they all get fed—a Buddhist "makes merit" by feeding them. Pariah dogs everywhere, even in portico of hotel. Cannot kill animals here—tho am told Siamese police secretly trying to round them up. Profusion of fruits and veg. in markets, constant impression of gaiety and sweetness of people. Far cry from the Japs. No doubt "Mai ben rai"—the Buddhists "makes no difference" phrase, can be trying for Westerners to live with.

(Alex MacDonald's book, on his paper, *The Bangkok Post*, very helpful on all this. 1949.)

Finally met up with General (Richard Partridge) bluff, pink-faced man, very nice, hearty and intelligent, about to retire. Embarrassed, since this boat had never disappointed before—and he is undoubtedly an efficient gent—but this boat disappointed nevertheless. Went home to his villa—wife in States—had enormous hooker of whiskey—a fine but dangerous way to begin morning—the others had gimlets, but gin in morning is not for me—and huge breakfast rustled up by his "boy." Again Maugham flavor—the military villa, set in a compound of others, all crisp and beautifully shrubbed and tended. Will try for boat again Tuesday.

Then Sanfords took me to the Temple of the Emerald Buddha, Wat Praker—like Wat Po but much more so. Took off our shoes and sat in the shrine among the faithful—Sunday families all around. Shrine has governmental presents in front of it—many 19th century—a huge ugly clock from Queen Victoria—marble group, from Italy no doubt, in between the innumberable Oriental guardian figures of every height. Chinese tiles line the steps and bottom of side-walls. In palace, the wall paintings of the Ramayana, strung out "comic-strip" fashion, legend of the monkey-people, etc., scene after scene, constantly re-touched since they fade in this climate. Outside, the wonderful pro-fusion—incredible gold pagodas rising, Ceramic pagodas—"boudoir pagodas" I called them, made of ceramic flowers, like French ribbon or like the insides of glass paperweights. Enormous multicolored god-figures, gilt guardian figures—the garuda—a sort of monkey-faced dragon with serpent tail, the canellas (kinellas?) gilt figures half animal-half not—some with tails like cocks, dragon feet, some with great curved dragon-tails—I loved these—on the sidewalls, reliefs of women dancers, hands in the Siamese dancing positions—a few with faces like Sienese paintings. Wd like to have a book on this palace—colored. Nothing like it anywhere. Scale model of Angkor Wat—everybody horrified I am in part of world where is and not seeing—and this I regret but no time. Two-day trip. Say it is vast and unbelievable. I love these temples, in fact all the gay S. rooflines—if one could put Chartres next to Wat Praker one would not have to say any more about East vs. West. Great coiled serpents, studded with colored glass, sinuate up either side of most of the steps to the pagodas. Many shrines, because one "makes merit" building same. Even the hotel here has one with a large gold Buddha, surrounded with cheap vases, joss, flowers, etc.—in back of the traffic policeman's post, and with a few pariah dogs handy.

Then went to Sports Club with Mary, long afternoon of swimming and relaxation. More Maugham. This is the Club where the love affairs start—saw the "Rita and Einar" to whom MacDonald dedicated his book—story runs she had been violently in love with MacDonald but he md a rich girl and is now in States. Pakistani Ambassador came over and asked to be introduced—great Don Juan, and very handsome indeed, but if only wdn't talk—keeps up constant flow of hammy badinage—as if he had learned the "French" style of flirtation—to which one must reply in kind. Asked where I was staying and for how long? Mary said he will undoubtedly call—am busy thank goodness. M. says flirtatious, but means business—this she had to learn. Lots of other people—Jim Thompson, who wanted to sit with us but had to sit with the Harveys—typical country-club set—MG and a brilliant sport-shirt of Siamese silk—which will out-brilliant any on earth—ass of a man to look at him, and name-dropping wife. M. said she wd be dropping mine tomorrow. I get fonder of M. who has such a nice sharp wit, and is such a warm, thoughtful person. We get along so well. Asked Cecil once in car how he managed to wear all his "hats"—he has several distinct jobs and functions—SEATO, USIS, Embassy —M. laughed and said "One for each head."

Had curry for lunch, served by "boy" to reclining sahib-ladies in swim suits, then pigged it at hotel with tea and a pastry at the tea-shop —so elegant with satin sofas, embroidered linen—America cd use an occasional one of these. Then out to the Prems for dinner at 8. Dull affair, too many people, buffet-style supper, took the Siamese food (they had Western also) but not as good as at Jim's, though loved a kind of leaf they fry stiff—they use all sorts of plants and flowers—

even fry lotus and frangipani. Prem nice really, she too. House large, with ugliness typical of Westernized anything, in Orient.

From now on it will be a whirl—rather a senseless one. Today, shopping, lunch at Rachel McCarthy's, who wants me to see her Thai-style house in afternoon, cocktails at Bruces (Br. Council). Tomorrow we try boat again, then dressmakers, then Fulbright affair which, Cecil informed me, has burgeoned into three—we have to go from there to the Br. Amb, then to a USIS dinner at Casanova's, wherever that is.

Wed., Nilawan is gathering some author-ladies (the women are the better writers here, I'm told). Tonight we go to the Ungers (Deputy Ambassador) for dinner. Seni Premo (phonetic sp.) will be there—former Foreign Min., etc. Met his wife at a luncheon—her name "Usna" —either a Princess or a Momrajahwong, or a Luang—think the latter, title recently awarded.

Time for me to get out of here. I shall no doubt regret the lovely bathroom—(in the Tabriz one described by C.), and maybe the swimming pool—and certainly the Sanfords. But I long for a quiet life with C. Hope have seen the end of the R. business—he may not tell her until I'm away. Or not at all? This unlikely, since to tell wd be to his advantage with her. Still think he's nice, but terribly fuzz-minded in some way. In this way they probably are suited. If he does tell her, shd not be surprised to hear from her. Luckily, am dated up, God knows.

*Monday Night—11 p.m.*

Am to get up a 6:30 to have a try at the General's boat again, but must write down tale of a fairly exciting diplomatic evening, for Bangkok. This morning went to J. Thompsons and bought cerise material for suit, then took Mary to lunch at Mizu's. Long talk with Victor Jansen, married to Puckpring, divorced wife of prince. V. born in Tashkent, speaks 8 languages, including Walloon. Seen better days, now on the drink, works for KLM. One of those charming, sad, unhelpable souls, very intelligent. Thence to siesta. Thence to cocktail reception at the Bruces (Br. Council) for a new recruit to the council, appropriately named Mr. Tongue. Just in from Ghana. Inquired about Polly Humphrey, but no news. Large reception—at first lighted by spotlights, since electric power was weak, as it has been all past few days—then lights went up—there were the R.'s—he opposite, so I nodded, she behind. She saw me, but I managed not to catch eye—was embarrassed—shall have to do so if we meet again.

We left early to go to Ungers—Senator Fulbright there, as well as Amer. French and Chinese Ambassadors and wives, etc. Our table— Ambassador at one end (Amer.), me at other, flanked by M. Breale the French Amb., Conte Pontecorvo the Italian Amb., Mme Han-Lih Wu, the Chinese Amb. at Breale's left. Lively conversation mostly upheld by Breale—from opium-smoking to cinema. At Bruces, had heard that Quemoy bombing resumed 8 hrs. before.

By time we got to the Ungers however, more pressing news—a coup in Bangkok—a new one. Our Amb. left at once—did not reappear, and Unger left shortly after. Most exciting guest Seni Premo—former Amb. to U. S. during war, Foreign Min. and Premier here at various times —a lively versatile man—lawyer, violin-player—recited S. poetry asking me to note internal rhymes, and translating. Brother of the famous Kukrit. Wife (Lady Usna) had met at lunch and drove me home a few days ago—had a nice chat. (Correct title KunYing Usna.) Also nice Dutch-English couple—Vixteboyses—6 yrs. in N.Y. She had read my book.

So leave me there, at the abrupt end of my only journal, in the midst of the only time I have been "present," or with the inside bystanders, at an international "coup." One so tame, that hindsight on that part of the world—and on the U. S. there—makes one weep for it. There had been a show of tanks in the streets, no blood. At the end, I am left sitting at table with our hostess, Pontecorvo, and Senator Fulbright, all the diplomats having hurried to their offices. (The British Ambassador, invited to dinner, hadn't turned up; very smart man, I was told; no doubt had wind of it.) Neither Fulbright nor I can know that seven years later—when C., now legally my husband, using his

journal to me as notes, publishes his memoir of an American in Persia—
he, Fulbright, will write him an admiring letter on it (perhaps in
answer to some in Washington who were disturbed at C's now
prophetic remarks on the U. S. role abroad).

So the lights go out, and on again all over the world—and I have had
my small taste of it. And I will get to Persia.

I leave now.

.
●
.

WELL, SCATHED or not, I get there—for a few remarkable weeks. Then
the children's father cables through the consulate: Our daughter, who
had had a breakdown at seventeen and is now twenty-one, has again
dropped out of college—he cannot cope. I return to the States, taking
her to live with me in New York, since the old homestead up the
river is barred to me; until the divorce is final her father and I cannot
share even a twelve-room residence without nullifying same, and he
will not leave.

In the school holidays, my son joins us in the pleasant enough flat
I have found us; he is a bracing boy, but fresh from the close, eupeptic
life of a big New England school, and a country boy before that, he
finds this New York gray and depressing, though he does not say. I
have no way of letting him into the delights of a youth-in-New-York
I remember, and his own friends are elsewhere—we three are off the
family circuit, and know it. I begin to understand the life of women
so situated—a story called "The Scream On Fifty-Seventh Street" dates
from that time. I am not teaching. Purposefully I sink myself into the
role of mother; it is lonely. Now my daughter is healthy again and
dating, and difficult; my jollier second child is again away at school.
Sundays, those cold Sutton Place winter Sundays, are the worst. The
trip down the block to the stationer's is the event. Tabriz and I correspond, in faraway voices; we shall meet again of course. But for me,
with my family as it is, motherhood is the waiting-game. Christmas,
with such kind guests as let me scrounge them, has been grim. I re-

learn a lot, even that city loneliness has its savor—one that a mind like mine, however, has to be wary of. I don't remember working.

Then, in the New Year, my friend writes asking that we marry. He suggests I fly over during Nan Rooz, the long Muslim holiday, during which he can be absent from the university, to meet him and marry in some country where we have never been before, perhaps Greece. A mad idea, I decide, knowing how mad it would be, not to. It is a case of the pearls all over again—I know my answer. And then, only then, I am free to remember Tabriz—in words. I write them—from memory. The "husband" is of course C.

Over the queerly even cones of Cebu in the Philippines the plane dipped so low that we could see the branches of trees; hail to Okinawa, at one moment a jade-purple coastline denying all bloody history except the natural, at the next the "restricted territory" of a waiting room whose showcase wares of brown tins of Droste and subfusc "native" jewelry attracted only the wanderlust of flies; farewell to Hong Kong, enormous dream harbor over which one sailed three times, still choked with history, descended to buy a typewriter ribbon cheaper than anywhere else in the world, have a hot bath, and move on. At Taiwan, standing on a landing-strip stacked with fighter-craft as pretty and gauzy as mayflies in the sun, one held on to last week's *Times*, eyeballs converging on a headline, "Trouble in Taiwan," and knew the newsprint Taiwan as still distant, more real than this. Such travel is lucid only in the sense that it is a shared insanity—everyone else has his feet off the ground too. And nowhere of course are there any real people, only other *doppelgangers* like oneself.

Technically we were going around the world; in actual terms of sensibility, as we were reclined, fed, deplaned in orderly dislocation, meanwhile incubating what mental life we could, the world was going round us. Karachi passed us—a half hour's wait, one lemonade, two turbans, but no exit; our bed was not to be in India, nor yet Teheran. But then, finally, we boarded a plane at once less tranced and more intimate, not only because it was a single-engine job and bumpy, nor yet because the hostess, though beautiful as any, wore hair and cap humanly astray, and wrapped us in blankets that smelled definitely of burro, nor yet even because the desert flowing beneath us was as familiar as a Sunday-school engraving. This vehicle, moving umbilically along to a firm terminus, was the *last* plane, ready to berth us out of the scenic into the static, back into a daily living, however rich and strange, in which we might presumably clasp hands again with our domestic selves.

The city of Tabriz (Pop. approx. 350,000 local, 100 foreign—all real) lies in the northwest corner of Iran (once Persia) in a high valley of the Caucasus not far south of Russian Armenia, some miles from the great salt lake, Urmia, and some 18 hours by rail from Teheran. This is Tabriz by atlas. But my Tabriz (which I was to have to leave unexpectedly after a month—perhaps the ideal interval) lies in that never-never corner where we collect the house we grew up in, the one where we spent *that* summer, all those homes perfected forever by the fact that we shall not or cannot return. Mine is situated more precisely in one wing of a house where, on a certain afternoon, I might have been found sitting back of two high windows that give on a long garden which is in its turn behind the inevitable wall concealing it from *koutche* Ark—the Street of the Ark—which except for the high, rubbled ruin of the Ark itself is a yellow-dusted continuity of such walls, behind the main street, Pahlevi.

Persian style, everything here is behind something else, including of course the women inside their enveloping *chedurs,* each a shroud walking, deep above whose facial crossfold, held in the teeth, there gleams, coal-pot brown or pale Kurdish aqua, the Eye. Occasionally there gleam both eyes, a sight at once lowercase and less eerie, but small reassurance to any shy dog of a foreigner. How is it then that as I sit there and will for three hours, while the burning welkin above the Ark declines magnificently toward the blue dye of the tea-hour anywhere, I begin to feel a certain burgeoning of welcome, the first intimations that even in this land of many screens I am no longer so coldly in front of the scene but perhaps a little way behind it? The answer lies behind me, in an oddly burbled noise which, as might be expected, is the sound of a cake. At home—or rather, in the never-never of North America—cakes make no sound except the hush in which the children are warned to tiptoe past the oven. But this is workaday Iran, where the economy is oil and I have no oven, only three wicked burners with characters distinct as the Fates: Sometimes Steady, Always Hot, and Out. This sound, halfway between cauldron and cabbala, is the sound of a cake *boiling*.

It had taken me three weeks to get this far, by some hypocrisy and in a state of mind—often read about, recounted by grandmothers—best described as "suffragette." Traveling alone until now, I had only once or twice delicately been reminded of the status of women in the Orient —on the night for instance when, while sharing a second-class sleeper to Kobe with three Japanese gentlemen, one of these, seeing that I was unfamiliar with their prerogative of removing trousers, donning kimono, at ease in the aisle, had reached over and sternly pulled down the curtain, not to his bunk, but to mine. Here in Tabriz, however, I had joined my husband.

Back in the States, boning up for our projected visit, my husband and I had noted in a study collated, I believe, in Princeton, that "In Iran, the roles of the sexes, as traditional in Western eyes, are reversed. Both sexes see the image of the man as that of the poet-dreamer-philosopher, that of the woman as the hard-headed realist whose business is to deal with the practicalities of life." Or some such. What the report had failed to emphasize (or we to note) was how wide a latitude the dreamer seemed to have for his business, and conversely, how impracticably narrow the orbit in which the realist might take her exercise. To be sure, it was only natural that my husband, arriving first, had hired the flat, the services of the gardener-houseman, Hassan, and his faceless female adjunct, even christening the latter "Bodji" (in rude translation, "Maid!"). He had arranged with the landlady such details as what space belonged to us in the communal refrigerator, which afternoon she and daughter might spend in the only (ours) bath. With a month's seniority in Turki bargaining phrases, it was merely sensible that he go before me in our first dips into the bazaar. Since Hassan, our shopper, did not buy our meat, our needs there being harder to pantomime, my husband would—I was to cook it, but one sight of the butcher's bloody-wagon and I mightn't be able to. Also, *un-chedured* as I was, it would be politer all round if I did not go out alone; later on, during Ramadan, when native tempers were frayed by fasting, it would be advisable for women in Western dress to stay off the streets altogether. All in all, my husband seemed to have acquired the most delicate sense of the proper thing to do here, expressed largely in terms of what I couldn't.

My husband would be back from the university at four, at which time he would take me out for my airing, on foot perhaps for some miles down Pahlevi, peeping like any trippers into coppersmiths' stalls, saddlers, silversmiths, a few crammed with West German *kitsch* and electrical appliances (an ice cream freezer once, but never an oven), returning by way of three shops where, bypassing Hassan, we got our daily loaf of bread, bottle of local wine (hopefully labeled *Chato-Ikem*; wine snobs are everywhere) and clay pot of *mast* (yogurt). Teahouses abounded on the way, but of course only for males. Or perhaps we might go by droshky to the Blue Mosque, or jog along under the moth-eaten fur rugs to the very outskirts of town to watch the sun go down behind the range of the Elburz, on the other side of which lay Russia. These were not afternoons to be despised.

But except for Hassan, Bodji, and a student who called one afternoon, I had met no Persians, and beyond the few Europeanized ones to be met at Western parties, was not likely to. The previous week, grabbing even at this straw, I had gone to a reception for our ambassador, only to find that Americans and others had been invited from seven to eight, Iranians from eight to nine. My path was clear: Either I must join up with the "others"—wives of consulate, of missionary, of Point Four, or else I might stay as I was, in *purdah*, in a harem of one. A concubine, I amended. A harem was at least crowded—with other women. Now *they* would be interesting to meet. Even Europeanized Iranians sometimes still took a second wife in spite of the practice being frowned on. It was certainly going to be lonely here being the only concubine-wife. Catching myself in this train of thought, I suddenly stood up, put down the Presto pressure-cooker book of recipes, in which I had been looking for yet another way to render meat germless, and went to get my coat. For the good of everyone concerned, it was time I leapt over the wall.

Hassan had looked at me dubiously as he unlocked our wall door for me. Much taller than most Azerbaijani females, I was able without too much craning to exchange glances with a seven-foot Kurd. My coat, voluminous as any cotton *chedur*, was like these, hooded, but double-thick woolen does not sit well in the teeth. Below were my shoes, Abercrombie's desert boots for ladies, but to Middle-Eastern eyes a ringer for the U. S. army-issue for men. And above all were my eyes—two—goggled not for chic but for glare, with lenses aviation-size. As I left, Hassan cast a curious glance at the red pamphlet I was carrying—perhaps a part of our Koran. So I fared forth. Probably no one before me had ever tried to get acquainted there via the Presto pressure-cooker recipe for White Fruit Cake.

On that first day I had really no trouble. Dried fruits abounded; as for nuts, no Westerner, unless he had grown some in his garden perhaps, has ever tasted any like the Persian ones—the very soul of nut. I knew that stalls selling both were at the bazaar's entrance. The latter was some distance and I had no sense of direction, but I had only to use my ears, following, above the general hullabaloo of a Persian street, the bazaar's steady, subterranean roar. Arms full, I returned safely, thanking Allah that we lived near a landmark like the Ark, intoning which phrase I had buttonholed young and old, and once, myopically, a burro. My purchase method had been simple: Point, shriek the scale to stop, extend a hand with an assortment of coins. Once or two merchants, literally unable to believe we were not to bargain, would perhaps suffer neurotically from their encounter. Any money transaction draws a participating audience in Persia; life under the spiritual flatness of the *prix fixe* would be unimaginable. American prestige would go down another notch, but Point Four largesse had already weakened it beyond what I could repair; I was a bit more rueful about the prestige of women. When Hassan let me in, he looked embitteredly at my packages; there was no sentimental question of trust between us, but he had lost his cut. Tomorrow, when he bought our onions and eggs, he would be told the full extent of his loss—and ours.

I put away my trophies just in time. "Well," said my husband, entering, "and what have you been doing with yourself?" This, a query of which he had never been guilty prior to Persia, is a question asked only by a man utterly sure of the reply. As both expected and deserved, he got it. "Oh, mmmmm," I said. "Nothing."

On the second day, according to my recipe, you get lost inside the bazaar. This time I was hunting a container (to hold the batter inside the cooker), about the size of a pound coffee tin, of a metal strong enough to resist ten pounds of pressure for three hours—surely an object easier to pantomime than a cutlet. I had only to find it and point. Pots and pans stalls, however, held nothing small enough that was not as big as a bass drum. The Tabriz bazaar is not an open arcade but a labyrinth. I nosed deeper, peering at chamber pots, poking at silver censers. As I progressed, sellers came forth in droves to harangue me; behind me ran an increasing retinue of the small boys used as runners, holding up everything from mosaics to goatskins, here one trundling up a cauldron to cook a flock of hens in, the next tugging my sleeve to tout a tiara for the cook. Yesterday's réclame had preceded me; there was a woman loose in the bazaar who would pay the price of a horse for a pomegranate. Meanwhile, I had penetrated to the huge, vaulted core of the place, where the fine rugs were hung in an atmosphere thick as Rembrandt, almost Parke-Bernet: Very hush-hush, no hard sell, no goats. It took me ten minutes and three circuits to realize that I could not seem to leave it. But if one has the recipe, no need to be downhearted. Here came a last urchin, towing a young man. I scarcely had time to hazard what this might mean, when the young man spoke. "Cyrus Shabusteri. Student of English. Son of general." His lineage, it developed, was better than his English, but somehow I had dropped the word "coffee," and in a trice we were at a stall that sold it. Only in the bean, but there, next the jar, was my answer—Middle-Eastern answer. Tea of course, a brightly painted round tin canister of it, expressing itself in exotic French as the very best, which I somehow rather doubt because of the picture on it, a heavily embossed one of a girl in a two-part bathing suit, reclining on a beach between two palms—not my idea of a tea-picture. But my

thumb tests the girl with satisfaction. Thick tin. Very heavily embossed. Cyrus escorts me all the way back to our door. That day
Hassan does not look at me at all.

After that it is easy; the trick is to be hunting something indescrib-
able and to get lost at it—extemporaneously if need be. This is possible
even on a street as straight at Pahlevi where, after two days hunt for
the "heavy waxed paper" that the canister must be covered with, I see,
in an oddlot shop between some binoculars and a jar of Max Factor
face cream, a dusty packet of Peek Frean biscuits whose inner wrap
will just do. The owner and I, both speaking a little German, have
one of those nicely limited chats: He has never been in England; I
have never been in Germany—whence comes the natty Opel in which
he returns me to *koutche* Ark. On other days I arrive by various means,
often with child guides, once in the well known Rolls of the lady
beer-magnate from behind the wall across the way, although the lady
herself is not in it at the time. As I get to know Tabriz, it appears that
Tabriz, on certain levels, is getting to know me. True, most of my
encounters have been at point of purchase, but I am learning enough
of the place to know that this is a very Persian point. In fact I feel
almost at home here, or about to be. Home is the place where, when
you can't find it, they have to bring you back.

But there is an end even to fruitcake, and now mine, blended of so
much, is done. As I unveil it, the sun has just set behind the Ark; now
the blue at the windows is total. The hullabaloo from Pahlevi has the
gloaming sound of tea-time anywhere. I find that the girl on the
canister has lost the bandanna half of her enameled-on bathing suit,
and is now nobly tin above the waist, nobly nude. But the cake is quite
perfect, even looks occidental. It is not; it is a Persian one; Alt. 4,500
ft., Temp. Sometimes Steady, Time—three weeks. Ingredients, endless.

Just as I light the lamp in the window in its honor, my husband
enters, suggesting that we drive down to the consulate, where they'll
give us a cup of tea. At my answer, that we can't because we're having
people in for it, his query is natural—whom? Invitations go by note
of hand here, there being few telephones. I have been my own day-
by-day messenger, and the RSVP's are all in. They're delighted to get

a closer look. Nobody's been in hiding except us. "Let's see," I say, "first there's Mr. . . . Jamshid, I think it is. He has been in Germany. Very lively. Then there's little Shaké—her parents have the nut shop. Armenians, I guess. Shaké is only 12 but she already has been through one whole French reader. Then there's Mrs. Vartanian." This is the beer lady. "I don't yet know what she speaks, but her chauffeur is certainly very courteous. No doubt General Shabusteri already knows her. And his son Cyrus is studying English. Altogether, we should do very well." I unwrap his muffler from beneath his dreaming gaze, take the briefcase from that abstracted hand. "Oh I know it's all rather humble, compared to the university. But it's a beginning. And besides—" I add this last very practicably, "you won't have to run out and get a thing. I've whipped up a cake."

Two weeks later, in a hotel flat in Manhattan, on a raw Sunday, I sit re-reading yesterday's letter from him. *January's sea of mud is upon us, days the color of same. Hard to believe that come spring this is the land of the peach and the rose. A shame you shan't see it, but perhaps someday we'll return here together. As plans go now, I should join you in New York by June. Love from me and the tea-girl. Today I ate the last of your cake.* Before flying to America in answer to an emergency cable, I had made him another cake. That time the tea-girl had lost the other half of her suit. Just to think of her made me homesick. He was wrong about the color of days in Tabriz of course. I looked out the window—how gray the dusks of the East Fifties! At home in never-never they are always blue.

As I prepare to go, my daughter threatens to fall ill again, as she will do through the years; doctors have long since explained to me this strange dependency—"as for the womb" the first one said to me—in which a stay of even a day away from her, on my part, is a desertion. (And to which, I myself, through all the pitiable times of her troubles always subject in a way to that bitterly gleaming intellect, and temperament so much my twin, have fallen too deeply in thrall.) How can she or I know that my friend, more than any of them, will help both her and me with it? Meanwhile, since for my life I cannot help going,

a friend, Holly Roth (herself later to die mysteriously, lost at sea in a
storm off Morocco, from the deck of her schooner, her new husband at
the helm)—will watch over her.

On the lighter side—during what I suppose might be called the
engagement period—I go to a party composed mostly of women
poets, given for an acquaintance, the painter Tobias Schneebaum, who
is going to Greece—in a ship's hold, as companion to and wrangler
in charge of some bulls being exported to Salonika by the F.A.O. Not
pushing the analogy, he asks if he can in any way help *us*. And sure
enough, in due course his letter arrives. Marriage between divorced
persons is difficult in that Greek Orthodox country; other than a
marriage by a ship's captain at sea—shall he arrange for it? —only one
minister, the Presbyterian one, will oblige, and he is very busy; we had
better write at once. Since the Persian mails are so untrustworthy, I do,
in stilted language. Conscious that this is usually not the bride's function
(I believe I asked him to "favor us") I promise confirmation from my
intended, later. Tobias' letter has added that the head of CARE "is
very interested in you and would like to give you a champagne party."
We balk at that, but are sent a limousine to take us to Kafesias, nevertheless.

There the minister takes us into his study, for a little talk. Perhaps
it is exactly what we need. At one point, when he is saying that daily
we must take some moments out of the worldly day to brood on
things of the spirit, I burst out with a joyous "Oh, but we do, you
see—we are writers!" To me it is an honest approximation of what is
done in those mornings—and I suppose I think people ought to know.
A minister especially, should be pleased to. My friend gives me a
strong look. It says SHUT UP. Or the man won't marry us—is what
crossed his mind, he says later. But a pattern is set.

The minister's wife limps in, in polio-braces, to witness us. The
vice-consul, Mike Bank, also attends. Toby is our best man. I see from
his taut expression that what we are undertaking is serious. The mar-
riage-certificate is a long, accordion-pleated affair, exactly like those
postcard Views which fold to mail. I am wearing the "cerise"—from
Bangkok.

Later, going round the islands by steamer, at every stop, the shores are lined with people crowded on quays, clinging from the cliffs, with banners and dulcimers, cheering themselves hoarse. It is only for General Grivas, just out of exile, who is on our boat. But it feels as if it's for us.

∴

A GHOST I once knew—a man who did "autobiographies" of famous people, told me his hardest work came in making them interesting "afterwards." People only want to read about their upward climb. "Once they've made it, forget it. Or if they're *ha-appy*." He snarled the word, with the artisan's hatred for poor material. I heard it drag its peacock feathers in the dust.

A sense of loving and being loved doesn't change one's "nature." It gives men and women what it gives children—a confidence in what they are. And more openness in being it.

Memoirs, I see now, aren't formal compositions of what you re-member—and what you care to say of it. A memoir is your own trembling review of what you did and do—what you can bear to say of it. In so much of my life, as here and now, the saying *is* the act. In varying shades of distinctness, it is my public life. No matter how private it seems.

No life can be seen in a straight line, even afterwards. From the first, my stories and novels took this for granted. As I gained "worldly" knowledge—which means any kind one doesn't begin with—they often took this for theme, or for part of it. After my new marriage, as was remarked, there was certainly more of them: so far five novels, a brace of novellas, considerable critical work as well as some prose and poetry never shown—as against a novel and two short-story collections mostly written between the first book and 1959. Serenity is good for work you already have in mind, or for summoning it; performance is nourished by a calm under whose routine, not dull but reassuring, all the blood can run into the book. Certainly I was freed of the lovehunt, and with a companion whose life-hunt was kin to mine. Since all our professional and "living" connections were in New York, we had settled there. Neither of us wished to return to the West, and though we flirted with suburbia and countryside, except for the long summers when we immured ourselves on islands in the sea or the woods, nothing came of it.

But avoiding the New York litry life, which so many writers take postures on, has never been hard for me—so often those writers are not natives. To me New York is quite another thing—a home town, a habitat, full of ordinary people and *their* parties. As well as all the other arts—and theirs.

Meanwhile, as a mother I could live less wastefully or oddly than I had had to do. My son could go on to school and college without feeling himself the preoccupation of a lone woman; for whatever his need, there were now two of us, actively. At any time, my daughter's disease could rampage through her life and ours, and often did; our quiet periods were rare. Yet for her, as for me, there was now a solid aide, who could often do more for her than I. Slowly too, he helped free me of my own guilty dependence in that direction, doing it with honesty and good will toward her. All of us learned to trust his firm fairness, and lean on it. I learned from it. As I still learn from her illness, and from her death—the only tribute I can give. But all this, though so much, so much, is not the full point of the years since that second "extreme" change.

The inner life of an ego has to be phrased otherwise. Mine seems to me a pilgrim still in progress, shedding fears like skins, which with age—and if life is as spherically returnable upon itself as I think it—may well form again, in old age's version of them. I had never had purely sexual fears or puritanisms—I'm not sure why. Neither the restraints of a middle-class girlhood, nor the reprobations of a Germanic mother, had made me doubt my own candidacy or capacity. Maybe Jewish training doesn't scar the child with sexual sin—as some other religions do—and perhaps my father's Edwardian gaiety had helped. But otherwise, I had grown up, intelligent and a woman, in a country which wasn't too sure of its respect for either condition. In a way—I have had to acquire the confidence in me that it hasn't had.

By this time I had passed through my fear of not being a writer, and of not finding a lover. Now I would have to pass through my fear of being a woman writer. Which by this time had less and less to do with the external limits dealt us, or the statuses. The real danger had always been that it would restrict what I wrote. What I *wrote* would have to pass through this. The real limits of art are always self-imposed.

In the next years, and next two novels, it is my luck to pass through this almost unwittingly—partly from circumstance, and partly because my aggressions have their eye on something else. True, I have joked to friends that after years as a male narrator, my next book (*Textures of Life*—1963) would be as "female" as I could make it, but I had also written that it would be about "the little things that push life on while we are waiting for the big ones to happen"—which, if books have a major theme, was its. Actually, the praise for *False Entry* has been a liberating one, and all considered, remarkably uncondescending as to what sex I was—in whatever areas I explore I have no fear of being dubbed a "kitchenmaid" writer. Meanwhile, if other woman writers here seem to me off in corners too balladeering, grotesque, or minimally satirical for me, I have enormous admiration for what they do in those corners, and haven't yet logicked out for myself why they are in them.

Certainly, in a third novel (*Journal from Ellipsia*—1965), I have no intention of writing a feminist one. Art is still not a standing together, even with them. Later, when a critic tells me it has been the first feminist novel of the decade and the new era, I am surprised. In it, I have had some fun with the taken-for-granted divisions between the sexes—and high time too—but the locus I have in mind isn't even American, but "the world." True, I have made use of an interplanetary visitor of undifferentiated sex, who had come here to find one, in exchange for some female scientists intent on emigrating to a planet where they could lose theirs. But to me the book really takes place in that terrible but thrilling gap between the word-masters of the human condition and its math-masters, between the humanists and the atomic symbolists—that gap whose consequences, pointed out to us by C.P. Snow, had been with me ever since, as a young philosophy student fresh from Kant and Hegel, Schopenhauer, and all the other beloved anagogues in whose word-systems I had hoped to revolve endlessly nearer the touchstone, I had come up against the Quantum Theory and Max Planck—and had first understood the barrier nature of that other visionary side of the universe, over to which I could never travel first class unless I reversed my life, to learn *its* instruments.

Expertise interests novelists, who usually despair of having all of them. Novels spring up in those gaps.

I am feeling my oats because I am writing them.

Chronologically, American writers of the era seemed to peter-out earlier than those of other nations. Perhaps not so much because of the nature of American success, or even of failure—but because continuity is not being expected of them. Some, only in their forties and fifties, already retreat into literary make-work, or sit on the one book, or find their idolatrous claques. But because of my late start, I am just beginning to expand. At an age when some writers mire, circumstance has so arranged it that I seem to myself to have just begun. Ideas in work ferment as fast as I can write them down; afterwards, I sit on in their buzz, their swarm. I tell myself sternly that any writing which happens after "the work" is only accessory—a leftover energy. Sainthood must be like that—it feels so good you want to be at it twenty-four hours a day.

When you're not on Sinai, you exhort. I still feel that for a writer, reviewing (or even other critical work) is in a sense going over to the enemy (and I will never quite lose that feeling) but when I do, I find myself hewing my way toward some body of ideas I didn't know I had; during all this make-work, I must be formulating them. I write long letters to friends, and begin correspondences, the most continuous with Mary Sanford, a keen observer in foreign parts. And a vice which had first surfaced early in my writing days, begins to grow.

Letters Of Indignation—from time to time, I write them. My friend gives them their name, when in the process of our living together, he finds out. A psychiatrist might say that I am merely releasing a basic anger, in a number of quite various but ever more socially acceptable guises. They do seize on me in the early morning—after who knows what dreams of insufficiency, unremembered? (But mornings is also when I work.) If I'm not careful, I'm likely to spend the day at one. (But then, I have often spent as long on letters of a few lines and of quite other kinds—one, for instance, that has to turn somebody down.) Maybe they surface at those times when I'm afraid, for all the reasons writers often are, to go on with what I'm working at? For we all know that anger is fear. Yes, partly.

But outside the work, there are also real things to be afraid of, personally or socially—and at times I remember them.

Though some portion of this enters the work. I no longer see the work as totally sourced in early angers which have been decently, *artistically* extended. I have departed from that early self-interpretation. Injustices, social and private, ferment in me, but I am incapable of writing a work about any *one* of them—a reason that does have to do with art, has protected me. No work I admire is ever really about one thing, in the sense that one can pluck its subject between forefinger and thumb, like a tiny, screaming homunculus.

My mother used to accuse "all the Calishers" of "Jewish self-righteousness." (Typified for me by my Aunt Flora, who simply *had* to make the best soup. Everybody conceded it. But she had to make this clear.) My friend agrees that Jews appear to suffer in a way peculiar to them, over having to put things right according to their lights, (but adds temperately that this is biblical.). Only then do I recall a passage in *The New Yorkers* where, after a long interchange, Austin, the young Quaker lawyer, replies to the Judge, a Jew—who has twice said to him "Well, that's honest of you."—"No. You people mean to be honest. We only mean to be fair."

In a chapter called, "The Honest Room." These days I am brooding on honesties—of a writer's life, of a Jew's, of a woman's life (in the novella called *The Railway Police*), of an American's. In and out of books.

As I look over these letters now, I see how the tone changes, or lapses, with the target. I have tried not to put in only those which make me look good. I see how, taken together, they make me look *too* good. With a strong flavor of Aunt Flora's soup. Yet, snappish or high-and-mighty, or trivially insistent, they're a part of me I cannot leave out. What is it they really want—justice? I leave them because, in a small way, they are a sign to me. Of what I want more than anything, morally. That my books and my life be—not discontinuous.

I remember when the habit first seized me, a snowy blue day on the river outside my desk-window in Grandview, with the cardinal and the bluejay swooping contrapuntally in front of me and my wasted morning. And the letter, long since lost or torn up, boiled up in me without notice, from that black roux that must be at the bottom of all of us, of me. At the breakfast table, we had now and then been reading aloud from the music reviews of a daily critic with a ridiculously euphuistic style; in his hearing no one ever played an instrument—music was "elicited" therefrom.

When I was eleven, this man, then training to be a concert pianist, had been my first music teacher, and a baleful one. Obscurely, I felt he was willing me not to learn. I was wistfully eager to, and under later teachers became one of those amateurs able to play the Beethoven Sonatas with fairish bravura to close relatives—but under his baiting eye I was kept witless. One day, with a "Hang it!" he slammed down the piano lid not quite quickly enough to catch my fingers, and I was scared enough to ask my parents for somebody else.

Of the letter, which must have poked fun at his style, I recall only the last sentence—"Isn't it nice, Mr. X., that after all these years, you now write about as well as I play?" —and my shame at this nursery eruption, which left in its wake the same hangdog exhaustion as after a useless quarrel.

I didn't mail the letter, and that annoyed me too. How cranky was I?

Some years later, I told the story to Virgil Thomson.

"Poor man," he said. "Prison broke him."

I was horrified then of course, at my pursing vengeance.

"What was he sent up for?"

Was there a spark in Virgil's eye? "Molesting little girls."

None of the letters was written for publication. Each was in response to a circumstance. Each had two addresses, one being the receiver, the other myself.

*Exhibit A:* Written to *The New Yorker*, in the person of my editor there, on the matter of *In The Absence of Angels*, a story they had congratulated me on, accepted, and then decided not to publish because of *New Yorker* editor Harold Ross' fear that it would contribute to already dangerously excited public opinion. (I cover the details later on in the excerpt from "Ego Art.") "Marion" refers to my then agent, Marion Ives.

Dear Mr. Henderson:

Marion's told me that you are writing me a long letter about the decision on "In the Absence of Angels." As you know, I've never before broken protocol by answering a rejection—and never thought to do so until now. But this time I feel I have to do so —and before I receive what will undoubtedly be a kind and considered letter from you—because I think that this time it is perhaps as important for you all to hear what my reactions are, as it is for me to voice them. Believe me, there is not an ounce of personal resentment against any of you involved here—it would be very much easier if I could write it off as such, or could dismiss it as outraged vanity or disappointment on my own part. It is precisely because I know what serious consideration you all have given this, and because from the length of time given it, and your and Mr. Lobrano's comments, I think that I can assume that the quality of the piece was not the question here—that I can write you at all. I should appreciate it if you would let this be read by anyone who has had any part in the decision, including Mr. Ross. I know that, normally, he is pretty much protected from the hazards and complications of writer-reactions, but I should be grateful to you if you could arrange that he see this one.

For a long time now, I've been telling anyone and everyone who would listen to me that *The New Yorker* was the one magazine

I knew which could be trusted to make its decision purely on quality, on its own judgment of that, within the reasonable limitations of length and fitness for inclusion in a national magazine. I told them that, granted that a piece satisfied your critical standards, you were the one magazine which could be trusted not to refuse, for commercial convenience, a piece which might alienate or disturb a portion of your readership. You took "The Middle Drawer," despite what you called its grimness, and despite the cancer taboo, and it is just possible that two stories on a similar theme by other writers, one in *Harper's* and one in *Bazaar* which appeared not too long after, may have been helped into print because you did it first. You took "In Greenwich," which had ticklish material too. And, in discussing "Old Stock," when I told you my admiration for the magazine in doing that in the face of obviously expected reaction, you remarked that, from your own experience, *The New Yorker* had no concrete taboos, but demanded of a story with a ticklish subject only that it be done extra-ordinarily well.

I have told people too, and will continue doing so, that the impeccable, honest, and deeply thoughtful editorial guidance of all of you, has been of inestimable value to me in my own development. As a matter of fact, I am glad to have the opportunity of saying to you, with thanks, something which reticence would otherwise prevent me from saying. With you, the editorial process which at first, in my inexperience, I found so harrowing, (as you remember) had become something I relied on, welcomed and trusted. If I've become gradually aware that style, however interesting to the writer, must subordinate itself to theme, if I was finally able to make the transition from reminiscence to real fiction, and if, finally I felt strong enough to tackle bigger themes, it was in a large part owing to the confidence and help which grew because of what I could expect in interest, taste, and rectitude, from *The New Yorker*. It's an odd and unhappy state for me to be in —to feel compelled to tell you how seriously you've undermined a confidence you helped me so much to build.

It's strange, too, that this should come about over a story which concerns itself so intimately with the importance of a writer being allowed to say freely what he feels he must say, and with the larger significance of that for everyone in the world today. Censorship begins when a writer is denied an audience, not on grounds of craftsmanship, but on grounds of what is cautious and politic. We do not yet have despotic government censorship in this country, but we do have a growing censorship of another kind, sometimes frankly commercial, sometimes misguidedly benevolent, which is exercised by those who feel that, for one or the other of these reasons they have the responsibility of protecting their public from what the public is supposed to be too unready, too unenlightened, too weak to consider.

When a magazine, out of the most benevolent intention, begins to underestimate and overprotect its public, then it has taken a fatal step. When one such as yours, which has always been so conspicuous for making up its own mind, begins to take soundings, test out opinions, then it had better take its own pulse too. For this is what the slick magazines do every day. They tell writers that they desperately need "good" stories, and subsequently they tell them "This is a very good story; but not for a mass audience." I submit that, from the best motives, however well rationalized, this is what you are doing here. It is unthinkable that, with you, it could ever end in any appreciable depravity, or even mediocrity of purely literary taste—but it could conceivably end in *The New Yorker*'s being left with only its justly vaunted good literary manners, from which conviction has subtly slipped away.

For me, it means that when I hear a revered and respected editorial mouth say: "Miss Calisher, we hope to have something from you very soon. We desperately need good stories!" my inner comment will certainly be "The hell you say!" And that is the very worst thing that can happen to me, and all the writers like me. Bonuses for production are a fine thing, and no one appreciates or needs them more than me, but the best stimulus for the production of "good" work, for the serious writer, is his awareness of the existence of a market which is incorruptible against "popular" demands, however judiciously disguised these may be, and which, as one of your editors once memorably said to me "may make errors of judgment, but never of justice."

I am sad to have to admit at last, and to you, what I've been so long denying to myself—that it is not arrogance, but wisdom which dictates that the writer put trust in no one but himself.

Sincerely,<br>
Hortense Calisher

Best as always, to you all personally. I guess I had almost rather have had you say it was a bad story. This way I feel as if Grandmother had kicked me, and had fallen and cracked her own spine in doing it.

They printed the story (*In the Absence of Angels*).

*Exhibit B:* Written to a reader who had protested that the first line of a story called "Mayry" made it impossible for her to read on—though she wrote on.

April 14, 1961

To Mrs. X
Etowah, Tennessee

Dear Mrs. X:

Your letter, forwarded by the *Reporter*, interested me very much, since, as their reader, you can't be that "stereotype" Southerner against which you quite properly inveigh. A point of the story was that although an attitude deep and general enough to be called stereotype does exist among intelligent, literate, kindly Southerners, it is a very much more subtle one, miles away from the Simon Legree, white trash kind of thing. What is it? The story, since it is fiction, does not attempt to define it, but merely to show it in action.

In the ironic "My father was a Southerner, but a very kind man," the "but" was of course expected to detonate in the reader's mind, make him wonder why the narrator feels the need to apologize, "does he mean that to be a Southerner means that one cannot be kind—what nonsense" etc. In real life, it corresponds to the apologetic "but" that often sounds in the minds of those of us who are

constantly called upon to explain, often abroad, the peculiar division in the mind of that very Southerner whose personal culture
and conduct is of the highest (in our history some of the best we
have) yet who on one moral point has a beam in his eye that
contradicts all the rest of him. Yes, we must apologize for that kind
of Southerner—as we would be unable to do, or might not bother
to do, for others. As a Southerner one step away, I have had to
do so all my life.

Since your letter assumes, as Southerners so defensively often do,
that any criticism is likely to be from ignorant visitors comparable
to those touring Englishmen who used to write such confident,
superficial quickies about the States, I must therefore be personal
enough to make it clear that such is not the case here—knowing
that you will forgive me if I do that very Southern thing, talk
ancestry. My people came from England to Virginia shortly after
1800, and I'm the first generation to be born away from it, though
not actually bred so. Even in New York as a large family constantly replenished from the South and visiting back and forth,
we remained Southern to a degree that now seems astonishing.

To a child growing up in Northern schools, this divided heritage
was often confusing. My father *was* the kindest man in the world—
how could some of the things he thought be morally wrong? We
were very much more responsible about our Negro servants than
many Northerners—just as some of the South is at this present
moment more paternally responsible to its Negroes, within certain
limits, than much of the North. Yet, as a Northerner, perspective
made it possible for me to see the stock attitudes on both sides.
When I enter a rest-room marked "White Ladies," I know both
a Northerner's shock, and what my Aunt Flora's response would
be if I expressed it—for I know all the rationalizations with which
"good" Southerners must defend themselves, and dare not let themselves see behind. One of these—the story tries to show it—is that
Negroes are "children," incapable of the grown-up emotions, and
are best "handled" so. But I had been made to see, even in an only
partially desegregated community, that any section of the human
race shares its whole range of emotion and intellect, low to high,
remaining only as "different" as it is kept. All this is no particular

credit to me; it was forced upon me. It wasn't so daring to think it, as it would have been in Tennessee—and much easier to see it since the evidence was all around me.

So be fair to me, Mrs. X, and honest with yourself—and read the rest of the story. Perhaps you may still find it "not short enough" for comfort. For it was written, not by that vacationer you hopefully posit, but by someone whose accent returns to its origin after five seconds with a Southerner (and will never in life be able to put a proper Northern "i" in a word like "five").

You'll find no easy stereotypes there either, other than May-ry herself, who like many Negroes of her vanishing class in real life, is something of the stereotype we have made of her. The Southerner you *will* find there is unfortunately not one to be dismissed humorously, but a decent, honorable, cultivated, deservedly beloved man—whose manners restricted his humanity. In fact—since it isn't that stereotypes are getting "thicker" but that defenses are getting thinner—you will have to summon all your "sense of proportion" and "humor" not to let yourself know what I mean when I say again: "He was the kindest man in the world, but a Southerner."

Sincerely,
Hortense Calisher

I have known many respected editors—and respected them. Some more than others. Their general trouble is industrialisation. Plus the totem of the late Maxwell Perkins, who carved Thomas Wolfe's books from logorrhea and morass. Probably young editors still invoke him even as they pick up the Sunday carving-knife. Knowing that on Monday morning they have to meet with Sales. And at Monday lunch with author—who may regard them as fundraiser, party-giver, alter ego and psychiatrist. Who may even want them to help write the book.

Editors used to be the recipients of books—in Britain, at the time of this letter, they still were. Now they not only tailor them as Perkins very specially did, they expect to potter with any book, as a matter of course. Often they initiate one—even a work of fiction intended

to be "literary." I hadn't known this until I myself was propositioned.
I had thought we were going to talk about something of my own.

It was one of those browngold, dripping days, when New York
rains autumn outside, even offices take on a darkly double look, and
men like these, kindly enough, can convince themselves they are still
in libraries. This one—suddenly but delicately—tells me he is dreaming
of a novel, that could be written about student riots. He so admires my
work—and was so excited to hear I was a professor. Don't I think such
a novel needs to be written? (And may have been, by now). Would it
interest me to?

I smell the elusive, cardboard odor of highclass offices; it must get
to a man's mind. A man who can ask me to write a novel to order will
never understand my shock. How can I explain myself to him? (And
why should the onus always be on me?) And why do I feel so sorry
for him?

"No, no," I say. "I have to gnaw my own chains."

Here I am doing it.

*Exhibit C:* Written to my then agent, Carol Brandt, herself new to
me, when, after *False Entry* I was being solicited by publishers and
had some thoughts about leaving mine.

January 26th, '62
25 West 16th. New York, 11, N.Y.

Dear Carol:

A courteous reply from X—he will eagerly await word from
you or me. Meanwhile, perhaps some line from me on the "editor"
business might be of use, and certainly will concern me.

Little, Brown and Co. has one great advantage to me which
they don't know about—and I'm certainly not going to tell
them. They leave me entirely alone as far as critical suggestion
is concerned. This is no doubt by default, since as far as I know
they have no one "in authority" who feels able to cope with such,
on my stuff. In any case, it means that I have in effect a "British"
situation. When Bernice (Bernice Baumgarten, then my agent)

sent in *False Entry* in toto, she told them that I knew one chapter had to be much cut, and probably some at the end. They were quite willing to take it as was. The stipulation that it *must* be cut, (as was done, by me) was mine—a reversal of the usual situation. I work best that way, in the long run.

Now—with editors of high literary intelligence—like X—there is an opposite dilemma, which I should want to consider very carefully, and have my views very clear to them at the start. Most of them expect to work "with" an author. Most delicately of *course*, with someone like me, and of course, author always to have the *final* word. All of them will say this, and mean it. It will be our problem to explain that I do not ever work "with," either on work in progress *or* work completed, and that no matter how much I may respect an editor personally, I don't want any "words" at all. What they think, beyond "yes" or "no," will be a matter of interest to me only well after the event.

This is not because I arrogantly think the author is always right. But I know with every fibre, and much experience, that I must reserve the right to make my own mistakes, to *be* wrong. Otherwise, I am nothing. And once one embarks on any kind of suggestive discussion, the erosion begins. An author's sense of autonomy is maintained with difficulty from day to day. All good sensitive editors will tell you it has to be handled ve-ery delicately. To my mind, it is best for it not be be handled at all. For, on work in progress or just finished, most of us are indeed not arrogant, but far too amenable to suggestion—and all the more so when we respect the source. This I learned at *The New Yorker*. It's not the dopes who are dangerous, but the men of taste. And in the end, a writer always loses more by consultation than he gains.

X, for instance, wrote me a fine letter re *FE*, containing an observation that was absolutely just, re the fact that the high point of the book dramatically, the hearing, was so high that there was of necessity a drop afterwards. He was quite right; it worried me endlessly, with my final decision that it was a correct progression for this book; that the more orthodox way, of a gradually rising dramatic interest, was not feasible for what I wanted most in terms of this book. Other things could have been

done—and if an editor had got to me in time, I might have done
them. Or I might have decided as I did, or *we* might have, but
I would never quite have that fine, unequivocal sense: On my
head be it. And the next time, not trusting myself, I would lean
just a little on a sympathy and taste I know to be so good, and
eager to *help* . . . etc.

A good editor would be one committed to the author's work,
who also wields influence in the house—they must be in good
supply. An *ideal* editor would be one also committed to standing
by the principles above, even against his own finest inclinations.
I do not ever expect to meet him in this life— at least not in
America. The smarter they are, the more they want to use *their*
talent; the more admiring they are of yours, the more they want
to help. And they are quite right to say, or secretly believe, that
"the work does not exist that is not improvable by editing." Including Melville, Shakespeare. The only damage is to the author,
if he has the misfortune to be still living.

I shan't always be writing these declarations, God willing. But
we are just getting to know each other, and this is a matter so
important to me that is better voiced for whatever use it is to
you in deciding among these gentlemen. The dilemma of course
is that the editors who don't "speak one's language" are naturally
less willing or able to go to bat for one—and the ones who do
are always too bloody eager to speak it.

The best we shall probably be able to do is to enunciate as
clearly as we can: that Miss Calisher regards the descent to hell
as so easy she thinks she can make it without guides.

They won't hear us.
Best,

H

.
●
.

"Granny—what did you do in the war?"

I wrote. And wined and dined, and walked about, slept with a
man, agonized over children and took pride in them, built a house

and traveled from it—suffering and enjoying the common experience
of almost all people living off the battlefield in a land whose war they
cannot tolerate.

If my grandchildren and I ever co-exist, that's what I'll tell them.
In case not, I'll say a little more.

I do not know what the position of honor is. Few writers I know,
or the public knows, went to prison for long for peace, though a few
were kings for a day there. Paley and Levertov were devoting their
lives to anti-war activities. Lowell, remaining a poet (and a consci-
entious-objector in a prior war), spoke out most clear. Mailer, like
Hemingway, became a correspondent, ruefully at home instead of
abroad—but in the way of the world, peace gained less than literature
and he did. Ellison, stoutly refusing to be caught in a popular position,
bravely defended his own. Updike, in one letter to the Sunday *Times*,
seemed to me to want most to disassociate himself from the *kind* of
people who were against the war. Some never in any way lent their
presences, or voices. Most of us who did, shambled about in the wake
of organisers and occasions we could tolerate.

The Town Hall Read-in is the one I recall best. Most of "us" were
there, minimally nodding at each other like people who meet only at
parties or wakes—or on these lists—and in any of these places, know
how minimally we are there.

Children, when you in turn come to it—you can usually count on us.

Your granny hated going. To sit with bowed head until her turn
came to mount one of those mock barricades that are never composed of a barricade's rightful ingredients—which the dictionary will
tell you are barrels, wagons, and stones. And an enemy, very near.

As it happened, we were all herded into a kind of basement green-
room, there to wait our turn, listening to the program meanwhile, via
the public-address system, while one after the other of us went upstairs to read, and came back. Downstairs, we hullo-hulloed with the
sheepish looks of people accustomed to thinking of themselves as
original, come together to share the same painfully undistinguished
thoughts.

"Granny, don't you remember anything nice?"

Yop, I do too. So-and-so kissed me, jumping from the chair he sat in. No I don't either—that was on another barricade.

"Granny, remember anything *ghastly?*"

Well, not really. Downstairs, we festered familiarly along, as always in these dragged-out rituals, in which the effect was as if we gave ourselves the bastinado—a kind of foot-cudgeling, dears—with our own tongues. (I recall the kindly, sad face of Stanley Kunitz saying that many who hadn't been asked, had demanded to read, in order to get in on it.) But as I turned to go offstage after my own stint, I saw the backdrop, one huge "atrocity" blow-up, in which the dead and wounded bodies had been grossly magnified in the media manner— yet could one say *vulgarised?*" I couldn't decide.

"And how about funny, didn't you ever see anything *fun—?*"

Yes, the look and shrug Lillian Hellman gave me as she held a friend's jelly-jar of whiskey for him, while he went up. Why a *jelly-jar?*

"Granny, is there a moral to it? What are we supposed to *think?*"

You're supposed to see what we know deeply, that reading one's work aloud, *being* there, is not the same as writing it. A writer is not *what* he or she writes.

And yes, there's a moral.

We had come there, all of us, a good portion of the writers of the nation, under agreement not to speechify, but to read from our own works. Glumstering over books thick or thin, or patches of paper rousted from pants-pockets, we did so. Only Sontag, chin Jeanne D'Arc high, and hands free, spoke—a speech as from an impulsive heart too *feeling* just to read like the rest of us.

And next morning, that's what the *Times* remembered.

Then, while a poet was reading, a man, later identified as an un- employed detective, jumped on the stage and asked the audience to sing God Bless America.

And next morning, that's what the *Times* remembered.

I had been in straits between "liberal" action and writer-action be- fore this—remember? If I record these new trials of ego, it is for a reason. In the Gallup-poll of consciousness, writer's egos are no different from other people's—except in their ability to record.

In no war I had read about, or lived through, had the collectively expressed peace-consciousness ever been less than several respectful or frustrate years behind the starkly moving events. I had long since concluded that "made" events, such as the Read-in, did not make history. We were only having a dialogue with our own need to have a part in history. (As no doubt our grandchildren, if they exist, will be able to testify. To want the "real," and settle for the unreal, *is* part of that history.)

So I began writing letters—for publication.

*Exhibit D:* Excerpt from *The New York Times*, dated December 10, 1965.

### EDUCATORS BACK
### VIETNAM POLICY
*190 Professors Sign Petition—They Defend Debate*

One hundred and ninety professors representing Harvard, Yale, and 15 other universities announced yesterday full support of the Administration's Vietnam policy. . . .

The statement of the professors, while welcoming debate, expressed serious concern, however, about the tactics of a "small minority of the intellectual community" in opposing the Administration on Vietnam.

These tactics, they said, led to exaggerated estimates of their numbers and could cause Peking and Hanoi to underestimate seriously the extent of the American commitment, thereby prolonging the war.

The signers included Max Lerner, who is also a political columnist, of Brandeis; Morton H. Halperin and Henry A. Kissinger of Harvard; Harold Isaacs, Max Millikan, and Myron Weiner of Massachusetts Institute of Technology; Bruce T. Dahlberg and Thomas C. Mendenhall of Smith College, and Gunter Lewy of the University of Massachusetts.

Exactly half of the signers are professors of government, history or the social sciences, and almost one quarter are political scientists.

Dr. Wesley Fishel, chairman of a 10-year-old organization known as the American Friends of Vietnam, which coordinated the petition project, contrasted the signers' with those who have signed academic petitions opposed to Vietnam policy.

"Opponents of U. S. policy on the campuses," he said, "are largely teachers in fields unrelated to political science, international relations and Southeast Asian affairs.

"The further one gets from the subject—Vietnam and U. S. foreign policy—the more opponents among campus teachers there seem to be. The reverse is equally true. Most of the teachers of government, foreign policy, and international affairs support U. S. policy or accept it as necessary."

Dr. Fishel is a professor of political science at Michigan State University.

Letter in reply:

205 W. 57th St.
New York, N.Y.
December 10, 1965

The Editor
*The New York Times*
New York, N.Y.

Dear Sir:

Dr. Wesley Fishel's statement (p. 16, *The Times*, Dec. 10) that "opponents of U. S. policy on the campus are largely teachers in fields unrelated to political science" and that "the further one gets from the subject—Vietnam and foreign policy—the more opponents on campus there seem to be"—is interesting on several scores. It attempts to suggest that political science is an exact expertise which can tell us what to do, rather than merely the *study* of

politics—an intermediary and quite ordinary subject, which often
stands on just as illusory ground as any other. By implication, the
statement carries also that latent contempt for the humanities
which pure scientists have long since deserted, plus the same contempt for these scientists. But most of all it reveals the true limitations of those who put themselves forward as the only "informed"
men, and therefore the only competent judges of what the body
politic must do.

Historically, political scientists have often been used as apolo-
gists for the status quo or military ambitions. It is less easy to
name those conspicuously chosen to lead nations in peacetime—
perhaps because men who have at their fingertips all the reasons
for past wars, are by habit of mind that much closer toward proclaiming a particular war "reasonable." On campus, a political
scientist is merely a man with a doctorate, like the rest; except
for his small ballast of scholarliness he is as much at sea in human
affairs as any, no better than they at the "practical," and hopefully no worse at the "ideal."

The educators who have signed Dr. Fishel's statement, though
implying that their colleagues in the pure sciences and the humanities must not be taken seriously on matters outside their ken, very
graciously award us the right to speak out without being called
Communists. In Dr. Fishel's capacity as chairman of the American
Friends of Vietnam, one must award him the same—and imply
the same. But beyond that, any educators who so suddenly separate
themselves from the rights of their colleagues, who so impugn that
medium of total knowledge or inquiry in which they have spent
professional lives to date—are at once suspicionable. To give them
the status they demand is like awarding the exclusive right to serious statement only to pure scientists because they are "purer" than
other men, or to us of the humanities, because they are more
"humane."

Most shocking of all is to see how such a statement fails to recognize that to categorize whole groups of men as incompetent to
judge, is only deviously different from stigmatizing them politically—the intent to muffle or nullify being the same. For these
educators not to see their own pronunciamento as a classic one of

all war periods, is to be far farther away from their own subject—
from a sense of history—than any of us.

Sincerely,

Hortense Calisher

None of my anti-war letters to the *Times* ever made it. I don't blame
the *Times,* which was never *for* the war, and hadn't yet expanded its
letters page. A more ancient force was at work, in journalism as well
as history. People *believe* in war. They only dream of peace. In time
of war it is always the believers who get the podium.

Three years later, long silent in this neighborhood, I wrote again,
on entirely another subject, and this time the *Times* printed my letter.

Its genesis was simple. Two speaking engagements of mine that
spring had coincided with two deadly week-ends. Just after Martin
Luther was shot, I had to speak at Brandeis—a reading. Just after
Robert Kennedy was shot, I was scheduled to address the Alumnae
of Barnard College—and spoke out against the war. (Not receiving
the usual thank-you note, or any, from the college, afterwards.)

Kennedy had been my candidate. I had met some of the people
working on his Bedford-Stuyvesant project, and been heartened. Certainly he stood for my hopes in government more than the others.
Because of his stand on the war, I had volunteered to work for his
candidacy in New York. Though I was not part of the writer-artist
"in" group around him, I knew most of them, as well as the exact
nature of the glamor-glue that held them there, and had drawn them,
in richly collegiate bonhomie, from "the Vineyard"—to travel west
with him. Except for Jules Feiffer, a serious man, none I knew had
had any political commitment before—even if old enough to. They
were "casserole" Democrats. No other candidate would have drawn
them. In personal grief—and yes, snobbery, they would now disband,
fall apart. Yet their vital force, together with the young people who
had been for Eugene McCarthy, might tip the balance against Nixon.

For *another* Democrat. No pearl. But no Nixon. I doubted the young collegians could see this either, or bear it. But hating to be only a fireside Cassandra, I wrote.

*Exhibit E:* Letter to *The New York Times,* dated Aug. 29, 1968, from Monhegan Island.

To The Editor:

Millions of anti-Administration Democrats now face a terrible disfranchisement. If we stay away from the polls, we shall most certainly help to elect Richard Nixon, who will most certainly mistake this as a sign that the temper of the country is with him —so to let loose in 1969 a violence sure to be worse than what we have seen.

Politics is the art of working with what you have. We Democrats now have an organization man, nominated under circumstances which no apology of his can disavow. Yet it is rumored that he had a noble youth. And it is said that the Presidency often brings out the better in a man.

Yet I cannot vote for Hubert Humphrey unless he and all know what my vote means. The duty now of all anti-Humphrey Democrats is to help us express ourselves in vote.

The mails exist, as a start, and they can be powerful. We must be provided with some immediate *en masse* means of saying to the nominee and to the party: "I am a Democrat opposed to Administration policy. Although you were not my candidate for the nomination, I plan to vote for you because I cannot on any score vote for Nixon. Sir, if you get the people's mandate, remember me."

Some such memo should be put in our hands as soon as money and mimeograph can make it—as the start of a program to provide us with a positive *modus vivendi* for the next two months. Democrats for the memo, and Republicans it may be, can be a force within the election, to be reckoned with now and after.

We, the deciding, independent voters, must at once have some honorable expression made open to us—and made clear to all—

which will allow us to work with the Democratic party. Apathy now—which everyone of us feels—could be tragedy by winter.

Hortense Calisher
Monhegan Island, Me.
Aug. 29, 1968

No doubt the Maine postmark had helped. Or the heart of the *Times* letter-sifter who always returned mine (I seem to recall a lady named Martha) had been touched. The one-room Island P.O. sagged with mail from those who had been—and wanted to help, offering everything from money to mimeographing.

Winnie, the postmistress, said to me "What did you *do?*"

What had I?

Three years before, when an Air France plane, due to fly a group of us, publishers and writers, from London Airport to Orly just in time to connect with a once-a-week plane to Zagreb, had defaulted, I had suddenly heard myself say to the Air France hostess, "You must hold the Paris plane!"—and supply us another Channel one. "We are Marshal Tito's guests—we have to be there."

Technically this was true—we were five out of perhaps a thousand at the P.E.N. conference. Luckily I had spoken in English; when I saw the hostess had caught nothing but the "Tito," I repeated it, many times with increasing authority. The plane was held for us on the other side.

"It's that black raincoat of yours," an English publisher whispered. "She thinks you're Madame Tito." But as guards met us at Orly and whisked us forward to where the huge immobile thing waited (with Arthur Miller, due to be elected P.E.N. President and all the rest of his delegation sweating inside, though I didn't yet know this) I had that sense of power (Is it merely a modern one? I doubt that.) which comes from having for once stopped the hostile clockwork of the irreversable world. Not by being somebody—that would spoil it. *By being nobody at all.*

"I wrote a letter, Winnie," I said, taking the string-bound piles of them she kept handing over the counter. "And people answered. *You see it happen all the time.*"

As I laboriously answered them until they outran me, yes—it did feel a little like Orly. And this time, by God, an act of the pen. Looka me. Except that now, it would seem, I had to have an organization. Did *I* want one—or want to start one?

No. (I *had* hoped that the Democratic Party might use my suggestion.)

A lady came forward, just in time to save me—if not them. Wife of a Princeton professor, she wrote for permission to use the letter as a statement to be published in a Princeton daily by a group there, faculty and others, who wished to organize around the letter's suggestion. Ultimately the *Times* ran a news story on the Michel Balinskis—to me, when later we met, the prototype of those young, energetically concerned Americans who ought to be one of the glories of our political life, but are increasingly scorned there (for being college-connected "intellectuals") by a country which deeply mistrusts the "universal education" it is committed to.

Through the efforts of the Balinskis, and others on campuses all over the country, the campaign spread to many college and small-town newspapers, and just before the election, I was told, the use of such a form-letter was being considered by a Democratic caucus held in New York State, and by some other states. Too late.

Meanwhile, to help out as I could—with the pen, which still seemed to me the proper way—I wrote the editor of the *Times'* Op-Ed page (now expanding), asking to report the progress of this campaign. Electioneering—but why not? This was refused, but with the request that I write something for them on some other subject.

Months later, I did so. It wasn't what I had asked to do—now a dead issue. But there was something else I wanted to say on civil rights, so I took the opportunity.

This, a short piece on "Civil Rights in Black Hands," as the *Times* called it, was much reprinted nationally, though Southern newspapers cut some of it.

To what end any of it?—I begin asking myself. I can now see cynically clearer the odd paths to public expression; once you have been certified by the press as of sufficient interest or vigor, you can speak up on anything (and might learn to on everything).

Twice more in time of student riot, I wrote in. Once, from the City College, in defense of an open admissions policy. And once from Columbia, my own university, whose record on freedom of opinion had long shamed me, when it at last came out against the war. At the time, I was teaching in both of them.

If I hadn't tired as suddenly of published letters as years ago I had of organizations, I might have been ready for one of the next steps in pop American personality. Public office. Political or educational.

God is my witness I wasn't smart enough to think of it. When, not long later, a man tells me my name has come up for the presidency of a good university, I say "You're kidding." Indeed not; he is on the search committee; I need only encourage him. When I still laugh, he says stiffly "Maybe you don't realize what a good image you have."

Good? For an artist? I feel just as I had when the Nyack Library, putting in the basement some writers' books as unfit for the young, hadn't included mine. (Perhaps since repaired.)

American life often gives one these raw glimpses of the ski-slides possible between its professions and its powerlines—to the alert. Between being a film actor say—and a governor. Or a district attorney—and a President. Do you have to be what the public wants, or simply a hard wanter? Do you have to be charismatic to the public eye, or merely be there?

Artists often go pop, once they have money or fame—or enough of whatever else they came for. But often too it comes upon them out of their eagerness to be effective in the public world.

One step nearer, and I wouldn't be sure what *was* pop. Except that my letters would be, if I brought forth any more of them. In public. In private they could remain what they had been. Sometimes an honest wrath, sometimes a self-righteousness that has soared past soup. Sometimes the ignobler part of the process by which I find out what I think.

A letter of indignation is its own best answer. Protests that require another's answer aren't indignation but controversy—wherein somebody else finds out what *he* thinks. I don't mind.

(My friend says reflectively, later: "They are part of the writer's soul, that cannot elsewhere be utilized.")

But one day after (I confess it was on many days) I awoke feeling that in my pilgrim's progress I had strolled too far from my first writing-innocence. The air was like that, Bunyan-clear. I felt print-sick. Inside me, it was all paper news. How could I get back? Once, on a peace march, I had felt the same.

On that wistful, fashionable day (is it five years, seven, since a whole world of city thinkers with peace raging in them gathered to stand like angels on the daffodil pins of Central Park?) at precisely 2:28 in the afternoon, as our horde, every one of us an individual and finally on the move, oozed inch by proud inch from the field onto the open land of Fifty-Ninth Street, a bride and groom came out of the Plaza Hotel—it was thought to be from there—and briefly walked with us. Had they floated down to us from those reception rooms just over the canopy, which are so neuter-bleak to the morning walker, but at dusk such a champagne shadowplay? Nobody around us strictly saw. Each of us could see only the pilot cerebellum in front of him, or laterally the member profiles from whatever unit somebody had soul-attached to us by phone the night before. No, we couldn't say from where or how those two added themselves to our number, (in itself a count never to be settled in the newspapers) and walked with us, beckoning from a romantic distance, a personal one, against which we for the day had absented ourselves. Who invited them, where did they go to, when did they disappear? Nobody quite said; we'd been standing since 7:00—most of us—or even the laziest liberal among us since 9:00. Who else saw them too, that Houdini couple? Have they gone?

We live two blocks from there, the two of us, ten flights up, or is it twenty, impaled on the stakes of the city, beleaguered, but we're city thinkers, we'll last. Hopefully, each as long as the other will. Our bedroom is a helicopter garage or nearly, but the mood between us is like any couple who have lived and loved gently lapped on the breakwater of city acquaintanceship: which one of us will go first, leaving the other to last? We can't hope for the Titanic, so we never say.

But we know the cold-hot sea of city thinking the way you know that book you lost as a child of ten on the subway, and can pick up any day. We are companions in observances whose bond will never end. We're that modern pastoral couple you know so well if you marched with us, or are marching presently. I could keep our genital particulars dark; as companions in this we could be anybody. But why deny that we two are a woman and a man? Consorts. Married maybe, now and before. Not much interested in weddings, never were. (Last one we went to was our butcher's, our *family* butcher, if you please. In that Catholic church somewhere in the Fifties off Ninth Avenue— the baby's now two. That day in the park, their love affair wasn't even born yet. And Ronnie's a hawk, even now. A Jersey-living Daily Newser, who gets up at 6:00 to cross the river for the whole-saler—and for us. We are the city. You always get a special greeting, coffee in the back and a special cut—for us. They come from Alsace or the Piedmont, or somewhere. A real family place). . . . Since I have to march today, I went there yesterday. They want Ronnie to marry. We had their *boudin* for breakfast just a few minutes ago, that's blood-pudding; we're international. We're the city, that couple. And we are standing just inside the park entrance, on this corner that the journalism of life has brought us to—at about 8:00 A.M. Of a wistful, fashionable day. The day you two got married, you brilliant Houdini pair.

The park looks like a vulnerable pastel. Not overcast, but no sun, and the day unlikely to go any further either way—though if you two came to the Plaza from Houston, or Connecticut, you mightn't know that. Or even from Roslyn, or Rahway. Muted day, blended, ready for its promenade. Where our morning walk usually takes us is now a multitude far as the eye can see—or to Central Park West and the Mall. There's a constant whirlpool eddying at one meeting-point, between the steady current of those who feel they must be a-moving, a-moving because that's what it is to be serious, and the slow strollers —heads up, lids lowered as at intermission—who are waiting to see who they are here with. We're not daunted though, any of us; we're inside what a parade does for you. We're not doing it for ourselves. What did it do for you two, when you came from wherever?

Did you feel that the wedding notice in the paper later—you were the kind of couple who would have had one—made you as you were and would be—or that *you made it*? To wherever you are. What did you make of it, and yourselves, later? Did you do it for yourselves?

We weren't feeling much. We had been here before. One of us had been to a war directly; the other hadn't. But we don't know any-body who hasn't been to a manufactured event. Once, during a war, one of us had even had a wedding reception right here in the Park, in the Tavern on the Green, so never wanted to stop by there for a drink. What is a manufactured event? What is this journalism they say is eating the real ones, eating couples, eating the book I left on the subway, eating my life? Eating yours? Does it? Now? (The butcher's had his baby—it's been five, seven years. He doesn't read much, but even so, the wolf of newsprint is at his door.) And you looked like the kind of alert, aware, liberal young pair—Ted & Molly? Mark Smithers and Janie Grosbard? Oleg Peters and Ava-Lou Jones? Hedda Goldberg and Abel Cohen? Sweet Caporal, Idaho, Lattingtown, L.I., Berkeley, California, Bruckner Boulevard? ... John and Mary Doe, temporarily of the Plaza Hotel. I don't want to know your names, please. Oh, Mr. and Mrs. Houdini, marching became you! And us?

In all they say is happening to us, the books dying like the robins, the grass withering like the books, they can club my psyche with the hard facts like they do the baby seal, but I'll still hunt my private Cyclades. When I saw the two of you, I thought "This is the day that pair go public. Even though, standing here by the thousands, we're

SEIZURES OF LOVE AND WORK

just newsprint to them. This is the day for them, maybe. After this, will they just wait for the manufactured facts?" I still can't believe that people only do. I see them standing lone and aside, trees that will not be a wood. I see them looping the mist from the monument around a finger, and spinning it into a hair thin enough to string an insoluble equation on, or to service a guitar.

(Strikes me you two might be too young to know who Houdini was. He was a magician, who got out of trunks. His hands being manacled first, by experts. "Life's not all fact," he said, and slipped out.)

At precisely 9:10 then, for those who must have it so, or after we'd been for an hour or more in the tepid cage of the crowd—always warmer there—we came to our first familiar face, a man called Bob Brustein, then or about to be dean of the drama school at Yale. I mention names because this is journalism; there's to be no clouding-it-over from Olympus, that old pattern-studio. Also because, since his was the first known face I saw on my first peace march, whenever I think of that day, I think of him. And because the expression on his embarrassed face was the same as on ours, on mine. . . . At one time, on those morning paths which stand so still and waiting even while the press of us wanders, we collect a whole group of such faces; for the record there was Ann and Christopher, Philip and Anne, Ann and Alfred, Judy and Jules, and John and Anne. And maybe Ann and Bernie, though not for sure; the fact remains that facts are always a little interchangeable . . . *Our* crowd, it must have seemed like to others—and even warmer there. But in truth we only meet for a minute, stand for a minim in the pool of stasis a park meeting makes, and skitter on, pleached by what we cannot bear to think is politics, squinting with what we hope is allegiance to all. At noon, or perhaps 12:35, I share food with whichever of the group is near—some who, to appear feckless of spirit, came without, and some who like us, have brought a campaign lunch. And some who, having been seen, leave early. "British biscuits," one who stayed says, taking one. "*Too* chic." And chocolate is for soldiers. Would it have been better to have been embarrassed in private? After automated war, an automated peace always follows. But we are the pen-pushers of our own lives, the storytellers of other peoples'; we can't believe that the real events are artifices. We're too smart to be caught *in context.*

My companion, who has been to war, whispers, "Be better when we march."

But maybe it's you, Houdini pair, that we're waiting for. There is a time, maybe, when all the facts chiming together make a creation beyond themselves. To be sung in part-songs later, in all the places where life hides from the record. Behind the veils of old brides. In the ink-music at the bottom of a brain. In the marching fountains that once were literature.

So here we are, at 2:28 precisely, in front of the Plaza, waiting for the word to move, massed at the border of the park in our shimmering thousands—which is the way a crowd looks from above. Well dressed, this one. Told to. Though such as it is: deans and writers, social workers and students, CPAs and scholars, actors and teachers and their children—we are unlikely to impress a President. Some people are city litter, admit it, but there's none of that, there's not a submerged face here. College people. Not rich enough, not poor enough. But up there, at the punchbowl of marriage, we impressed you. What did you say to the parents who paid for the Plaza: We want to march?

Suddenly, skimming from the plush steps, or maybe floated down in a Chagall balloon from that window just over where the evening hustlers check in—you two are here. Oh Houdinis, you got out of the trunk the wedding pictures were going to put you in! The snapshot of you among us, smiling, beckoning, bidding us begin our parade —somebody must have taken one—is different.

You're a slight girl in a Juliet cap; you carry your token train over one arm and lean on the groom with the other; is there an easy suggestion that you are a little urging him? No, he's a slight boy too but taller, you're a matched pair; his hangdog look at what you've got him into is only what all grooms of his kind have, nothing to do with politics. As the two of you walk toward us, among us, he gains jauntiness; your private, almost shamefaced smile is for each of us, but he can't be as public as you. (In the Ninth Avenue church, last wedding I was to, the totem bride entered with two great pom-poms of veil hiding her votive face, and the groom strutted twice-as-alive in his black-and-white, like a guinea-hen—thirty-two of whose heads he had chopped off for the wedding-feast that morning—but over there the facts are different.)

You stand very still, Houdinis, in our votive light. In the place where the horse-cabbies usually are. The bride's cheeks shine like small peach-halves. The crowd holds that silence one can hear. Her bodice is a heart. She raises a fist, her lace train dropped, sliding maybe into manure, and there it is— the peace sign, the V—the victory!

We knew it! You are Americans.

Suddenly everybody bursts out cheering. . . . Not singing . . . *suddenly everybody burst out singing,* that's a line from Sassoon, and from that book, *Poems Children Love,* that I left on the subway. And from the first World War. But what difference can it make? Above my head, my own arm is up, and back of me, back, back, on and on behind me the V's are spreading, waving over Central Park, all the way to the Mall. Near me, an Anne whispers, "It's *May-Day,* to the life!" Oh everybody's waving, Scott Fitzgerald too, and why not, it's everybody's war. And at last we're moving. Off cobble and grass, and the old park design of L'Enfant, onto a street where once were the steel lines of the Fifty-Ninth—a trolley-line, not a regiment— then onto manure, and rounding the corner of Bergdorf's, to where Fifth Avenue still leads to the spire of St. Pat's, Childe Hassam even in this gray light. *Our* lines—we're in lines now—are destined for the U. N. of course. The Hassam series, *Fifth Avenue in Wartime,* are all a striped, waving red-and-blue, the flags hanging to a point, in the solemn, seventh-seal way flags used to do. I have his lithograph of Armistice Day, in it this very bit of park we're leaving. Signed. And if the ticker-tape falling now on my face from above is all from paintings and from what the ads call the world of books, what does it matter—we're marching. My companion, whose hand I hold shy and tight, whispers "Better now?" It is precisely 2:59.

The Houdinis are gone.

Forever?

Worlds shudder and join. Streets go jagged, girls get knocked up, and are healed over with a sealing flag. Slowly, in the Cyclades, in the butchershop, the dynasties push on. It's time again to drop a name.

Ronnie's next will be christened for a saint, like the first one. On the march—at half-past four, on Forty-Ninth Street, we ran into a man named Anthony West, who for some minutes marched abreast with us, his face the only clear, unabashed one of us I saw that day, but he's an Englishman. (Ronnie's family never march civilian, but last week two members of their family flew over from Italy to see the Muhammed Ali–Frazier fight; they're an entirely different readership.) On the march, it began to rain, I had an umbrella, but at 5:51 we copped out for our dinner-date, when just in sight of the side-street leading to the U. N., solid with motionless people under their parapluies and bumbershoots; that's the way it shone back to us, international. In the subway, there are like breadlines for tokens, but my companion has two in his pocket, and in twelve minutes we're home—which is just over the BMT—and out of our marching clothes into evening ones. Catch a cab, and in two shakes, or eighteen minutes more, we are on the top floor of a townhouse in East Eighty-First Street, sitting on a sofa, bathed but footsoldier-sore, next to the ninety-year-old man the party's for, Rudolph Hempel by name—he has always regretted that his parents, who knew Mr. and Mrs. Stanford, wouldn't let him go to "their" university—who says, when he hears where we've been, "Oh—you young people." Suddenly, we burst-out laughing. At approximately seven o'clock.

On the march—I remind my companion—we whispered. I ask him why. He says nobody's forgetting the war, nobody's forgotten it—but your experiences are your own. My name is Hortense. His is Curt.

O posterity, who will not know us, this is all the names we were. Or almost.

There is a pair to whom some have given the name Houdini. From another legend, farther back. They reside in another area now, beyond the city limits. (Once, not long after I met them, Ronnie's father, the old boss, says to me "Couple my customers, they say they know you. Newlyweds." and my heart shot up like the cardinal just now at my window, against the thermapane of its own fear. I don't want to know the trunk they're in now. "College couple," the old boss said. It wasn't them of course; it can never be.) So if you are some college couple reading this, and think you fit the facts, *please do not write in.* Fall in each other's arms, gather your children into that circle, tell them. The Houdinis are another pair now, entirely. The record will do them justice. I am making my peace with it. I can't let in any fact that wasn't there then. But I must let in all the facts that were. I'm not making my peace with the kind of history they say is eating us. I want to march on.

For the record:

You stand there. We stand there. In the Childe Hassam light of former flags. At 2:28. Always somewhere, standing on the manure from the horsecabs, a yard from the lamp where the hustlers meet— you give the signal. The V'd hands fly up, a bird-cloud wavering back, and back, and back. The leaders have let us wait too long, but suddenly because of you we're cheering. The air looks grainy, as if, through its dirty, pointillist specks, a first cause is trying to say something. Under the asphalt of that street, a trolley-rail strikes through. The broken pavements of Fifty-Ninth Street, I stand and weep for them. Maybe only the blood-pudding is real. But we march.

And it was a famous victory. You are never lost, Houdinis, even on the subway. This is how we bring the news from Ghent to Aix, to all the butchershops. In the poems children love. Stand there in the sawdust, Houdinis, in the pure, fictional light. Bloom forever, from the dust of literature.

Worlds shudder and join. Why do I whisper, even now?

PART IV

# PUSHING AROUND
# THE PANTHEON

E<small>VERY</small> art is a church without communicants, presided over by a parish of the respectable. An artist is born kneeling; he fights to stand. A critic by nature of the judgment seat, is born sitting.

We're hierarchical animals; none of this is new. Why though is the artist as a person as well as a creator, endlessly anatomized, while the psychological make-up of a critic is let go hang? Who has investigated the oedipal pulsings of a Sainte-Beuve? Or the possible anal indelicacies of a Saintsbury? Or the Gestalt of all our critics who wrote a novel once? Nobody hangs *their* laundry out. Or sees them as men and women for a' that, outside the hall of fame like everybody else, beating their little welfare fists against the big bank door.

When the Reform Bill goes through on Olympus, all critics and certainly all biographers, will carry their non-academic *vita* with them at all times, to be checked as freely as the tag on a decanter, before it pours forth. We shan't want to see their medals. What we'll want to know is the state of *their* beds, *their* dreamgoals and psychic pocketbooks, before we listen to them freudenize Twain and stack-sullivanize Keats. What is home to Harold Rosenberg, we'll ask, that Barnett Newman is *this* to him? Where were you, Edmund Gosse,

Maurice Bowra, Brander Matthews, *when the lights went out*? And who has collated Arnold Toynbee's "analysis"—a Jungian one, I was told—with his version of history?

Oh, I can see all the arts then, a proper Disneyland, with all the worms turning animatedly to say to the spades "Kindly present a psychiatric background of *your* prejudices. And in print please!" Before you dig *me* up.

Trouble is, would we read it?

Perhaps all artists have to settle for the fact that they don't get justice, but treatment. Sitting men will always see themselves as Jovian. The artist's concept of himself tends to be cruciform—as befits a hanging one. Both will be even further shaped by their situations. The critic spreads bottomwise, into scholarship. An artist's best mobility is above the neck. Often when he has enough work behind him, he grows a second head on it.

I begin to remember how many artists of the past have had two of them. My prejudice is that we should always carry our critic head a little negligently under the arm, like a collapsible top-hat. In the nineteenth century, the writer-artist sported his less self-consciously; the poets wrote the best literary criticism of the age, and even in the letters of George Eliot (who all her life, according to Gordon S. Haight in his preface to her *Letters*, suffered from "a morbid lack of self-confidence" in her work), we see nevertheless how widely and naturally she expects any writer to range. Europe expected it. There are periods that tolerate this, just as the gardener is allowably the authority on roses, the vintner on wine. Ours is not one of them.

To do this of course, one must have formidable artists. I think I would always rather read the notebooks of Matisse than the essays of Roger Fry—and a look at Fry's paintings in their room at Kings hasn't disabused me. (Though I would also rather read Hindemith on music than E. M. Forster; an artist has to be in his own art, for this kind of authority.) To have a fan's passion for an art, or even like Fry to help disseminate and explain its new forms, is a kind of hostess function, never to be confused with an artist's data on art's essences.

Literary criticism has yet another confusion at its very heart, in

that anyone talking about the medium seriously is in effect using it—
and had better have the powers of the artist as well. This often convinces literary critics that they are artists. It convinces me that artists
are the best of them. Only the artist can be trusted never to confuse
essences with statuses. And every judgment he makes involves him.
This is true of the most minor review or conversational flight. *He has
no light words.*

The French understand this. To the end that some become exag-
gerates of it, as the later Sartre becomes the art-spider who must cling
to the corpus of Genêt for his energy while his own work in art
dwindles, appendage to that suddenly monster second head. (At a
certain point in that sort of game, perhaps there is no turning back.)
Yet when we say then "But *au fond*, he was always *philosophe*," something is added. We are subscribing then to the abiding continuum of
human thought.

When I was sixteen, Jules Romains seemed to me both boring and
mysteriously seductive; I sensed that he was part of some luminous
tradition my own hadn't prepared me for. A few years on, Gide
bowled me over, above all for his seriousness; for his hairsplittings in
the realm of orthodoxy I cared nothing. What was this temper of
mind that suited me down to the ground though I might war with
its contents? Or feel outside it, as with Simone Weil, whose atmosphere I nevertheless *recognized* to the point of shock—for I was no
*religieuse.*

I had been a philosophy student though, happy to deliver a paper
on any closed system, from Schopenhauer's *The World as Will and
Idea* to a flirt with Kant and Hegel—always holding my breath in wait
for that wonderful, acolyte moment when I would see the angel-plan
spread out before me, and could hope to believe. Spinoza, as a Jew
and hence somehow already in my blood, didn't interest me—perhaps
here as elsewhere I always had a taste for Christian boys. Mystics like
Jacob Boehme drew me, but uneasily, as half on the road to art and
artists like Blake. In the French attitude what I had found was what
the world had long recognized as a perfect agar in which critique
could nourish endlessly: the spirit of *rational* inquiry, in a *religious*

temperament. It was my air. I too wanted to lay my life on a line.

But did I want that same air for art?

English after all was my language and spirit. Once past Spenser, or midway in Shakespeare, the air turns Protestant. Since Dr. Johnson, a large part of literary talk had been just that—talk, coffee-house common-sensical, with heaven around the corner in Grub Street. Then had come the message of Matthew Arnold's muscular speeches—we must cope—then Ruskin's sentimentality of the chaste, and Pater's watered-down Marcus Aurelius—a whole silly-season of flowers set in a dry sink. Shaw had been a journalist, D.H. Lawrence a bitter heckler; though coping was glorious at times, nothing I saw in English criticism matched the high, tonally fixed seriousness of the French. But the language itself was a fountain to be leaned upon, not formless but forming—always literally more words in it than French, looser, more open to change, yet not as heavy-spawning as German. A fine wool of a language, English, to which cockle-burrs can cling, yet which still has the watercolor vowels and voice-syrups of a Romance tongue. Its writers of the twentieth century have leaned on it like a rationale. And I with them. It suited what we like to think is our lawlessness.

Yet somewhere is a thought-continuum we too yearn for and must have. Nowadays the phrase "He's a renaissance man" is slang. Said not as if we are the forceful owners of a world on the way to knowing everything, but like men who wish that all knowledge once again was one. Or that one man—each—could have a "universal" portion of it. We think of Goethe, the poet-dramatist and novelist of *Elective Affinities* who could also discover the intermaxillary bone in man and quarrel with Newton over their theories of light, as able to do this, aside from his gifts, only because he lived at a time when the intellectual life could be the size of a duke's court, under smaller astronomies than we shall see again. But because knowledge is "larger" now, and no part of the world is sealed to it, must this be the end of seeing the connection of art, philosophy, and yes, science—as real as they ever were in that smaller continuum? Surely the closer interconnection of the physical world is telling us otherwise. In *death* and life.

I begin to see that agnosticism is a pale life unless, like any other religion, it is lived. Because I broke through the egg at the chickhole marked Art, doesn't preclude a temperament as religious as the churched, or an inquiry as rational as—the rational. In my work, it begins to seem to me, I am no longer the "novelist" or "short-story writer" which the American mode likes to have me. Nor even a writer only, though for passports and pickpockets that will do. I am the thing being written at the time. I am *this* one, now.

Going back over one's work, one can see from earliest times certain para-forms emerging. If one is crazy, these are *idées fixes;* if one is sane these are systemic views. A mind is not given but makes itself, out of whatever is at hand and sticking-tape—and is not a private possession, but an offering. Every "essay" I had ever written was in effect a way of telling *what* was offered to *whom.* I had always had to write everything, no matter the subject, as if my life depended on it. Of course—it does.

My father once gave me a fine sled, a Flexible Flyer. Though he'd often seen me ride bellywhopper on the old one, now for some reason, perhaps because I was a girl, he knotted two thick ropes through the steering wing of the new sled, one to the hole in each side. Once he had done this, I took to sliding down our steep hill sitting up holding the reins—which earned me the jeering name "High Coachman." I persisted. I liked the view.

About the same time, the Irish "Director" (an actor I imagine) whom the Mt. Neboh Sunday School hired every year to stage its elaborate children's musical, had a chat with my mother. As a fair ballet student since I was six, I was trying out for the star part—and for the blue spotlight on the rose-sequined tutu. Poor man, he couldn't tell her that my long ten-year-old bones and solemn face, plus a certain soft-shoe expertise I had concealed from her and the ballet-mistress, made me a cinch for the comedy trick—or that the other part was always slated for the President of the Congregation's little blond cuddly. "Why do they all want the classic stuff!" he said, clutching his bald spot. "When she can tapdance to hellandgone'!'

So now and then I say a funny thing in the forum. I have since learned how serious the comedy trick can be. But my taste for the High Coachman view remains.

This then is my vita. I have no light words.

But outside the "work," the words turn different, differently.

Anti-criticism is the one great dialectic tradition within which an artist can afford to be. Men who go to war for their convictions too often become the monster they meet.

Yet, in art, surely one doesn't fight the human soldier but the killer-process? Surely no one critic is *digne* enough to be the great enemy. And the killer-spirit may invade from anywhere. In the arts, nowadays it seems not to come huge on all fours, breathing false flame from fine nostrils. Rather, it tends to inhabit small, wan people, bilious with desolation, whose demon keeps them building matchstick bridges across the bloody flux.

In anti-criticism, I begin to see there are only two causes for going to war:

The proposed or predicted "death" of an art, or of some part of it. The setting up of "boundaries" which an art "must" have.

Neither of these propositions understands the very nature of art. The nature of the killer-spirit is that it will always find a dead art, or a caged one, more examinable.

Anti-criticism has therefore only two positives:

Art has no law-and-order per se—being a *way* to it. In art, death does not die—is not a dying.

During my first teaching year, I was asked to inaugurate a series of lectures on the novel to be given by experts in their fields: Leon Edel on James, James Clifford on *Pamela*, etc. It was suggested I speak on the novel generally. "But I haven't yet written one!" I stammered. That didn't seem to be a prerequisite.

I spoke from the one point of view I thought I could contribute—a writer's. My tone—which struck the note for all work of this kind I would do later—was personal. For a writer, the editorial "we" is a falsehood. We have only "I."

I often wonder why people are always being so much more solicitous about the novel, than of other forms of literary expression—always giving out greatly exaggerated rumors of its death, always rushing to resuscitate it, somewhat in the way worthy matrons used to rush hot soup to that rather deplorable family at the end of the town. Meanwhile, look around you. Poets are often still reduced to reading each other; Broadway is always complaining about the dearth of good plays, yet no one ever seriously proclaims the death of either drama or verse. No, the truth of the matter is that the novel has only lately become respectable, worthy of being talked about in the universities. The kind of people who in their hearts still believe that "real" knowledge can't reside in the specious world of the imagination, who will pay lip service to poetry and drama because these have been going on long enough to have anthropological value—(you know: the kind of man who would be ashamed to say aloud that he never reads a poem or sees a play, but who tells you virtuously that he "has no time for novels")—these people sometimes manage to make us feel that the novel, like that deplorable family, might, for its own good, be better dead. The truth of the matter is that the novel is as protean as any other form of expression. Like them, it does die sometimes—but, take heart— only, like them, when it becomes too respectable, in being the thing done at that time. Then lo, one day another changeling is found under a cabbage leaf somewhere—in Dublin or in Mississippi. . . .

I'd like to tell about some particular novels and what I got from them at certain times.

One of the first things we are told is that novels are useful as an accessory to history. By this people usually mean that when we read a novel written in a vanished era, or retrospectively *about* it, we can acquire, and painlessly too, *first* a mass of concrete data on how people lived in those days—the cut of their clothes and their manners, the slant of their architecture, the cadence of their speech—and *secondly*, a much more amorphous mass of data known as the "spirit of the age." The first kind of data, the concrete, might be thought of as the "Did they or did they not have bathrooms, and what kind?" department—certainly it would be for our era—the second kind of data, the "What did they say to themselves in the mirror when they were shaving"—that is, in the event that they shaved. The first category I won't belabor; certainly novels do provide a great deal of such material, in my mind, although the account books and all the other minutiae that people leave behind them do this in more detail, and although the novel—and this is important—always provides such material "by the way." The second category—the "spirit of the age" and how a novel interprets that, bears more explanation and examination. For the fact is that novels, good novels, are *not* accessory to history but in themselves a very special kind of history, in which the people always take precedence over the era. Such novels don't tell us how people lived and thought, but how *some* people did so, and—as it happened—at a certain time. They do give us the spirit of the age, but only as subsidiary to the "spirit of human beings." No doubt this is why certain people regard novels as untrustworthy.

The truth is that a good novel, like any work of art, is not an accessory to anything. It stands alone. For two reasons. First—it is an artistic attempt as opposed to an inclusive one; it abstracts from the world to compose a world of its own; it does not attempt to give all the facts but the pattern of some of them. Second—no matter how deceptively objective in method, the novel always has a stance. It is rooted in the peculiar semantics of a special kind of mind—one sensitive to the overtones of facts and to the overtones of people—and to the odd sonorities produced when these two combine. Its comments on the history of human beings are always, in the highest sense, prejudicial—no doubt why I regard them as so trustworthy.

I might say a word here about modern so-called "historical" novels, and about the special dissatisfaction I get from them. By this I mean the novel not written in a past era, or fairly close to it—within say two or three generations—but the novel which goes back an untouchable distance to recreate an era that the author can know only through other people's facts and other people's books. Some time ago, when a friend gave me for comment his new "historical" novel—one that had taken four years of research, and in the writing of which I knew there would be considerable ability, I accepted it with a sinking feeling and protected myself by saying, "You mustn't mind in case I don't enthuse; I've a blind spot somewhere, or else my standards are inexcusably lofty —anyway, about the only historical novels I want to read are *War and Peace, Henry Esmond*, and *The Virginians.*" He looked at me blankly and said: "But of course they aren't really historical. The Napoleonic wars were only 25 years before Tolstoi was born, and as for Thackeray —the period is only *back*ground for the people!" And of course he was right—it was I who was confused.

But I think I know now why the modern "historical" novel, no matter how exquisitely recreative of detail, usually sets my teeth on edge in some indefinable way. It is because this kind of novel is almost always an accessory to history—the era takes precedence over the people. Therefore the novelist, not being concerned primarily with his characters, cannot really imagine the truth about them as people—they remain lay figures, however beautifully reanimated and dressed. Such novels also violate those other tenets of which I have spoken. In them, the writer doesn't venture to compose a world out of the flux close to him, but plumps for a world already long since composed for him. Thus he tends not to use freely his own sense of proportion; his canvas is at once enormously wide and tempting—think of all that wonderfully available material; how can one leave any of it out?—and at the same time his choices, set within limits not imposed by himself, do not have the tension of suspense—because, after all, history tells us things did turn out a certain way. Above all, he can't use, except retrospectively, the superb struggle of values still under question. No, his era becomes his hero, either in itself or in some *post hoc* analogy with ours, and that is not enough for me. I am very prejudiced. I think novels should end up in the libraries, not begin in them. That's why I look blank when someone says, "Ah, you're researching, are you?"

Yet, nevertheless, all novels worthy of serious study are in their sense historical. In that respect, they attempt a number of daring things, although all of these may not be present in one novel. First, the novel attempts to write the story of a person or a group of persons. Whether it is their inner or their outer story, or some combination thereof, varies with the literary fashions and predilections of both the writer and his day. Sometimes a novel tries only to particularize these individuals, so that they live for us. At other times, it may also so generalize these individuals that, no matter what their "period" is, we identify with them—we recognize some continuity in the human psyche that we and they share. For isn't it a peculiar fact that although we make many formal surface protestations over our inability to "change human nature," at heart we love to see its very sameness explored? We love to see the old striations picked over again, reassembled in the light of another mind. The process entertains and instructs us with our own foibles, sometimes it comforts us—"there, but for the grace of God, go I," and sometimes it inspires us—"there, in the grace of human beings, I go too."

And, because no individual can be totally divorced from his situation in time and circumstance, the novel, sometimes inadvertently but more often not, gives a picture of his period. A great novel often does all three: the individual story, the human identification, the era. Parenthetically, the great subject of the novel in our day is the relationship of the individual *to* his time—to political time, dimensional or psychological time, to "no time left." But no matter how the focus of the novel shifts, no matter what subject it prefers in one decade or another, it shares, with poetry and drama, the great advantage of all art over the assemblage of literal fact. It makes use of the fact, in any or all assemblages of them, but it dares beyond the fact. Like all art, the novel's obligation to reality is obscure. It can therefore be more real than real.

Let me tell you briefly about four novels. I did not choose them because they are necessarily great ones, or because they clearly contain one or more of the elements of which I have spoken—any good novel does. In fact, I thought I had chosen them at random, out of the genial but practical impulse which leads us to press a book on a person, saying "Read this. You must read this"—and which has caused me to buy copies of these four rather often. Purposely, these are novels

written well in the past. You know all about the others. These have
settled down; they have perspective or in one case are ignored. They
span almost exactly one hundred years. After I chose them I saw that,
if taken chronologically, they do show certain changes in the focus of
the novel. Since, also quite by accident, they happen to be respectively
English, Russian, Italian and American, they show, by chance in a
comparative sense, that enormous versatility which causes some to
say that the novel is the art-form of the middle classes, and causes
others to question whether it can strictly be called a form at all. I
cannot synopsize these books for you, because no good piece of fiction
can be in any very useful way; I can only say what I perhaps might if I
were lending you them.

There is a certain book that, if there were still any desert islands to
be shipwrecked on, I would hope to have with me at the time. First,
frankly, because of the company—it has so much of it. It has two
heroines, one blond and gentle, of the pretty sort that dark women like
to think of as ninnies, and one dark, fiery and *ve-ery* slightly masculine
—of the type the gentle ones like to call "bluestocking." Its heroes are
two also—brothers, Robert, a mill-owner, tradesman, Whig, an un-
romantic man of action who "seems unconscious that his features are
fine," and Louis, the tutor, the seeming misanthrope, who really has a
"quiet, out of the way humor"—one of the typical *hommes fatales* of
nineteenth-century novels—those gentlemen whose attractive morbid-
ity proceeds from the possession of qualities superior to their station
in life. I leave it to you to guess which of the four marries who. In
addition to these, the large cast includes three comic curates, three
spinsters, two rectors, a country squire, a pompous baronet and a
modest one, a mischievous scamp of fourteen and several other charming children, various supernumeraries drawn from village life, etc.

This is a novel full of that coziness which the psychological novel
has lost, a novel truly crammed with the furniture of daily living.
Reading it is like walking into a series of genre pictures, into parlors,
salons, kitchens, schoolrooms, and yet, because it was written in 1849
and is set in three towns in the West Riding of Yorkshire, it is per-
vaded too by those great secondary characteristics of nineteenth cen-

tury English romanticism—the wind and the weather. Its plot is of
the period, an entirely unselfconscious blend of melodrama and sociological observation in which there is a mystery of parentage for one
heroine and the dread risk of hydrophobia for the other; yet, under-
lying these, one of the most solid representations we have of England
at the time of the industrial revolution—the period when the woolen
trade was suffering from the effects of the Orders in Council, the wars
of 1812 and the riots of the workers over the introduction of new
machinery. The novel has humor too, high comedy and low, that its
author intended; second, for us, the unconscious humor that we now
find in those stilted mores of the emotions that we have learned to
call Victorian. It has everything.

It remains only to tell you what the name of the book is: it was
written by a woman who was born in 1816 and died in 1855; it is of
course Charlotte Bronte's *Shirley*, to my mind a book grossly neglected
in favor of *Jane Eyre*, and I send you off to it without further ado,
stopping only to quote its first line—one of the most enchanting beginnings I know—"Of late years, an abundant shower of curates has
fallen upon the North of England."

We come now to one of the great novels of the world—as I say that,
I always find myself thinking what a singular treasure one has when
one is able to say such a thing almost without thinking, without question. Criticism is a defensive procedure, beset with the never quite
submerged antics of the ego, for in judging we know full well that we
judge ourselves. But on those occasions when we meet a truly great
work of art and can subscribe to it fully, then judgment quite literally
rests. By this I mean that such a meeting rests us—we find ourselves
suddenly in that area which is below ego and above fashion, where,
unutterably relieved, we can declare for the absolute. We are surprised by the lasting. We've been muddling along with the transitory;
we are suddenly suspended in what is sure. It is no less difficult to talk
about, however.

I first read Turgeniev's *Fathers and Sons* when I was about seventeen; I was reading it in the family living room where my father was
also sitting quietly reading, and when I finished the next but last

chapter, which tells of the death of the medical student Bazarov, in the house of his parents, I found myself crying hard, openly, in a way that I had never before cried over a book—and perhaps not since— and I sneaked out of the room so that my father would not see. At the time I no doubt cried partly because the death of the young and untried is peculiarly affecting to those who are the same, who perhaps have already imagined themselves on a similar bier. And partly, I suppose, because Bazarov, the nihilist who denied filial love even while he suffered from it, had something to say to me; although I did not see, as an older person might, that his nihilism was only that of the young, I recognized the suffering. No doubt I thought too that *I* would have loved and understood him, as Madame Odintsov, whom he loved, had not. I was later to see otherwise, that their tragedy was that they *had* understood each other, and had parted for this, not for the lack of it.

But, to return to that living room, I often wonder now, in the way that we like to rearrange the past, of what conversation would have ensued if my father had caught me sneaking away, and if I had handed him the book, saying: "Read it. And explain to me. Why am I crying?" For the simple and eternal subject of this book, set down with the Russian genius for depicting the concrete in the terms of the illimitable, is this: two generations, and the gaps and ties that lie between them— between the older, rebels passé, who have *settled* with life, and younger revolutionaries with the short future of revolutionaries, who think they will not settle. And how this has gone on, two by two, and will go on, two by two. And how, in Turgeniev's mind, it perhaps does not go on in vain.

About seventeen years later I re-read the book, and was shocked to see all I had missed in it. "I read too much too young," I thought to myself. I think otherwise now. Such books should be read first when one is young enough to care without quite knowing why, and again during those smart years when one thinks one knows why one once *did* care, and again—and this I look forward to—when one is too old *not* to care, and *not* to know why. Meanwhile, every time I re-read *Fathers and Sons*—I did so again in order to be able to talk to you about it—I see something I missed before, and I do not expect ever to read it without doing so.

Let me tell you, briefly, what it concerns. Nicholas Petrovich is awaiting his son Arcadi, who has just graduated from the university and is bringing home for a visit his friend Bazarov, son of a retired doctor, and himself a medical student. Arcadi, a sweet and simple young man who "loved nature although he did not dare avow it" and is doomed by his admiration of Bazarov, the brilliant disciple of scientific materialism pushed to the nth, ·who believes, or thinks he believes this: "I do not believe it at all necessary to know each individual in particular. . . . Moral maladies spring from a bad education, from the absurd condition of our social law. Reform society and you will have no more of them . . . in a society well-organized it will be all the same whether a man is stupid or intelligent, bad or good." "A good chemist is twenty times more useful than a good poet."

Arcadi is ashamed to let his friend see the depth of his love for his own father. The two friends visit Bazarov's parents, and there we see that Bazarov also has not been able to quench his family feelings—his tenderness toward the worth and the foibles of his father, his inability to be harsh to the simple, doting attentions of his mother. Meanwhile, we see the two fathers, good fellows, not really old—Nicholas P. is still in his middle forties—but both of them retired to those compromises that individual lives sooner or later make. Arcadi's father, full of vague, well-intentioned efforts to manage his farm under the recent rulings which have freed the serfs, is abashed before the sweeping theories of the young men; Vasili, Bazarov's father, retired from practice, but still doctoring, is outmoded in his son's eyes. The sad timidity of the fathers before their critic sons, their sense of failure, of compromise, of not yet being wholly negligible—and this complicated with an insistent love of their critics; opposite them the young men, bent on changing the world, despising their elders for their abdication from it, unaware that they themselves hold the ovum of compromise—and this all complicated with a love for those whom their theories teach them to despise—all this Turgeniev does in the round, as the whole novel, separate its facets as we may, does. Do not think that I do it any sort of justice here.

The action of the novel occurs entirely in the series of visits paid by the young men; on one of these, to the house of Mme. Odintsov, Bazarov falls in love and "recognized with a sombre indignation that romanticism had gained on himself." Mme. Odintsov, beautiful, rich, has, after certain difficulties, attained her defenses, and means to keep them; for her "tranquility is better than anything." She is one of those subtle people who choose the expedient thing even while they are well aware of what they lose by doing so. In the account of their love affair, as in the account of the fathers and sons, we hear, with the same extra-sensory perception with which we hear it beneath the concrete action of all great fiction, the sound of the mills of the gods grinding. Here it is the sound of what people must give up, or will give up—in favor of what they cannot give up. But I am way ahead of myself. That happens to be what I saw in last week's re-reading.

What I saw in the second reading was entirely different. It was then, say 1948; by then, a whole generation of students, locked like me in the ivory towers of literature had had to become "politically conscious." And I saw with amazement that I had entirely missed seeing the extent to which this is a novel of political and social ideas. Perhaps I may be excused for this because, as with the "historical" novel, I had been trained by this time to think of the "political" novel as a separate entity, where the people were always pastiche to the ideas. Whereas, in the 19th century Russian novel, although the air is political, the garden is political, and social argument streams through the Russian temperament like arterial blood—man as a human animal underwrites it all. *Fathers and Sons* takes place during the era of reforms that began with the accession of Alexander, when the serfs were freed, the peasants allowed to pay for land and given courts of justice— you may remember the reference in the first paragraph of the book, to the domestic, "a servant of the new generation of progress." Turge- niev's *Sportsman's Sketches* played an important role in bringing about these reforms, for which he later was punished, and his portrait of

Bazarov so outraged his friends that he went to live abroad. All his work is documentary in the narrow sense as well as the large. Yet I had been so interested in the people, it had all seemed so natural, that I had hardly noticed. As I have said, this is a great novel.

But, during those years over here after the iron curtain fell, when people wondered what the Russians were like now, when later one heard it surmised that the Russians were still Byzantine, still Slavophile, still in fact Russian, I often wondered why the knowledge that censorship denied us was not more sought in those books that ignore frontiers, in a book like this, where the author can say, in a casual aside: "The city of X, to which the two friends went, had for governor a man still young, at once progressive and despotic, as so many are in Russia." Or where Bazarov can say of "Liberals"; "You gentlemen cannot go beyond a generous indignation . . . or resignation, things which do not mean much. You think you are great men, you think yourself at the pinnacle of human perfection when you have ceased to beat your servants, and we, we ask only to fight with one another and to beat. Our dust reddens your eyes, our mire soils you; you admire yourselves complacently; you take pleasure in reproaching yourself; all that bores us; we have other things to do than to admire or reproach ourselves; we must have other men broken at the wheel." Does that sound familiar?

Later on I saw many other things in this book. Once, when I was reading another favorite, James' *The Bostonians*, I thought suddenly of Eudoxia Kukshin in the Turgeniev book, the emancipated woman, and of how Turgeniev had done, in ten hilarious pages, so much of what James had done in 378. And I thought of Turgeniev's portrait of Arina, Bazarov's mother, the simple, household woman, whom he has set down forever in two pages of short sentences bright as silk, in a way that James, for all his long and marvelous respirations, perhaps could not do. Still later when, having become a writer, I was reading with a certain professionalism, more aware of trade-secrets, as it were, I saw how Paul, Arcadi's uncle, the frustrated *elegant* of whom Bazarov says "his nails might be sent to the Exhibition," a man who in a lesser book would be made to say all the properly wrong things that would conform him to type, is here made to step out of character now and then,, to speak on the side of the angels, to say some of the right things that make him a man. Bazarov, of course, does speak in a straight "line"; the secret here is that while he does so, we watch him feeling in another.

But the story must end. Bazarov returns to live in his father's house and help him doctor; he contracts a surgical infection from an autopsy on a typhus patient, and dies—untried.

And now I shall have to reverse myself. I've been telling you that novels are neither political tracts nor historical ones, are stories of individuals, not eras, and I am now about to tell you of two modern novels, one of which began as a political tract, and another, in which an era—ours just past—is the true subject. But "modern" means in part a "reversal." And, as I have said, the novel is a protean form. If *it* won't remain consistent, there is no reason why I should.

I was in Rome during the spring elections of 1953. The city, with almost every building plastered from roofline to pavement with election posters, looked like an enormous mosaic. Almost all the posters had that wonderful Italian versatility of design and color, and many of my American friends were making collections of them. This was the period of McCarthy at home; it came uncomfortably to us to admit that the Communist posters were by far the handsomest and had the most effective slogans. A friend and I were sitting in his car, parked off the Piazza del Populo, looking at some of them. My friend was an Englishman, a Catholic who had spent some of his boyhood in Italy, had worked with British Intelligence there during the war, and was now a critic and editor specializing in Italian literature. We were looking at one poster that had a photo of a banquet table surrounded by members of ducal or princely families—one was a Torlonia. The name of each man was printed over his head, and beneath the photo there was a list of figures, enumerating the taxes each of the men should by law have paid, and the actual smaller amounts each had paid. "Can one trust those figures?" I said. "Is this true?" My friend sighed. "Yes," he said. "Unfortunately, there is no need to exaggerate them. You in America have wealthy men, but you cannot understand the kind of wealth a man can have here. None of your American millionaires is rich the way Torlonia is—in privilege, in land, and in human men." Just then, a group of young boys and girls surrounded our car—it was not a pretentious one—and spat into it. After they had gone, and we had cleaned ourselves, my friend said: "I don't suppose I can make you understand the basis for Communism here. I love southern Italy, yet I cannot bear to stay here long, because I know how the peasants have to live. I'm a Catholic, but if I stayed there for any length of time, I would have to become a Communist too. Not in any intellectual way, in theirs. And in spite of all that we all well know. But I don't suppose you could understand."

But I did understand, because I had read Silone's *Fontamara*. Fontamara is a town in southern Italy, and this is a story of how Fascism and Communism came to that town, and of what was there before. It was written in 1930, probably when Silone was still a member of the Party, but although he may have begun it as a pamphleteer, he finished it as a novelist, and the reader does not have to know or subscribe to any Internationale except that of human beings in order to participate. What Silone has done is to show how some people have to live, and he has done it from the inside of the peasant mind, using the choral dignity of a people who have no written language. As he himself says, the story is "woven"; it is *told* by three people, as an old man, his wife and his son, each of them handing over the next chapter to another: "my wife will tell you what happened next"; "my son will tell you what happened next." And they do. And you see. As Silone says in his preface: ". . . let each man tell his story in his *own* way." Many years later it was reprinted, not long ago, in a revised version I did not read. It did not seem to me to need revision.

And as each man tells his story in his own way, we are beginning to see, perhaps without even having paused to note the great landmarks of Joyce and Proust, what a long way the novel has come. People are still its subject, but now it is people in the aggregate, almost in the mass, as if the individual no longer has enough weight to hold a story together, against the single all-face of the human condition. The arena has become more compelling than the gladiators—as it had in the Malraux novels. Or the novel takes to an old and tried way of handling men in the aggregate—to satire—to Orwellian returns to *Erewhon* and *Gulliver's Travels*. Or in those novels which cling, however tenuously to the story of the individual, we see the powerful, nullifying mask of the real hero—our era, our "spirit of the age"—peering always over his shoulder. And then the novel perhaps tumbles toward essay.

In 1949, a novel called *Do I Wake or Sleep* appeared under the name of Isabel Bolton, a pseudonym. Since then she has published several others. All of them were written during her sixties or later, and all have a similar scheme—a tenuous, brittle plot, touched upon sometimes faintly, sometimes luridly, and always transmitted through the mind of one observer, who is always a woman looking back upon her past, out upon her world. All of the first three novels were set in New York—*Do I Wake* opened at the World's Fair in 1939, just after Hitler entered the Sudetenland. What she did with the New York scene was to make it no longer a scene only, but a fusion of the sensations peculiar to a city strung upon the nerves of its inhabitants. She had a style that, like all the best, seemed fatally wedded to the meaning it carried, the one inseparable from the other. Its nearest antecedent was possibly Virginia Woolf, the Woolf of the last extraordinary novel, that ought to be better known—*Between the Acts*. Like Woolf, she used breathless, cumulative phrases, flashing with participles, whose almost wearing cadence seemed certain to topple, but built instead into sentences whose strange effect is to make the present, our present, constantly palpable. "But isn't this poetry?" it was said, and the next instant—because a strong analytic intellect, prosaic enough when it wished, was working there—"But isn't this essay?"

What this novel was, was an essay of the emotions—ours—the haunted esprit of our age, expressed by an intellect wedding itself constantly to the immediate, like some antenna, some thinking reed drawing together the vibrations in our air. So just as we had begun to tire of the narrow limits of the stream-of-consciousness "inner I—me," this novelist took up the method again, with all its limits, but transposed the subject—to the inner "we." Her characters were dangerously limited—they stood on a single premise; what drew the reader was the acuity with which he found phrased for him those very limits, that very premise which, as a citizen of our time, we all share. The writer seems to have caught for us, in her half lyrical, half philosophical net, the "we" of her era and of ours—that individual whose private self appears to be shrinking in the face of all the mass-media obligations and terrors of his public one. It was one of the earliest novels of this type, over here. Now we are all too well acquainted with them; many a novel may be named for one man, but he seems to speak in the voice of the aggregate, as a prancing symbol of what we think we are. I think that too will change.

And so, the novel goes on. In fancy, I lend you these four. Each of them says to you what Turgeniev remarks that little Fenitchka, the mistress of Nicholas Petrovitch, seemed to say when she became respectable: "Excuse me, I am not here for nothing."

.
.

BY 1963, when Robert Hatch of *The Nation* asked me to review a clutch of foreign novels in any form I wanted, I had imposed certain rules on myself: never to do a review in order to blast someone or some book, never in fact to review anything not liked, only to review at will and at some length—and presumably for literature. (I had also kept off contemporary Americans—the only way I saw to keep friendships and avoid tea-pot tempests.) *The Nation*'s proposal seemed to me just on the order of what my British writer-friends might do—covering foreign news as it were, for a small, decent paper, at a thin, honorable price. ($75.)

I started out bravely anti-critical, fell into complacency over books I could easily despise, and was gratefully redeemed by a book I could praise, Gunter Grass' *The Tin Drum*. (And by the Germans—for me so long an *idée fixe* by way of war and family, that the slightest snuff of them hurtled me into the long view without half trying.)

*The Nation* asked me to continue, perhaps in a column, but I had had enough. Meanwhile, toward the end of my connection with *The Reporter*, I did some drama reviews.

As a dance-student since the ago of six and as a high school and college actress, I had had the amateur's "inside" whiff of the theater; as audience, I had started as a patron of Gray's Drugstore's cut-rate tickets when I was twelve. After my first book, at the instance of Cheryl Crawford, who hoped for a play, I had attended the Actor's Studio for about a year, but was not deflected—I still had too many novels to write. And I knew the theater would take all my devotion, not half. If I ever again wrote a play (in college I had been a student of Minor Latham) I would attach myself to a repertory theater. Meanwhile, at the studio, I had seen how a working theater can serve novelists; they see their own limits—and avenues—better defined.

To review a play was refreshing; it took me "out of my field." (By now, having written two or three novels, I had almost accepted the category thrust at me.) But a thinker's only boundaries are his own. I had a vigorous sense that I was testing these—or else constructing them. For "the Germans"—actually my own compound of a childhood hatred of their bourgeoisie's servility and "schmutz," their evil history and my perverse love of their language—had appeared again. This time, I thought I was ready for them. The subject was Peter Weiss's play about Marat-Sade. I called the review, "*The Agony of The Cartoon.*"

Some poets, painters, thinkers represent mankind always with the *risus sardonicus* of death and corruption on its face, whirling in a society which is a death dance. Others trace this face with a certain tenderness of perfectibility on it, and see the society too as teleological, pushing along that famous incline toward the stars. Between these two views lie all the gradations of art. In Peter Weiss's play, *The Persecution and Assassination of Marat as Performed by the Inmates of the Asylum of Charenton Under the Direction of the Marquis de Sade* (and as performed with disciplined rage by the Royal Shakespeare Company under the wizardry of Peter Brook), the stage at the Martin

Beck Theatre is a pitched one, for real and for metaphysical, angling
its inmates *down,* and toward the audience. Musical accompaniment
is fifed and tympanied, or rattled from the metal sheets used so often
in productions of *Godot,* by inmates placed in the boxes, while a
Brechtian chorus of four more sings and mimes from the stage or from
trapdoors below. Coulmier, the director of the mental home where
de Sade, as an inmate after 1801, wrote some of the theatrical enter-
tainments that were produced there as therapy, sits onstage with his
wife and daughter—as indeed the fashionable Parisians who came to
watch the antics at Charenton did sit. There are incursions of actors
into balcony and orchestra, wherever sit the aristocrats of the Martin
Beck. For, as in Genêt's *The Blacks,* the audience is indictable. When
it claps the cast at the end of the play, the inmates clap back.

The intent is "total" theater, and in production terms—short of a
possible spastic song-and-dance response from the ticketholders—the
play gets it. Everyman is onstage in all the grotesques of his overt
and hidden lunacy—the obsessive, the autoerotic, the weeper in her
mobcap, the drooler with the thick tongue, all performing their silent
rhythms, and attended by coifed male nuns and butcher-clad nurses;
the mime chorus is Elizabethanly drunken or whorish; other types
and professions pass behind in Molièresque charade. Directorial in-
vention underscores the author's intent at every chance. Where the
author himself, careful not to have his play "about" one thing or any
actor speak for only one, specifies that the Girondist deputy be played
by an erotomaniac "in the smooth, tight trousers of an 'Incroyable,' "
then the Royal's customary fondness for humanizing touches of
bawdry improves upon this suggestion very versatilely; in a play
which as much as anything is about revolution, then the blood poured
from buckets at intervals is of course red, white, or blue.

In the modern theater, where so much device is available (and for
all the complaints, so much money for it), audiences have often to
quarrel over whether the play is really the thing in a new production, or whether directorial energy has made it so. When the two
are so merged as here, that question may remain as unanswerable
as the dialectical questions in this play itself—and like them, sets up

one of the vital tensions which make theater. For while it is evident at once that this play is not, like *The Royal Hunt of the Sun*, a weak-minded pageant in which the elephant spectacle is poised on the butterfly wings of bombast, nevertheless the visual and aural confusion is at times overwhelming—too close to circus for us to get it all at one whack. This is an old Brechtian trick, but an older theatrical one. In a sense the play here is swarmed over, even attacked by the production ideas it itself invites, but not swamped. Sometimes, in one of these three-ring whirligigs, there is clear contempt for the play's words, but here the important monologues are delivered at as staid a pace as Hamlet's, underscored by the choral flow. Even in the din at the finale, when all might well be chanting "O Sophonisba! Sophonisba, O!" with all Jamie Thomsons anywhere, instead of: "Charenton Charenton/Napoleon Napoleon/Nation Nation/Revolution Revolution/Copulation Copulation"—one wishes the best wish, to come back for another performance, or to go to the text.

London critics have argued that the play itself derives from a number of fashionable sources; so it does, along with those I have indicated. But it is not merely an adroitly composite echo, though it is composite and does echo within itself. One brilliant idea sustains it: we *are* in the asylum; de Sade *is* producing his play; Marat (at whose actual funeral the real de Sade did deliver the oration) *is* in his bath (to which the real Marat was confined by a skin disease) before us, but in the bathhouse of the asylum, ready to be murdered by Charlotte Corday, toward which event all continuity proceeds. The aristocratic onlookers *are* watching, onstage and off. Marat is played by a paranoiac inmate, Corday by a sleepwalking upper-class girl, costumed like an Empire nymph and singing her somnambulist horrors to the lute. The director, always ready to speak for conventional political and social order, must by his very role interrupt at intervals the actions of the "disturbed." The audience has its half-knowledge of history, and an awareness that both history and itself are to be manipulated. So the play at once acquires a juggler's multiplicity of levels, and any idea extractable from it is intended to be seen in movement with the others.

Many so extracted are not new to the world's logic: revolutions return rich and poor to the status quo, achieving nothing: money is Marxist in all its implications: man is a mad animal with further plans of madness. No criticism here, at least from me. Precisely because most ideas are not new to the world, ideas alone are unbearable in art, which must clothe and externalize them, it doesn't matter how, as long as a forceful unrest is successfully raised under and around them. Mr. Weiss's juggling is one way of doing that; he is not interested in a longitudinal play which progresses toward a resolution in the key of C—or even C sharp. "The important thing is to pull yourself up by your own hair/to turn yourself inside out and see the whole world with fresh eyes" (Marat). Well and good, so far as it goes, and with a sop to existentialism too: though the pointlessly horrible aspects of our world are on record, they bear repeating. And although the energy with which both language and action here overstate, restate, and confuse themselves is familiarly Brechtian in mode, it is merely one of the many methods of drama, used to send us in pursuit of these elusive balances, these words lost in excitement— that is, back to the play.

Here, I suspect one will find that Weiss has a multiplicity of very realistic images, but after that brilliant beginning, no metaphor that would sustain it toward greatness. Nobody is asking for "answers," or a play with a literal "point," which is why I say "metaphor." Ideas may not resolve, but once the chaos of our world has been established, plays still may, and not necessarily on an up note—as Genêt, Sartre, and Beckett have shown. This play is not surreal *enough*. The "chaos" is as well ordered as a concertmaster's. And though Weiss clearly knows that "total" theater is not just "everybody running," his play's total statement falls far short of Brecht also, absconding, as is currently fashionable in so many of the arts, with an implied: "Get excited. Start thinking. But don't ask *me*!"

As the uncurtained scenes progress by topic and harangue—Stifled Unrest, Corday's First Visit (she has three), Marat's Liturgy, A Regrettable Intervention (a paraphrase of the Lord's Prayer, e.g., "forgive us our good deeds and lead us into temptation"), Marquis de Sade

Is Whipped, Song and Mime of the Glorification of the Beneficiary, to quote a few—the most interesting and best-maintained dialectical balance is that between de Sade and Marat, the freshest antitheses being there. In Conversation on Life and Death, de Sade, who hates Nature, "the passionless spectator" who "goads us to greater and greater acts," complains that "even our inquisition gives us no pleasure nowadays . . . our postrevolutionary murders . . . are all official. . . . There's no singular personal death to be had." And Marat replies: "If I am extreme, I am not extreme in the same way as you/Against Nature's silence I use action/In the vast indifference I invent a meaning . . . work to alter . . . and improve." Later, de Sade says: "Before deciding what is wrong . . . we must find out what we are . . . for me the only reality is imagination/the world inside myself." And Marat replies: "No restless ideas can break down walls/I never believed the pen alone could destroy institutions."

We appreciate this for a number of nicely posed—and mixed— reasons. Clarity, in the midst of a continuous-movement play, is welcome. We rise to how neatly Jesuitical it is that de Sade, that doctrinaire of the perverse and the exaggerated, should be made to speak for or stand for the inner imagination (usually assigned to gentler lyrists), and that it should be Marat, apostle of revolutions artistically complete to the last blood-drop, who itches symptomatically on the cross of that bloodletting, and dreams of action—in his bath. I say "stand for" with intent. For the counterside of plays which juggle, raise the hair, and leave us is that if the smoke clears for even a moment, the people tend to stand and stare at us from under the paternal arm of the playwright, as the adroit antitheses they are.

Weigh these as one may. Weiss's stance is clear enough without statement. He writes of humanity in those ever-resuscitated grotesques of flesh-hatred which, in the long line from Bosch to Breughel and before, we used to call medieval. It is of course a genre which must accompany us forever, like our own smell. Lately the Germans have done it best; between wars they have an especial talent for it. Curiously, whether done by a Jew who lives in Sweden, or a half-Pole, it is recognizable as German still. Günter Grass's robust humor gives the genre more depth; what grim jokes there are in the Weiss *Marat-Sade* are very like those in the Royal Shakespeare Company's recent London production of Brecht's *Puntilla* at which American audiences seem to laugh timidly, at least in this kind of play.

To be able to speak of the *Marat-Sade* as "this kind" of play may also be a measure of its scope, and of Brecht's "epic" theater in general. Must it always be couched in terms of the cartoon? Or is that why, though the artist is not obliged to answer his own questions, "this kind" of play seems to truncate the question before it is asked? The power and agony of the medieval cartoons of humanity is in their assumption, under the grimacing flesh and the snake-scales, of a spiritual antithesis. Mr. Weiss neither demands nor assumes *any* antithesis, which is why his play remains one-dimensional and he correctly describes it as Marxist. Within that span, it has the mesmerism our own caricatures always have for us. We see the normals regarding the lunatics regarding the normals. It is no wonder that *everybody* claps.

Censorship, when not too serious, is often fun to watch. The modern version of the sport, now that sex has less shock to it, will be to catch onto whatever else will be sex's substitute, not in the great arenas of politics and civil law, but in the small daily mind.

Once upon a time, in the story "The Hollow Boy," *Harper's* Magazine hadn't let me, then a new writer, say a girl had her "monthlies"—which was the idiom proper to the story—but had insisted on the word "period." In the Weiss review, *The Reporter* had balked at letting me say that Peter Brook had improved on the stage directions for the erotomaniac's trousers by having him wear an erect penis, presumably wooden, inside them. "Improved upon them very versatilely" was all I could think of—a fine example of how Euphues takes over when you can't be direct.

Yet in another piece, *The Reporter* let me speak of buggery—and even the arse—I was talking about homosexuals in literature—perhaps because the legal abrogation of homosexual freedom was just then under scrutiny in Britain, and therefore a liberal cause. For, what we were going through over here, especially in the theater, was that period of heart-in-the-right-place sentimentality which always precedes admitting a wronged sector of humanity to its full rights. As a Jew traveling in upstate New York, and a woman traveling in literature, I already knew that line. One day, but not quite yet, I would write at more length of homosexual writers, and of what American sex in general has done to its literature. Meanwhile, in a piece called, "Will We Get There by Candlelight?" I had this to say:

In a recent week I spent approximately seven hours of an otherwise idle life at two of John Osborne's plays then running concurrently in London, the West End production of *Inadmissible Evidence* at Wyndham's, and *A Patriot for Me*, in repertory and out of the Lord Chamberlain's clutches, at the Royal Court's "private" showing to the members of the theater club we had joined at least two days previously, that being the length of time which must lapse legally here between desire and performance. With the exception of *Epitaph for George Dillon*, seen off-Broadway, and *The Entertainer*, which I missed altogether, it has been my luck to see Osborne plays on home ground, beginning with the 1956 production of *Look Back in Anger*, which I was fortunate enough to catch on one of those celebrated Monday nights when discussions were held after the performance so that patrons coul relieve their outrage at what the playwright was doing to English life, society, sex, youth, the class warfare, the welfare state, death and taxes, red-brick universities, the owners of sweetshops, middle-class girls who marry them and have therefore to do their own ironing—and general hard times for anti-heroes all.

In the 1956 *Look Back in Anger*, not all of the audience's rage was caused by attack on institutions precious to it, or even by Osborne's wickedly skin-raising flicks of line-to-line dialogue. Instead, it was in part teased out by the antics of the "anger" in the play itself, as it flitted restlessly from target to target like a bird that defecated intelligently from the air but never perched, or like a floating paranoia that never revealed itself centrally—what made the patrons sore was that what cannot be grasped cannot be attacked. In discussions of last year's *Tiny Alice*, Edward Albee's reply to questions on what this play was about suggested that this was not necessary to know; if the audience would but "think" along with him *he* would be satisfied—and, he hoped, they would be too. Thus he very cannily and properly avoided saying whether he himself knew precisely—for any artist is a fool who is willing to state his subject except in the work itself, or at least in another work as long.

Osborne's case was different. He seemed not to make distinction between the world's confusion, his hero's, or his putative own, not even to perceive it or care. However, when "a pox on all your houses" is stated with such wit, vigor, and passion too, it makes for a rousing evening. Some audience irritation derived from having to admit it, particularly in the case of the hero's famous soliloquy, which went on and on with such an intimacy of nagging that one began to need either to answer back, as in a family quarrel, or else leave the room—and then had to remind oneself that to make a theater seem a room, or an audience a family, is virtue indeed. Here what the author had done was to use sheer length and circuitous repetition in even greater proportions than Wagnerians are used to, or families either. And here, too, our itch went unappeased, for though Osborne might seem to be seeking a Tinker Bell rapport with us, he never gave us the satisfaction of being asked the question out loud.

In *Inadmissible Evidence*, Nicol Williamson brilliantly plays a solicitor whose hysterically egoistic need of both office and home entourages —mistress, wife, daughter, clerks, and secretaries—demands that they dance attendance on his twenty-four-hour daily merry-go-round of broken promises, until the clock runs down, the luck runs out, and the dread blow falls: he is alone. The promises are of varying sorts. He has an inability to keep appointments with clients in jail or at his office, he runs very near the law regarding trumped-up evidence; he doesn't write his own briefs or study them, and meanwhile twits his junior and senior clerks for the hard work they do to keep the firm in order, plus the dull lives they must lead in consequence; his clients do not get a fair shake, at least from him. Nobody does; he cannot keep his appointments with life, though he presumably has a rare old time in the evasionary hours between.

For, mainly, his broken promises are to women; being late or never home to dinner with the wife is the least of them. He "stays late" at his office twenty-four hours a day for the usual reasons: he can't get to the mistress with whom he pleads each day to stay home for his call; he has outgoing and incoming mistresses among the secretaries; even his own daughter is kept waiting so that he may be seen breaking his promises to her (or perhaps as excuse for the long digression—in this case on the younger generation—of which there is at least one in each Osborne play, often the liveliest part of it or the most worthy of serious attention). Always the broken bargains are plastered up with charm and/or argument, and the boundless energy of a personality whose energy can exert itself only thus and has done so since schooldays; he is an emotional athlete while obviously believing himself to be a sexual one.

Williamson's job is to make us believe in the hero's basilisk effect on others. The problem is somewhat akin to that of bringing on-stage a "great man" already known to us from the annals of history or art and having the greatness weigh true. For almost three-quarters through, Williamson, if not the play, gets away with it. Of course every energy and bit of brilliance is tipped his way; the other males are mere placatory figures and the women either telephonic devices or plasticine presences; the departing and pregnant office wife bows out in a tantrum; her successor complements the hero's monologue with the complaisant gestures, almost in tutu, of a ballerina choreographed for Hot Young Thing and Has to Have It. (If a woman had written the play, which is somehow quite imaginable, she would rightly have been accused of seeing all "obligation" only in the context of what is due the female.)

What defeats both actor and play a good hour before its end is its monologue. For while Osborne, plainly narrowing his boundaries if not yet in control of them, has settled for the inadequacies of one man over those of an entire country or world, it can now be seen far too clearly that his real talent, even more especially when he is dealing with a modern man than with a historical one, is still for soliloquy. The play is actually a monologue and certainly in monotone, with any roles other than the hero—or male lead, as one is continuously tempted to call him—performing as little more than subservient projections of *his* will (and whose metaphysic?).

Meanwhile, I had begun to learn what I thought of Osborne's metaphysic, or perhaps "moralities" was the better word. Hide as an author may behind his naughtiness (a word that would never occur to me except in England) or behind, say, his strenuously *risky* modernity, why did both these words, searched out to express his style, bring to mind such an opposite as "morality"?—a nineteenth-century antique that has not yet come back into its own in America. The answer may be that nursery-naughtiness brings on nannyish moralizing, in the reviewer as in the reviewed. Following this train of thought in the entr'acte, I recalled how many recent British plays did go back to the nursery in the end for emphasis—remember Osborne's own squirrels and bears in *Look Back*, or Dorothy Tutin kneeling down to repeat "Dod bless Mummy" (as example to be taken, Dod Wot, of a pre-suicide's mental state) in Graham Greene's *The Living Room*. (American authors don't go back to the nursery; they go back to *childhood*, which can be orful, but is not the same.)

"He's trying to write *Everyman* with one character," I mused, "in this case Vanitie"—but this didn't seem quite enough either. Suddenly there came to mind a favorite set of illustrations in an old bound *Harper's* of the mid-1860's—a double-page spread of drawings showing the progressive corruption of a provincial young man, his rise in city sophistication and champagne wickedness, and predictable fall. As with many nineteenth-century cartoons, the style of these was a kind of bowdlerized Hogarth, still teeming with an eighteenth-century cast of characters, but all arranged now according to a virtue and a vice that plumbed the depths of neither. It had always typified for me that exact limit of "Victorian" sentiment in which good and evil become the tamed gorgons Naughty and Nice, watching over that slough of dismay (not despond) where, sadly but never quite tragically, the good people are uniformly dull and the wicked have all the endowment of vitality and charm. This seems to me both the range of Osborne's "anger," and how it stratifies itself also, which may be why it originally bewildered audiences used to the newer psychological mixtures. It may also be why Osborne's comic comments have a persistently topical superficiality, and why his tragic ones never really hurt. I'd certainly never thought of him before as one of our more eminent Victorians, but take away the shrewd or shrewish patter of the language, especially as it attaches to sexual matters, and remember that our grandfathers never went undistinguished for stàyın power or long breath—and see what you see.

The second of these two plays, *A Patriot for Me,* tells the story of the rise within the Imperial and Royal Army of the Austro-Hungarian Empire of the nobody Alfred Redl; of his fatal flaw of homosexuality which leads to his spying for the archenemy Russia; and his ultimate fall.

Aisde from the documentary technique that divides the scenes (those screen flashes: "Prague 1896," "Vienna 1897," which are always such a deadly impediment to the natural flow of "legitimate" theater that so knowing a dramatist can surely have used them only in haste) there is nothing here that devotees of Victor Herbert might not take to, except, of course, a slight sexual displacement. Alfred can't love the Countess because going to bed with a woman gives him the willies (we have already had a scene with a whore, a tender one of course). And Alfred's dear friend is a dear boy—Flash, Vienna, 1902! Plus any modern analogy the author would not be sorry to see us make.

And meanwhile we have the monologue again, this time Alfred's. For monologue is what it really is—though in intent he speaks *to* people rather than *at* them, and the fast blackouts of the staging help by breaking up what might flower into soliloquy. Despite whores and nightmares, Colonel Redl takes ten scenes to discover his own dark secret, though the audience, being much wickeder, has long since jumped the gun. After that, why, the downfall—gradual very, and with flourishes, not infrequently, of violins. Surely even the Greeks, who made so much of fatal flaws, including this one, never followed one so dead straight to such literal consequences as the simple Osborne psychologic does—or with such deadly obvious development of event and retinue. Colonel Oblensky, the shaggy-friendly, cynic-sinister head of Russian intelligence who recruits Redl by blackmail (in a scene in the snow of winter, what else?) is himself a man of parts, many of them previously played and written by Peter Ustinov. Actually, all the sins against believability end by giving the play a kind of grossly reverse artistic form all its own, as we learn to deal with the difficulty of believing in light opera and psychology at the same time, with the oversimple scarlet-letterdom of the psychology itself, plus the unfortunate fact that, unlike Williamson, this time even Maxmilian Schell cannot make the hero as Dick Deadeye a fascinator as all the other actors keep saying he is—perhaps because vanitie allows of more inflection than sodomy.

That time should soon come (or may have) when homosexuals and heterosexuals alike will be bored at the recurrence of homosexuality as the dark secret or the fatal flaw of current dramas. For any such labeling of a man or of a life by a single quality is not only to patronize human individuality but also to sacrifice any artistic one, to melodrama or perhaps naughtiness. In the same way, to jot in a little anti-Jewishness—Redl is a concealed Jew, and the generals are made to make such anti-Semitic cracks as one expects of "the period" —is no automatic passport to drama or even sympathy; here it remains one of Osborne's digressions, notable only as it suggests that where once these were almost arrogantly designed to kill our sympathies, now they seem complaisantly to bid for it. Too late, for, prefaces to the contrary, this is no story of a Jew in that army, or a man of any kind anywhere in history or out of it. Take the young man of my old *Harper's* magazine cartoon, which was called "The Drunkard's Decline," change the accent, the army, the sex of the whores, and the vintage of the champagne—but keep the sentiment—and call it "A Fairy's Fall."

Nevertheless. Nursery or not, buggery fascinates us all. It is a word I never think of except in England—perhaps because it suggests a verbal bluntness, possibly a specious one, common to English sexuality in general. As against the brilliantly emotional or religious logistic with which French writers depict the homosexual, or the shadowy, sometimes subcritical murk the Americans use, it does suit the bracing English style, half music hall, half Elizabethan clown, with which Osborne stages the one lively scene of the play, a cruelly funny one, where Redl attends a party "in drag." There Redl, in uniform, fades from the play altogether; it is the supernumeraries in their transvestite array who are the thing: the false soubrette who warbles, Lady Godiva with rope tails hanging indecently from "her" pink tights, the classic whore telling of "her" first fall, and the Baron, a boxer-shouldered dowager in white satin ball dress and tiara, hilariously queening it over all. In spite of plenty of material from the good old folklore—"He wanted to be a homosexual but his mother wouldn't let him"—or perhaps by a canny use of it, here is a scene that should be the comic set piece on the subject for quite a while, though I can't see it being performed even in those "progressive" schools at home (where I hear they sometimes do Genêt's *The Maids* with girls, a lovely confusion which would never occur in the land of Sir Andrew Aguecheek). For though Osborne's patriot has all but disappeared—and it has taken the playwright how many miles to get to this Babylon?—the scene has brio, to put it politely, and it's certainly worth your time, though its full zest may not travel. Remember, that though the Lord Chamberlain might not get at us in our club, it couldn't have been the aura of censorship that had so sharpened the author's wit or our reception of it, as much as the aura of crime. For if there was brio here there was good reason; where homosexual practice elsewhere may be illstarred, in Britain it is illegal. It is necessary to understand the place occupied in *this* empire by a question that Parliament itself studies from time to time.

As we left the theater, trying to pin down between us the exact nature of Osborne's *Sachertorte*, we heard a native voice bluntly do it for us. "Bit like *The Merry Widow* arse-backwards, wasn't it?"

Goes to show what can be done on home ground.

Anticriticism, like other mischief, attacks the idle—like me when between books. At one such a time, *The Kenyon Review* asked me to contribute to a symposium on the short story. The symposium, like the Festschrift, is a device to keep a literary magazine going, as well as a straight road to the highest form of nonsense without humor. It appeals to vanities who don't mind sounding off in a crowd of them. I refused, but the idea smoldered, until I wrote the following, under the title "Talk Given In Heaven After Refusing To Go There"—(which the Sunday *Times* "Speaking Of Books" column called "Writing Without Rules.")

To write about "the" short story or "the" novel as an entity—an actual "art form" wandering the Aegean or West 44th Street and only waiting to be drafted for the literary wars—is an ancient kind of high-altitude nonsense. From which the artist unerringly excludes himself, every time he sits down to write a manuscript which shall be as single in shape and essence as the mortal coil will allow.

He wants every work to be a reformation, and to come like Luther's, straight from the bowel. Secretly he hopes people will get to understand it because they too have bowels—which is one of the connections between literature and the world. Only one of course. And mentioned here merely to anticipate a volume of essays shortly to be published on that subject by Marvin Mudwrack, Leslie Fiddler and Steven Muckus—to be entitled "OUR Mortal Coil: A Symposium." What is a symposium? It is an attempt to arrange in orderly theory those very works that are alive because they are singular. And to put down the artist for disorderly conduct unbecoming to a symposium.

There is no "the" short story. Or novel. More than a foot away from a particular one, we are discussing the nature of art—another fooler. The nature of art is that, one foot away, it can best be talked of only in terms of what it isn't. For the artist knows that a work of art is everything else but what can be said of it, one foot away. What he says of it—meanwhile standing on his own navel to get close enough—is what he makes his art of. He doesn't waste time dreaming of the realms of "the." Insomniac that he is, he's forever working on a "this," beautiful as a skin without pores, and to the words of anyone else—not pervious.

The symposiast of anything, however, is an old-fashioned Platonist. He believes in Rainbow's End. Clinking up there among the other absolutes is the final Smasher Short Story and the definitive Nevermore Novel, at which writers down here are to aim as faithfully as they can. The symposiast's job is to establish their pecking order. He does this very simply. First he sips, from any blushful cup of Hippocrene proffered. Then, like any winetaster, he spits. . And here I am back at the bodily functions again. It will take a critic to tell me why the very thought of criticism so often leads me there.

For the critic's job, as some see it, is to tell all of us not only what we and the artist are to believe—but what the Artist already does believe about the Art Form he's working in. Against that Ammunition, the artist can only say, in the lowest case possible: i don't. Or he can sit and think about his immortality—that endless and useless chance to talk back. For if he opens his mouth to shout to the heavens what he doesn't believe in, he can never command the decibel of those crying aloft what they do.

I don't believe that the short story or the novel—or the symphony, or the sculpture of object—should ever stand still enough in artistic time for us to say unequivocally what it is, or should be. For that is the End, whenever that happens, isn't it? I don't believe in any comprehensive methodology of any kind—even if you say I've used it. What you really see, if a piece of work is good enough, is the particular order it has self-imposed.

"Point of view"? In the professorial anthologies, every story has one, narratively speaking—whatever that is. Often the prefaces still urge that a story has or should have only one point of view. Readers of these should remember that the commentator is urging strictly his own limits, not the author's. No reason why a story can't be told from 80 points of view if the writer can manage it—the best are as spiny with viewpoint as a porcupine, as whorled as a whelk's idea of a whelk. Even in a work of the smallest scope, the daring attempt is to do as many things as possible, and to do them inseparably. I once said as much, to the first students I'd ever addressed. One said thoughtfully, "That's not what Miss Rubaker said." My answer was awed—we were from the same city. "You had Miss Rubaker too?" I guess I never listened to her. But in some quarters, I hear her yet.

I hear other voices too. Mr. James, striding to dictate, stares across the Channel and says, "Today, I shall write a story with an 'omnipotent narrator.' Or is it 'omniscient'?" Mr. Joyce scowls myopically higher. "Mine ends in an epiphany." Now I'd advise both those eminences not to be too sure of what they've done, before looking it up in Northrop Frye. I've not read him myself. All those people are too smart for me. They know everything—except that their business is fantasy. Of a purer, more restricted sort than mine.

The writer should flee confrontations of that sort in the manner that Blake fled Joshua Reynolds; he should beat down classifications, or any gnomic effort to put it all in a neat nutshell. Read it all if he must, and learn to spit it out. Write a story like a nutshell, and another as fleecy as the top of Mount Ida, if he chooses. If he's lucky, he isn't even an iconoclast. That's for the converts to creative freedom. If he's blessed, he has a more congenital disorder. He doesn't even see the rules that are there.

I treasure the categorizers, nevertheless. Like weeds in the garden, they tell us where the flowers are. For, little as a good writer should know about the general logistics of the Elysian field, while he writes he has to be cocksure about his own. Afterwards—when he is telling himself and humanity how he did it, in the exquisitely punchy journalese which comes to all of us at such moments—then maybe it is healthy for him to read what one of those cats may have written of him. Let him read all about how he did it, and in the best Latinate agglutinate. That'll humble him, back to his own vernacular. And maybe send him on, to a kind of book he himself had never thought of before.

For the writer knows well enough how he did it of course, from the first reveries through the rheumatics of the daily chair. His dilemma is that he can't really talk about his work in any words or terms but its own. If he were seriously to try, his "extrapolation"—more exhaustive than any outside analyst's, though maybe not as lengthy—would be to reconstruct, step by step, the work itself. And he doesn't want to bother, but to do something different. Not merely from other writers' works. From his own. Something different from last time. Which will again make its own rules.

Is this anarchy? Yes, of course. And no. The anarchic appearance of experience is what stimulates a writer to regularize it in the telling—and to tell the world. The ways of doing that, when seemingly inimitable, make writers who are "new." For the moment. Then somebody smells out a few "theories"—for which read mannerisms and preoccupations—and the imitative race is on. After a lapse of time and dust and followers, a few writers remain who are not merely inimitable, but of whose work it can now be freely admitted—that it was not done by rule. These are the great.

The ordinary artist however—that is, the live one—will never persuade the world that his magic calculator and charisma computer isn't somewhere—and somehow communicable. The sadder likelihood is that the world may persuade him. People will pay him to teach them his secrets, for one thing. He can usually fob them off with his own personal ambience, or with his convictions about other writers' works.

Yet one honesty he will never be allowed. He will never be excused from explanation of his own work by lazily pointing to the work itself. If he insists, a variety of vengeances are taken, the most indulgent one being also the most irritating: writers, like the dear saints, don't know how the mystery occurs. From which it follows, that if the poor naif doesn't know how he does what he does, then he can't know what he's said, in its true and full significance. If he answers in a rage, as I have often done, "The book is what I am saying. That is what a book—a novel, short story is!"—well, watch out for that kind of stuff. He may be illiterate.

Once, at a party for the first issue of Discovery, in which I had a story, I was led humbly up to an Authority. I mean I was humble—there were about 400 other Discoveries there. He watched my approach with a gaze I know better now—the true appreciator's air of having discovered himself. Then said, down his Apollonian nose (it was John

Aldridge): "I wonder. If you really *know*. If you really *saw*. Everything you said in that story. I can't think you really *saw*." It was my
first encounter with internists of this order. (And of course it occurred
to neither of us to question whether *he* had seen everything there was
to see.) For days after I thought of replies both deep and brittle. Like,
"Oh well, the midwife is the last to know." What I said however was,
"Well, unh, I wrote it." He smiled. And like a deb who'd tripped over
her train, I was led away.

That's all changed now. Or is it? In a way. They used to warn
writers not to "talk it out" and so waste subconscious material—until
we learned this was merely "their" way of pre-empting the field—for
talk. It would give us "blocks," they said. But writers are quicker than
anyone to know where the power is. These days I can count on a hand
the quaint characters who have blocks. Once I'd have needed an
abacus.

Talk has done it—and the breakdown of the distinction between print
and talk, between "fiction" and "autobiography." Nobody has to
wonder which he's doing anymore; it's all reportage. Poets have
helped. "Readings" have made us all troubadours. Sound is king. And
on the terrible bandwagon of present-day politics, quite a number of
johnny-come-latelies to the world of social concern have rediscovered
themselves—in a kind of talk-print-feint social action, which is a
medium all in itself. The new slogan for the writer is "Don't just complain; *Explain*." We're invited to do it endlessly. Writers are almost
their own critics now.

They have often been the most prophetic ones, against all the stand-
pat formalities of the lawgivers—Blake against the whole eighteenth-
century academy, Proust retroactively against Saint-Beuve. Uncommitted to any theories but their own—and uncommitted to the perman-
ence of these. A writer's arrogance toward the present is often really
a humility toward the future. And very hard to maintain. For it's such
fun to be easily doctrinaire, most of all about our own work. Especially
now. America, always hungry for a Left Bank, now has one. The
college is the café now—and offering the talk-print *carte-du-jour*.

Writers have helped make it so. We now have the classic two establishments, money and the salon, to help us contend with what we are. Wherever a glass is drunk to the Muse these days, the circulation manager of some modish mag stands ready to foot the tab. The café categorizer has even higher aims. He wants to make us like himself—a man who understands the "the" of everything.

How can we tell him our aims are infinitely lower! To flourish as we are. Magicians whose pockets are literally empty, until the next time. Apostles of what is unphrasable to us except in those primary manuscripts. Before which, all others appear to us secondary.

So gentlemen, my thanks to your symposium, which I leave just in time to escape. Your job is to clean up the past. Ours to keep the future clean for possibility. Meanwhile, very humbly, I toss a lion to you Christians. Here's a book.

I sent my friend on *The Kenyon Review* something else.

Sometimes art has to be defended even from the young—as from any who confuse it or associate it inseparably with living either the "arty" or the "revolutionary" life. Here, as quoted by John Leggett in "Metamorphosis of the Campus Radical," is a student, now a senior, looking back on her year as a freshman radical: "It was really nice then. They were the bad guys and we were the good guys. Everybody who was a writer or an artist or smoked dope was us."

I was always glad that the young thought writers were good guys generally. It spoke well for both of us.

I took it for granted that some people assumed that all artists doped or drank or did something to excess, their work being the product of it. (And that the possibility of art itself being the "excess," never occurred to these outsiders.)

But be damned if I'd let them say that taking dope *made* you an artist.

I was hearing a lot of that, from the young especially. And had heard it before.

In "A Five-Sense Psyche" I answered them.

When I was twelve, I spent a lot of Saturdays at the museum, staring at the Corots. Until recently, I had gauged those half-dull, mindlessly brown reveries as the first clear signs of an aesthetic feeling separate from all the other lymphatic swellings of the adolescent self. It would be possible, of course, to interpret into that communion with those cob-web Barbizon forests, landscapes carefully dreaming as only the nine-teenth century could dream, the first properly saloniste stirrings of sex. Fortunately, my fantasies in that direction took place in quite an-other red room of verse, sound, sobs, and touch, all floating with the naked human figure, male and mine, in which I had as yet no interest one could call classical. No, what I was seeing in those paintings, and with the exquisite recognition of relief, was something much more literal than either case—the trees. At the time, of course, I must already have been suffering from some sensibility. But also, in those days of irregular eye-tests, I had a mild myopia, as yet uncorrected by lenses. I knew what trees tended to look like "artistically" to other people— from the wintry black-and-white of etchings at home to the luscious green clumps of colored advertisement. But here on the museum wall, if I got close enough, was comforting testimony that once upon a time another vision, and one considered worthy, had seen real trees exactly as I saw them, on my walk in Central Park—now.

What I was experiencing, as I would later be told in college, was the well known phenomenon of the "element of the familiar" in art—in visual art, or perhaps in any art, the prime satisfaction of the novice; but to the artist himself, and to the people who can learn his vision, the most primitive. "It's what makes people say, 'Look, just like the barn at home!'" said the instructor. "But you can find that satisfaction on a postcard. If postcard naturalism is all you are able to see, or have learned." He was being loftily modern. And he went on to be what he thought was witty. "But, until you can also see the composition and color-relationships the artist poses, you too will be up against a barn door!" Unknown to both of us, we there in front of him were already hopelessly far beyond him in what our eyes saw as reality normal to us—and in the music that would seem sonically normal to our ears.

and in the literature already dropping unalienly into our minds, as well.

For he, born circa 1880, was talking principally of the components of objective art—which to him was still the principal art. And we, still gazing so innocently up at him, according to *his* own predilections, with Greuze-blue eyes perhaps, and here and there a Jacques David curve of odalisque above our wool kneesocks, already had the cells of almost another reality—non-objective, atonal, anti-heroic—in our bones.

Between our cradle days and our instructor's, reality, that open secret, had once more been changing its terms. At the time of his birth, the impressionists had already broken up light. By the time of ours, the a priori tenets of all the arts had themselves been smashed to bits— in music the scale, in language the words. And the dimmest of us, from the most conservative backgrounds, had taken some of this, like fluoride slipped into a city's water, into our mental lives. I still knew nothing of "modern" art, but in ballet school I had long since danced to Stravinsky, as nonchalantly as the ballerinas preceding us had to Chopin, and those before them to Rameau. A foreign girl next to me in the dorm had Max Ernst and Kurt Seligmann on her walls, and both our mercantile fathers, before they retired, would become used to ads no longer couched in the visual terminology of Landseer or even Marie Laurencin, but in the poster techniques of Stuart Davis.

Outside the school where we studied Spenser to perhaps Whitman, we ourselves and our men friends were reading Eliot. In philosophy, we had long since given up teleology or else had never even experienced the feeling—by instinct already sensing that even in science the world wasn't progressing on any upgrade toward heaven, utopia, or peace. In religion, we had given up church, or had never had it. In literature, where I was, we laughed at continuity in any form—of moral view, or of form itself. Or, rather, we were puzzled by, or doubtful of, it. Secretly, we sometimes mourned the death of character, which had become fluid, vaguely attached to regions or to dissenting opinions, or to violence, but rarely personal enough to be great or even interesting in the old style. But there wasn't an apple-cheeked one of us who didn't know that reality, or rather the ways of proving it, was radically different now. If we were to have heroes they would have to be nonobjective ones, for that was the way reality was expressing itself and affirming itself to us.

And, as we gazed up at the art instructor with his slides, this was really all we knew. Since we were university students, we would try to clock what we were pedantically, as in terms of an educated vision which had come upon us consciously. Actually, all our habits of reading, viewing, and discussion, and the conclusions, too, were only after-the-event expression of what had already effortlessly happened to us in being born when we were. This we did not suspect, either. We would have denied with vigor the shocking idea that every human being is already a participating member of the rearguard the minute he is born.

Actually, the visions and insights of art-in-general—plastic, musical, or literary—are ways of expressing reality, which is to say, of *proving* it. And while individual artists may seem to be ahead of the general current, or enough out of it to be individual, they are all the while actually augmenting it with their work; the seepage of that current is continuous, and waits for no man, educated or not, to be born. The most important fact which the instructor or we might have mentioned had escaped all of us. For in fact, by then, even thirty years ago, even the "postcard" people were no longer looking at visual reality in strictly postcard style.

But all we stubbornly knew that day, and for the conventional number of years after, was how modern we were. And how old-fashioned "Mr. Slides" was. As old-fashioned as I am now or appear to be, as I sit here, in the new world acoming, stubbornly ensconced, entrenched in my mere five senses—limited as a stereopticon facing whole nebulas of radio-telescopes, all of them lodged in one room. As I sit here—lodged merely in my five senses—in any one of the sugar-cube, hemp-sweetened parlors, conversational or actual, of the "psychedelic" world.

As I sit here, what am I trying to do? As usual with humans, I am trying to assess the "new" reality, more than likely either by refusing it or asserting mine. Dr. Johnson, confronted by such Berkeleyan conundrums as where the room went when the observer was out of it, was able to prove the existence of matter, and of himself, by kicking a stone. But he was a lexicographer, and a critic, too. Being what I am, I might do it better via art itself. But art is long. So as I sit here in the potclouded room, with the cubes of "acid" scattered delicate as sesame on the table, and the needle-and-spoon in its ready little box, stashed say at the bottom of the baby's bassinet (all of which, for the sake of the Feds, shall we say is imaginary, excluding only the baby?) —I shall settle for one or two insights which anybody might have, on reflection. How did I get here, for instance, in this peculiar position, re-fusing the glorious sense-data of the unknown, standing on the mere equipment which nature has given me—and will shortly take away—as on a beleaguered isle? Is nature still the newest, freshest thing around —or a has-been? In the role of artist alone, am I at worst a coward before experience, at best a fool, at likeliest a conservative? Or is it still possible that I can get as much out of my five senses and brain as anyone who gives up his autonomy over them, such at least as he was born to have? Will it one day be seen that this room—like vomitoriums, saunas, the baths of Caracalla, the chapels of the flagellites, the mas-sage-room at the New York Athletic Club, or you name it—is only modish in its turn? Or only valuable when it is not communal but tragically personal—as, say, the bedroom of Thomas De Quincey? Am I really, in my isolation, gloriously reasonable—an angel who re-fuses to be confined to the pinpoint of a needle, or a pill? Stop the questions. Let us see how I got here.

Take a look at historical reality, which, whether you consider it most influenced by the battle, the plough, the apse, or the monumental person, is ever in a state of change. Alongside its panorama goes that other, more single-file drama, preoccupation of the philosophers—the problem of the observer versus the observed. Like the question of the existence of God, the problem is pitiful in that it is unsolvable, wonder-ful in that the mind subject to its condition can still conceive of it. Meanwhile, man, who has to live under the assumption that reality is fairly stable, has always had spiritual-physical ways of relieving him-self of the dailiness of his own psyche. These vary from time to time,

in means, method, and popularity. But that we should want to escape
from our self, or to enlarge it, is eternal. This particular room, in its
clouds of acrid smoke and sweet illusion, its pleasure in the possible
company of the foul angels or lucky devils we are sure to have within
us, is nothing new. Nor is art's specious presence here new, nor
youth's. Like so much in life, it is merely new to us.

In the youth of many who are now middle-aged, Sex was the respectable way to be revolutionary. This was especially so for those not
involved in "pink" politics, but often was a sideline or indulgence for
those, too. For some of the literati, both practicing and fringe, assertive
Sex was a way of proclaiming that literature *was* life—or that one had
found this out. Or that one was a member of the literati. In the other
arts, and gradually for much of the populace, the mystique went much
the same: sexual conduct, though still pretty much a private flight of
the psyche, was publicly meaningful, and in certain places an avowed
synonym for poetic pioneering into both Eleutheria and *la boue*—into
both the mysteries and the mud-slush of life. A current mystique always is. (Just as it is always a sign that mystique and mysticism have
once more been confused.)

Nowadays, of course, sex is for everybody—either everybody's Eden
or everybody's duty, seems to be the line—and to capitalize the word,
as was then often done, seems scarcely amusing. But to do so is owed
to history, and helps to note that Sex, to those pioneers (and for that
reality), had in the main a holy, male-female connotation. Not to say
that other forms of love or orgy were unknown or not busy at their
mystiques; at any time in the world all of the latter somewhere coexist.
But one may always recognize the fashionable, the Mother Mystique,
by the difficulty of slanging it without being thought "not with it"—
as is the case today. Youth particularly tends to revere the connection
between the orgiastic and the serious. Innocent as we might be of
sexual orgy in the old days, we were chary of kidding it. But only yesterday I heard a young "swinger," to whom "turning on," whether or
not she does it, is still the sacred key to Eleusis, say laughingly of the
other, "Oh yes, that. Group-grope."

In the '40s, alcoholism was particularly fashionable for writers, and some of them made art of it. Other writers tried to inherit these men and women's demons intact. But men's personal demons, or the art that may go with these, are never heritable in a straight line. A writer-cum-bottle is now old hat, as "out of it" as any member of Rotary. Those demons are the property of any club car, now. The furies don't come in a bottle any more, or in the pure-and-simple bed. Sex as revolution, alcohol as the black-mass acolyte of the soul are both supremely out of style.

Looking back on our era, it may one day be said of us that *travel*, both literal and poetic, was our major attempt at once to extend bodily sensation and to relieve ourselves of the pains or burdens of the inner dialogue. New estimates of the nature of time and space, new powers over distance, have been with us scientifically for more than a generation, and the "new" time-space metaphors engendered by this have all but been exhausted in the arts. However, it takes a while for metaphor to seep into the general populace, and this, of course, includes the non-artistic side of the artists and scientists as well. Just at about the time the early intellectual intuitions of an era are codified and on the way to senescence, they become part of generally accepted reality. Like any other discoveries, once implemented or open to all, they are regarded as commonplace. Travel to the moon may remain poetic for a time, the moon being what it has been to humans, but it can scarcely remain mysterious.

Once upon a time, the tour—the literal kind, on land, by sea or by air —was for fun, education, or rest. Now, even in this mode, it often has another aim. People go touring for the significant experience, as to the *kibbutz*; the idea is not to escape from responsibility but to find it. Or one vicariously follows the bloodbaths of the world as some follow sporting events, to be where the action is; yesterday's papers report that voyeur tourism in Vietnam is on the rise. Voyeurism is of course deeply connected with the "real" experience that one dare not have oneself, or with the lost innocence of the real emotion that one cannot have any more. There are so few unspoiled private places any more—as the travel-agents used to say—short of other people's graves.

But there is one. The psychedelic "trip," being limited to the self, must remain more arcane even than moon-going—until, at least, we perfect even other ways of self-peeking than those electronic buggeries we now have. As a testimony that travel in perception is as possible as travel by miles, the drug-trip has its dignity—though one not unique to it, surely. It is versatile, since the individual can travel either alone, or alone in a group. One advantage of the group is that it has a special attraction for those who have trouble with such relationships, or are limitedly seeking them. Philosophically, the drug trip has deeply seductive roots in the experimental psychology of us all, as drug-taking has had down the ages. For what could be closer, more clairaudient to that classic dialogue of the observer and the observed? Finally, the drug-traveler can give the white feather at once to those who stand and wait for experience to happen; he coins it, courts it by a process for which the word "happening" is so apt, advancing like Stanley into the inner darkness of himself. And, so doing—at once actor and audience, novel and writer, poet and poem (like Swinburne, like Coleridge, see?)—whether or not he already is an artist, or wants to join up, he has imposed an extra handspring on the processes of art. Hasn't he? For he has used the very stuff of himself creatively. And that's new, isn't it?

Having listed all the virtues of psychedelia, except the obvious one of escape, it now occurs to me that the process of ordinary thinking has most of these, and indeed travels by the very same routes and means. But it *is* so ordinary. As for Coleridge and Swinburne, one can no more measure what portion of an artist's imagination is under stimulus, rather than native to it, than one can weigh the contribution of Dostoevski's epilepsy to his. Except perhaps to remark that when a poet is also avowedly his poem, he is often at his worst. As an abstainer, it is even possible that I need feel no guilt at all.

For those who hope to make psychedelic connection with the arts, where other means have failed, the estimate is more certain, and has nothing to do either with moral wrong or with health. Great artists have been thieves and drugtakers, have starved or grown rich, but neither thievery nor poverty, wealth nor poppyseed, makes artists.

or any coterie of circumstance or even intellect, or other laying-on of hands. As a fashionable mystique among artists themselves, psychedelia is as phony and temporary—and as ancient—as any other. There is nothing more innately artistic about drug-taking, solo or in soirée, than any number of modes of conduct, given the proper aura and spice. Naked communal birdwatching, say—in front of the Plaza. So many delightful ways of enlarging the perceptions are possible. But no more artistic because artists may be doing them. For the artist, once delivered of his insight or apart from it, is vulnerable to the reality of the day, like any other man.

It has taken me a long time of sitting here in this room to see this. And it now occurs to me that I have been in such rooms, or ones very similar, before—often on greater occasion. I was here in the '40s, when it proved guiltily impossible for me to transmute my young ache to help the needy into Communism's doctrinaire. I was here once as a Jew, when, for all my will to build Zion in the name of the martyrs, I could not manage to see Zion as merely and only Israel. Every time I am tempted, either from ambition or solitude, to join a sympathetic or powerful coterie of artistic conviction, I am here—innumerable times. I am here every time I am tempted to give up my absurd autonomy, which any man may have: his reserved right to go on seeing the *differences* in the world, and to see it differently from the rest.

This can be saddening for both sides, joiners and non-, as it has been since the beginning of the world. Moreover, that sort of dissidence can come, not worthily, from intellectual choice, but merely from a nasty sense of one's own boundaries—as any yearner who sees the front lines of so many fracases dissolve into the *arrière-garde* before he can get there, well knows. Ours, however is a generation trained to fear a mysticism which thinks democratically, in groups—which is what Fascism was. From there, we have gone on to mistrust group thinking altogether; at least some of us have. Often, the mysticisms of ordinary people *are* frightening, precisely because they have little or no spiritual or intellectual content. The psychedelic movement is unlikely to shake

governments or affect too many more than those engaged in its taran-
tella. But mass-moods toward mindlessness are scary, at least in the
Western world.

There is a certain snobbery, though, in insisting on the antennae of
one's own senses only. They afford no surety. After a certain age,
surely, mayn't the data of one's senses be as decadent as any provided
by $C_{17}H_{12}NO_4$—old-fashioned cocaine, once thought the height of
psychedelic sophistication? And even when one is young these days,
the hillside is no longer that dew-pearled; what does all that cleareyed
gandering bring one except the stench of other peoples' blood, or at
best food already corrupted at the chemical root, desensitized sex, and
bad air? To all this kind of argument there is no answer, not even to
remark perhaps that nature corrupts and purifies itself faster than we
can ever—for we are back at the duet of the observer and observed.
It is a matter of temperament.

A charming couple had lunch with me yesterday. Just out of grad
school, they are as conventional for the breed of the times as any I
ever saw. Husband is a physicist, where the best butter is, but is also a
fiend at the guitar. They speak proudly of a working-class background,
but find the actual Czech parental pad in Yorkville as stifling for a
really groovy home-visit to New York as any rebels fleeing Scarsdale.
(They have made the ritual visit to Paris and are now perhaps a little
more European than their parents—in the way of food. He loves it,
better than haircuts, and she, neat as a phoebe, is already watching his
weight.) They adore each other, obviously. They are wise enough to
sense that "folkies"—the "life-pattern" they have somewhat subscribed to—are on the way out, but their alert sense of style will keep
them "with it," totally unaware that this merely means being one's
age, at *that* age. She has a degree in home economics, but need not be
ashamed of it. For, of course (not too often, as a matter of modernation
and economy), they are in the habit of turning on, and that one symbol
makes everything right. In ten years I see them, succumbed, as they
already have, to that greatest of drugs—convention. There'll be another name for what they'll be, and no opprobrium for it from me.
But they'll be what they are now. Squares.

They in turn are clearly disappointed in me. Introduced by a friend, they know better than to expect antics of all writers. They don't mind the lunch being good. But they are astounded at my attitudes as expounded above, and coming from someone who has published in their Koran—a magazine so hip that they don't have to read it. They have listened politely. They speak of the material that turning on might bring me. I agree that bizarre thoughts and perceptions, which thank God I have constantly, are a fine matrix for creation, but useless when the controls are absent. "I like to be *there*, you see. When I have them." But their eyes are onyx; in fact, orthodox. They're in that room. And, as usual, I'm outside the church. Later, our mutual friend reports their puzzlement. "You wore an apron, you dog."I can play roles as well as any—and I did cook lunch. "They can't understand it. You were a *sweet lady*, they said."

Who of us knows for sure a revolutionary when he sees one, even if it is himself? I had my first experience with drugs at twenty, when an appendectomy went wrong. After days of dosage for the pain of having had intestines reeled out and put back again, and violent dope reactions of which I was totally unaware, I woke to an old harridan of a head nurse leaning over me. "Why didn't you *tell* us," she snapped, "that you were allergic to morphine?" Even my incision wanted to laugh, and answer, though I couldn't, "How the hell should I *know*?" I had never had anything more vicious than aspirin in my life. "Trauma," said the doctor at her side. "Next time it may be different." And he was right. It is a question of the patient wishing to go under. Some rooms can be entered after all, at will.

That is why the thought of death so troubles me. If I am in pain, I shall certainly want painkillers. But a mere five-sense psyche is always untrustworthy. Its trouble is that it never wants to die. And it never confuses nirvana with experience. Or lethe with life. That's hard going at the end, that is. So I see why people might want to study the ins and outs of turning on and turning off, to learn how to prepare themselves early. Otherwise, even at the bitter end, one might not know how to go gracefully under. One still might want to rise. And kick the stone.

(Thus spake who?—not reminded he was daily slave to a boiled egg.) Certainly what I am slave to is clear. I still want to kick the stone.

I had never really looked back before, at my own literary history as entangled with others. I seemed to me just getting to be of an age to have a history, though not ready yet to embalm it in conventional auto-biography. There have been eras, like the 1920s and 1930s, when certain writers have done that extraordinarily young—and some, having expended their stamina and lifescape, live the rest of their lives collecting their medals but without conclusive work. My era, elasticized by literacy, media and an ambivalent life-expectation—die older, *if* you dodge the bombs—seemed ever more hypnotized by the future. Art was at best a present seizure.

The past for some artists was entirely a dead lava-plain.

Oddly enough, their future looked just like it.

Ego art. We know we are the era of it. Naturally, our reasons are compassionate: in clouds of self-media—but only after the death of certain gods, and under continuous war—we take on ourselves, as the supreme burden. Our century began, after all, with the great re-entry of Self into art. . . . Eras, before they decline, exaggerate. Ego art occurs when that great art-of-the-self becomes a trade.

A writer is expected to use his ego like a great probe, suffering diagnostically to record the world. He always expected to, but now he must do it by convention. The "world" in turn no longer feels itself reportable in third person, or in imaginative art: everything must be first-person in order to be believed. Imagination as willed fantasy, or fantasy wilfully shaped, is therefore false: the "conscious" artist must fall back before the scrupuously accidental action-painting of "life." Reviewers cannot read novels which present themselves as more than this or different from it, and novelists, quick to catch the blight, cannot write them. The suspension of disbelief is willing no longer. A writer must be his own character, so thinly veiled that we know. Fyodor Dostoyevski—give him his *full* name—can still be his underground man, but how can one Dostoyevski be Raskolnikov? Was he ever? Satire, always closer to the critical faculty, is still reputable. But once the imagination shaking free of the ego-possible, strays past "It really happened to me" into those mysteries which lie beyond, or once the writer declares his intent to make a world that lies beyond, made perhaps of third-person-reported pysches, or not clearly based on his journalistic ego—then he has crossed the Styx, into the world of ghosts. The facts are against him. The critical faculty—in novelist as well as critic—coaxes us to mistrust what cannot be explained or has not been literally lived, and to deny that powerful art is made of it. Non-ego art is still here, as it has always been. But speaking up for it, to those for whom the journalistic "I" is now the sole category of literary belief, is like trying to describe what even blind men can see with their eyes closed, to a very visual elephant.

Modes of writing really have very little to do with the quarrel. "Fiction" and "non-fiction" are magazine words or workshop ones, indicating only as always that business is perfectly capable of influencing art. The real bite is not between novels and history, or journalism and novels, or even between confessional and "constructed" art. (Any more than that there exists a real quarrel between poetry and prose—instead of a teasing, constantly changing, pingpong difference.) All are sides of the writer-animal, evoked as the spirit moves us. Or as the battle does. Or as the wind turns. The real tussle—paradise lost, hell regained—is between the orphic and the didactic poles in all of us. Literature is all the gradations between. Yes—all.

Time was when the novel, that bastard upstart, was more clearly a poor fictive thing, and belles lettres—always doing what it could for other forms—more surely sublime. As almost always, the lettrists are still in power, and as always have to be reassured of it. For though men of letters start out from interest in the conduct of values, the conduct of their lives is often such as to persuade us—and even themselves—that power is what they are primarily interested in. The change in them is—that the lettrists of today, or critics once *pur et simple*, will do anything to keep from being genteelly called belles. They learn their tough stance, of course, from the novelist.

The old New Critics, less genteel than predecessors like Irving

Babbitt and Paul Elmer More, were still formally on the side of us
angels, the *pur et simple* writers—although the effect of their honest
dissections was usually to show that an angel is a winged creature
who cannot walk. Men like Van Wyck Brooks went on to explore
their own nervous crises as artists did—and men of letters often have,
or wrote their critical work under the assumption that this too was art.
Edmund Wilson, with the sincerest flattery, now and then wrote
"imaginative" books. Why not? A critic attempting a work of imaginative art is only as assumptive as a writer attempting literary criticism.
Each may be assuming that he can have or get the best of both sides.
Or each may be freely reveling in the continuum that is literature.
In which writers might more keenly remember that the limits of
a critic's generosity show up as quick as those of his intelligence.
And critics might be warned that imagination never conceals what
you are. And is most nakedly what you are. What is required of
either of us is a soule—though *soul* is welcome too.

Today's men of letters want that as much as ever; only the form
of their desire is different. As usual they copy those who, in the
bitter nature of things, precede them by writing the books on which
their own must wait. Today's lettrist can't be belle, not only because
the world isn't, but because the writers aren't, anymore. He wants
to be an ugly lettrist—a true-blue plug-ugly whom nobody gets to
imagine, mind you, but himself. Where, if he talks about himself instead of books, as the critic does so much of nowadays, it is with a
lash aspiring to Swift's and a whine he hopes is Rousseau. Again, he
gets this harsh-tender stance on himself from the novelist. On whose
attitudes he must wait, before he can react, shadow-box, kill—per-
form. The meateater smells of his meat. Often tainted with the "put
up your dukes!" reverse romanticisms of the day (as in *Making It*,
where a sensibility as conscious as any maiden's becomes an *in*sensitive
ego sensitively recording). He craves the same wounds as the "imaginative" artist, given and taken in the same ring. Or the self-
inflicted ones. *Particularly* those. So, the critic too, ends up writing
ego art. He has to tell you about his psyche before he• can render
his judgments. Often it is very interesting—because psyches are.

But when he gets around to the books again, to that other-directed artist to whose north pole he is south—watch this *jolie laide* very carefully. He himself has claimed the free man's heady right to an obsession with his own life; now, for the novelist, he may stipulate it. He mistrusts the objectivity of another man's imagination, on the same terms as he mistrusts the objectivity of his own intelligence—nothing will convince him that these objectivities are not the same. So, ten to one, he will be telling you what the imagination can't do anymore. He never sees it as the other writer sometimes does—illimitable, grossly and gloriously unfactual. To him, the nonreal is never a true source. Artists must no longer invent. Novelists must report only their own dilemmas, in the appropriate areas, ages and sex of their own true lives, otherwise he can't believe it—he won't. Twain is not Huck; Anna Karenina is not Leo Tolstoi. It's over. And of course it is. For this psyche is projecting. It is timid about imagining imagination. People who have to wait around for other people's often are.

Yes, watch the ugly man of letters. How he craves imagination's risks!

And watch me. How sometimes I, at the other pole, crave his.

In school and early childhood, fantasy is sometimes coddled, but the didactic is what we are urged to trust. Early on, I ran from it, as from what teachers and other crocodiles fed on only to regurgitate a dead corpus of that literature which I had to find out for myself later was still painfully alive. Fantasy, imagination, whatever you called it, a great free river of possibility in language, was what you could trust. Once you learned to swim and mull there, life and feeling accreted to it. From its dark shallows came those anode-cathode associative bounds, those sudden firm ledges of insight, of something put into the world that had perhaps never been there before. A small babe of vision might be made. After a while, I never read critical comments any more; their comparable river ran so sandy and thin. Critique was a game that I had played at in college, trifled with as a possible vocation, and done too wildly well at: "You certainly sling the King's English--but what is *this* you say!" I was too young to confess that the only authority for it was myself. Or others like me but better at it. Even later, I would always rather read what I still tend to think of as the *primary* manuscripts. And if confined to hard choice—rather write them.

What I know now is that one need not make it a hard and separate choice—indeed one cannot. Slowly, all those categories the crocodiles put in me were one after the other to melt away. Grudgingly, I would see that in the greatest of writers, the fantastic and the didactic combine. (Not always, surely, in the first person singular, or any of its facsimiles. Sometimes in a wildly differing array of personae, not all of whom could possibly be her or him.)

For if criticism doesn't precede writers but follows them (never a popular theory with those "influential" reviewers, who prefer to project a more innocent version of their influence), then writers do not consciously or collectively know the change that is coming upon them, at the time. And prefer not to. Talk can kill verbal art. That blind orphic impulse wants not to be phrased, but to phrase.

But one inescapable way of learning what literary change is, is to live through one. Unconsciously.

Category, I can tell you, is the only real crocodile.

In 1948, it was astonishly true that the reigning ideal of the "proper" short story—not only at *The New Yorker*, which published my first few, but generally in America—was the absolute reversal of what I have called ego-art. *Author should not appear*. A story, a novel, possibly even a poem, was designed—*should* be—to drop from a hand which was nowhere, as a *Ding an sich*, a globe maybe ready to burst inside the reader from its own hot internal pressures, but meanwhile wholly contained, even coolly so, by only its own symbolic skin. Later, when I was more knowing if not wiser, I would term this method "the oblique." It is one of the great modes of art, and at first I was writing in it, but I didn't know that. The one supernal fact about any mode of art is that it isn't the only one—but I didn't know that either. (Not consciously, though an inner tug was soon to move me).

At this time, I knew no writers, only a couple of very restrained editors whom I saw rarely, in fact almost nobody who "talked books," and this isolation was to continue for some time. Further, I had read almost nothing of the "modern" short story, American or otherwise. I hadn't known I was going to write any, for one thing, and even if so, hadn't the temperament for research. Even then I was perhaps self-protectively reading books strangely unallied with what I was doing, and always books a little behind or tangential to "current" ones—a habit that has persisted, and one I often suspect other writers of. It keeps you out of the collective *conscious*.

First influences, they say, are always the deepest. Well—for a time. Back in high school, I had read much on my own among the Russians, but only the novels were important to me. Chekhov I absorbed silently along with the rest, but in college, where I found him in the curriculum, I immediately backed away. I had a tendency to back away from whatever was touted there. James (except for *Daisy Miller*) was not yet studied there. Sometimes I touted him (and other stumbled-upon oddities like Gide and Colette) to them. But at home, much earlier than any of this, what I remember is the thumbed small book of Hawthorne's stories, and one of Flaubert's (containing "A Simple Heart," "The Legend of St. Julian the Hospitaler" and "Herodias") which I still have. Also Wilde's Fairy Tales (I *knew* "The Nightingale and the Rose" was a sexual dream though I didn't know of sex yet), some Jewish Publication Society folklore where the one-level characters never grew, so rather bored me, but I would read anything—and a corner of tattered paper Nick Carters, where I much lived.

Make what one can of it. The likely truth is that any actual influences were outside "the short story" entirely: in the Bible (mostly Ecclesiastes and the Prophets), whose rhetoric I was never to recover from—and a complete set of Thackeray, read and re-read by the age of ten, in which I was quite as happy with "The Yellowplush Papers" as with *Vanity Fair*. Thackeray keeps appearing in his own pages, remember? (Always welcome too, except when he quoted Greek.) And the Bible, though pithy, keeps saying what it thinks.

This was soon to cause differences of opinion between me and *The New Yorker*, the causes of which neither of us really knew. On my side it was not yet opinion at all. I had a rhetoric not always calm, though it did tend to collect. At the ends of stories. Stories? When I wrote them, I wanted to *end* them, and often in a burst did so. At the time this was felt to be unsuitable. Why? Because in her way, though still so anonymously, author did appear. I had violated the oblique, as I was increasingly to do. (To the point of finally breaking away into other forms, novel to essay, where there was more natural space for it.) Twice, in two of the earliest stories, editorial suggestion (which, apart from the fact-questioning done by the checkers, was never concrete, always delicate, rather like a maitre in an atelier flicking with his pointer a passage in the nude drawing, here, there, which had *not quite* fulfilled itself) got better endings out of me than I had first put there. (Once, with the first story written, "A Box of Ginger," where I took a corny sentence out and felt much the better for it. And once, with "The Watchers," justifiably rejected for not being quite *finished*, where, after some months' mulling I found the right sentence—while looking into the toilet as a matter of fact—and put it *in*.)

But with "A Wreath for Miss Totten," a story bracketed in two paragraphs, opening and concluding, which are quite plainly both rhetorical *and* moral observation (shoot the oblique from both sides), when it was flatly suggested that these be removed, though I was of course otherwise "free to send the story elsewhere"—I sent it. Not merely because I knew that the story, unbracketed, thereby fitted nicely into these memoirs-of-a-memorable-old-character which are a *New Yorker* genre. Something else in me, an instinct not yet formulated, lurked beyond that. Several stories on, with *In the Absence of Angels*, there was to be another controversy, this time in a way political. It was the time of the first SHELTER signs in public buildings, when

New York City feared Russian bombing (*Collier's* printed an entire issue devoted to a mythical such bombing). My story (of Westchester under totalitarian rule), though already much praised "at the office" was finally regretfully rejected on the grounds that the magazine wished to do nothing to contribute to that fear. I replied with a letter of protest suggesting the magazine's obligation to print what it had on all other grounds highly praised. Later, on telling an editor there that I was abashed over the letter (I am always abashed, *later*) he replied, "That letter did you no harm." And indeed the story was later printed, the delay and soul-searching on their part (or on Harold Ross's part as I was told it was) being in a way a credit to their still admirably sustained conviction that the pen is or can be—a sword. I agreed with them. During our correspondence—for the total of nine stories they ultimately printed there was quite a lot of it—I several times wrote to tell them so. These early statements were my first letters of indignation. The burden of them was "It has to be *my* sword."

I felt pretty shaky about it. It seemed that I would have to do—what I had to do. In whatever guise—some of which I am not yet sure of—whenever author wanted to appear, author would. But I wasn't at all sure I had the figure for it—as a dancer, I knew that those girls who didn't, were often the ones most willing to strip. Later still, I would often wonder how some editors could be so knowing, why they never were as shaky as me. Simple. They don't appear.

By which a writer meant—in what he writes. Which then meant—no commentary of any kind. Nothing on literature, neither of the world or one's contemporaries, and no comment on one's own work—above all nothing on that. In the American convention of the time (to which, from an inclination to privacy that still persists, I inarticulately subscribed to without knowing it) "author" like his works remained oblique. He had almost a responsibility to, which went far deeper than the mere preservation of a private life, or a dislike of public "personal" appearances. Superficially among lesser writers, the attitude may have had to do with snob dignities. Going down or out to the litry hustings, they surmised must indeed be a descent. For the "best" writers, hunted in picpost flashes, or traced in gingerly answers to news interviews, still were aloof. Except when acquiring Nobel prizes, they kept their thoughts on literature—and on life—to themselves.

There were good reasons for this, practically and psychologically. Even on the eastern seaboard, American literary life couldn't concentrate as it does in Britain and France; the distances between writers, in backgrounds as well as miles, were often vast. Often, and most poignantly before the 1950s, American artists had gone to those countries half for art maybe, but also to meet those semblables, themselves. At home, for discussion companionship a writer had a choice of small letter-united friendships, or perhaps a provincial group (agrarian or not) attached by ethnic origin or to a "little" review, or else a social life essentially unserious, ranging from the New York martini, to the leftovers of Boston tea.

But paramount; in the realms of opinion, the American writer per se, had long since lost his supreme authority or relegated it. In the academy the critics cluster, in the reviews they bluster; to them now belong the barricades. Except for James, a special case, American writers had never much had an authority in the European tradition of a Goethe or Gide, or of those dozens of minor writers who by aristocratic right would both formulate over the corpus of literature and create it. Or of those like Lawrence, who were savagely and openly anti-critical. When the American writer finally appeared to explain or defend himself, or to express judgments he had perhaps been nourished by, it would more often be in posthumous letters like Hart Crane's, or post-hoc crackups, or in memoirs which were the pre-death flare sent up to show that his work and his quarrels were done. Now and then, in interview, to a younger person or in a foreign country, a Hemingway or a Faulkner unbent. But characteristically they hoarded their *mana*, like men who had wiser uses for it.

A writer may well mistrust literary companionship. Talk *is* bloody hemophiliac. The orphic in us is a pulse; the didactic is a code and a restraint. All work involves pre-judgments too delicate for aeration perhaps, or which codify best of themselves. Gestation goes on best in the dark. When it is over, you are already gathering energy for the next, in the usual anxiety over what you can't do, arrogance over what you can. It is then, idle and meditating, that an urge to write *about* books may arise. An intent one, gaze bent on the dark coil that makes books.

The counter-urge—*not* to spill the seed, *not* to expend the love—is one of the strongest I know. And comes from the same fear—of not having enough. Enough energy and time (a day's writing is a day) and enough fertility for both art and analysis. Yet, sometimes, one has the wild urge, need, to assess or correct the critical attitudes of the day—which almost certainly are not one's own. Why bother?— they never will be. I suppose that is why.

Professionally, in America, you ran a risk. Since you were not an equal-opportunity critic, having neither the lingo nor the connections, you could not really be talking to them, about literary concerns. It would be assumed you were really talking to reviewers, about your own concerns. You could earn equal time, of course, by constantly writing reviews yourself and joining in all the litry cabals, on the principle of the partygoer who by accepting all invitations, both insures himself against gossip behind his back, and makes it known he's been asked. If you don't want to be an underdog of literature, hadn't you better set yourself up as the watchdog of it? I have heard many writers shrewdly take this into account. There was of course the chance, especially if you had never before spoken up about books, yours or other peoples, that attention might be paid because of the oddity of it, and those who respect your work might respect your views. Never of course engage with reviewers on any score—and not merely because of these obvious revenges—silence, or the last-word slash. Even if you respected a reviewer, and he you, it was dangerous. The American gap was still too wide for it. If you respected yourself, you would know enough to keep your pose arcane. You might not think you were lowering yourself by speaking publicly to him. He would.

That hasn't much changed since the '50s. Slowly, other author obliquities which also had nothing to do with literature itself, did seem to be giving way. Media has had much to do with it. University teaching has had more. With a press and a pulpit, many a silent writer has learned to talk—and talk always enlarges itself. The habit of the lectern instills the habit of knowing. The habit of writing instills the habit of finding out. As in my own way I was enveloped in the usual media-clouds and university respectabilities, I sometimes knelt inwardly, praying to remember the difference.

Meanwhile, for me and others, a categorical silence familiarly imposed on short-story writers was breaking down—as it could not help but do. Perhaps because we were in a short-story renaissance, it was felt that writers of them should not—in fact could not—turn into novelists. When the novels did come on, good or bad, it was always keenly observed that they were "not the same," although the one sure difference between the two forms—length—insures that they can never be the same. Looking back it is clear that stories were getting longer everywhere; writers were tiring of the short stint. On my own side, almost at once I felt I had finished with the "Hester" stories, typically a young writer's autobiographical material which I no longer wanted to stay in, but also the "environment" I was told *The New Yorker* had bought me for, never having seen it "done" before. For me it was merely my childhood; I felt no obligation to stay in it. Already stories had shifted subject—and *were* getting longer. It felt like Alice, I must say, or adolescence—gawky skeleton enlarging, qualifications crowding in on childhood's gospel, and in the half-poemed cherub's enclosure that so many stories of the time stayed in, the long gaunt boots of another kind of prose. (By 1953, I would begin the novel *False Entry*, whose related novel, *The New Yorkers*, written years after, would finally return in part to that never-since-used environment, now altogether transfused out of the autobiographical.)

Paradoxically, stories were having to be defended—were they really as *good* as novels?—meaning were they as important on the literary scale, and in a *Times* interview I was asked that. My answer was much what it would be now, "Whose scale?" As another complication, many of the best story-writers of the day were women, and this was seen as a sign of special affinity between the form and the sex, rather than as part of the greater intrusion of women into general literature. Actually, once again the real truths went deeper. (Deeper even than sex, which is pretty far, but a distance writers are used to.) . . . Why list the old false imperatives though, if you never believed in them? Because you didn't know that, at the time.

All over, in the same way that scientific discoveries ignite simultaneously half across the globe from each other, writers were not merely going from short forms to long, which they classically do; they were getting damned tired of the oblique. Which had been perhaps a rather specifically American reaction to rambling Victorian morality, had never been as tightly and totally the thing in European writers anyway, and was now over. From then on, author would appear on his pages in that capacity when and where he chose, commentating on absolutely everything. And stories in this style, soon in its turn to become a category, would appear in the best magazines.

For there were other sides to the explosion, far more important ones—political and sexual revolutions, and the last throbs of the Freudian one. What one must say ultimately has the greater effect on how one says it. And should. When numbers of writers begin to think the same about the world, then a literary tradition is made without their ever having corresponded or met—and one not really based on expressional modes. Explaining why is like answering the question, "Why I had the baby," and of about the same use—it makes ya think. The material of the world—which precedes art—was forcing us all to be more dogmatic, open, shrill at any cost, and committedly personal. We had to give the picture of our own pain. In the name of all of it. Art for art's sake? Ah, that was an ivory tower, belonging to Anonymous.

Well, here we are not so many years later, and in the name of either world or personal pain, a great many writers have since appeared both on the platformed page and in the world publicly, as authors who are themselves continuously. And on the page, in all guises and pronouns—as "he," "she," "you," "we," and even "they"—as long as it is understood that these are all surrogates for the most popular pronoun, the out-and-out confessional "I." "Fiction" and "non-fiction" (those words made of plastic elastic) now do not merely combine. Nor yet see themselves as inter-mirrored in any of the ways that normally have confounded philosophers. The only fiction now worth writing *is* from fact. This has made all the difference.

A reader-critic must now be able to feel that any of the "old" pronoun approaches to experience really are masks for the literal "I" of the writer. The experiences described must have happened, or be conceivably happenable—to him. So why bother with those other approaches, which no longer seem to work anyway? (As indeed they don't, under such an assumption, since they are avenues out from the solipsistic world, not toward it.) Since they no longer seem worth doing, why bother with "fiction" at all?

Why indeed? This is segregated art, with all the limits of art wherever artists are so confined—this time to their own autobiography: to black-white, male-female, national, ethnic, country-city writing, to the end that only a pup called Rover can truly tell you about Lincoln's doctor's dog. The "fictive" world, whatever that is, must never sound imagined beyond the life-mobility of the author. The story or novel, to be living, whatever that now is, must never be—oblique. It must spurt, hot and unwilled, uncorrected and undirected by art (which is only a fake word for artfulness)—the real red-ink blood of a poet. Into your honest hand. You've got the real thing now. (Don't ask how he got it to a publisher.) The burden of belief a reader once had to carry is lifted. You don't any longer have to be guilty of that lie, imagination. Know what? You're not *vicarious* any more!

This is the willing suspension of our disbelief *now*.

And if the novel (whatever that is) won't do that for you in that way, or begins to bore you at it—then it is soon to be very dead. So it will be. *That* way will be. It is one of the great modes of art, but it isn't the only one. Segregation, in art as any where, is a straight road to escape. For a time. Look back on how, in painting, the human body, once individualized, canonized, was finally impressionized out of all personality. And now, unerringly, returns. The human figurative always does. And in any art, it also knows how to hide. The novelist (whatever that is) is also and always has been a quondam-diarist, proto-historian, part-time pundit, pseudo-dramatist, and putative poet —he eats roles. And frequently smells of them. He as often wants to conceal himself in his work as to reveal. Give him the wide-open chance to be himself on a platter and he may take this as his right; compel it and he will as soon chuck it back at you, in exchange for the delights of being a hunted, wanted man, and for the sheer professional practice of peering at you from some other bunghole.

What is the fictive world? Does a fact, the moment it is phrased, start to be imaginary? Does the imagined earn reality through very language? Where, on the street of shadowboxes that is now our life, is the non-fictive world? Can you and I tell each other sometime? Don't bore me, I'll bore you. I'll tell you about I.

I was well used to finding out in my books what I dreamed of the world. Slowly, at another point of the pen, I began to find out what I thought of it. At times it was almost as if those old philosophical divisions, in the anatomie of our melancholy intelligence, were true. There were two rivers in me, two pens that dipped in these, very separate and entirely alternate. The connection between them—for there is one—could give a critic no cheer. A writer's critical ideas were always preceded by his books. (I don't do as I say. I say later what I can then see I hoped to do.) Special pleading? Of course. A writer would be mad not to. He has an obligation to keep the field free, always to enter it against those who knew too well how to do precisely what. Generalized pleading, toward a system, was for the critique, and not his affair.

There's peril in it—in that second pen. I have never got over my fear of it. Too much logic destroys the image, which is a fusion of the vague. Imagination had its own precisions, which a habit of critical thought could blunt. There is a certain amount of hermetic air around us at the beginning of things; once carved into attitudes, could it ever return to the nobility of an emptiness waiting to be *made*?

Long ago, describing how a story began, I said, "One wants to *show*

this thing. One feels a clean . . . strong . . . almost anger, that this half-
visible thing is not yet known. It's a paranoia *toward*, not against.
One has seen. One must rescue it." A story, a poem, a novel was a
rescue of life, a muckraking of it, or even a letter of indignation—to
one's friends. Criticism still seemed to me more like a lettre de cachet,
meant for the enemy, which might turn out to be mine. I might end
up outside the beloved prison, looking in.

At the same time the conscious feeds the unconscious; that stream
is not always one-way. The creative in us (I knew we would come to
it) is not always the hothead part of a writer, the critic in us not
always the objective and willed. Each passes through the sieve of
the other. Outside in the world, wars between the two come less
from the critic's secular power than from his assumption that he is
there to instruct. When he loses his cool, dropping into the ego-
explanation, the life justifications that afflict other writers, I find
that encouraging. It is a sign that, at his pole of literature, he is
aware that no man can be its procurator; each man may add to it.

But when I write with the second pen, I still think of it as ego-art.

Once, wandering into a round-table conference, I came upon a
rising young American critic who was addressing a group of European writers. "Oh, h'lo," he said over his shoulder, when the rest of
us entered, and went on: "We—" he said, and at that pace, "—who
are working in literature—" I stood behind him, uncredentialled and
feeling it. He sat. *Who* was working in literature, dammit? Suddenly
one of the others at the table, not a critic either (the blessed Richard
Hughes as a matter of fact) winked at me. It was better to be uncredentialled in that way. Better to stand behind.

And once, I was taken down in the bowels of the British Museum,
where by law a copy of every piece of printed matter originating
in England, broadside to ballyhoo, had to be kept. Libraries all over
the world were choking on their own goods, and reaching for the
microfilm. Yet as I stood there, it seemed to me that I could hear the
huge, rosicrucian murmur of language reincarnating itself in the old
habit; what was Cheapside down here would someday be taken into
a poem upstairs.

Literature is a continuum. We can only continue it.
I thought so. I dreamed it.

Am I coming to the end, for me, of one more kind of expression? In my other work, this displacement process has become a familiar one. Though I don't want to investigate why I write what when, in fact want to be the last to know consciously, I can't help an awareness as innate as any body-rhythm, that after a long or massive and perhaps "irregular" piece of work, I will want to do something "small and finished," or that after some concentration on the "inhuman" or meta-physical, I will want most to "get back to people." Or that after work in which I have tried most of all to invest the ordinary with strangeness, I may find myself stretching toward the reverse. Each time, the feeling, physical and plastic, is that I break the mold *in the act* of making it—leaving it behind me. (Just as, nearing the end of this book's auto-biology, I already know that if someday I should have a further span of life to report on, biographing that in this way will no longer be possible.)

The sensation of leaving, dependent of course on one's private admission that one has soared a few feet up, and not too badly—is rather as if one has been an eagle-for-a-day in a certain vicinity, and is now bored with eagledom *in that neighborhood*. I am able to get away, perhaps, because each piece of work, like any living organism —which for the time being it is to me, somewhere contains the seed of the next.

Anti-criticism, I begin to find, won't remain fixed for me either. At first, as a squib tossed out to set fire to some too-fat-and-fancy bottoms, it can progress to avuncular chat, dangerous though it is for the writer to be sage uncle rather than fresh green nephew. But after two or three such anti-rounds, even anti-criticism has to be something more.

Under the working title *In Full View Of The City* (which I sometimes wish I had kept) I had just done a long novel, in some ways set in a "real" New York I thought I remembered. I labored for that realism, not only to capture a period now gone, which I had in part inhabited, but also because the people in the book, the two principal women especially, were thus set off in their own strangeness—in its turn that very human oddness which the "realistic" side of any environment tends to create.

Behind these forces within the book, there was another influence I had never worked under before. This book, *The New Yorkers*, was in a sense a sequel to my first novel, *False Entry*, though actually prior to it in time sequence. Since either one could be read alone, before or after the other, their permanent intersection lay somewhere in space—in the reader's mind after he had read both. Both were intensely concerned with the notion of "place." For my generation, changes in that concept had become the number-one trauma, outdistancing even the touted changes in our concept of the psyche, secondary only to the traumatic looming of death itself, personal or racial—and in some ways allied to both.

In the earlier book, "the real place" was that romantic, metaphysical or spiritual one we all yearn for, often confusing or combining it with other elsewheres seemingly *in situ*—notably "time." The later book was concerned with that actual place which is so much where we are that where treated in the novel it does better to be *more* real than real. In the first book's climate—one essentially still prevailing when I appeared in the world—the spaces between rich and poor, grandee and dressmaker's boy, England and America, were still fixed enough for encounters between the two poles of social class to have an exotic flavor—as for North and South, I remember thinking that its "Knights of the Midnight Mystery" (drawn from actual Ku Klux Klan records still in force when I wrote) belonged as much to the gothic novel as to mine.

The second book explored that class where the novel is said to have begun—the middle. Not so much in its social relations as in its dreams and textures—to outsiders always furnished to the nth, and full of its own darkness. Almost unconsciously, I used everything my class had accumulated in its carpetbagger progress and crisscross realms of perception—because I too had them, in our mutual background.

Here in my book were the talk-thought marathons of the novels *our*

PUSHING AROUND THE PANTHEON

youth had admired, the chapter alternations *our* shared reading had been fed on, plus one of those culminating dinner-scenes in which everybody arrives (an integral part of middle-class life in any time) and two of those long monologues which novelists from Richardson to Joyce have unerringly given to women characters—perhaps in recognition that free association and internal monologue are part of the essentially feminine.

As always with me, the style or form had aped its material, or inflected with it. This time, I seemed to have made the novel's ontogony —where it and its people were "now"—echo their joint phylogenetic history—what both they and the novel in general had come through, to what they were. This is what living people do every day, so acquiring a more than present-day density. And this is "where" the book was set.

Taken together, the two books were in their way a recapitulation of what the American "mind" of my time had come through. Afterwards, I began to think about that. Because, once again, I was leaving.

That year, in a hired hall somewhere, or maybe the "Y," three or four writers got together and more or less reported the death of the novel. A lot of people paid to hear. I didn't go, because I already knew about it, but I read the account the next morning. What these sighing Alexanders had said was that "modern times" wasn't good for novel-making. They were right, of course. Modern times never are.

If a writer sees himself too regularly as an inhabitant of this, he may well be in trouble. An Era is such a dull place for a book to be. Once, when I told a "serious" novelist he had a talent for the comic he oughtn't deny, he took it as a put-down. "I want to make a *serious* impact on my times." He and I clearly differed on what comedy was, but still I was awe-struck. He sighted "the times" along the barrel of his .22—bang! Meanwhile I was up to my neck in it—it was having such an impact on me.

Modern times is a bad place for seeing the great metaphors that all art must have. In the mixed media that modernity always inhabits, God is often very possibly dead, but the arts are surely. They are so because they form part of the tangible godhead of that daily life which all men, including artists, are trained to see small. There, in the slim incarnation of our lives as we can see them now, painting is always on its last pop cycle, and music, shorn of the "ancient" melodies, is silent. Even the past is never as rigid as modernity is. For, looking back, we can see without pain that art is fluid, or even celebrate how art has united with document. But for *today*, the arts are always catatonic —fixed. This comes about because the document of our own time affrights us all. And the idea that art must be document, or should be, or *will* be—cuts at the very wrist of the artist, as his hand grips what it can, midstream.

A novel is a kind of enclosure. So of course is a poem, a watercolor, a fugue. But the novel, whether it maps by way of people or dream, or in the very essence of the void, still sets itself up as taking place somewhere within the human stockade. So, in effect it always takes place within that prison. It makes a place for itself there, sometimes cosmic or international, sometimes parochial, in a street or a town or a childhood—or in the great savannahs of a single mind. But always, the novel in some sense will tell us about a place, actual or metaphysical. For the novel, place is the devouring unity. The nature of the novel is to tell us what the nature of some part of the prison is.

"And it was so much easier, wasn't it," you hear people say, "when the enclosures were there for all to see—and almost certain to be strictly regional. When the world had *useful* boundaries, never seeing itself too large or too small—look at Barchester! While look at us— fragmented, moonborne, yet at the same time colonized to the inch, tape-recorded in every known Babelese, and *shhh*, worst of all, *on camera*, down to the very declivities of our newly-to-be-exchanged worlds—or hearts." I think rather that the people of an era never really see themselves as living in those neat amphitheatres which art or history will later assign. Where are we to find again the tidy Barchester of yore? In the reminder that Trollope—a man of many other milieus by the way—gave us it.

In the nineteenth century, a novelist expected to depend on the dignity of a literal setting, often an agreed-upon reality gained from what men already knew of such a habitat—from which starting-place he might then go on. The degree to which he could depart from it into further recesses or heights, would determine the greatness of his work, and this is what keeps great novels accessible. Agreed-upon reality never stays the same. Places disappear. But in time, a great novel sheds its literal place, whatever that may be, for an eternal one.

To that modernity of the moment—us—it is the concept of place itself which has most altered. Will we ourselves be magnificent in all those spaces that are to be—or only ever more cramped back into what we miserably are? In literature, has even the most traditionalist sense of a particular place long been swamped by those other unities, action and time? What's going to go next? For the world and the novel, what is "place" now?

I guess we see clearest what it no longer is. As late as 1932, there was another English novelist in the tradition of Brontë, Winifred Holtby. Her much praised *South Riding* could subtitle itself *An English Landscape* and mean it, in the old exhaustive way from manorhouse to councilhall, squire to alderman. Reading it now, one suspects that for many in its own time it was already *déja vu*. For by then, the concepts of place and place-time had so altered that novelists either were affected, or had already helped to alter them. For all men, the old Aristotelian unities were shaken forevermore—or again. By 1930, Robert Musil had already published *The Man Without Qualities*, where a 1913 Vienna vibrated with all the interpenetrations of a "modern" city, and chapters had headings like "If there is such a thing as a sense of reality . . . ," or "Which remarkably does not get us anywhere." Proust had written. Joyce had given us his Dublin of the mind, and Kafka had given us a paralyzed geography in which man stood on the pinpoint of himself. Some of this had already been done before—some always has. But for the art of the future, and the man— the psyche was to be the recognized "place" now.

So, it's come about that literal place-reality in the novel can no longer impose the same dignity or force. We can neither read nor write about it solely in the old way, without that unalterable flash of *déja vu*. New enclosures, long since sighted by literature, make this impossible. And these in time become the new convention, as we have it now: "Better to ignore place altogether now. Or make it metaphysical." For of course, a convention is an either-or proposition. It never lets you do both.

And in the American novel, the dilemma has been particularly sharp. For we were still lagging in the pioneer's lively enthusiasm for *real* places, new ones, and for that "American experience" so rooted in them. No one wished to annihilate this, or could. What happened was simpler. Certain places, mostly urban, became proper literary; "modern" novels could take place there without fear of ridicule, or damwell had to. The rest of the country could go back to pulp, and damnear did. The West went into the westerns. The South redeemed itself, as the special home of our guilt. The small town disappeared down a trap-door marked Babbitt. And nobody heard tell anymore of the farm. Not in high places. And so arose a new American literary convention, of unparalleled naiveté.

A "regional" novelist was now a man born in the sticks and doomed to write about it, under rhythmically weathered titles: *Hardscrabble Sky*, *A Light Sweat Over the Carolinas*, this to let the reader know that the book's prostitutes would come from the fields and there would be no highclass restaurants. Metropolitan novels meanwhile, even if bad were never *regional*. The provinces had too much parvenu respect for the city, and the city agreed with them. Across the nation, the whole literary push had been toward the cities—as in Dreiser, whose novels were saved by that fact. Or toward Europe—for experience of which Cather, Anderson and Wescott could be condescended to, and Hemingway praised, for having once again (after Wharton and James) brought Europe back to us. For thirty years, literature rushed east, and many writers sank there, in all the artificialities that a buried nativity can become. But, as with any convention, all writers have been affected by it. For, if "rural" now meant "rube" forever, the city now became the very citadel and symbol of Nowhere.

It has been several other clichés in its time. Once, as in Dos Passos, it was the Great Collage. Before that, the abattoir, and the "teeming poor." Or in a later frivolous era, the Penthouse. For the real American nterest is in change, and the city is the place that changes most, and most "modernly." In time, the city has become the best place for an American novel to be, since all psyches of any importance are pre-sumed to be there. At last it has escaped the old dilemma of place altogether, by becoming *the* existential Place. Totally surreal, of course, never parochial; the absolutist novel cannot be both. Personae in the novels of this type wear their eyeballs on stalks and float down nameless avenues, like paranoid balloons. The Action: Unisex in Night-town. Probable Title: a single symbol, maybe &, or $. And, presto, a new cliché, of sorts. Natives of the city will once again recognize an old one: The City—by an author who comes from somewhere else.

A writer's region is what he makes it, every time. Great novels will not be impeded by the presence of cows there. And the absence of them, or the presence of pavement, has never kept great urban novel-ists from a kind of rural concentration. Dickens, Musil, Biely, Proust—are all great regionalists of a city kind. London, Vienna, St. Petersburg, Paris all "live" in their pages, through people who if written of else-where would not be as they are. Looking back to those eras, the perfumes and stinks, and the ecology, are all clear to us now. The people live in the scenery of those cities, and the city now lives in the people, tangentially, through their eyes and minds, or as in Biely, like a hero itself in the wake of the supernumeraries, its streets following like waves the little people it makes flotsam of. Simple. Yet for our times, our own times always, what a balancing! For a novel at best is never a historical or descriptive thesis, but a sub-news or a supra-news of the world, which all but drags the novelist down, or up and out with it. The novel is rescued life.

What a novelist must trust to is that continuity exists somewhere, somehow to be seen, perhaps as a useful terror strikes his heart. Casting ahead, in order to *see* change in the name of intellectual duty, will not help me. Nor will going back—to such as West Egg or Wessex or Yoknapatawpha; these and their kind hang like mosques made for once only, above their own documents. The novel never goes back in that sense, just as it never leaves the documents as they were. After *seeing* an enclosure, which means making one, a writer may then choose to leave it, as a philosopher leaves a fully expressed idea. Or he may elect to spend his writing life there. But except as a reader, another writer will not be able to accompany him.

So, every age is a sighing Alexander—how can there possibly be more than *this*? Yet every decade brings in more documents. Ours asks the literary artist in particular to shiver and to bow before these —forgetting that the "facts" of the past are often very much what art has made of them. Sometimes, one is tempted to say that all art of any kind is an attempt to make the unimaginative imagine—imagination.

And there's no perfect time for it—except now. "Modern times" sees itself as the time of the breaking up of the myths. That may well be its. The age which my own most reminds me of is the medieval—the same brutality and enchantment, the same sense of homunculus peering around the cornice of a history happening far from him—and the same crusade toward a heaven not here. It's chill, lone, and wuthering for some, an overheated faeryland for others, and running with guilty blood for all. An age when change can be caught like quicksilver and held up against the gloss of what we think we remember, where all the gauntlets of starvation and curtailed freedom are still thrown down to us, while sex will be our aphrodisiac and the documents our earthly paradise—who can fail to recognize that description? It is a marvelous time for art.

.
.
.

I WANTED more. But I had no idea where I was going next.

I had always loved slang, collecting it as the energy of language— and of the nation. It keeps your ear to the ground—and to the groundlings, on whose side I most wanted to be.

We were coining slang very fast now, hacking it out with the coughs and cheapened body odors of the television ads, or buying it up bright and carbon-streaked as the goods at a firesale—wonderful mobile images whose jokes or poignancies were dead in a month. For our reactions to such language ran the same quick course as it did, from natural to fashionable, from honest to false.

There was a phrase of the day—did it come from Harlem street-corner or Hollywood press-agent, out of "real" jive-ass music, or from the curly boys at the recording studios?—"Let it all hang out."

Such a phrase means what you make it, depending also on what you are. We coin ourselves from day to day out of such phrases, which interlock enough to keep us going and understanding one another. So if I am feeling false-rural or mock-naive—or if on the other hand I am merely young enough to be nearer the slang—such a phrase may perhaps conjure up women at the washline of the ancient grievances, freed at last of their corsetry and proudly breastfeeding their babies in public places. Or men with bellies hanging easy over their beltlines, from all the good greeds of simple, open life. But if we are merely feeling jazzy, city-corrupt, for today, then the words, jumbling from the crowd, say "Stop the Mafia-style whispering, let down your hair and/or your pants, admit old sins, like maybe that you still say cullud quicker than black, stop being a closet-queen, roll the shirtsleeve from your junkie-arm—be anything you weren't allowed to be yesterday, even if it's bad news or badmouth taste, which it is bound to be, for all honesty is really shame." Shake with "natural" music—even if unnaturally! And above all, loose the pajama string. On anything from the genitalia to literature and politics. For connections between the three are once more being made.

From as far back as Cole Porter's "Let's Do It," American popular-sexual slang has had its own brand of coyness, odd if one considers that most of such slang probably comes from the male side. Bottom of it all is the dinky phallus that the country has kept in the dark of the bedroom, or in the decent jockstraps of the lockerroom, and has shyly immortalized best perhaps in its skyscrapers (with plenty of heavy money at their roots).

Some of this is what I was thinking. And that not all the modesty in the country was male.

Let it all hang out. Rather a fine phrase, that one.

So, gathering my own echoes together, I did.

Sex. Literature. American.

A mug's idea of it, I always thought. Whenever I saw any two of those words paired together.

Sex was never just a topic, to me. Literature doesn't move by topic; critics do. Our literature hadn't been all-American since well before I was born. And my fellow-American writers, who so often fought out their friendships in the magazines—or their judgments—had never been joined there by me.

For two and a half years, until that summer of 1968, I had scarcely read any of them. The novel I had been working on had become a meditation enclosing all I could handle of a sustained metaphorical world: I wanted no interruptions except from life. Increasingly, for the duration of each book, I had found myself doing this, perhaps ever since that first novel of 1961, after which I had been made to see (if I hadn't seen it before, or not as parochially as the commentators demanded of one) that I too was writing about "America."

Every writer is a loner in his own way. By circumstance, I had been a late and fairly innocent beginner at an age when others were professionals, belonging to no school except in the minds of those who fixed on those eight early stories in *The New Yorker*, by temperament alien to the nitpicking of the quarterlies, by sex a woman in a period when the short story was a great female province but the novel was felt to be male, by heritage European, American Southern, and a Jew. When it was complained that I couldn't be trusted from book to book to hold my own "image," I gratefully agreed. Yet I could see that all of them were as much American as anything else, and as much about America, as anything else. In this latest book, I had faced that in a way I hadn't before. Or rather, the book had led me to this conclusion, one outside its own pages or purpose, because it was a chronicle of the past, done in terms of the hot present of the past, but not of the now—in a way I had never attempted before.

But now it was done. We were in summer, on island. I was a reader again. Each morning the postmistress handed me a bundle from the New York Society Library, and I returned her one. I groaned in empathy over every book. As for their "status," that lay embalmed in the silurian light of the winter claques.

Then—for the record, while pausing in James Purdy's *Eustace Chisholm and the Works* at a sentence—I happened to look into the eyes of a deer.

In June, those deer who all year have the run of that island come to the porch to stare. Behind them, their dark wood nibbles our scent. We have left the city of literature. Bringing with us our pathetic fallacy that nature is *not* watching us. They have left nothing. They bring the gloaming. So, under their eyes—there was now the doe, the fawn, and back in among the trees the stag—I closed that day's book, on that sentence: "I could drink your come in goblets"—said "millionaire Reuben Masterson."

Why a goblet, I thought irritably, why not a plain glass? Why does he have to be so *fancy?* Then I burst out laughing. "Oh, well"—I said to the vanishing scuts of the deer "these days there are millionaires everywhere."

The idyll was over. The reading had become the meditation. For days I took notes on the flood of it. At first I seemed to be writing of Sex in American Literature, but as other sideshows advanced, I let them, and writing for myself, I named names. Sex, literature, America, I was seeing as sideshows in a circle. Male, female and otherwise, created He them. He was looking for His image. I went looking for mine.

Finished with my orgy of judgment, I made no rewrite, and hid the packet away as one does the minor madnesses. From time to time, hoping to understand what it was to me, I took it out again. I saw nothing in it but what any critic has—ego and empathy, prejudice and taste. Yet perhaps one slim advantage. The creative critic will sometimes do a showy interpretive dance around another man's book, reworking it in rather the same hungry, possessive way in which certain Freudian biographers seem to want to relive the very life. Writers have small interest in such recreation.

Some of what I had said had not yet been remarked as far as I knew, or not in this way. Or not by a writer. A critic usually thinks he is objective. A writer always knows he is not. At any given moment he can tell you where his ego is. But the empathy wrung from him by the work of other writers tastes of his own sweat. And the balance between these is his brand of scholarship.

I saw too that such notes as these ought to be left in their original circularity. The silent jumps between sections seemed to me to make of themselves a kind of connective current, and the repetitions also. My contemporaries and I knew well enough what it is that "order" destroys.

Meanwhile, I trembled at what I had said of them. For whatever axes I had ground, in the end they ground me. And by now, I was on another book. An odd one, for me. Or odd in a new way.

But until well after its completion, I had no realisation of what the following pages, since transcribed, really are to it.

There are writers whose blessed perversion is not *extra* the universe which they "share" with "the rest of us," but total. A writer like Firbank is not only eccentric to the marrowbone, though he may seem merely that, in the first freak delight of encounter. He takes us into the marrowbone. Where exists no "the rest of us," but the same unity anyone feels when man can take us into his universe. Social and sexual distinctions do not weigh, except in laughter; the sociological or religious critic would be absurd here; delicacies and profundities create themselves according to the relationships in this world, astonishing and fresh as any art new to us is, but no more mixed and polyglot in the end than incontinently truthful art is anywhere.

A writer like Angus Wilson—who in political discussion with a stranger I have heard interject matter-of-factly "Well, I'm a homosexual, you see"—is as an observer and recorder so thoroughly upheld by a particular tradition—here the whole background of the British "class" novel, that his satire is impersonally directed outward, no more homosexual or less heterosexual than a mythical anybody's; homosexuals in his gallery get the same shrift as everybody, and if the compassion, when it comes, is a bit directed also, that too is British to the core.

Is an American like Albee less lucky for not being centered in such a tradition, or more? He gives no affirmation to any sex, but has used the heterosexual cliches to bitter advantage. When it is complained that he is not only constrained but compelled to do his work in these terms, even to obscure or hide it there, what is really being asked of him? Is he being asked to declare a sexual bias—which is a personal affair, and to couch his work strictly in terms of whatever it is—which is an artistic one? Or is he being asked to affirm—which is a national affair as well? It seems to me, that like the rest of us, he suffers from his Americanism on all these scores, and where he can, also makes very good use of it.

By contrast, Tennessee Williams seems to me more simply a writer of a kind, much gifted with feeling, whose personal vision, whatever its sex, sometimes transcends into poetry and sometimes not—in which case it does become ridiculous. The absurdities do become sexually divisible along a line that one can after a while predict—the girls gone dippy or bitter over homo husbands thrust on their innocence, the bull-like uncles and butch husbands, and with increasingly baby-blue religiosity, the young men always assumpting toward heaven in gilt-gesso featherbeds. If Williams' work, always heavy on the symbol and the Freudianism, now seems old fashioned, that is why—and really most why the adoration of boy-muscle seems outmoded too. Theater treatment of homosexuality has meanwhile become more liberal. But I never feel that Williams is writing of the homosexual world. From *Streetcar* on, I have felt that he is writing of "the world" in the heterosexual terms in which it couches itself to *him*. Sometimes he gives us poetic moments, a kind of intensity-to-the-left-of-feeling—rather like a radical poet in a roomful of Republican ones, certain of whose sensitivities he shares. But I have never seen a play of his which I didn't feel was akimbo emotionally, or that stayed with me after-theater, to be returned to—as the major intensities anywhere do. He has always made me feel that he has got "our" world squeegee, and is stuck with it. The worst of this being that the "our world" he brings out in me is a false one too. Oftenly too narrowly heterosexual by far.

I think that the heterosexual artist himself rarely sees the "breeding" world—which is basically as far as I care to define the difference—as narrowly as the consciously or secretly homosexual must. Basically, these must deny the breeding world all its implications of feeling or worth. All their satire will proportion itself toward that, and all their self-exaltation away from it. As for that part of life—death, war, taxes, money in general, and even birth—which is only peripherally sexual, or asexual, or a no-man's-land mixture of the *comedie humaine*—they are forced by circumstance to deny that it exists nonsexually, or to castrate themselves from it; they must take a sexual stance on everything. By its nature often an hysteric one. For the world do breed—and is not altogether to be talked out of it.

At present. As food and good rivers grow scarcer, maybe sexual difference, already on its way to optional, may sink the whole frame of reference we now know, in a puree of pills. (Even now, what is a "heterosexual" writer—a man who copulates with women strictly non-anally, if not in the missionary position? Is a woman writer, after a certain mild point of subject and aura, dubiously heterosexual altogether?) Meanwhile, if the English-speaking world, and American literature in particular, has undergone a sexual revolution in the last fifty years, then it is the homosexuals who are its latest suffragettes.

Like all writers, their position toward society—intellectually, emotionally, influentially—starts from their place in it as people. And is altogether different from the suffragettes who preceded them. Women, however kept to the back stairs in the pantheons of art, are admissible to society as people, if only so far. The homosexual, as a person forced into underground alienations or flashily outsize compensating reactions, can feel closer to the categorized—to the black and the Jew. Art, however, has always accepted him as a fully participating member of at least the world of art. Where the women writers, still somewhat relegated to their end of art's living room, must earn their way across it much as in that kind of segregated American provincial society (and with the same mixed results), the male homosexual writer's place in the pantheon—and in the host of earthly connections which arise from that privilege—is still with the gentlemen. He may or may not also have additional "homintern" access to spheres of sympathy and influence. The female homo writer, even if a type bold enough to assert its place with the men, also instinctively tends to align herself with that "homintern", thereby acquiring a coterie to face the world with, much as Southern women writers, linking themselves to the Southern Agrarians, or linked by the critics to that renaissance, were enabled both to escape the stigma of female, and to achieve the connections.

One pays for any connection, of course—is the usual moral tone taken. One pays in a narrowing of sympathies, in exchange for sympathy, and in a loss of autonomies important to artists—in exchange for not being literarily alone. So be it—if it is also admitted that all writers in America, and the heterosexuals as much as any, suffer from their connection with a society which in the most rigidly gross way arrogates what shall be considered male or female in people, taking no note that the antipathies which it has manufactured for itself: soft-hard, virile-weak, delicate-strong, sheltered-experienced, etc., etc., are elsewhere much more loosely defined—as in Europe even of the nineteenth century, or are partially blended or altogether reversed—as historically in Asiatic and Muslim countries everywhere. (What would be said of a flower-arranging American who spent his days in exclusively male cafés, or walking hand in hand with a male friend, meanwhile expecting his wife and her female relatives to run the family business and practical relationships? Or of a country where the practice of medicine and dentistry is more for the female, and a poet can therefore tell me "I am free to write of course, and have this beautiful house, since my wife is one of the best dentists in Manila"?) That so-allotted sex characteristics vary wildly with geography is still a matter of merely anthropological or travel interest even to the educated here—rarely entering their thoughts about themselves. And the democratic fear of acknowledging that money makes us different *really*, shuts off even the artist from freely admitting in his work that where you dig your ditch or your dough has more to do with some so-called feminine-masculine divisions of personality than human nature does—or than personality does. American society, certain portions of it, can take up sexual "looseness" for fun or freedom's sake. Or it can learn to let fathers change diapers, for dear psychology's sake. Or

it can admit that there's a little feminine in the best of us, and a little
heterosexual in the worst of us. What it fights to the death, even on
the highest intellectual levels—literary critics, say, or really male
novelists—is any admission that those ingrainedly fem.-masc. activities
or movements of the reason, which our lifestyle apportions as such
and takes for granted—are actually "so-called."

What these binding divisions of sexual characteristic have done to
American writers goes deeper than what is in their books—because it
apprehends it. Deeper even than the dreary round of fictional orgasm
or bedsheet romanticism, or the use of sex as the sole revelation. (Or
the near ruination of pornography—ordinarily one of life's more aristocratic or subtly private adornments—by practicing it on a dull mass-
scale.) Whatever the physicality in question, or the mind, a cloud of
these stipulations obscures them. Sometimes, writers have been the
greater for not knowing that nothing is new under the sun—in youth,
a writer might otherwise never begin at all. But none ever draws
strength from keeping to concerns defined as proper to what he or
she is—except the negative strength of doing the opposite. Which turns
some into narrower polemicists than their talents call for, or into
stunted followers of the very opposite. But by and large, American
writers have kept to being men, women, or homosexuals, as the case
may be, very much in terms of what the times have told them that
they are. In fact, doing what one is told, in this area, seems perhaps
the primary *secondary* sexual characteristic of all Americans.

We already know how doing what society expects of the male, or
overdoing it, works with those male writers who get sucked into the
virility calisthenic. These are the writers, some still extant, who are
doomed to hunt deer in Brooklyn, or fish for cunt in the Caribbean, or
to make the cock itself their Chantecler—all with the penis-envy of men
infinitely grateful because they have got one. All because, we say, they
early got hung up on Hemingway's jockstrap. What we forget is that,
prior to this, something in the society hung up him. Behind him at
home was the conviction that artists were sissy (and drink and the
shotgun were dashing), ahead of him even a Europe in which Freud
was prying into the neuroses of art, and Mann was perpetrating his

own guilty notion that art was neurosis—wasn't any artist deserting life by not "living" it? Was art life? A *man's* life?

Women writers in America have acted expectedly also. In the nineteenth century, women here, when not poets either hidden like Dickinson or album like Hemans and Ingelow, were journalists, to either the philosophical passions of the hour, like Margaret Fuller, or to the political ones, like Harriet Beecher Stowe. All the rest were ladies, in a three-named tradition that was to survive well past the age of Adela Rogers St. John—and never quite die. None were novelists with the breadth of experience or daring of the European Georges, or even with the formidable pomp of Mrs. Humphrey Ward. As women passed through the period of the expansion of women's rights, they might be expected to take the right to be an artist as one of these: many did, and have, and do. But the freedom to be an artist is not granted like a vote—it is made. And women continued to make it, most of them, in terms of the sexual image allowed. In the early 1900s, before sexual taboos were broken—by men writers always remember, but *not by Americans*—the gap between what either sex could say of experience was narrower. When so much of life had to be left out of art, there was naturally less surprise or threat in the idea that the powers of women artists might be up to it. For a while, the image allowed them was actually less separate, more equal, than it has ever been since.

Cast back. To Wharton and Glasgow, and Cather. The first two, as women of means and position, were part of a society which, with its confined sexual mores, was the world of Howell and James as well. Lucky or not for all of them, the shades of sexual difference in terms of subject and language, were not as severe as for women of Twain's day—and far less violent than in the days to come, when the major division was that women didn't go to war, to sea, or to any of the "virile" professions. If Wharton wrote restrictedly of war, so did many of the men; in *Ethan Frome* she did try "the poor," attempting a break from the social world rather than the sexual one. She wrote no *Golden Bowl*, but she did write a *House of Mirth;* though as a writer she always went for the circumstantial intensity over the psychological one, the sexual ground treated was much the same.

Glasgow's sexual boundaries were smaller and the experiential ones also—she went to the history and nostalgia of a tapestry past. But neither the experience expected of a writer, nor the language, had yet so exploded over here that Cabell couldn't say of a book by Glasgow that it was so much like James it could have been written by Mrs. Wharton.

Cather was saved by "the land." It allowed her to speak from a major vision, and for that, even from a woman, to be acceptable—more acceptable than it is now. As to sexual material per se, *A Lost Lady* is no more delicate than much writing of the era, and *My Mortal Enemy* a psychological masterpiece of great power, done without any of the overt sex which would have spoiled it (Fitzgerald was to do the same). Though small in scale, these two short works were still tied to the pioneer experience, or to the provincial one. The larger novels seem to be thinned less by reticence than by a blurred or cramped knowledge of how people are—thin in proportion to wherever "the land" is no longer artistically enough. As that vision recedes, a writer of less authority begins to appear. But as woman of her time, her consciousness that she could speak for the country, and for its cosmos, gave her the confidence to write "like a man". To the country, she would be no more unfeminine than some of their pioneer grand-mothers. And her male colleagues, whether from city, town, or open boat, still were allowed a dignity sufficient to them—as "men of letters." The society had not yet placed them in the bind where they must defend their part of life or literature as the important whole.

But these days, art takes more responsibility for what is said of it, and has more influence. If, once past the basic physical facts, society is what makes children "manly" or "womanly," "black" or "white," "Jewish" or "Christian," artists too are molded by the times in their very expression of these, often reporting back to the society in terms of what it has made of them. Academy-culture is merely popular cul-ture early aware of itself; these days the roads between are very quick. American society at present is provincially cowed by the artist in gen-eral and the successful one in particular—this meaning one who makes either money or news. If he blows the horn loud enough, society will now accept what it has made of him (occasionally even of *her*)—and looks to him to tell it what art *is*.

The male hetero writer no longer has to apologize to America for being unmanly. But he still may have to overcompensate for it, to himself. New elements have long since crept into the lifestyle, and into that yearly Christmas package, the American ethos. The jokes are not on the equality of women, but of the sexes; women are getting equaller all the time. Teachers, mothers, dominant purchasing power and stockholders, overbearing even in the life-expectancy statistics—there's no end to it. The Freudians have told them and told them that they have nothing to waggle in front of them. But they seem to have got used to it, in favor of a better 'ole. He doesn't want to hate them for it—that would be homosexual. So he approaches the subject of women in art very cannily—on the highest plane possible. And the most objective. Let them remember that they can never make major art. Not without cocks. And *cunt* is a pejorative.

Major art is about the activities of men—that's why so much of it is about women. But not by them. For major art includes where women can't go, or shouldn't or never have. There are no places where men can't go or haven't been. Childbed is not a place or an event; it is merely what women do. Major art is never about the activities of women. Except when by men. Women are household artists; Austen's art is a travelogue between houses. Dickinson hid in one all her life, Emily Bronte too. Colette had to be locked into one, before she would write. George Eliot had to be *persona non* at some of the best London ones, before she could write a study of marriage like *Middlemarch*— and change her name. Let's face it, dear ladies—a house is not a cosmic home. Notice too, that the women who do write scarcely ever have guts enough for the full, real life of a woman—of all the women writers so far mentioned, plus the recent generation of Porter, Stafford, Welty, McCullers, O'Connor—only Colette had a child. And she was AC-DC—talented women usually are. That extra chromosome coming out in them. In the wrong way. Art is really wrong for women. How otherwise could it be so right for the men? And Marianne Moore? —she never went to war.

To which those critics who model themselves on the male hetero writers of the day (and perhaps once wanted to be one) add, "And look at their style!" Critics of this type always know what major art is —and wish to discuss only major artists. (That's how they know they're major critics.) And a major artist writes only in a "masculine" style. Which uses short words—like Faulkner. Whose sentences don't inch forward on little iambs, but are rough and clumsy—like Hemingway. What the masculine style of major art must never be is jeweled—beg pardon, lapidary. A jeweled fancy is always feminine. Like Shakespeare. And Melville. And Sir Thomas Browne.

Most symptomatic of all, when I say any of this, I must joke as I have, though a riffle through the reviews of any modern female writer, major or minor, would give me all the citations needed, all of the most serious intent. The bind here is extraordinarily interesting—if only to women and anthropologists: *Women who complain of injustices done to them as women are in reality not angry at the different or inequitous treatment of women, but at the difference between men and women—which of course is ineradicable. The subject of female injustice is therefore innately ridiculous. Women who act as a group on any subject are also innately so—even to women. They are being* personal. *Men, men writers for instance, never allege injustice on the grounds of being men—even the homosexuals. They pick something sociological, something sensible—like being black, or Bahai, or poor. Men are* impersonal. *That's why they can afford to act sociologically. Women can really only act sexually—that's why they are the* same *everywhere. Women are not sociological creatures—that's why they are funny in groups. That's why men take any rise in their status or opportunities not as a sociological threat, but as a sexual one.*

For a woman, a woman writer for instance, never merely wants her work to be treated equally with her peers of any sex (with a due allowance for the sexual bias of all), allowing her then to be a writer who is a woman. She wants to *be* a male writer. In her body, she has the mind of a man—and she wants a you-know-what to go with it. And don't let her tell you that they order these things differently in France. All that means is she wants a *French* one.

So does the tangle, sent up by the society and implemented by the male artists themselves, gather around the woman of good mind until she half believes it—or more. Women writers in America, by the evidence, are often made to believe it totally. Partly because of the real present differences between male and female in their attitudes toward the public world. As artists, women can learn pomp, but from a long history of humility generally, they begin with less of it.

As they still do in science to a degree, and of course very largely in politics and government. In a democratic country, where women cannot expect to be queens and have never been presidents, how could this be otherwise? England has a minister of culture, but if Americans were to create such a cabinet post, it would probably still be better for "culture" for the post to be filled by a man.

As artists, women can also be made to feel that the honesty of their work is impugned by their affect as women—particularly if it's a good one; dare they have beauty, style or the vanities approved as womanly, or must they bloomerize? Historically and now, both men and women have dressed to show the fashion of their convictions; after which women usually get the credit for the fashion, and men for the convictions. The ringlets of George Eliot, say, were affectation, the beard of Walt Whitman sincere. So, just as men have worried whether art in a man isn't affectation, women wonder whether their affect as women can coincide with art.

In reaction, some literary women become scholars, or Xantippes of the quarterlies, or salonnistes. Or males. Or use their profession to fend off the female experience. "Hortense, did you *want* yo chi'drun?" Carson McCullers once said to me. "Ah didden. Ah always felt they would innafere with my *woik*." Honest to the nth, we are. We lack the pomp to be sure that when we spread our breast to the world as *ourselves*, a major eagle will come and peck at it. We have been taught to lack it: that a man's role is to hunt experience, a woman's to let it come upon her—and that this makes all female experience less exciting document.

Women are constitutionally immersed in and interested in the minutiae of daily living; so are artists and writers; a great deal of Dickens,

Balzac, and Tolstoy takes place in the Dutch interiors of life. But in women artists this is called domesticity—of subject—and women artists themselves fail to see scope there, or give it. They fear the lady-writer in themselves. For what society says to the American male writer, via his sex, is Watch Out—maybe you shouldn't. What he says in turn to the woman writer is Hump It—you can't.

Not anything important. You are the little jewelers. Of little experiences. Once, when a renowned poet and a writer who had just written her first book were guests at the same house, the poet one morning reported to their host that he had stayed up all night reading it—he was an old man, and slept little. "Very fine," he repeated several times over. "Very feminine of course! But still—very fine."

For a long time, this puzzled her. Some of her stories were autobiographical, as with any young writer, but some were about men, some were about "the society," one was indeed the very essence of the woman's side of an affair and as feminine as she could make it—in just the way that a male writer, on love, might be male. None of the stories were more miniature than most short ones are, nor had even the reviewers called them ladywork; the title story, as it happened, was political. Whereas the body of the poet's work was very autobiographical and very delicate—and included some famous miniatures. Perhaps all this worked differently for poetry. Later, she thought not. Even at eighty, a male American artist daren't be a miniaturist. He has his cock to think of. Which is always very large.

So, very naturally, we come back to the queers, who are now in the process of telling us, in their own way, what all this has to do with America. Or showing us. Not the writers themselves (who for all we know may be as hetero American as a Legion commander after church, in bed with his wife—*and* a floozie). Their books. I say "queer" because the word at least says what it means, where the homo-hetero language, once straight biological, now belongs to the psychologists—and *all psychological language implies redemption to a norm.* Queer literature, in its own way is now preaching redemption for the American norm. Not only for sex. For all American life.

So is everyone else of course. But not sexually. Why, the sexual revolution was won some forty–fifty years ago, wasn't it?—with Freud and Joyce and Gide and Proust and Havelock Ellis and de Montherlant, and D. H. Lawrence and Bertrand Russell and all those freelove people—and Freud. And lots of Americans?

I myself have certainly never scanned back over the so-called "pantheon of American writers" in terms of their sexuality before—first off because I am an enemy of any who look at literature topically, second because anything monosexual to me is a bore. But one glance, and one realizes that whoever made the revolution, American writers didn't. And at one glance, the whole "hoorah for bed and basic language"—which *has* been mainly American—becomes clear. *We came in late.* And on the hoorah score, mostly with secondary or second-rate writers. Among our good ones—it was quite possible to read both *The Sun Also Rises* and *Sanctuary* (and especially if reading it before the deluge had made expectations clearer) with at first some wonder over the guy's lack in the former, and over who was doing precisely what with the corncob, in the latter. (Nor is it certain that on the part of Hemingway and Faulkner this was all merely artistic restraint.) Meanwhile, only gradually did Americans readers learn to lean over the bed, unpartisanly cheering. Over what the 1950s would tell them at once. And the '60s? With pictures. We develop slow.

Take a further look. Only the heterosexual revolution was "won" by whomever, in those days. Gide made his living out of his neatly Calvinist self-torture, straddling the bisexual see-saw. And Proust made his Albertine a girl. Colette did as she pleased, but revolutions are not won by those not interested in them. Except for *Cheri*, her work was narrowly known here (mainly through the fashion magazines and a later movie made on the least of her works, *Gigi*), and was altogether out of line for critics like Wilson in his Marxist period, or for the later historicity of Kazin and Howe. (Plus all those sub-emendators who were out for "American Studies" buffalo—and picked their comparative literature along related lines.) Trilling might have done her, in his Forster period—if of course we could be sure that he "knew about" Forster. (When I lived in England, in the '50s, I was regularly taken aside by writers or dons, and hilariously asked, with covert or plain reference to the novels Forster was rumored to keep locked up at Kings—"*Does* Mr. Trilling know?") Certainly the New-Critic commentary which took *Howards End* to its heart in the forties paid no mind to the diaphanous sexual qualities in *The Longest Journey* or *A Room with a View*, in their ardor at discovering a book in which sex too was treated entirely as a matter of social class. Meanwhile Wilson kept any trenchant sexual comment of his own to his fiction: *I Thought of Daisy* and *Hecate County*. It looks better there generally, I agree.

American criticism in any case spent scant time on queerishness, maybe because, according to the style of its segregations (and of the review journals) Catholics tended to write on Catholics, women on women, etc.—and it mightn't have looked right. The college critics and litry journals would treat even a great queer like Gide more for the style of the revelation than for the revelation—recording perhaps how the *tradition* of *Si le grain ne meurt* opens its heart in the manner of Rousseau—but letting the matter go. The "other" side of Gide (say that side of *The Counterfeiters*, or *The Immoralist, Lafcadio*, et al) which had nothing to do with litry methodology, had to wait for the younger crowd—and for the paperback. (As much queer writing has.)

As for pornography and perhaps the Marquis de Sade—he became a *philosophe*, entirely. And therefore a man for the avant-garde-academic curriculum. In the sixties, pornography-*not*-per-se would be taken up by just that university crowd, in their forties say, post-social-conscious and even post-Freudian—for whom sex was now *the* respectability. (College departments and newspaper staffs will recognize some of them, as the men who got drunk once or twice a year with Mailer on the symposium or party circuit, and afterwards wrote articles saying "Norman said to me—") And as with all such respectabilities, the subject matter was not merely newly decent, but *new*—to the respectable. They had discovered it.

For such as these, who had perhaps read Frank Harris in their youth rather than *Mlle de Maupin*, and whose idea of homosexual critique is still Fiedler's little divertimento with Huck Finn, pornography is still by and large "square." A beast with two backs—but the pudenda don't match. And queers are taken care of more or less manly-classic style, in terms of the old question turned answer: "What *they* do". In the "male" novels of the era, any lucky Pierre still gets where he gets by accident. Either by way of adolescence, or merely in the happy melée of the accident school of writing, whose later name, black comedy, was actually a loose term for a number of old genres. (Some-times nothing but a professor poking the eighteenth-century ash-heaps for some old Humphrey Clinkers. And sometimes pornography, look-ing under the bed for art. Which it found there, sitting in its own middle-aged white skin, reading *Lolita*. In the early Paris edition.)

But meanwhile the younger people, and the old Dostoievski-lovers, and the good Bronx social workers and the beautiful boys flocked East to find out what they were—and all the other elements which make up off-Broadway theater audiences—had long since been read-ing or seeing Genêt. Once more, in that long inheritance which, only yesterday it seemed, had brought Sartre to the intellectual Jews and Céline to Kerouac, American literature was being seeded from abroad—and this time the dramatists were the most accessible.

The picture is still near enough to see how mixed it was. Certainly the idea of politics blending with sex, as in *The Balcony*—of sexual force and allegory used to flay the *moral* vision, the moral-*political* vision—was new for Americans. And exciting intellectually—or exciting in those parts they had always taken to be intellectual. Genêt as thief and anti-hero was nothing new; even the avant-garde's anathema, *The New Yorker*, had had Cheever's story of suburbia gone thief. What completed Genêt's respectability here was *The Blacks*, which those Americans who saw it took to their hearts as the post-war Germans had taken *The Diary of Anne Frank*.

Guilt, in no matter what sexual expression, was the point—and certainly not sexual guilt per se, by now old hat in any form. Tangen-tially, black-white and queer-square antitheses were to shift into all sorts of new alignments and crossings-over, from new political alli-ances, to newly chic mixed couples: white girls with black men, bright white queers with passive black partners, or notably among Southerners, the reverse. James Baldwin, whose first novel *Giovanni's Room* had been cast in the old Gide pattern of sex severely (and romantically) apart from other life elements, indeed a "white" novel in every way, was to shift drastically in his second, mixing up sex, Whitmanesque brotherhood brought to bed, violence-vengeance, and all the old asseverations of extra "Negro vitality" (sexuality) got from the whites—in all of which the Esquire magazine squares now joined in. Sex was now how you expressed your *other* guilts.

Meanwhile: *Godot*—gone from Broadway into the universities (where I saw it in Iowa, in 1958), followed by the other Beckett plays, and to a smaller audience, the novels. . . . And altogether—in spite of Irish quirkery and French logic—an asexual art, surely an art whose device and delight was to show how nearly it and man could be, or were, solipsist. Absolute personality, on a pin in a void, watched its own neutral despairs, with a faintly giggly cosmic hope. Maybe even theater art then, much less the novel, didn't have to be sexual? Or human beings didn't, or not as much as had been thought— what was this hollowly taped cosmological echo-of-a-breath saying in its writer-translator English?

And don't forget the English—not that we've been allowed to. Any change in the class-structure tosses up art with it—witness us Americans ourselves, at least in our beginnings. That change took the English once more by the throat—in the spoken word. And from theater-stall to the lumpkins of country or town, the sexual attitude is much the same. What Pinter is saying about sex is as obscure as the rest of him, except for one surety; he's not saying it separately, that is, apart from the rest of what bothers the human hegemony—and not differently for women and men. His whole metaphor is to realign the old emotional proportions of things. In that metaphor, individualized sex seems to be going out. Which also seemed to be much the tone of whatever else was being said there in the *kitsch* of that time, from the Sassoon haircuts of the girls to the Carnaby Street modsters, and even the Beatles' trail of bobby-soxers, whose yowl came straight from still undifferentiated sex, a mass sex in which the other girls around one are part of it too. The line between this and the old upper-class sexuality—hockey-girls and Oxford dramatic societies—is not far.

Returning to the theater proper—it's noticeable that Frank Marcus' *Sister George*, technically a quite ordinary comedy in the old style, at times almost music-hall (and not at all that serious-play-which-fell-short-of-itself which, because of its sexual material, Walter Kerr in solemnly called it) was remarkable not only for the frank tongue of its Lesbians, but for its flat-tongued pursuit of people as people, in a notable lack of tea-and-sympathy guilt wringing its hands in the wings over the pity or evil of it all. Charles Dyer's *The Staircase*, of perhaps more serious intent, or less televisionery method, did much the same for a pair of queers. Osborne's *A Patriot For Me*, did go at it in the old grand style, tracing a Prussian Officer's slow self-revelation of homosexuality—here that word suited—while the audience went raving bored with unsurprise, but then topping it with a drag-ball scene, extremely funny—and entirely in the "square" mode. (As over here, Warhol's *Chelsea Girls*, a window-dresser's idea of a documentary, was entirely not.) In all the English muddle, it was idly funny that one could see *Sister George* in the West End, but for the old-fashioned *Patriot* had to join a club—it's guilt that's private in the end, according to Lord Chamberlains.

So, as might be expected of the English, they have finally been the first to redefine the third sex's legal rights in their nation, openly linking sex and law, and politics—precisely as they had for women, once. The key to English emotion is perhaps not sexuality anyway, but sympathy. Character in the end takes preference over difference. In their literature, presently their drama, the language itself, backed by an hereditary eighteenth-century dryness and Congrevian sharpness, leads them into attitudes which show once again how European they are—while we are still mired in counter-Victorian.

And so—around the rim of the circle, the new suffragettes arrive. If irreverent or anti-social sex is now a vehicle for protests *other* than the sexual—who better can express to the extreme their horror of *all* a society's norms than those who will have nothing to do with it? They don't have to join that bandwagon; they are already there. (For among the repudiations of society which are possible to humans, surely a refusal to have its children, therefore its future, must be a basic one.)

Meanwhile, since nothing in art or life stands still, the stance of homosexual repudiation has shifted also, away from the old-fashioned guilt and alienation, and toward social protest, their own stylized version of it—often still peculiarly square. Like the women in this country, homosexual men aren't allowed to go to war. But in the arts, war in the samurai sense is no longer possible (fashionable) as a direct and serious subject; the basically jingoistic "manliness" of the huntin' and fishin' set is artistically dead, at least for a while. (Even the commercial historical novelists don't celebrate the nation any more, instead bending their nostalgias toward how it went wrong, and may yet go right of course, or else deserting us altogether for the far Peloponnese.) More important, the nation itself has the horrors less over sex-in-any-form than over drugs—for which sex is subordinate—and over the newest bogey, violence-at-*home*. Sex isn't everything anymore.

Those homosexuals, and those artists, for whom it still is, may soon find themselves ranged with the middle class. In the most recent bohemias, where once the "beats" were an active protest still mainly artistic, the later hippies were a passive one, focused on a mandala-blur of protest, the weakest ray of which was sexual. Either has produced artists only in terms of those who, like Allen Ginsberg and William Burroughs, cling to some above-the-drug-reality—to berate or to engage. If Ginsberg already seems establishment to the rank-and-file of the young bohemia or the merely young, it is not only because of age and a verse-line like Walt Whitman's; it is because he still has a reality to berate—"ours." And if Burroughs doesn't yet seem *derrière-garde* to them, it is because, under the drugs and the inverted sexuality, and most profoundly, under the spiky shape of his art, he hides from them —not from himself—that he too is engaged with it. Past forty, these two, past any number of things; still, in their own fashion, Cynara baby—they too celebrate life.

All influences of course influence each other. Looking superficially backward over the novels of the '40s and on, for examples of homosexuality as subject, we turn up Gore Vidal's *The City and the Pillar*, an elegant Cook's tour of the queer world drawing-room style, as I remember it, and Truman Capote's *Other Voices, Other Rooms*, a coming of age and to an identity, one which however counts for less in the book, and less for us, than the plangent imagery and inimitably freakish youthful art. On to *The Roman Spring of Mrs. Stone*, and alas, to ridicule. No matter who is sexually envying what, the menopause, when circumlocuted in the hushed, veiled tone of Bulwer Lytton on the mysterious East—is funny. This novel's elevated tone toward it reminds me of a host whom I once heard excuse his wife to her arriving guests because "It's her time of the moon." Equally, "Mrs." Stone's excitement, when she sees the Italian boy pee against the wall, is not really female-sexual as intended, but has all sorts of swelling montages to the left of it. We laugh at any art that risks intensity, if it is imprecise. Here, "society" is ruthlessly seconded by our own knowledge of human nature.

A good deal of queer literature has this kind of cross-wiring intentionally—becoming a kind of *roman-à-clef* of the emotions inverted, from which the reader, potentially queer or in the know, is to get his titillation. Unintentionally, queer writing for queers has the same effect that any writing has when it is intended for one sex, the nearest analogy being the "kitchenmaid" novels of Queen Victoria's day—any sex can be "Victorian."

John Rechy's sentimentality is borrowed from elsewhere. The tone is tender exposé, plus special pleading—oh the agony that is here, sister! There is an attempt to make the drag world a microcosm for us all—which should be possible. (As, in a way, Genêt's *Madonna of the Flowers* speaks for cunts.) But Rechy the writer adopts the contortions of his own exhibitionists. What it reminds most of is Nelson Algren—a sentimentality which is butch. Even so, we are now approaching the world of social protest for everybody—done on queer terms. In the work of Purdy, it is reached. (*In Cold Blood*, aside from

its marked resemblance to *The Fifty-Minute Hour* and similar docu
mentary, may suggest itself as deriving from homosexual sub-sympath
with its protagonists, but surely in its method, from social-worker
through the waving Kansas wheat of its lyrical breezes, it is man
aged on cannily square terms.)

Purdy's work has always veered interestingly, beginning, in th
shorter stories of *Color of Darkness*, with those gothic depths o
childhood where so many good writers start, but in the longer *6
Dream Palace* giving us another kind of lushly invertebrate, Frenchi
fied fancy, as do Alfred Chester's early tales. Comparing Purdy'
*Malcolm* with Chester's earlier novel *Jamie is My Heart's Desire*
perhaps that same literary derivation comes out in the kind of pretti
fication that overtakes the one, and the uglification that somewha
conventionalizes the other—for where Purdy by now is playfull
shocking, in that fancy undersense of the word which Schiapareli
once gave to "shocking" pink, Chester chooses grotesquerie in th
relentlessly *gris* style of Genêt, always consciously underground,
world of subways.

In Purdy, one may see some Firbankery too. *Malcolm*'s allegory i
however, middle class. And with him, Purdy begins his own succes
sion of those painfully golden male innocents, half Pamela and hal
Jesus-boy, who are so often the symbolically pure heroines of th
most sophisticated homosexual. Against these, his novel *The Nephe*
is the real shocker; its writer hasn't forgotten that he is from Souther
Illinois, and now any literary tradition invoked comes twining fror
the haunted porches of the Middlewest, from Wescott's *The Grana
mothers*, Ruth Suckow, Sherwood Anderson. Not yet from Dreise
that determined face already turned to the urban and to the caseboo
sociological—a great digression which Purdy, like so many other
will finally join.

When a writer returns to his origin, or stays there, he is never a lon
example; rather, he is alone with literature. But after *The Nephe*
most of Purdy's work has the emigré tenseness of the early denizer
of Greenwich Village—of those who had had to come to urbs, urbi
but never grew too sophisticated to forget what they had left.

The eastward-to-Europe drive of writers like Hemingway and Fitzgerald was met by some ethnic surprises on the eastern shore of their own country, as "American" literature finally lost its New England character and became the literature of New York. Antiposed by a powerful wave from the South.

In this pinch, the literature of the Middlewest began to be identified with "farm" literature, with "growth of the soil" stereotypes like Hamsun and early August Derleth—actually a stage which it had long since passed through. (As, in the '60s, the work of Lois Hudson, Curtis Harnack, William Gass, would show.) It remained chic enough to come from the Middlewest—as dozens of well-known journalists were doing—but impossible to write about it. In a curious about-face—and against all the industrial socio-economic facts, as well as the hordes of flat-tongued middlewesterners in all the Departments of English in the colleges—the center of the country as literary subject matter sank either under the smalltown stereotype Sinclair Lewis had made of it, or under the label "regional."

The South of course had never allowed itself to become merely that; any writer who came from there spoke from a proven civil agony against which a merely sexual revolution would have looked small. And in prose, after Faulkner, its outstanding writers were women— Porter, Welty, O'Connor—who again had other things to win. In all this, we curiously tend to forget, because New York is the center of literary activity, that the literature of "the city" can be as regional as anything which comes from the farm. As practiced in some quarterly reviews, it was to be so.

The Jews of course were to be our next mainline local-colorists— though never named so. (Or not perhaps after the era of Samuel Ornitz, A. Singer, and Israel Zangwill.) In the quarterlies of the '40s and '50s, the Jewish urban childhood became "the farm"; the gutter-ghetto and peddler-pavement became the new "soil." So tenacious was the image of "the city" as taken to be that of all literature—and so largely urban both the Jew and his reader each to all intents a "New York Jew," wherever he came from—that they too escaped the label "parochial." Also, like the Irishman and the Southerner, the Jew can be broadly funny—as those writer-heirs of Transcendentalism, or of more generally white-American-Protestant sociologies, so often could not—and the country-at-large had long loved his vaudeville. Finally under Hitler, the Jew became our Everyman—as the black is becoming now.

Actually, of course, there were to be hierarchies among Jews-as-writers, as among Jews anywhere. For which read—difference. Aside from I.B. Singer—a beautiful throwback to a classic distance preserved and Bernard Malamud, whose work, heir in part to a less rabbinical side of the folklore, is also a complex of American "academic" strains—most of the others are heirs to Bellow, linguistically the most gifted, who also from the first had the prescience to write with European politico-philosophical scope—not as a Jewish writer, but as a writer who is a Jew. Wryly verbal, this group's contribution to the many genres of black humor was to be mostly via language and metaphor (as a vaudevillian's is), using that poetic argot which is as much Russian, Polish and even post-First World War German as it is Jewish—the bitter, broadly peasant argot of European *Untermensch* any-where. Plus all those changes that arise when the practitioner is both American and on the way to being economically comfortable.

But sexual revolutionists they weren't, as it is often said Jews seldom are. Freud himself saw the importance of Christian sexual guilt to the Judeo-Christian ethic, all the more plainly from the Judaic side. In writing of sex, the younger writers like Heller, Friedman, Roth, and the older Golds, Herbert, and Ivan, use all the freedoms and attitudes that a much prior revolution has provided, from the flower-decked pubis à la Lady Chatterley, or from the chamberpot humors of any folklore, or from psychiatry—or from whatever the virility disease which Norman Mailer, early on writing as the middle-class Harvard boy he couldn't bear to be, first caught from Papa H.

Mailer's own cancer metaphor was to be far more original, when applied to America's sense of itself—as well as closer generically to his own modern-middle Jewish fears. He had a litry interest in queers Coupled with his avowed cult of women in her basic functions only and his use of "writing like a woman" as a sneer against male rivals, some said that he protested too much, and took this as a sign of something latent. If so, it was not in the sex—which was monumentally old hat—but in the ego, which at its worst, but at its artistic best also, pushed against proscribed boundaries and greedily seemed to want to be what it saw. Mailer's view of women is essentially suburban Talmudic. As a Jewish Don Juan, he always laboriously marries them.

He empathises toward homosexuals, however, exactly as he does to blacks—and from his canny power-sense that they are going to be of new importance to literature. They are those aliens which birth hasn't sufficiently allowed him to be. Has anyone noticed, for instance, how *Why Are We In Vietnam* imitated Burroughs? The gag is great —analyze American aggression via Texas sexuality and the whole Southern stereotype (to be seen any day in televised field interviews in Vietnam) of sexy war. It's a typically sharp Mailer choice, in which he may at first appear to be as usual—imitating himself. But the use of violently linguistic sexuality as *propaganda* in this serio-comic, demonic way, is pure *Naked Lunch*. (Whose author, Mailer has said, may be a genius.)

Yet in *Naked Lunch*, the note of anguished power is authentic; Mailer is energy trying to *be* anguish. Burrough's ultra-high-pitched language works through confusions and exaggerations to a terrifying assemblage in whose hell we must believe. Mailer's language is as clear as gag-style always is, the tone assumed being that of the "best" gutter lingo, peppily poeticized—does anyone really bother to refer to a woman's asshole as her "dirt track"? (Or sometimes an oddly dainty jocundity: "elegant as an oyster with powder on its tail.") Although Mailer too, tries to command the blind force of that every-which-way physicality which Purdy and Burroughs have—which masticates as it fornicates as it masturbates, all in a delightfully polymorphous mud-slinging at the target—what emerges is only fecal pie. As a friend said of it, reading it is like eating crap. (If so, very Jewish in its alimentary concentration. Kosher crap.) What we really see is "the writer" going at his "subject" with cannibalistic empathy, and that fake-Southern talk-talk which is one of his oldest charades—most of it unreadable not because it is dirty but because it is old-man-dirty and other-generational, a gritty banjo-uke getting up the last of the poontang blues.

Where *Naked Lunch* is a cry, Mailer is all elocution, the spiritual difference being that try as he may, he is not sufficiently underdog to anything; born to be linguistically on top of everything except death, all his other humiliations always sound just a little *arriviste.* His achievement is peculiarly elsewhere, and never where he would want it to be—in the sexual, emotional sphere. He cannot create the presence of common life, in literature. What he can do is no mean thing, but quite inverse to that. What one feels in each successive book, even this one, is the *presence of literature,* in common life.

Sexually, only Malamud and Singer write out of "orthodox" Jewishness—by which I mean from feelings born of the Jewish law. On the rest, including Mailer, an appropriately funny destiny has converged. When they try to make sex their "main thing" they can't—and for good or bad art, that's Jewish enough. But there's worse to come. Sexually, they write exactly like Christians.

All of them pure white American Sex One.

And now, what of writers Sex Two and Sex Three?

One of the advantages of the writer as alien—of the disinherited, disenfranchised or dispossessed—is that whether or not they themselves are great, they can write from some nearness to the open-ended world to which all serious artists aspire. They write from an intellectual and emotional diaspora, from a past which transcends the nostalgias of childhood, and toward a future which apprehends something better than they have. Satire—the worm's eye turning—comes to them naturally, as it does to those without full passport privileges, or else they have the kind of neutral perspective that attaches to small borderland nations. At the same time, they have the furious energy of the repressed.

Women, as comparative newcomers to civil rights (some of which, like full employment in the professions and equal participation in scientifico-military researches, are still in limbo) and as artists still shrinking back against their own meager history in the arts, have easy access to minority feelings—not the least of which is their own superiority in numbers, wherever it is used to make them feel extra, rather than universal. Homosexuals, if they stick to their last, are in an even purer and sadder case; they are forever barred from reproducing themselves.

Both they and the women have certain advantages. Freed of that birth-envy (envy of the physical capability of birth) which sends so many unfortunate American men, writers among them, into parabolas of virility-thinking and war, they can transmute their energies all the quicker into envy-for-a-cause, envy-for-a-cross, or merely envy of the square-peg in the square-hole. It may be of course that all the sexes have had their envies misnamed or misapplied. For, among the phallus-worshippers, even the inverts run second to ordinary men themselves. Organ envy is a natural fantasy of the "haves," who conveniently can also then visualize the "have-nots" as wanting what they cannot possibly give.

In minorities, however, envy attaches most and first to what they are not allowed to do or be—especially when they can see there is no solid reason for it; except perhaps in the case of eunuchs, or a few Lesbians, a sexual 'have-not" doesn't really want the organ, but the role. And the social privileges. Women do not suffer from penis envy, but from a lack of allowable birth-pride. Meanwhile, they and the queers can use all these advantages to make close little parochial worlds to live in and write about—as the Jews have classically done. Except that they don't have to emigrate or be martyred first. They don't have to move an inch. Like the blacks, they can get it all at home.

So far, women have done less from outrage at being Sex Two, than might have been expected in the verbal arts. Unless raised to the level of great satire, outrage at what one is may be a dead end, in a woman giving rise to that henhuffing of the feathers, suffragette in the worst sense, and anticipating the worst—a desire to write "like a man." (Vide a passage I recall from a "female" novel of some years back, in which the mind of a male character said "crud" to itself every ten paces—creating a page on which the word stood out like button-tufts on a French pouf.) Woman's passivity may work out to be of more use to her; if the shape of human physical equipment is of as much importance as men have said it is, then it may be that those ovoid inner conformations of which a woman is always kept aware by her oval outer ones, may push her sanely centerwards—for what she has is not a "tool" or a "weapon" but a confluence much more resembling the omphalos. (In the plastic arts one sometimes sees clear variants on this consciousness; once Edward Dahlberg has called Georgia O'Keefe "the vulva-artist" it is difficult not to see that, and the sculptress Lee Bontecou seems preoccupied with frighteningly saw-toothed holes, suggestively vaginal.) The oestral tide—that grandiose attachment to the stars which civilized women have learned to deplore—may be a basic tidal sanity which men are powerless to denigrate, but keeps women where they are. Even Lesbians generally menstruate. Their half of the birth-machine—which they may not want—is in a child-bearing woman considered merely unnecessary to tout. (Particularly by the male half, which must gaze at nine months of it.) Which makes for earthmother serenity in their sex, but less chance of art?

That's a suffragette idea, and like another idea often projected on women artists—that in a kind of compensatory barrenness they must sacrifice to the Muse any creation of their bodies—is partly male. (For male depletion, and a plaintive study of the married writer who "leaves it in the bedroom"—see Moravia.) Neither men *nor* women seem to think that sexual activity depletes the woman artist, (or I have never heard it propounded.) A suffragette idea is one in which a woman changes her real conception of herself in order to counterattack the male idea of it. Writers expect to deal with the world as writers. A woman who is a writer may find that the literary world expects to deal with her as a female. (After death, she may be taken into the pantheon, but in America not usually before.)

On the fictional work of Mary McCarthy, it was for years the critical fashion to say that it (she) "lacked compassion," a phrase I used to think revealed a lack of knowledge of what satire was—until I caught onto the fact that it was never used on male satirists. What I saw, maybe as a woman, was that Miss McCarthy, (how hard it still is to leave out the "Miss"!) though in command of extraordinary powers of mind, and a sentence like a lance, often bent it on subjects smaller than need be. (A man would have had more "pomp"?) Later, her novels would be given the attention they deserved as satire, but very much because she had won her spurs as critic and journalist. And now had more pomp. In *The Group*, it was still the historical minutiae which were fascinating—an age disinterred in its artifacts of advert living and advert meditation—by a memory as careful with that dust as an archeologist.

Whatever, no one could deny that she had a major energy, which exerted itself with a European range, always refusing that crutch of the "one image" (in the sense that galleries currently exact it from painters) which can give a minor air to any artist's work, even while it be a source of the deepest parochial strength. F. O'Connor had the Catholic faith, Welty the South and the Southern one; Miss Porter was its self-proclaimed classic storyteller, at best with the objectivity of the *diseuse*, always in danger of a balladeering coyness—and of the set piece. Alone among them, McCarthy wrote of sex apart from love, as a Frenchwoman might, or as American males tried to—copying not the manner but the privilege. Porter wrote of "love" either in the Habaneras of the peons or with fairy-tale cool. It was never Welty's subject. In O'Connor, a sexuality not really Catholic at all extruded its allegories from within the snake-dark of the Baptist basilica.

A man might see a spinsterish limitation in all of them, nothing to do with marriage, but much as if one midwife word might shatter the glassy page. (And a woman is tempted to.) Only McCullers, more naïvely honest than any of them, more lyrically endowed than any, and with an asexual mobility which could seem both childish and adult, wrote of "love" as undifferentiated sex. Whether or not her vague or weak sexual orientation made her sound the more "universal," she had the ego to write large. Where McCarthy prefigured a time, (really already well on the way) when the lines between pure fiction and pure journal, either public or private, would drop, McCullers used sexual love, "unnatural" or not, naturally—that is, in the nature of art—but bothering so little with the customary alignments of the day, that the day could do nothing but call her an original.

The psychic history of women artists since their so-called civil or psychological emancipation should one day be a book itself—by that time hopefully to be written in terms of its significance to the society itself—and always remembering that the history of art is nothing except as it attaches first to individuals. Meanwhile, watching the recent women of American writing, recalling the work of others like Stafford and Boyle (at least one of whose short novels is Laurentian) one seems to see a whole generation of marvelously endowed women, not holding their breath—which contrarily pours forth in a unity of language and sensibility that can arrive of itself at the small masterpiece—but holding still. In one way or another.

One might think that as heirs of so recent a civil victory as the vote, they might have taken up their political responsibilities, not literally maybe, but in terms of the energy with which it was fought for. But like American women in general, they have not much done this—Hellman in the theater, Rukeyser in poetry—but in fiction little to compare with the roaming conscience of the men. Physically, they were kept from the wars, for one thing, and this had its effect on them; they accepted the image given them, and forgot that experience-of-itself is not art, or can be countered by *other* experience. Saved from the virility disease of the men writers, they abjured those excesses of the language and of the ridiculous which went with it. Prose, in its many relationships—to poetry sometimes, but to the peasantry too, or to the locutions of a blended middle society—in their hands seemed to attain its true directional force. And became their forte.

Meanwhile, publication was no problem but sometimes might be a gift horse; avoiding the slick like any artist, they would still find the high-fashion mags (then foraging the arts for art-chic) more tenderly open to them, always eager to encourage their talent for minutiae—and to print whatever they wrote "about women." Some, like Djuna Barnes and Anaïs Nin, seemed to "come from abroad" even when they were here, always expatriate, not from the country but from the image it cast upon them. Others faded, still writing, in the magazines of taste, which were always in the market for any "fine" writer who could write of reality *objectively* (that is, from a *recording* sensibility but not a *judging* one) and would never get in a fight about saying "fuck."

But it was not "style" which made them mandarin. Reading much fiction by American women of the '40s and '50s (and of the men who imitated them, particularly in the "little" reviews), one can't help but be struck by the droning of the sensibility, on and on. (Most writers dispense with their own past work by dropping it out of their consciousness as a means of getting on to the next—and I am one of these —but on occasion when I have had to refer to certain stories, it is that tone against which my eye screws up, finding it unreadable.) One of the great "tones" of literature, of course—the sensibility—and perhaps common to most writing, but when pursued *en masse* like this, one wonders why. (And why it *is* a sensibility which seems to be standing still—*en masse*.) Partly it derives of course from the general nineteenth-century upswing of the individual. But a still later part of modern sensibility-writing comes out of the Zolaesque realism which was to treat even the individual as an object "found" in space. And for some women artists of the time, this has been ideal.

They are not going to be trapped into speaking for women only, or for any division of women—and in this, like any artist who avoids category, they are right. They are going to be objective, with a coolth the men can't manage, maybe—and long after the men in many instances have given coolth up. (Negro sociologists of the era, who hid their blackness under that everyman language, are the same.) Fleeing above all from the image that the society projects upon women artists, such a writer is not going to write, even in the deeper sense, as a woman—i.e., from her own preferential experience. She knows her own capacity for the universal, and will not have it contaminated with the particular—if the particularity is feminine.

Looking abroad, she can see what has happened, even in Europe, to women who do: de Beauvoir, tied in the inimitable French way to the coattails of a man. Lessing to the coattails of psychiatry, and the vaginal reflex. She herself has had her mental hysterectomy early, and avoided that. She is going to be a pure artist, i.e., a sexless one. (And since male writers of the time, like Hemingway and Faulkner, abjured criticism, leaving the impure or second-rate to practise it, she too will thus cut herself off from that philistine power.) In art, she will speak for anything but the literal female experience or female part in experience; she will not use any of her sexual power at all (much less in the extravagant manner of some men); she will be the angel-artist, with celestially muted lower parts.

Reading back among those wondrously endowed women of roughly the second quarter of the century, one glimpsed how they had perhaps helped to eunuch themselves. Powerfully gifted in eye, ear, and hand, they had self-willedly kept themselves artistically dead from the waist down. Thinking themselves to be countering that image which the society and the male artists had projected upon them, they had in their way really accepted it. And in wherever it was complained that their work remained beautifully "minor" or "mandarin," this may have come not from their womanhood, but from their lack of it. They had accepted their envy after all. Or had belittled their experience, or hunted it in male terms. To say this is however an understanding of their art, not a belittling. Art is a series of limitings; half of any work is the leaving-out. One of the great elements of form is the presence of the absence of something. From age to age, from writer to writer, this changes.

In Nabokov's work, for instance, the critique of literature was once more allowed to take place in the body of the work itself, as in ancient days it sometimes had. Long since, in America, critics and journalists had reserved critique for themselves, allotting novelists et al. only either the direct dramatic effect in which meaning must remain implicit, or the tensile powers of an ambiguity in which meaning could be trapped. (In neither case must it be stated—in the '50s, my friend Ken Stuart once said he'd heard a rumor that *The New Yorker* intended publishing all the endings of its stories in a supplementary volume.) In "pure" art of the era, formal resolutions were gauche, and "moral" observations of any kind, declassé. As editorial parlance had it, "author comment" was out. And in the curious misapplications of that policy, anything in a novel or a story which could not be made to seem the comment of the persona themselves, was "author." Ideally also, persona should make their comments as part of the "action"—as coming from characters so unaware, or so far immersed in life, that they could never make an intellectual or meditative comment upon it. That would spoil the "pure" effect. (Vide the work of O'Hara.)

Life-in-the-raw, as these literati saw it, could not be meditative too. (In itself, what a litry conception!) The voluminous, ramshackle world-of-comment of the Russian nineteenth-century novel, was momentarily over. Subtly too the reader was downgraded, or divided, into those who read for art's sake, and those who read for critique divorced as much as possible from an art to which it was very possibly superior—since it made the moral judgments. The literary artist, himself in flight from either church-pamphleteering or happy-ending art, found himself ruled out from direct statement. (As well as somehow politically committed to popularist readers—when a "review" intellectual asked me "Who do you write for?", my answer, that I visualized a reader sentient and intelligent enough for anything—was taken to be arrogance.) Concurrently, pure prose artists, "imaginative" ones, did not "write" criticism (which high as it was on the litry value-scale, was too low for them), meaning they couldn't expect to have all the art and the power too, or to be on both sides of the fence—as James and Flaubert, Tolstoi and Turgeniev had been. As writers, somewhere in their mutterings, always are.

All this was to change in a world not only troubled, but media-aware, and rawly or not—meditative. With science morally discredited, God in trouble too, the artists were looked up to by a materialistic world as interpreters from the one remaining medium which had no axe to grind. (Whether it did so or not.) And some writers of course had never abjured statement. Choice of subject is indeed a form of statement. On literature. *Pale Fire* moreover took in all the antic semantic of some critique, made shifts between poetry and prose (Nigel Dennis, in *Cards of Identity* had already included a poetry sequence very similarly), and made it plain that any of its critique of literature belonged there, being in its turn a critique of life. Pure critics would praise it, not yet seeing what prerogatives had been snatched from them—and some writers would not see what rights had been returned to them.

*Lolita*, wherein sex, however lepidopterously inspired, could be seen as a put-on directed at a sicklily material American gas-station civilisation, was a bonus for everybody. It was hilarious, and done in that nihil, non-person style of character, that rolling-stone rhythm of action, which was being called black comedy—nobody's yet defined white. Above all, it was sex with intellect—which the quarterly-review porns hadn't been able to make hilarious. Only by the way, it was a lovely work of art. In which the statement—in spite of all the scathing minutiae—was not strictly direct, the ambiguities pointing like a porcupine's quills. Heterosex—America's youthful version of it and denial of perversion in that, was somewhere being laughed at—or if sex with a barely nubile girl was perversion (Islam would not say so) then how natural! Alignments were being changed or crossed, both in the "subject" and the use of it. Sex was once more being used as a critique of life, both from within the core of the work and peripherally, at a point where the work of art itself was also the critical commentary (often of itself). Sex was the metaphor and the moral weapon—but the moral judgments made were never about the sex itself.

Those were as absent as in any scientific account of the stages of the butterfly.

Meanwhile, coming up again from the left: Sex Three.

There is no purely homosexual literature—once it becomes literature. Any more than a novel of note is ever "about" something, *on* one subject, or in any sense an investigative circling of the fields of fact. (In the way that a helpful reviewer tabbed Cozzens's *Guard of Honor* as "the best novel about the Air Force.") Values, the minute spoken of, derive from others—femaleness is never paid so much literal definition as at a drag ball. And the more a work of art spreads and runs into itself, like a sphere or a double helix or a polyfaceted net, the better it is. But one may see sexual focus, or proclivity, or wavering. Or the mirror-writing which would sink all sex in a vague sea of love or hate. We can never avoid seeing the selfness of a writer—what he thinks it is, and what he uses it for. Or what he sees as the objects of his hate, and uses it against. Sex in D. H. Lawrence is a hatred against, once one sees it outside the rosy penumbra of what it is for. It has sublimated—i.e., made the turn upward or outward from self-hate—to a propounded social usefulness. Just so, the Gidean self-hatred double-turns at the world which denies it, (as heterosexual guilt did after Freud). We begin to have books in which the dominant meetings and partings of people flow toward the homosexual ideal as clearly as old-fashioned love stories once flowed toward marriage. Where the old Yin and Yang sexual oppositions are as clearly no longer dominant—or are repellent or ridiculous. (Or old hat—and non-chic.) Or where the queer is no longer a member of a thieves' carnival, or an underworld. Or where, like everybody else nowadays, he becomes middle class, with as much right to make social criticism as anybody, and like all minorities, with a sharp tongue and eye for it.

In the Burroughs' world of *Nova Express*, the sex that is natural is homosex, but the battles between good and bad, paranoid-real and sane-real, still take place in a romantic no-man's-land of the spirit, countered by terrible physical honesties, always presided over by the cloud-cuckoo metaphor of the drug. The struggle is a spiritual one, in language which is mystical, or even built upon a theology which is traceable from book to book, and the end impression is of a struggle unabashedly toward some ideal which is "loved." Sex falls back, secondary, before the daemon of the drug. Lyrism, Byronic grandiosities, stagey asides, all have a place in this grim arena—and a humor like the chuckle of a prompter from below. It is proper. This is the cops-and-robbers posturing of the soul. Whose very existence admitted, whose utopia promised, dignifies all. Society in recognizable terms scarcely enters.

Purdy's world and its malevolences are altogether more concrete. They are staged in the mess men and women have made of the social world, by a writer who at first seems tough-minded in all directions. The manner is a mixture: Congreve without epigram, a Restoration esprit with a fondness for typifying, mock-naming, and highjinks in high places, and a rodomontade which stalks (goblets!), but also has a nose for the absurdities of the lower middle, and a special sarcastical talent for describing the city strata as seen through the shrewd, traveled eyes of once-beglamored Southern Illinois.

The game here is not grandeur, but the world *coccu*. In which nobody's redemption is urged. Specifically the "American" world—but as target of an objectivity which could go anywhere. Clearly the author's objectivity is not the usual "ours," but it is well defined. Is he really crying a pox on all our houses, his aim to cleanse the world of its constitutional horrors and cants? Or is his satire sprung from something far more parochial—the distaste of men who bug, for men and women who breed? Who's getting *coccu* here? And how?

Certainly the sexual symbology "we" are used to has changed, and the social structure with it. Here are no families based even in the beginning on the breeding purpose; we are in some outland of Babbitry, of which the people here are the detritus. Couples are composed not of the two "straight" sexes which have classically set themselves up as the center of things, but of all the oddments of the *comédie humaine:* men live with grandmothers who are rich, and bring their men home to mother; wives are elderly with income, with itinerant spouses from the heartland and not hip yet; or are Griseldas too farcically enslaved to give their husbands the status of sadist or pimp. Men living with wives slide off expectedly toward other men, as toward a norm. Cabot Wright sets about raping five hundred women, in a gagstyle romp aimed at American heterosex—a one-man gang-bang in reverse.

Sadism is humorous, but some of its sallies—like Maureen's bloody abortion, effected *commedia dell'arte* style by the black C. Clark Peebles, are more innately humorous than others—more so than say, the infinitely extended torture of the captain by the sergeant, which may or may not be a burlicue of James Jones. A different flavor hangs over the two; Maureen's scene is the funniness of the birth-process deranged; the long incident between the men has the emotional timbre peculiar to torture, and to that old Kafka-Gide staple, the gratuitous act. The sergeant, throughout all, is true to his back-home love, Amos. Amos is a virgin, a sleepwalker, a Greek and Latin scholar whose

simplicity, near birdbrain, has an undeniable something; people wash
his feet—he is a catalyst. Is he Jesus, or merely that pure golden boy,
our heroine? Or "any man's son", the ideational fantasy of all male
marriages which will not settle for poodles? Women are a bad show
in general, but like Maureen (a knockout portrait of a knocked-up
type) can be likeable if they belong to the bad show of things—and if
they are the butt and admit it.

But what is most arresting is the continuously off-key sexuality.
Off-key, not merely in relation to the dominant symbols in the
"major" sexuality of the world, but to any. The body processes all
seem to run together: Mrs. Masterson's coronary, Maureen's abortion,
Cabot Wright's hot flushes, all bear a less particularised sense of these
than they do of some intimacy they share with each other; they are
what the body does when it has no fixed image of its parts, or when it
will not allow its parts to have separated ones; blood comes from
any aperture, and every part of the body is one; even the sadism is
not violence but violent effort—a straining to be. Clearly we are participating in what is beyond customary sexuality of *any* kind, or maybe
prior to it. And when the fucking stops (if it has been that) certainly
nowhere does it much matter who fucks who. (Or marries who, or
lives with who—socially we are beyond that.) Here is no mere homosexual code-writing, no Roman Spring in which a middle-aged woman
may really be a menopausal man. The scrimmage is everywhere. And
it is not of the appetite.

In Albee's *Tiny Alice* there is a moment when an image fails of
the horror it asks, because it does not touch the predominate response: When the Cardinal reminds the Lawyer that his school nick-
name was Hyena, "Did we not discover about the hyena . . . that
failing all other food it would dine on offal . . . and that it devours
the wounded and the dead. We found that the most shocking: the
dead. But we were young. And what horrified us most . . . was that
to devour its dead, scavenged prey, it would often chew into it
THROUGH THE ANUS???" (after which the script reads: *Both
silent, breathing a little hard*). Lawyer (finally; softly: "Bastard.")

The capital letters are not mine. They would not be "ours" in general, I think. In the braw world of the "tochus," the "bum," the "backside," the "asshole," the anus is a somewhat mock-erogenous zone (being a less used one) not as all-important to straight sex as it is to buggery. Since the anus *is* for offal, the hyena's aim, to "us," might seem more accurate than not. Whatever, if horror was intended, it failed; muff horror and you may get laughter, as occurred the night I saw the play. Whatever the Cardinal's insinuation, it belonged like the play's wisecracks, to a world of the "in"; straights in the audience of theater or books may well understand homosexual symbol while quite unable to honor it with emotion. (If that hyena had gone THROUGH THE COCK or THROUGH THE VAGINA, it might have been different—but that would be  n another country, another play.) In *A Delicate Balance*, when Agnes accuses her husband: "We *could* have had another son: we could have tried. But no . . . those months—or was it a year—? . . . I think it was a year, when you spilled yourself on my belly, sir?"—the audience does shock, not only at what is not usually said in the middle-class theater, but somehow also at the over-elaborate phrasing, something in it not female to male. As in Agnes's rejection of her daughter's confidences, wondering if she herself would be better off as a man: "I shall try to hear you out, but if I feel myself changing in the middle of your . . . rant, you will have to forgive my male prerogative, if I become uncomfortable, look at my watch or jiggle the change in my pocket . . . "—where the shock is both at the terms of such a refusal, between mother and daughter—and at a transliteration of the sexes which seems not to lie in the "transferred heads" (and tails) of human imaginative desire, but to be author-enforced, according to some code he is following.

Shock is valuable in the theater, and in literature—but scale is important to it, subjectivity changes it and repetition dulls it—if it cannot attain to poetry. Much present-day drama moves in terms of the simple actions under or against the accepted symbols of things, or as in Pinter, in showing the actual simplicities of the symbols by which people move. Albee's strength comes, a lot of it, from these fresh alignments, coolly shocking to us not because they are sexual, but because they are off-base.

And they are not of the appetite. Rather, they are the comedy-of-error tricks, or incomplete tragedies of those who, for all their apertures, have no outlet in generation. Yet are not "impotent."

As heirs of Freud, we are used to seeing sexual impotence as a theme of life, in our friends, our books and in ourselves, in those husbands and lovers, who are the heroes second-class of a Laurentianism in reverse, in those spinsters whose bed is ice. And we are familiar with the "larger" litry themes that maybe come of it, anything from what "the rat-race" does ta ya, to the Identity Hunts of those who "cannot love." (Barren women are rather duller, dramaturgically speaking. Except in those biblical milieus where primogeniture is still of the first importance; we tend to see them as victims of the cell rather than the fates, who merely need to go to a good gynocologist.) In a society under protest homosexuals need not feel as alienated as once. They can refuse to have the "children" of its ideas. Leaving the sexual refusal with its attendant Freudian dramas, far behind. All those little boys who can't get born out of the spilled seed of the fathers, or who are revealed never to have existed except in the minds of their mothers, all those innocents dying on the milk-train of other peoples' charity, are psychodramas going over the old personal revelations—with here and there a hint of the world's disjointedness. In recent Purdy, it's a clean sweep into the non-sex of satire, or the "a pox on all of it" of social protest—a somersault over everything, into an impersonality that shock-deadens, fizzes out, sniggering all the way, into down-at-heel hatreds, crudely Gothic humors, rudely interrupted by prissy echoes of the once liveable world. Sex as hostility, as humoresque, is here only the beginning of it. It would be futile to ask of the people in these books that they be more than cardboard, or their blood more than the plasma of the world's generally laughable sores. Or to ask the style of expression—"amid the industrial world"—that it not waver as "fitfully" as the jewel on the finger of its millionaire. Waver it does; this pen feels less for the word than for the situation, and has no other focus for which it so much cares; it will hunt the ridiculous anywhere. (With, in *Malcolm*, perhaps the last gasp of a gravely Americanized Firbankery, fallen short of those silver flashes from the adorable to the ineffable, but with the same mordant method: giggle-pastiche.) The seriousness is in the intelligence—and feeling is anthropophagous. (Compare it with Bellow, in which intellect and feeling bleed *together*.)

Is this "white" comedy? One reels out of these books with the inner ear disturbed—not sure what has been intentional. With a sense that some of the failure may be in ourselves. We are still new to the non-directed. We would prefer though to be able to trust this intelligence more not to demean itself as it sometimes does—either by loving its personae too much, or too often the same ones. The barrenness of the world, as theme, is dignity enough. When a little special sex creeps in, or its propaganda, the satire turns silly. For the modest proposal of this satire at its grim-slim base is that *all* of us are eatable, from the anus if need be. When that intent falters, then what comes—in goblet or glass—is farce curdled by serious intentions. Non-ridiculousness won't do, in this exhausted air. Where it fails is when it inadvertently reminds us that all is not barren, and all is not ridiculous.

So, as in the old movie, we have circled *la ronde*—except that one doesn't exit the sideshows of art merely like any good pair taking childie away from the freaks of Eighth Avenue, back to the redempted norm of Queens. The literary thicket is thank God the same; no girl scout exits as entered, only an hour older, with everybody found. Or with a fistful of conclusions for the next troupe's safe conduct.

Do we live in an age of artistic license? I think so. I hope so. I find it exhilarating. One has only to look at the movies, the films, the ceenaymah—which are always so helpfully the *déjà vu* of the arts. Okay—of all the *other* arts. Literary people resent the lens because it is always so much their shadow, always dressing up in their last year's thoughts and saying "Look what *I* found!" We should be happier to see change so neatly documented. And at such a pace. Drag documentaries, pussy galore—and they only discovered heterosexuality last year!

At the moment, it may be that the really lively use of sex-as-theme and sex-as-comment is on the stage side of literature. Where an *Indira*

*Gandhi's Daring Device*—whose variously whirling copulations included a Marie Montez in drag, a satyriac with a yardlong penis and a bedstyle choral ballet—made sufficiently rousing comment on India's food-birthrate lockstep to draw protest from that government. Where the "chicken-in-the-basket" routine in John Guare's spoof on the American commuter, *Muzeeka,* could draw praise from the *New Yorker*—if only in paraphrase. And where, in *Futz,* a piglet-incest tale very reminiscent of an old one of Coppard's, the La Mama troupe demonstrated, as Stanislavsky often had, that "method" in itself might be a kind of literature.

In the academic "serious" American novel—which often means as written by humorous professors—the black-comedy sex-routines are at the moment still drearily grinding and bumping in a kind of ritual macadamese. (See Barth, where the goings-on might be called university-perverse.) The "popular" novel, carrying cash between its legs instead of metaphor, is often funnier. Abstract expressionism is never "over" in any art, but as the dominance in literature of the moment, it has had its day; as practiced, it is already second-rate. Man, whelmed by wars, by an astrological perspective almost too vast for him to carry, has periods when he cannot see himself as important enough to bother with—and great human perspectives come of this. But the figure willy-nilly always re-emerges again. In literature of the past, this has meant "character." But fixed character, as novels have known it, is now historical, no more possible than old melody is to music. What is authentic in environmental reality, and what is pastiche there, changes constantly. We are in one of the great eras of confusion partly because everything in the environment itself makes us daily more aware of that. McLuhan's acceptance of this was a paraphrase of what every tabloid-reader and televiewer, every purchaser of Tide and *Time* already knew in his bones.

The arts had long since phrased it. Since their impulse is always to spy out the organized in the confused, the philosophy in the flux of the now, they will undoubtedly once again rephrase the human figure—along with the society which will also. I should be surprised if Sexes One Two Three ever totally disappear from it—except of course under the dignified pressure of the millenia. But in this country and century, their present frameworks and boundaries well may—under the assault of more than art, more than literature. Sexual themes find their best proportion whenever *other* concerns overtake them.

Literature itself takes strength from its own catholicity. (How many times in recent years has the pictorial been predicted as its killer—yet it is merely the magazine that dies, not the Word.) In the end, it has no trouble taking anything into it. Or expelling anything. In practice, female writers may take their sensibility out of mothballs, homosexuals may broaden their spectrum past hatred, and males may narrow their fear of being otherwise; all the sexes may begin writing like each other, as with the journalists. (Not that I would necessarily fancy it.) Sexual demagoguery and cannibalism may pass into such bland ententes that their era may even be regretted. Or will sexual emphases shift altogether, as we pass out of the white ages into the era of blackthink? I doubt it. Sexual blackthink so far seems to be conventionalised right out of the departments of whitethink; only the language is more interesting. In Cleaver, the sex is tired, or the same; in Fanon the medical approach is. The originality of the black man seems to lie in his blackness; as with anyone, their best essence lies in what they humanly are.

In American society, that meretricious sexual image which it had made out of the pioneer platitudes, and which was to be direct ancestor of the maw-and-paw, covered-wagon sexuality of a Hemingway, is now more and more identified with middle-age or beyond; the young are no longer that provincial anywhere. Their hetero image is certainly changing, well beyond the mere costumery. In the colleges, it is often fashionable for a girl to have had a little lesbian experience and a male a little of the homosexual; it is chic to seek these as part of general experience. And in all the group therapies—the new touch-me disciplines, a vaguer, more diffuse sexuality is the likely result, if only as being more patriotic to everybody. Heterosexuality may not quickly disappear. But it could be the *last* suffragette.

What sex is art anyway? From art's annals, what we most want from it is to be taken into the involute of life. In that, we are all ultimately—square. But from those annals also, the genius of art is that when in search of itself it is always, part of the time—transvestite.

In this country, there is always a possibility that the constant fund of Comstockery may again find its senators (or its President), and we shall all be happily censored into old fashioned rebellions again, but it is hard to visualize. Since the Learned Hand decision on *Ulysses* there has been no seriously successful overt censorship in the literary centers of the country, let the local folklores go on as they will. (What with the movies, it is still harder to see how they can.)

Censorship, or the lack of it, certainly shapes literature; one might even note—if only in a low voice and to well-wishers—that literature has been known to thrive under its restraints. But they *must* be open ones. In my own time, the most powerful censor I have lived under or near, has been political. A *The Cancer Ward* can come of that. Covert restrictions, such as women are under, can only cripple—in the arts or anywhere else. They can determine one's scope. For a woman writer, in the place where it hurts most—by restricting her self-awareness of what her life possibilities really are. For it is one's sense of one's life possibilities that feeds imaginative work.

Yes, the literary establishment, back and front, is still as predominantly male as all the others, yet it has always seemed to me that writers of any sex are stupid to strive for that kind of power, in what for them can never be an a priori world. Because the power belongs in the book. To fight to the death for the right to say what I dare—yes —that is tonic, because it is basic. It is *my* kind of vote. To climb any of the more ordinary corridors of power in the literary world is to risk what any climber does—smallness of mind. It produces no *Areopagitica*. What would enlarge me as a writer is what would enlarge any woman, any man, anyone—the right to do and be, without scorn or sneer. The stretching of the flesh produces a stretching of the Word. In a world of astronauts, a Russian woman is born free to be one. In a world of presidents and premiers, the mesdames Ghandhi and Meir exist. That enlarges me, and all women everywhere. But I *write* in America.

If sex and politics now cross there, as they do, I take this as hopeful, as a sign of the country's slow recognition that the components of life do cross, and that sex is rarely ever sex alone. When anything gets freed, a zest goes round the world. What is most evident is that the old dictionary distinction between "license" and "freedom" doesn't do any more. As the Jew had come to know—and the blacks and the queers are now showing us, inside literature and out—"Freedom" is what you are given—and its iron hand often remains on your shoulder. "License" is what you *take*.

So I put away what I had written. Sometime later, I began a book. Once or twice, over a page, I startled myself with my own hooted laughter, something I had never done before. Sex, for me, had always had room in and around it for generous laughter. But my generation was not geared to see irony or fun in politics. I was finding the current blend of the two an irresistible burlesque.

The book was called *Queenie*. What I had written—I see now—was the preface to it.

PART V

# THE END OF
# THE PAST

EACH stage of my life has seemed to me somehow an ascent, and a surprise—since here in my country one is supposed to decline toward the grave at an acute angle, as everything in its popular civilization foretells. What has made this possible for me has been my peculiar "work," to which I have been as happily doomed as one of those children born with a religious sect, whom one sometimes glimpses on television, obscure and protected, for a time. When a child myself, I already knew I was a grudging one, thoughtless of others, yet as sensitive as if I had shingles all over, nursing all the ambitions of the envious but too easily humiliated to try my wings. In my adolescence, it was hard for me to give presents; I "forgot." Yet in the picture of me, one can see something—receptive. More open than watching, though a watcher I surely was. Waiting, rather, as if there is to be something more. There is a picture of me like that at the age of nine or ten, under the high crown and round brim of a hat that the grown have put on me, holding the reins of a pony that is not my own. I still know the feel of that cape I'm wearing. And I know that child's fortune. To be seized by work, and led through it to many loves. Perhaps the endpapers of this book, now that I'm closing it, should pose that early picture against the late one the publisher

will require of me, underneath each the same invisible title: Waiting
For More.

It's not death itself that I wait for. Though I expect it too will be a
surprise, nothing in my heritage has taught me to await it naturally.
Nothing, surely in my country, whose citizens scatter impersonal death
farther than Johnny Appleseed his pips, yet to a man, and to a woman,
stand affrighted to a sort of ghosthood before their time—of the personal one. No Jews I have known have been non-neurasthenic about
death; whatever remains of their orthodoxy shines with the virtues of
a non-acceptance which may have helped to bring them notably far
in history, but does not console. As for their modern philosophies,
these so far are stillborn; one may honor Buber, but find it hard to
believe in the people who say they believe in him. Probably my Southern inheritance, foolish and stoic (scan how it still adheres to the gun!),
looks death in the eye best—but I haven't much of it left in me.

I came on the scene, however mixed of heritage and in whatever
proportion of these, half of me still from an age and a century whose
thinkers, and even its bourgeoisie, took for granted (much though
they talked about it) the presence in their lives of a certain rationale
which no longer counts for much to my countrymen at large, or to
much of a world under their influence. Call it an aesthetics of *conduct*.

History has seen so many of these, often separable even from parallel
notions of "right" and "wrong." Courtly love in the middle ages,
Spartan infanticide, Japanese *seppuku*—all those rituals where violence,
masking as custom or honor, or even racial necessity, made use of
death-attraction. The way of the pantheist or the Buddhist is milder,
but still death-embracing. Western religion may see death as the door
to the after-life, but doesn't much live with it. Yet one may have an
aesthetic of conduct apart from any of these. Call it a sense of form,
applied to life. One models one's life in the shape of something. I
suspect that is what this book is about.

Any of us born in the first half of a century are in touch with the
preceding one. The nineteenth century, as it left off conducting itself
under the eye of Mrs. Grundy and God, or in that unholy alliance of

both which confused form with conformity, bequeathed us the malaise
of a noblesse gone a-wandering—how to model one's life when God
is dead, as well as all the other noblemen? At least, our talk is that we
are left with only the ordinary urges, to sex and politics, luxury and
war. And to art too, of course. To any of which we engage ourselves
only realistically, we assume—and without wonder.

Yet as far back as written work exists, one can read complaints
of the shallowness of "modern" life. Nothing but death has ever put
an end to that. Not all the deaths behind us have ever stopped our
urge to find a light in life-as-lived—the urge toward an exemplary life,
or a satisfied one. Toward—within the limits of eternity—a shapely one.
Resolved.

As I have been writing the confessive side of this book, I had been
thinking of death, taking my own more for granted, as one learns
to do in middle life, and brooding more and more on the death of the
race, as we have all learned to do. No doubt thinking of the one, helps
us not to think of the other; much of our mental life, or of mine, is
not repression but evasion.

The great lyric time for death-think is youth, when the concept is
new but far. Or it used to be. The second great time is late middle
age, when the friends begin to drop and one's own armatures to
loosen, when the idea is old and near. Perhaps old age grows literally
numbed toward death, or half easefully in love with it, or learns
better to live with the blessings of the day—and perhaps without meditation, rather than with it. The rounded elderly posture, those seamed
faces that we take for inward ones, may mean entirely something else;
surely there is some process, for I have never met a very old person
who seems death-scared—even in America.

Often now though, the young here seem older than many of the
rest of us. One day, it crosses my mind that perhaps the race itself is
now *physically* middle-aged. So this book too, along with the private
happenings that accompany it, has led me to another. In the deadheat of
summer, I leave it, to sweat over the new one at this same desk, a
novel I call *Standard Dreaming*. When I return here—to the landscape

I have laid out in this book, the row of impatience plants ranged along this balcony window, common to both of them, are in another growth, pink now against snow. They are like the relationship between the two books—seasonal and mysterious.

This book was begun just when we came to live in the house; carried back and forth with me to and from the city, in my mind it is half a country book. Though I have often "repaired to the country" in the last decade, it has been years since I have lived there, as now. Early our first winter, we saw the barn owl; he sat treed between snowy sky and deeper ground-drift like a buff-and-white waterfall in a drawing of Fuji. That was at the bedroom window. One dusk not long after, we saw a fox streak across the dark lawn like an orange lariat being cracked from above. That was in the sitting-room. Both owl and fox are said still to live here; though we no longer see them, we live somehow between. Now and then I think of how a book might be written in that space, to satisfy both of them, cold and simple yet with a wave of orange in it—a book written for the owl and the fox. Whatever, it is clear that I am leaving this one.

How does one "finish" an account of one's life? I suppose one does that best when one intends to write no more. I have not yet engaged for that. Autobiography is often an excuse for not going on any more, along the path of whatever one has done that might make people want to read of it. I can't conclude myself like that. Not yet. But this book has its conclusions, some still projecting for me, half unknown. One, I can see clearly. Perhaps my own process is not so much my own as I thought, nor even one that only artists know—but one that we share with other Americans, other *people*. Less and less do I see any gap—in the process of us all.

Yes, my book is my blood. But all those currents in me which I have for so long kept separate, begin to seem to me no longer so. This book has pushed that on. The book and the writer, the novel and the history, the autobiography and the biographer, the journalism and the poem, no longer seem so far from one another as they used to do. It seems all—our blood.

When you come to the end of the past—no more peroration. Tolerate life—a poem which annoys when it falls into grandeur. The past will come round again.

Until death do us part, then. Or I know your name.

—New York, March, 1972